Living with Earthquakes

in the

Pacific Northwest

Living with Earthquakes

in the

Pacific Northwest

_by_

Robert S. Yeats

Oregon State University Press
Corvallis

Cover: Downtown Klamath Falls, Oregon, after the earthquake of September 20, 1993. Automobile parked in front of Swan's Bakery was crushed by falling bricks from an unbraced parapet. Photo by Lou Sennick, *Herald and News*, Klamath Falls.

The paper in this book meets the guidelines for permanence and durability of the Committee on Production Guidelines for Book Longevity of the Council on Library Resources and the minimum requirements of the American National Standard for Permanence of Paper for Printed Library Materials Z39.48-1984.

Library of Congress Cataloging-in-Publication Data
Living with earthquakes in the Pacific Northwest / Robert S. Yeats— 1st ed.
    p. cm.
Includes bibliographical references and index.
ISBN 0-87071-437-6 (alk. paper)
1. Earthquake hazard analysis—Northwest, Pacific.
2. Earthquakes—Safety measures. I. Title.
QE535.2.U6Y43   1998
363.34'9572'09795—dc21   98-23913
                                                                      CIP

Oregon State University Press
101 Waldo Hall
Corvallis OR 97331-6407
541-737-3166 •fax 541-737-3170
osu.orst.edu/dept/press

"And ye shall flee to the valley of the mountains; for the valley of the mountains shall reach unto Azal: yea, ye shall flee, like as ye fled from before the earthquake in the days of Uzziah king of Judah."

Book of Zechariah 14:4-5, issuing the world's first earthquake forecast. The earthquake did not arrive until 31 B.C., about 500 years later.

Contents

~

Preface

At first, it was simply the excitement of a scientific discovery: that the Pacific Northwest, where I live, was wracked by great earthquakes in its recent past. During the 1980s, the U.S. Geological Survey held meetings and workshops to debate the possibility of catastrophic earthquakes beneath the magnificent mountains and verdant valleys of the land of Lewis and Clark. Then we held our own meeting in Oregon, and I became a convert.

But after a while, I began to wonder whether it was more important to discuss earthquakes with my scientific colleagues or, instead, with my wife, my next-door neighbor, or the state legislature. This question solved itself when, following the recognition of future earthquake potential, the earthquakes themselves started to arrive: Loma Prieta, California, in 1989, two Oregon earthquakes in 1993, and Northridge, California, in 1994. I found myself on the Rolodexes of media reporters, and I became a media resource (make that "talking head"), usually before I knew the details of the earthquake I was asked to explain.

In some respects, telling my Northwest neighbors that we have an earthquake problem has been like telling them about carpenter ants in the basement or about high blood pressure and high cholesterol as a result of high living. But the sheer size of the earthquake problem dwarfs other concerns we face: thousands of fatalities and tens of billions of dollars in damage. Suddenly, earthquake science stopped being fun, and as a scientist, I began to feel like the watchman on the castle walls warning about barbarians at the gate, begging people to take me seriously.

Part of my frustration was that, despite the scientific discoveries and despite the television images of earthquake damage, nobody seemed to remember anything. I could give a talk to a civic club in 1995, two years after the two Oregon earthquakes, and find out in the question and answer period that most of my listeners were surprised to learn that they ought to be taking some steps to protect themselves against earthquakes, just as they would against fire.

The solution to my problem came at the university where I teach. Oregon State University had recently adopted a baccalaureate core curriculum that includes courses that synthesize and integrate student learning at the advanced undergraduate level. One of the components of the new curriculum is a course relating the discoveries of science to their impact on technology and on society.

In 1995, I offered to teach a course that told the story of the scientific recognition of the earthquake problem and of how society responded to it in terms of legislation, building codes, insurance premiums, elementary school curricula, and individual and community preparedness. The course was first taught in winter term 1997, to a large class on campus and was also televised on three cable channels in Oregon. The class notes written for this course served as the nucleus of this book, a text for future classes. In 1998, the course was offered again on campus and on the three cable channels as well as four outlying classrooms via closed-circuit television.

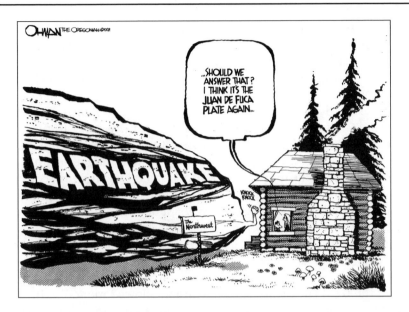

The course drew students from across the University spectrum. I required a five-page term paper on a topic related to earthquakes. Although the prospect of reading nearly two hundred term papers was daunting, it turned out to be the most gratifying part of the course. Students wrote lesson plans for third graders, retrofit plans for their parents' houses, designs for earthquake-resistant bridges, community response strategies and potential escape routes from an impending tsunami, even the feasibility of surfing a tsunami! Surfing a tsunami wasn't very practical, but surfing the Internet allowed students even in distant learning sites far from a university library to get up-to-the-minute information, so that in some cases, the student learned about new developments before I did. I was reminded again of the awesome creative potential of motivated undergraduates, some only a few years out of high school, others returning to school in mid-life. Some of these term papers enriched my own experience and knowledge and thereby enriched this book.

Although the book was written for the students in these classes, it serves a larger community as well: families concerned about earthquake hazards in their decisions about where to live, legislators presented with bills to expand (or reduce) earthquake protection, insurance actuaries wondering what premiums to charge for earthquake insurance, high school principals and teachers trying to figure out why they are told to conduct earthquake drills in schools, local officials considering stricter ordinances to regulate growth while avoiding lawsuits, and the growing number of people involved professionally in emergency preparedness. With better knowledge about what is (and is not) possible, people can make more informed decisions.

Writing the book led me into subject areas in which I was woefully uninformed, and here I had a lot of help from others in seeking out information, in guest lectures to my class, and in reviewing chapters. My thanks go to Clarence Allen of Caltech, Jeff Fletcher of Northern Pacific Insurance Co.,

Richard J. Roth of the California Department of Insurance, Ian Macgregor of the National Science Foundation, Bob Crosson of the University of Washington, Brian Atwater, Alan Nelson, Steve Obermeier, Bob Schuster, and Craig Weaver of the U.S. Geological Survey, Tim Walsh of the Washington Division of Geology and Earth Resources, John Beaulieu, Don Hull, Angie Karel, Dennis Olmstead, George Priest, Beverly Vogt, and Mei Mei Wang of the Oregon Department of Geology and Mineral Resources, Roy Hyndman and Garry Rogers of the Pacific Geoscience Centre, Kenji Satake of the Geological Survey of Japan, Chris Goldfinger, Vern Kulm, Bob Lillie, Lisa McNeill, Steve Dickenson, and Tom Miller of Oregon State University, Ray Weldon of the University of Oregon, Scott Burns and Ron Cease of Portland State University, Lori Dengler of Humboldt State University, Jill Andrews of the Southern California Earthquake Center, Jim Davis of the California Division of Mines and Geology, Diane Murbach of Murbach Natural Resources, Eldon Gath of Earth Consultants International, Walter Friday of Linhart Petersen Powers Associates, Jim Swinyard of Benton County Emergency Services, and Diane Merten of the Benton County Emergency Management Council. I learned much from the delegates to the annual meeting of the Western Seismic Safety Policy Advisory Council in Victoria, B.C. in October, 1997.

Illustrations make a book, and I received original photographs and drawings, some never before published, from Brian Atwater, Gerald Black, Lori Dengler, Chris Goldfinger, Bob Lillie, Sarah Nathe (of the California Office of Emergency Services), Gordon Jacoby (of Columbia University), Alan Nelson, Robert Kamphaus (of National Oceanic and Atmospheric Administration), Steve Obermeier, Rick Minor (of Heritage Research Associates), Kenji Satake, Karl Steinbrugge, Tim Walsh, and Pat Williams (of Lawrence Berkeley Laboratory). Original figures were drafted by Matt Gregory, Emily Oatney, and Mazhar Qayyum and converted to electronic format by David Reinert. The color slide collection of the National Oceanic and Atmospheric Administration, available from the National Geophysical Data Center, was the source of several photographs. Jack Ohman allowed me to use his perceptive cartoon that appeared in the Portland *Oregonian* after the Scotts Mills earthquake in 1993 and Morika Tsujimura and Chris Scholz permitted the use of their cartoon at the end of Chapter 7.

Thorough and constructive edits of the entire manuscript were provided by George Moore of Oregon State University and my wife, Angela, who pointed out my scientific jargon that got in the way of communicating to a lay readership. Jo Alexander of the OSU Press edited the final manuscript and carried the project through to completion.

The success of this book will depend on how successful I am in convincing individuals and communities to fortify themselves against a catastrophe that may not strike in our lifetimes. Ultimately, the book will be measured after the next large earthquake, when we ask ourselves afterwards, "Were we ready?"

Robert S. Yeats
Corvallis, Oregon

~ Part I ~
Introduction

We are not used to the idea of earthquakes near my home in the Pacific Northwest. Earthquakes are a threat to California, Japan, and Alaska, but surely not to Seattle, Spokane, Portland, and Vancouver. That was certainly my own view in 1977, when I moved to Corvallis, Oregon, even though I had been studying earthquakes for many years—in California, of course. My neighbor said, "Earthquakes? Bob, you gotta be kidding!"

On the other hand, the Pacific Northwest is flanked by a huge offshore active fault more than seven hundred miles long at the base of the continental slope: the *Cascadia Subduction Zone*. Subduction zones are where masses of crust collide, and a block of oceanic crust is forced down deep into the Earth's interior. Subduction zones around the Earth produce most of the world's great earthquakes. Unlike most of the other subduction zones, the Cascadia Subduction Zone has not suffered an earthquake since written records have been kept. Modern seismographs show very little microearthquake activity on this subduction zone. I assumed, as did most of my scientific colleagues, that subduction in the Pacific Northwest took place quietly, and that the oceanic crust somehow eased beneath the major cities of the Northwest without building up strain that would be released by earthquakes.

But in 1983, I heard a presentation by John Adams, a young New Zealand geologist transplanted to the Geological Survey of Canada. Adams stated that there *might* be an earthquake hazard in the Pacific Northwest. He had learned that a little-known federal agency, the National Geodetic Survey, routinely re-levels U.S. highway survey markers, and he decided to compare old level lines with more recent ones. Changes in the relative elevation of survey monuments and benchmarks along Pacific Northwest highways could provide evidence of the slow buildup of tectonic strain, ultimately leading to an earthquake.

If there were no warping of the Earth's crust, re-leveling highway markers would be a pretty boring job. Each survey would be exactly like the previous one. But the re-leveling done by the National Geodetic Survey in the Pacific Northwest was *not* the same between surveys. It showed an ominous change. The highways crossing the Coast Range are being tilted slowly toward the Willamette Valley in Oregon and Puget Sound in Washington. Could this mean an increase of strain in the Earth's crust, like a diving board being bent, and possibly a future rupture and earthquake?

As a student of natural disasters, I worry about needlessly alarming the public. What would be the reaction of people in major cities like Seattle, Tacoma, and Portland to such bad news? "Cool it, John," I said.

Good scientist that he is, Adams ignored my advice and published his results anyway. What was the result? Nothing! For the average person, the idea was too far-fetched. The media did not pick up on the story, and Adams' research paper was read only by other scientists. I breathed a sigh of relief, but I also began to worry that my early assumption of a slippery subduction zone might be wrong. So I waited for scientific confirmation from other sources.

Evidence was not long in coming. In 1984, Tom Heaton and Hiroo Kanamori, two seismologists from the California Institute of Technology (Caltech), published a comparison of the Cascadia Subduction Zone with others around the world. They knew that Cascadia was unusually quiet, but otherwise the geologic setting was the same as that of other subduction zones that had experienced catastrophic earthquakes, like those off the coast of Chile and Alaska. The oceanic crust in the Cascadia Subduction Zone is relatively young, which means that it has cooled from the molten state only a few million years ago (a short time for a geologist). Because it is hotter than other oceanic crust, it is also lighter and more buoyant, meaning that it is not likely to slide smoothly beneath the continent. (The comparison I use is that of trying to stuff an air mattress beneath a floating raft.) Other subduction zones similar to Cascadia have been visited in this century by earthquakes of magnitudes greater than 8. Could it be that the reason for the lack of seismic activity here is that this subduction zone is *completely locked*? Maybe the time during which records have been kept, less than two hundred years, is too short for us to conclude that the Pacific Northwest is not earthquake country.

Two years after Heaton and Kanamori published their findings, Brian Atwater of the U.S. Geological Survey in Seattle was paddling his kayak up the Niawiakum Estuary of Willapa Bay, in southwestern Washington. The purpose of his trip was to examine soft sediment along the banks of the estuary, which he was able to observe only at very low tide. This young sediment, only a few hundred years old, might contain evidence to support or refute the ideas that were being advanced about earthquakes.

There he made an astonishing observation. Just beneath the marsh grass is gray clay containing marine fossils, evidence that it had once been deposited beneath the surface of the sea. Below the gray clay is a soil and peat layer from an older marsh, together with dead spruce stumps from an ancient forest. These stumps had been covered by the marine gray clay, in which the present marsh grass had grown. Why are the fossil forest and the fossil marsh overlain by clay with marine fossils? Atwater concluded that the old marsh flat and the coastal spruce forest had suddenly dropped down and been covered by Willapa Bay. *Not gradually, but instantly!* What could have caused this?

Atwater talked about his discovery to George Plafker, also of the U.S. Geological Survey. Plafker told him that the same thing had happened after great earthquakes in southern Chile in 1960 and in the Gulf of Alaska in 1964. Coastal areas had subsided and been inundated permanently by the sea, drowning forests and marshes. Atwater made the comparison and thought the unthinkable. The marshes and coastal forests of the Pacific Northwest had been downdropped during a great earthquake.

The evidence for earthquakes that I had been looking for was falling into place. At this point, Don Hull, the State Geologist of Oregon, and I decided to hold a scientific workshop the evening before the Oregon Academy of Sciences meeting in Monmouth in February 1987, to address the question: *Is there a major earthquake hazard in Oregon or not?* We invited John Adams, Tom Heaton, and Brian Atwater, as well as other scientists who had previously advocated the idea that no earthquake hazard exists on the Cascadia Subduction Zone.

Everybody agreed to come, and the atmosphere was electric. The Portland *Oregonian* newspaper got wind of the meeting, and their science writer, Linda Monroe, wanted to cover it. I was nervous about having the press there because I wanted the scientists to be completely candid, not worrying about a front-page doomsday quote in a major newspaper. But Monroe asked me to trust her, and I did. Her coverage was responsible, and her presence did not detract from the give-and-take of the meeting.

As it turned out, Linda Monroe had a scoop. There was no argument, no controversy! Most of the scientists at the meeting were so impressed with the results presented by Adams, Heaton, and Atwater that the no-earthquake opposition retreated to the sidelines. The meeting marked a *paradigm change*, a fundamental change in our thinking about earthquakes in our region. Attendees at the Oregon Academy meeting and readers of the *Oregonian* got the word the next day. Oregon, as well as the rest of the Pacific Northwest, is indeed Earthquake Country! None of us felt as safe after that day as we thought we had been the day before.

This book, written more than a decade later, tells the earthquake story of the Pacific Northwest. It presents the evidence for earthquakes, the location of major faults, the danger from tsunamis, the importance of ground conditions, and what we as individuals and as taxpayers and voters can do to make our homes and our communities safer from earthquakes. There are lessons from the Northwest experience to be learned elsewhere in the United States, Canada, and other parts of the world where the earthquake threat is greater than that perceived by the general public.

We cannot prevent earthquakes, but we can learn to live with them and to survive them. When the inevitable earthquake strikes, we can be ready. But today, we are not.

❧ Part II ❧
Strained Rock:
Where Earthquakes Are Likely
to Strike

Earthquakes, like volcanic eruptions, are geologic phenomena, and to understand them we need a brief introduction to their geologic setting. This requires us to stretch our minds to think about moving masses of rock that are extremely large, more than tens of miles thick and hundreds of miles wide. We also must think of great lengths of time. An earthquake may happen in less than thirty seconds, but it is a response to the slow motion of massive tectonic plates on the surface of the Earth, building up strain over many thousands of years.

⏝ 1 ⏝

A Concept of Time

No one doubts that the Earth is the most hospitable planet in the solar system. We have a breathable atmosphere, and the temperature, as Goldilocks said about the porridge, is "just right." Venus is too hot, Mars is too cold, and the Moon and Mercury have no atmosphere at all to speak of.

But in terms of earthquakes, these planets could be considered safer places to live than the Earth. That's because the Earth's crust is unfortunately divided into great slabs called plates, that jostle and grind against one another like huge ice floes. In the process, all that crunching between plates forces parts of the crust up to create mountains—and causes earthquakes. In contrast, the crust of the other inner planets consists entirely of massive rock that experienced most of its mountain-building activity billions of years ago, soon after the planets were formed. Now the crustal movements on these planets have been stilled. There is no grinding of plates against one another to cause them to shake.

Of course, the Earth's crust seems pretty quiet most of the time. When I look at a map of California showing the locations of earthquakes detected by seismographs, I see lots of black dots, each signifying an earthquake. Many of these earthquakes lie on the San Andreas Fault. But you and I can drive to Los Angeles along a route close to the San Andreas Fault and never feel an earthquake. In fact, I lived in California for ten years and felt only two or three small earthquakes during that time. Had I stayed on for another four years, however, I would have experienced the 1971 San Fernando Valley Earthquake, and if I had been there during the Roaring Twenties, I would have experienced a large earthquake that destroyed part of the resort city of Santa Barbara. California was experiencing normal earthquake activity during the ten years I lived there, but I never chanced to experience a big earthquake.

How long is a long time? Let's take a look at Table 1-1 (on pages 8 and 9), which shows a series of time scales, each encompassing a longer period of time than the last.

Geologists have a different view of time than most people. I am a geologist, but I still consider it a long time when I'm stuck in a traffic jam on Interstate 5 and, when I was growing up, I thought it was an unacceptably long time until Christmas or my birthday.

You may agree that it is a very long time before you graduate from college, or get your kids raised, or retire.

Now that I am older, I have learned to take a somewhat longer view of time (except when I'm stuck on the freeway). I knew both my grandfathers, who told me stories about the horse-and-buggy days. I enjoy reading about the early settlers in the Willamette Valley and Puget Sound 150 years ago, and that, to me, seems an unbelievably long time ago. But in fact, our recorded history in the Northwest (Historical Time Scale, Table 1-1) is short. The stretch of the coast from Alaska to California was the last region of the Pacific Rim to receive settlers willing to record their history, a fact that will become significant when we consider the great Cascadia Earthquake of A.D. 1700.

Lewis and Clark arrived for a winter layover in 1806, complained about the rain, and went home. But they did blaze the trail, and fur traders set up posts at Fort Vancouver and Astoria. Soon after, many settlers from the eastern United States came to Oregon (which, as the Oregon Territory, included at that time most of the Pacific Northwest south of Canada). New towns were established west of the Cascade Mountains, and along with towns and farms, people built roads, established land claims, and started newspapers. By the 1840s, less than two centuries ago, people were keeping written records more or less continuously throughout the area west of the Cascades. This means that we know only that the Pacific Northwest has been free of great earthquakes since that time. To a geologist, that is not a very long time, not at all.

Native Americans were here long before that, of course, but they did not keep written records. Their rich oral traditions are another matter, though, and some of their stories suggest events that could have been great earthquakes and earthquake-induced waves from the sea.

To a geologist, two centuries is like the blinking of an eye. The Earth is more than four and a half billion years old. The evidence from the rocks shows that the Pacific Northwest is much younger than that, and only in northeast Washington and adjacent Idaho and British Columbia do we find rocks that are more than a billion years old. Most of the rocks in western Washington and Oregon are less than sixty million years old. But that is still an incredibly long time. A geologist can easily *talk* about sixty million years, but it is just as hard for a geologist to *imagine* such a long period of time as it is for anybody else.

If the length of time that geologic processes have operated in the Northwest is unimaginably long, the rates of these processes are incredibly slow, about as fast as your fingernails grow.

When I talk about the motion of the oceanic plate northeastward toward Oregon and Washington, and I say that

continued on page 10 ☛

Time Scales

*Table 1-1.
Different time
scales of interest
in the study of
earthquakes*

Historical

A.D. 2000	Age of computers, cutbacks in logging. Lots more people move to the Pacific Northwest.
1980	Mt. St. Helens erupts.
1960	Development of U.S. interstate highway network. End of World War II.
1940	Roaring Twenties followed by the Great Depression.
1920	World War I.
1900	Extensive logging and development of farmland; autos replace horses.
1880	Development of rail network.
1860	U.S. Civil War. Present U.S.-Canada boundary established after the Pig War.
1840	Pioneers head west to Oregon; settlement of Willamette Valley, Puget Sound, Fraser Delta, and southern Vancouver Island.
1820	Astoria and Fort Vancouver fur-trade centers established. Lewis and Clark winter over in 1806.
1800	Native Americans in charge, but they didn't keep written records.

Late Prehistoric

A.D. 2000	Today. Last great subduction-zone earthquake on January 26, 1700.
1500	Columbus discovers America, but not the Pacific Northwest.
1000	Earthquake of M greater than 7 on the Seattle Fault. Possibly a subduction-zone earthquake around A.D. 900.
500	Subduction zone earthquake about A.D. 300.

Late Quaternary

A.D. 2000	Today. We call A.D. 1950 "Present," before nuclear fallout messes up our dating scales. B.P. means Before Present.
5000 B.P.	Same as 3000 B.C., but 5000 years before A.D. 1950. Glacial ice caps largely disappear; Mt. Mazama erupts to form Crater Lake.
10,000	Beginning of Holocene, end of Pleistocene, sea level rising. Great Missoula floods 15,000 to 12,000 years ago; rapid sea-level rise.

15,000	Sea level is rising, ice caps retreating rapidly.
20,000	Glacial ice fills Puget Sound as far south as Olympia, Washington; shorelines nearly 400 feet lower than today.

Late Cenozoic

Age, in thousands of years.

0	Today. Sea level was 20 feet higher than today 125,000 years ago.
500	500,000 years. Several ice advances and retreats. Earth's magnetic field reverses at 780,000 years; compass needle formerly pointed south.
1,000	More glacial advances and retreats.
1,500	Beginning of Pleistocene at 1,800,000 years ago.
2,000	Pliocene Epoch.
2,500	First major ice age starts about 2,400,000 years ago. Still in the Pliocene, which started about 5,300,000 years ago.

Older Earth History

Age in millions of years.

0	Today.
2.4	Beginning of Ice Ages.
15-17	Great eruptions of Columbia River Basalt.
66	Asteroid slams into southern Mexico, dinosaurs become extinct.
245	Greatest mass extinction in the history of the Earth.
570	Beginning of trilobites and other shelled organisms.
4,600	Age of the Earth, 4,540,000,000 years.

the motion is a little more than an inch and a half per year, I sometimes lose my audience. Here we're talking about increasing the speed limit to 65 miles per hour, and this guy is worried about speeds of an inch and a half a year? Give us a break! But this is faster than the rate of a little more than an inch per year at which coastal California is grinding past the rest of North America on the San Andreas Fault. Even with that slow rate of travel, the San Andreas Fault has had great earthquakes in 1812, 1857, and 1906. If you continue this slip rate for 5 million years, coastal California will move northwest more than 80 miles. Keep that up long enough, and—hold your breath—Los Angeles will become part of the Pacific Northwest!

Let's suppose that one gigantic earthquake ruptured the Cascadia Subduction Zone prior to the start of recorded history in the region and caused displacement of 65 feet, which some scientists believe is possible. And let's suppose also that this earthquake relieved all the strain that had been slowly building up at a rate of 1.6 inches per year. Dividing 1.6 inches per year into 65 feet, you find that it would take almost five hundred years for the crust to recover that strain, so that the subduction zone could rupture again in the next earthquake. Now that's a long time, almost three times our recorded history in the Pacific Northwest since the expedition of Lewis and Clark.

But we've already used up 175 years of recorded history with no monster earthquake, and, as will be shown below, there is geologic evidence from Brian Atwater's subsided marshes that we have already used up about 300 years. Should we forget about it, inasmuch as we still might have 200 years to go?

Unfortunately not, because the repeat time of earthquakes can be highly variable. In southern California, a section of the San Andreas Fault ruptured in 1812 and again in 1857, just 45 years later. Yet more than 140 years have gone by without another major earthquake along that same section of the fault. We could have much longer than 200 years to go, or we could have the next great Cascadia earthquake much sooner, maybe in our lifetime, maybe tomorrow.

Another reason that we can't laugh at 1.6 inches per year is the massive amount of rock that is building up strain. The oceanic slab that is forcing its way under the edge of the North American continent is about 40 miles thick and 740 miles long, extending from Vancouver Island to northern California. So even though the movement rate is slow, the bodies of rock that are being strained are titanic in scale.

Because the times for geologic processes to work are so ponderously long, geologists have devised time scales (see Table 1-1), analogous, perhaps, to historians referring to the Middle Ages or the Renaissance. At first, this was done using fossils, because organisms have changed through time by evolution, and distinctive shells or bones of species that had died out were used to characterize specific time intervals called *periods* and *epochs*. In the past few decades, it has become possible to date rocks directly, based on the extremely regular rate of decay of certain radioactive isotopes of elements such as uranium. These atomic clocks enable us to date the age of the Earth at about four and a half billion years and, in addition, to date the age of trilobites, of dinosaurs, and of other dominant groups of organisms that are now extinct.

In our study of earthquakes, we do not need to be concerned about most of the geologic periods and epochs, including the ages of trilobites and dinosaurs. We do need to know about those times when the geologic processes that produce today's earthquakes have been operating: the Tertiary and Quaternary periods, together known as the Cenozoic Era. We need to know something about the geologic history of the later part of the Tertiary Period, but we are most concerned about the Quaternary, which started 1.8 million years ago (Table 1-1). We divide the Quaternary into the Pleistocene and the Holocene epochs, with the boundary between the two dated at ten thousand years ago. The Pleistocene Epoch, covering most of the Ice Ages, saw much of the evolution of human beings, as well as saber-tooth tigers, mastodons, and great cave bears.

But it is the Holocene, the last ten thousand years, that concerns us most. During the Holocene, there was a rapid retreat of the great ice caps, and sea level rose nearly 400 feet. During the last half of the Holocene, civilizations arose in Mesopotamia, Egypt, and China, and written records began to be kept. If geologists can show that a fault sustained an earthquake during the Holocene, it is placed in a special category of hazard, because if it ruptured that recently, it is likely to rupture again. This classification based on the time of most recent activity is written into law in many states and into regulations by federal agencies such as the U.S. Nuclear Regulatory Commission and the U.S. Army Corps of Engineers.

To date earthquakes, we have historical records only for the last part of the Holocene. But we can use one of the natural clocks mentioned above to date formerly living organisms for the last twenty to thirty thousand years. This is *radiocarbon dating*, based on the natural decay of a radioactive isotope of carbon (carbon 14) into stable carbon (carbon 12). Carbon 14 starts off as ordinary nitrogen, which makes up the greater part of the atmosphere. The stable isotope of nitrogen, nitrogen 14, is bombarded by cosmic rays from outer space, changing it to carbon 14, which is unstable. Organisms take up both the radioactive and stable isotopes of carbon in the same proportions as in the atmosphere. After the organism dies, the carbon 14 decays to carbon 12 at a precise rate, so that half of the carbon 14 is gone in 5,730 years. In another 5,730 years, half of what's left decays to carbon 12, and half of that decays in another 5,730 years, until finally there is too little radioactive carbon 14 to measure. We say that 5,730 years is the *half life* of the radioactive decay of carbon 14 to carbon 12.

Unfortunately, the radiocarbon clock is not as precise as we would like. Radiocarbon dating cannot get us to the exact year, but only to within a few decades of the actual age; an example of a radiocarbon age is 5,300 ± 60 radiocarbon years, an expression of the laboratory precision in counting the atoms of carbon 14 relative to carbon 12. Radiocarbon years are not the same as calendar years because the cosmic radiation that creates carbon 14 is not constant, but has changed over the years. Minze Stuiver and his colleagues at the University of Washington have designed a conversion scale that changes radiocarbon years to calendar years, and in most reports today, this conversion has already been made.

In addition, the geologist or archeologist must ensure that the carbon sample being dated (charcoal, shell fragment, bone fragment) is the same age as the deposit in which it is found. The charcoal in a deposit may have been washed in from a dead tree that is hundreds of years older. Or the charcoal may be part of a root from a much younger tree that grew and died long after the deposit was buried by other sediment.

To conclude our discussion of time, we need to think of earthquakes in two ways. On the one hand, an earthquake takes place in a matter of seconds, almost (but not quite) instantly. But on the other hand, an earthquake marks the release of strain that has built up over periods of hundreds, thousands, or tens of thousands of years. To understand the earthquake hazard, it is not enough to figure out *what will happen* in a future earthquake. To make progress in forecasting earthquakes, we need to know *how long it takes* a fault to build up enough strain to rupture in an earthquake, and how large that earthquake is likely to be. When? Where? How big? On the answers to those questions rests our ability to respond to the earthquake danger and to survive it.

Suggestions for Further Reading

Wicander, R., and J.S. Monroe. 1980. *Historical Geology*. St. Paul, MN: West Publishing Co., 578p.

Yeats, R.S., K.E. Sieh, and C.R. Allen. 1997. *The Geology of Earthquakes*. New York: Oxford University Press, Chapter 6, pp. 116-38.

⇜ 2 ⇝
Plate Tectonics

The Earth's Crust:
Not Very Well Designed

As an engineered structure, the Earth's crust is not up to code. From time to time, its design problems cause it to fail, and the result is an earthquake.

The principal cause of crustal weakness is geothermal heat. Isotopes of radioactive elements within the Earth decay to other isotopes, producing heat that is trapped beneath the surface. Because of this trapped heat, the crust is warmer with increasing depth, as anyone knows who has ever descended into a deep mine. Geothermal heat warms the City of Klamath Falls, Oregon, heats the hot springs of the Pacific Northwest and, on rare occasion, causes the eruption of great volcanoes like Mt. St. Helens.

Just as iron becomes malleable in a blast furnace, or hot silica glass becomes soft enough for a glassblower to produce beautiful bowls, rock becomes weak, like saltwater taffy, when the temperature gets high enough (Figure 2-1). Rock that is soft and weak under these conditions is said to be *ductile*. At lower temperatures, rock is *brittle*, meaning it deforms by shattering. Increased temperature tends to weaken rock, but, on the other hand, increased *pressure* tends to *strengthen* it. With increasing depth, rock is subjected to conditions that work in opposite directions. The strengthening effect of increased pressure dominates at low temperatures within 10 to 20 miles of the Earth's surface, whereas the weakening effect of higher temperature kicks in rather abruptly at greater depth, depending on the type of rock. The strength of rock, then, increases gradually with increasing depth, and the strongest rock is found just above the depth where temperature weakening takes over (Figure 2-1), a depth called the *brittle-ductile transition*.

Think about a bridge with a layer of asphalt and concrete overlying a framework of strong steel. If the bridge collapses, it will be because of failure of the layer of steel, not the weaker concrete or asphalt on top. So it is with the Earth's crust. The crust fails when its strongest layer breaks, just above the brittle-ductile transition where temperature begins to weaken its minerals. Earthquakes tend to originate in this strongest layer. When this layer fails, shallower and deeper rock fails, too.

Continents and Ocean Basins

Unlike the other inner planets, the surface of the Earth is at two predominant levels, one averaging 2,750 feet (840 m) above sea level, making up the continents, and the other averaging 12,100 feet (3,700 m) below sea level, making up the ocean basins (Figure 2-2). If you were able to look at the Earth with the water removed, the continents, together with their submerged continental shelves, would appear as gigantic plateaus, with steep slopes down to the ocean basins below. With the sea water removed, the dry land of the North American continent would appear as a high plateau relative to the deep-sea floor. It's as though people living on the Pacific coast were in Tibet, looking down to the plains of India far below.

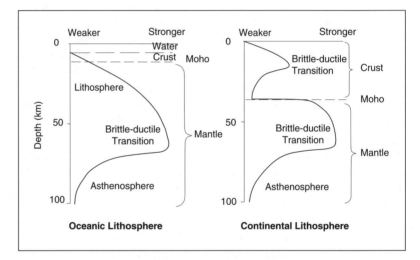

Figure 2-1. Strength of continental lithosphere (crust and upper mantle) vs. oceanic lithosphere. As rocks get buried, they get hotter due to the Earth's geothermal gradient. They also get stronger—down to a point, where temperature takes over, and they abruptly get weaker, at a level called the brittle-ductile transition. The Mohorovičić discontinuity (Moho for short) marks the boundary between the crust, made up of granite and basalt, and the mantle, made up of peridotite. Temperature softens granite at a much shallower depth than peridotite, so that the lower continental crust is a soft, squishy layer between the brittle upper crust and the brittle upper mantle. Earthquakes are limited to the brittle layers of continental crust, and they tend to nucleate at the strongest part, just above the brittle-ductile transition to soft, plastic lower crust below. For oceanic lithosphere, the Moho is so shallow that there is no soft layer. The hard lithosphere makes up the tectonic plates. The base of the lithosphere is where peridotite in the mantle becomes soft at high temperature. The soft stuff beneath is called the asthenosphere. From Yeats et al. (1997).

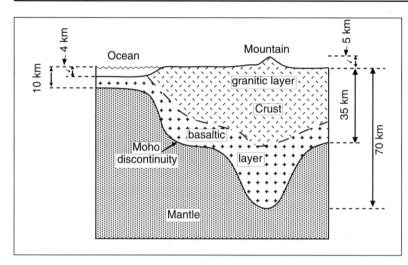

Figure 2-2. Cross section of oceanic crust (left) and continental crust (center and right). Continent is composed of granitic rock which is lighter, thicker, and more buoyant than oceanic crust, which is underlain by heavier basaltic rock. Both continental and oceanic crust overlie the mantle, composed of peridotite. The top of the mantle is the Mohorovicic discontinuity (Moho for short). The continent stands high with respect to the ocean basin, and for it to be in balance, it is underlain by a deep root of lighter crust. Mountain ranges stand above the continent and are underlain by still deeper roots. From Yeats et al. (1997).

The reason for the different levels is that the continents and ocean basins are made up of different kinds of rock. Continental rocks are rich in the light-colored minerals quartz and feldspar, which combine to make up the principal kind of rock in the continent, which is *granite* (Figure 2-2). You can find good exposures of light-colored granitic rocks in the Coast Mountains of British Columbia, the North Cascades of Washington, the Wallowa Mountains of Oregon, and the Sierra Nevada of California (which John Muir, because of their light color, called "The Mountains of Light").

Ocean-basin rock, on the other hand, is predominantly *basalt*, which contains the light-colored mineral feldspar but is dark brown to black, because its color is dominated by dark minerals like pyroxene and magnetite. Basalt lava flows characterize the Columbia Plateau and Columbia Gorge, although these rocks were not formed in an ocean basin. The mountains on the east side of the Olympic Peninsula, visible from Seattle on a clear day, also are composed of basalt, most of it deposited on an ancient ocean floor about 55 million years ago.

Basaltic rocks are common on other planets, whereas continental granitic rocks are not. (A Martian rock analyzed by *Sojourner* on the *Pathfinder* mission to Mars in July 1997 may change our ideas about this, as it seems to contain a lot of quartz.)

A third type of rock called *peridotite* underlies both the continents and the ocean basins, and this is made up of dense minerals such as pyroxene and olivine. This dark rock has no feldspar and thus it is heavier than either basalt or granite. Peridotite is also brittle and strong at much higher temperatures than either basalt or granite, a fact that will become significant when we consider in Chapter 5 the environment of deep earthquakes beneath the Puget Sound region. Peridotite does not form naturally at the Earth's surface. It is found at the surface only in special circumstances where great tectonic forces have raised it up to view. As it comes to the surface, it absorbs water, and the resultant green streaky rock is called *serpentine*. Serpentine and peridotite are found at various places in the North Cascades of Washington, the Blue Mountains of Oregon, and the Klamath Mountains of Oregon and northern California. From a distance, terrain underlain by peridotite or serpentine may appear a weathered reddish brown, and it does not support as much vegetation as other types of rock. The Twin Sisters range east of Bellingham, Washington, is made up almost entirely of olivine, one of the minerals in peridotite, and the mountains south and west of Mt. Stuart, in the North Cascades north of Ellensburg, Washington, are made up of peridotite.

During the four and a half billion years of Earth history, convection currents sweeping at extremely slow speeds through the Earth's interior have resulted in the gradual accumulation of granite and basalt near the surface, much like scum floating on the top of a large pot of slowly boiling soup. Granite and basalt float on top because they are lower in density than peridotite.

Basalt and granite make up the *crust*, and the underlying heavy peridotite makes up the *mantle*, which extends all the way down to the top of the molten outer core of the Earth at 1,800 miles (2,900 kilometers) depth. The boundary between the crust and the mantle is called the *Moho* (Figure 2-2), shorthand for the name of the Croatian seismologist, Andrija Mohorovičić, who discovered it in 1909. The Moho beneath the continents is commonly at depths of 20 to 40 miles (35 to 70 kilometers), deepest beneath mountain ranges, whereas the Moho beneath ocean basins may be no more than 6 miles beneath the sea floor.

The continents, made up of granite, which has relatively low density, stand higher than the ocean basins underlain by basalt and peridotite for the same reason that icebergs float on the ocean, or ice cubes float in a glass of ice tea. And if you look at the ice cubes in your tea, you will see that there is quite a lot of ice below the surface of the tea. This ice of lower density beneath the surface balances and buoys up the ice that sticks up above the water. For the same reason, the granitic crust of the continents extends to depths in the Earth much greater than the basaltic crust of the ocean basins. The basaltic crust beneath ocean basins is relatively thin, and its relation to the mantle is more like the water freezing on the surface of a pond.

But how can we use ice and water as a comparison with solid rock? Water is a liquid, and the crust and mantle are solids.

This comparison is valid for two reasons. First, rock at great depth is weak because it is subjected to blast-furnace temperatures below the brittle-ductile transition. Second, the tectonic processes that cause continents to rise above ocean basins are extremely slow. We know from experiments that, if the temperature is high enough, rock can flow as a solid, although it does so very slowly, fractions of an inch per year. This process, well known in metalworking, is called *hot creep.*

We have seen that earthquakes occur in the brittle upper crust, but not in the hot, plastic lower crust which is too weak to store strain energy that could be released as earthquakes. The reason for this is the abundance in the crust of the light-colored minerals quartz and feldspar, minerals that become soft and weak at relatively low temperature, about 575° F. For this reason, the upper crust beneath the continents is strong, but the lower crust is soft and weak. Oceanic crust, on the other hand, is so thin (Figure 2-2) that *all* of it is strong, and so is the upper mantle. Peridotite, the rock of the mantle, is made up of olivine and pyroxene, minerals that are still very strong at temperatures that prevail below the Moho, as high as 1,400-1,500°F. These temperatures are reached at depths that may be as much as 60 miles (100 kilometers).

The parts of the outer Earth that are brittle and strong are called the *lithosphere*, and the parts below are called the *asthenosphere*. Beneath the ocean basins, the lithosphere includes the thin crust and part of the upper mantle. Beneath the continents, the upper crust is brittle, but the lower crust is not. Below the Moho, the upper mantle may be brittle and form the lowest layer of continental lithosphere.

The flow of solid rock in the asthenosphere produces strain in the strong lithosphere. It is the response of the lithosphere to this strain that produces earthquakes. All earthquakes occur within the lithosphere, including slabs of lithosphere that have penetrated deep into the asthenosphere at subduction zones.

The Dance of the Plates:
We Know the Beat, but Not the Tune

It appears that a very slow flow of solid rock in the mantle is the dominant cause of the tectonic activity that takes place at the Earth's surface. This leads us now to a discussion of *plate tectonics.*

We would have no earthquake problem if the lithosphere, 60 miles thick, completely encircled the Earth without any breaks, as it does on the other inner planets. Unfortunately, though, the 60-mile thickness is not enough to withstand the stresses coming from the slow, roiling currents of the asthenosphere below. The lithosphere is broken up into gigantic *tectonic plates* that grind against one another, producing earthquakes and volcanic eruptions in the process (Figure 2-3). Most of these plates are of continental size. The Pacific Northwest is part of the North

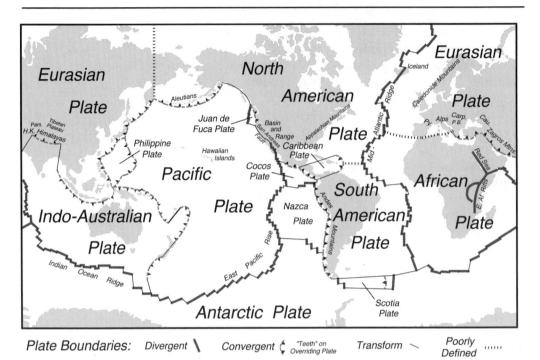

Plate Boundaries: Divergent \   Convergent ⊱ "Teeth" on Overriding Plate   Transform ‿   Poorly Defined ……

Figure 2-3. Lithospheric plates and their boundaries. The Juan de Fuca Plate is a fairly small plate between the gigantic Pacific Plate on the west and the North American Plate on the east. From R.J. Lillie.

American Plate, which extends all the way across the United States and Canada to the middle of the Atlantic Ocean. Most of the Pacific Ocean is underlain by the Pacific Plate, the world's largest, which reaches to Alaska, Japan, and New Zealand. Other plates are smaller, like the Juan de Fuca Plate off the Pacific Northwest coast, which is a little smaller than Washington and Oregon taken together.

Running down the center of the floor of the Atlantic Ocean, like the seam on a baseball, the Mid-Atlantic Ridge is formed by the upwelling of hot material from the asthenosphere, which broke up the supercontinent of Pangea, starting about 180 million years ago. North and South America, fragments of Pangea, moved away from Africa and Europe, and the deep Atlantic Ocean floor began to grow in the widening rift between them. The Atlantic Ocean Basin is still widening at a rate slightly less than an inch per year. The Mid-Atlantic Ridge is a ridge because the newly formed oceanic lithosphere is hotter and thus lighter and more buoyant than older oceanic lithosphere next to the continents. There are hot springs along the ridge, and new basaltic lava flows erupt on the ocean floor at the ridge. All of the ocean floor of the Atlantic has been created as basaltic lava in the past 180 million years. Atlantic Ocean crust is still being formed today as the Americas slowly move farther away from the continents of the Old World.

There is also a ridge in the Pacific Ocean called the East Pacific Rise, but this ridge lies toward the eastern margin of the Pacific, not near the center of the ocean, as the Mid-Atlantic Ridge does. But the origin is the same: oceanic crust is being formed at the

East Pacific Rise, and it moves away to the east and west. That part moving toward the west becomes part of the Pacific Plate. That part moving toward the east becomes part of several smaller plates off the west coast of North and South America, including the Juan de Fuca Plate off the Pacific Northwest. The local ridge where oceanic crust is being formed, a remnant of the East Pacific Rise, is called the Juan de Fuca Ridge (Figure 2-4). To the north, adjacent to British Columbia, it is called the Explorer Ridge, and to the south, off northern California, it is the Gorda Ridge.

But if new crust is being made, then old crust must be destroyed at the same rate somewhere else, because the Earth has remained the same size through time. The destruction of crust takes place at *subduction zones*. Most of these are found around the edges of the Pacific Ocean, which leads to the name *Pacific Rim of Fire* because of the abundance of active volcanoes and earthquakes, including the largest earthquakes experienced on Earth. One of these subduction zones, the Cascadia Subduction Zone, lies off the Pacific Northwest, where the Juan de Fuca Plate is being driven beneath the North American continent.

At some plate boundaries, lithosphere is neither being created at a mid-ocean ridge nor destroyed at a subduction zone. Instead, two plates crunch and grind past each other, producing earthquakes in the process. These boundaries are called *transform faults*, and on the ocean floor, they are called *fracture zones*. The best known example is the San Andreas Fault of California, where the Pacific and North American plates move past each other. Off the Pacific Northwest, the Juan de Fuca and Pacific plates are in part joined by mid-ocean ridges, as described above. But part of their boundary is made up of fracture zones, with the best known being the Blanco and Sovanco fracture zones (Figure 2-4). These, too, are transform faults.

During the past two decades, scientists have been able to determine the rates at which the plates move with respect to one another. This is done by observing changes in the Earth's magnetic field preserved in oceanic crust and by drilling core holes in the deep-ocean floor to determine the age of the oldest sediment overlying the basaltic crust at various places. In the last few years, these rates have been confirmed by direct measurements using space satellites through the Global Positioning System (GPS) and by the relative motion of radio telescopes with respect to quasar signals from outermost space. Using high-speed computers, all our information about relative plate motion can be fed into a computer model that tells us the motion of any given plate with respect to any other. We can even predict with some confidence the plate configuration of the Earth millions of years from now, which allows us to forecast that coastal California, including Los Angeles, is moving inexorably toward the Pacific Northwest.

Figure 2-4. Plate-tectonic setting of the Pacific Northwest. (a) Map. (b) Schematic cross section along A-A' of map. Sovanco, Blanco, and Nootka fracture zones and San Andreas Fault (map) are transform faults; arrows show relative movement directions. New crust is created at the Juan de Fuca and Gorda ridges. Oceanic crust of the Juan de Fuca, Gorda, and Explorer plates (shaded on map) are subducted at the Cascadia Subduction Zone (heavy line with teeth on map). As part of the subduction process, molten rock is carried to the surface to form the volcanoes of the Cascade Range. After R.J. Lillie.

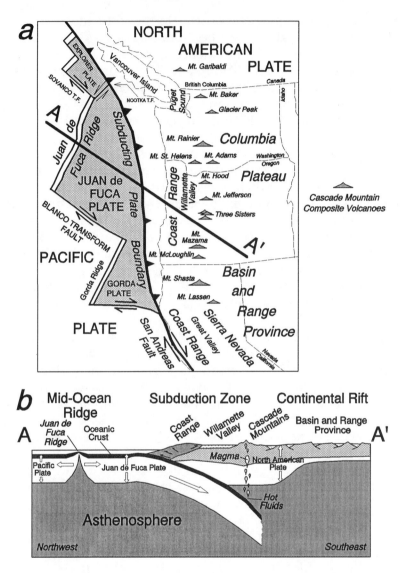

However, we have no underlying theory that explains *why* the plates move as they do, which leads to our description of the dance of the plates: we know the beat, but we don't know the tune.

So we can say with a fair degree of confidence that new oceanic crust is being created at the Juan de Fuca Ridge in such a way that the Pacific and Juan de Fuca plates are spreading apart at a rate slightly faster than 2 inches (60 millimeters) per year. We also know that the Juan de Fuca plate is moving toward and beneath the stable North American continent at a little less than 2 inches (about 45 millimeters) per year. Unfortunately, we know much less about how the motion of the Juan de Fuca Plate with respect to North America is distributed between the subduction zone itself and active crustal faults east of the plate boundary, which extends from the base of the continental slope all the way across Washington and Oregon. If some of the plate convergence is being taken up by these crustal faults, then slightly less is being taken up by the subduction zone. If we knew the rates of movement on crustal faults as well as we do the rates of plate motion, we would be much farther along in forecasting the future behavior of crustal faults and of the Cascadia Subduction Zone itself.

Suggestions for Further Reading

Glen, W. 1982. *The Road to Jaramillo*. Stanford, CA: Stanford University Press. An account of the plate tectonics revolution.

Kearey, P., and F.J. Vine. 1990. *Global Tectonics*. London: Blackwell Scientific Publications, 302p.

Lillie, R.J. 1999. *Whole-Earth Geophysics*. Englewood Cliffs, N.J.: Prentice-Hall, 361p.

⌁ 3 ⌁

The Origin of Earthquakes

Elastic Rocks:
How They Bend and Break

I f you blow up a balloon, the addition of air causes the balloon to expand. If you release the balloon, the air whooshes out, and the balloon shrinks to its former size. If you take a thin board and push the ends toward each other, the board will bend. If you let the board go, the board will straighten out again. These are examples of a property of solids called *elasticity*. When air is blown into the balloon, or when the board is bent, strain energy is stored inside the rubber walls of the balloon and within the board. When the balloon is released, or the board is let go, the energy is released as balloon and board return to their former shapes. Figure 3-1 shows another example of elasticity, the squeezing of a ball between two boards.

But if the balloon is blown up even further, it finally reaches a point where it can hold no more air, and it bursts. The strain energy is released in this case, too, but it is released abruptly, with a bang. Instead of returning to its former size, the balloon breaks into tattered fragments. In the same way, if the small board (or a pencil, as illustrated in Figure 3-2) is bent too far, it breaks with a snap as the strain energy is released.

It is not so easy to picture rocks as being elastic, but they are. If a rock is squeezed in a laboratory rock press, it changes its shape slightly, much as a rubber ball changes its shape when it is squeezed. When the pressure of the rock press is released, the rock returns to its former shape, just as the balloon or the board does, or the ball in Figure 3-1. But if the rock press continues to bear down on the rock with greater force, ultimately the rock will break.

After the great San Francisco Earthquake of 1906 on the San Andreas Fault, Professor Harry Reid of Johns Hopkins University compared two 19th-century land surveys on both sides of the fault with a new survey taken just after the earthquake. These survey comparisons showed that widely separated survey benchmarks on opposite sides of the fault had moved more than 10 feet (3.2 meters) with respect to each other even *before* the earthquake, and this slow movement was in the same direction as the sudden

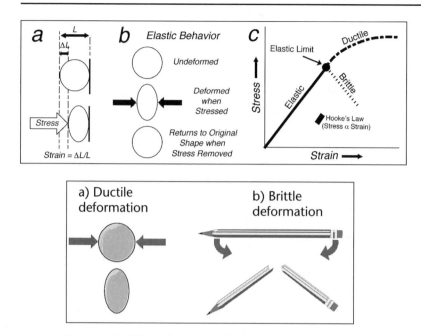

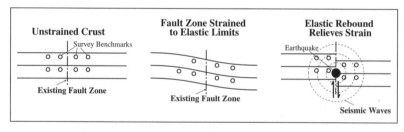

Figure 3-2. When the elastic limit is exceeded, the ball in Figure 3-1 may remain squashed, as shown in (a). In (b), the pencil breaks when the elastic limit is exceeded, showing brittle behavior. From R.J. Lillie.

Figure 3-1. Elasticity. In (a), a ball (or a balloon) is squeezed between two boards, causing it to appear a bit squashed. But if the boards are removed (b), the ball returns to its original shape. The diagram in (c) shows that the amount of strain (squashing, in the case of the ball) is proportional to the amount of stress applied (how hard the boards squeeze the ball). But beyond a certain point, called the elastic limit, the ball does not return to its original shape, but will remain in a squashed shape, or if it is a balloon, it will burst. From R.J. Lillie.

Figure 3-3. Illustration of elastic rebound theory of Harry Reid. The map shows the San Andreas fault, and the small circles represent land survey markers. The crust is deformed elastically as two tectonic plates move past each other on the San Andreas Fault. With continued plate motion, elastic strain energy is built up in the crust, and the survey markers slowly change their positions with respect to one another. The elastic limit is reached first along the old fault zone, which is weaker than unfaulted parts of the crust. When this happens, the fault is reactivated, and it ruptures in an earthquake, as it did in 1906. The strained, bent rock releases its stored elastic strain energy and rebounds to an unstressed position, as illustrated by the sudden change in position of the survey markers.

movement *during* the earthquake. Based on these observations, Reid proposed his *elastic rebound theory*, which states that the Earth's crust acts like the bent board mentioned earlier (Figure 3-3). Strain accumulates in the crust until it causes the crust to rupture in an earthquake, like the breaking of the board and the bursting of the balloon.

Another half-century would pass before we would understand *why* the strain had built up in the crust before the San Francisco Earthquake. We know now that it is due to plate tectonics. The Pacific Plate is slowly grinding past the North American Plate along the San Andreas Fault. But the San Andreas Fault, where the two plates are in contact, is stuck, and so the crust deforms elastically as a result. The break is along the San Andreas Fault because it is relatively weak compared to the parts of the two plates that have not been broken repeatedly by faults. A section of the fault that is slightly weaker than other sections gives way, releasing the plate-tectonic strain as an earthquake.

If we knew the crustal strengths of various faults, and if we also knew the rate at which strain is building up in the crust at these faults, we could then forecast when the next earthquake would strike. We are beginning to understand the rate at which strain builds up on a few of our most hazardous faults, like the San Andreas Fault. But we have very little confidence in our knowledge of the crustal strength that must be overcome to produce an earthquake. Crustal strengths are different for different parts of the crust, and are probably different on the same part of a fault at different times in its history. These are problems being addressed in current earthquake research.

A Classification of Faults

Most damaging earthquakes form on faults at a depth of 5 miles or more in the Earth's crust, too deep to be observed directly. But most of these faults are also exposed at the surface where they may be studied by geologists. Larger earthquakes may be accompanied by surface movement on these faults, producing damage to structures under which they pass.

Some faults have a vertical dip, so that an earthquake at 10 miles depth is directly beneath the fault at the surface where rupture of the ground can be observed. Other faults dip at a low angle, so that the fault at the surface may be several miles away from the point directly above the earthquake (Figure 3-4). Where the fault has a low dip or inclination, the rock above the fault is called the *hanging wall*, and the rock below the fault is called the *footwall*. These are terms used by miners and prospectors. Valuable minerals are commonly found in fault zones, and miners working underground along a fault zone find themselves standing on the footwall, with the hanging wall over their heads.

If the hanging wall moves up or down during an earthquake, the fault is called a *dip-slip fault* (Figure 3-4). If the hanging wall moves sideways, parallel with the Earth's surface, as shown in Figure 3-3, the fault is called a *strike-slip fault*.

There are two kinds of strike-slip fault, *right-lateral* and *left-lateral*. If you stand on one side of a right-lateral fault, objects on the other side of the fault appear to move to your right during an earthquake (Figure 3-5a, b). The San Andreas Fault is the best-known example of a right-lateral fault (Figure 3-5a). At a left-lateral fault, objects on the other side of the fault appear to move to your left (Figure 3-6). Strike-slip faults tend to dip nearly vertically, but there are exceptions.

In dip-slip faults, if the hanging wall moves down with respect to the footwall, it is called a *normal fault* (Figure 3-7). This happens when the crust is being pulled apart, as in the case of faults in southeastern Oregon or at sea-floor spreading centers. If the hanging wall moves up with respect to the footwall, it is called a *reverse fault* (Figure 3-8). This happens when the crust is jammed together. The Cascadia Subduction Zone is a very large-scale example of a reverse fault. Where the dip of a reverse fault is very low, it is called a *thrust fault*.

The 1983 Coalinga Earthquake and the 1994 Northridge Earthquake, both in California, were caused by rupture on reverse faults, but these faults did not reach the surface. Reverse faults that do not reach the surface are called *blind faults*, and if they have low dips, they are called *blind thrusts*. In most cases, such faults are expressed at the Earth's surface as folds in rock. An upward fold in rock is called an *anticline* (Figure 3-9), and a downward fold is called a *syncline*. Before these two California earthquakes, geologists thought that anticlines and synclines form

Figure 3-4. The focus is that point within the Earth where the earthquake nucleates. The epicenter is that point on the Earth's surface directly above the focus. The focal depth is the depth of the focus beneath the Earth's surface. The earthquake fault on which the earthquake occurs has a low dip angle so that the surface trace of the fault, R, where surface rupture may be expected, is displaced from the epicenter. The block above the fault is the hanging wall, and the block below the fault is the footwall. Modified from R.J. Lillie.

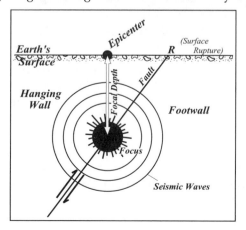

Figure 3-5. Right-lateral strike-slip faults. (a) Aerial view of San Andreas Fault in Carrizo Plain, California. Fault is marked by a linear zone that can be traced from left to right across photo. Two streams crossing the fault have been deflected to right. Last rupture was during an earthquake in 1857. Photo by U.S. Geological Survey. (b) Offset of furrows in a cultivated field near El Centro, California during an earthquake on October 15, 1979. Photo credit: University of Colorado, as reproduced in National Oceanic and Atmospheric Administration Natural Hazards Slide Set: Earthquakes in Southern California 1979-1989.

slowly and gradually and are not related to earthquakes. Now it is known that they may mask blind faults that are the source of earthquakes. Such folds cover blind faults in the Pasco Basin in eastern Washington and at Stonewall Bank off the central Oregon coast.

Figure 3-10 is a summary diagram showing the four types of faults that produce earthquakes: left-lateral strike-slip fault, right-lateral strike-slip fault, normal fault, reverse fault, as well as a blind thrust fault, the special type of reverse fault that does not reach the surface but is manifested at the surface as an anticline.

Figure 3-6. Road displaced to the left during an earthquake in 1990 on a left-lateral strike-slip fault on the Island of Luzon in the Philippines. Photo by T. Nakata, Hiroshima University.

Figure 3-7. Normal fault scarp at margin of Pleasant Valley, south of Winnemucca, Nevada. The fault scarp formed suddenly during an earthquake in 1915 during which the hills on the left were lifted up with respect to the terrain on the right. Fault dips (slopes) toward the right. Truck is parked in hanging wall of fault; left skyline is part of the footwall. Photo by Robert Wallace, U.S. Geological Survey.

Figure 3-8. Reverse fault in the San Fernando Valley, California, formed during an earthquake in 1971. Fault extends from left to right. Buckling of sidewalk indicates compression, fault dips away from viewer. Hanging wall (in background) was at same level as footwall (in foreground) before the earthquake. Ruined building in left background was part of a convalescent home in which several people died. Photo by Robert Yeats.

*Figure 3-9.
Ventura Avenue
Anticline in
southern
California. Folded
rock layers were
formerly
horizontal,
deposited on the
floor of the ocean.
Folding is
controlled by
displacement on a
buried reverse
fault, called a
blind thrust.
Photo by Robert
Yeats.*

What Happens During an Earthquake?

Crustal earthquakes start at depths of 5 to 10 miles, typically in that layer of the Earth's crust that is strongest due to burial pressure, just above the brittle-ductile transition, the depth at which temperature weakening starts to take effect (Figure 2-1). This is too deep for us to study directly by deep drilling, and so we have to base our understanding on indirect evidence. We do this by studying the detailed properties of seismic waves that pass through these crustal layers, or by subjecting rocks to laboratory tests at temperatures and pressures expected at those depths. And some fault zones millions of years old have been uplifted and eroded in the millions of years since faulting took place, allowing us to observe them directly at the surface and make inferences on how earthquakes occur on them.

An earthquake is most likely to rupture the crust where it previously has been broken at a fault, because a fault zone tends to be weaker than unfaulted rock around it. The Earth's crust, like a chain, is only as strong as its weakest link. Strain has been building up elastically, and now the limit of the strength of the faulted crust directly above the zone where temperature weakening occurs is reached. Suddenly, this strong layer fails, and the rupture races sideways and upward toward the surface. The motion produces friction, which generates heat that may be sufficient to melt the rock in places. In cases where the rupture only extends for a mile or so, the earthquake is a relatively minor one, like Oregon's Scotts Mills Earthquake of March 1993. But in rare instances, the rupture keeps going for hundreds of miles, and a great earthquake is produced. At present, scientists can't say why

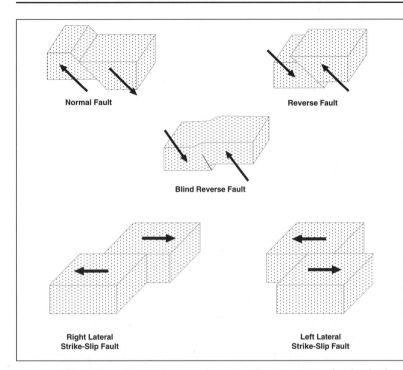

Figure 3-10. Diagrammatic representation of the four types of faults that produce earthquakes, shown as block diagrams: left-lateral strike-slip fault, right-lateral strike-slip fault, normal fault, reverse fault, as well as a blind thrust fault, the special type of reverse fault that does not reach the surface but is manifested at the surface as an anticline. Arrows show relative movement.

one earthquake will rupture only a small segment of a fault, but another will rupture a fault for hundreds of miles (but they are working on this problem).

The rupture causes the sudden loss of strain energy that the rock had built up over hundreds of years, equivalent to the snap of the board or the burst of the balloon. The shock radiates out from the rupture as seismic waves, which travel to the surface and produce the shaking we experience in an earthquake (Figure 3-11). These waves are of three basic types: *P waves* (primary waves), *S waves* (secondary waves), and *surface waves*. P and S waves pass through the body of rock to the surface, whereas surface waves travel along the Earth's surface like the ripples in a pond when a stone is thrown into it.

P and S waves are fundamentally different (Figure 3-12). A P wave is easily understood by a pool player, who "breaks" a set of pool balls arranged in a tight triangle, all touching. When the cue ball hits the other balls, the energy of striking momentarily compresses the next ball elastically. The compression is transferred to the next ball, then to the next, until the entire set of pool balls scatters around the table. P waves pass through a solid, like rock, and they can also pass through water or air. When earthquake waves pass through air, sometimes they produce a noise.

An S wave can be imagined by tying one end of a clothesline to a tree. Hold the line tight and shake it rapidly from side to side. You can see what appear to be waves running down the line toward

Figure 3-11. An earthquake produces P waves, or compressional waves, which travel faster and reach the seismograph first, and S waves, or shear waves, which are slower. Both are transmitted within the Earth and are called body waves. Even slower are surface waves, which run along the surface of the Earth and do most of the damage. The earthquake focus is the point in the Earth where the earthquake originates. The epicenter is that point on a map directly above the focus. The cross section (above) shows the P and S waves. The diagram (below) is a seismic record, reading from left to right, showing that the P wave arrives first, followed by the S wave and then by surface waves. From R.J. Lillie.

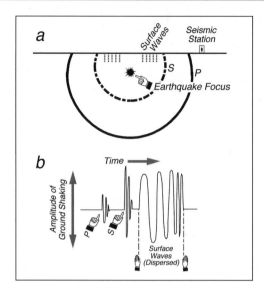

the tree, distorting the shape of the line. In the same fashion, when S waves pass through rock, they distort its shape. S waves cannot pass through liquid.

S waves are slower than P waves, and the seismologist uses this fact to tell how far it is from the seismograph to the earthquake (Figure 3-13). The seismogram records the P wave first, then the S wave. If the seismologist knows the speed of each wave, then by assuming that both waves started at the same time, it is possible to work out how far the earthquake waves have traveled to reach the seismograph. If we can determine the distance of the same earthquake from several different seismograph stations, we are able to locate the *epicenter*, which is the point on the Earth's surface directly above the earthquake *focus*. The focus or *hypocenter* is the point within the Earth's crust or mantle where the earthquake initiates (Figure 3-4). The depth of the earthquake below the surface is called its *focal depth*.

The surface waves are more complex. After reaching the surface, much earthquake energy will run along the surface, causing the ground to go up and down, or sway from side to side. These waves produce much of the severe damage caused by earthquakes.

An earthquake releases a complex array of waves, with great variation in *frequency*, which is the number of waves to pass a point in a second. A guitar string vibrates many times per second, but it takes successive ocean waves many seconds to reach a waiting surfer. The ocean wave has a low frequency, and the guitar string vibrates at a high frequency. An earthquake can be compared to a symphony orchestra, with cellos and bassoons producing sound waves that vibrate at low frequencies, and piccolos and flutes that vibrate at high frequencies. It is only by use of high-speed computers that a seismologist can separate out the complex

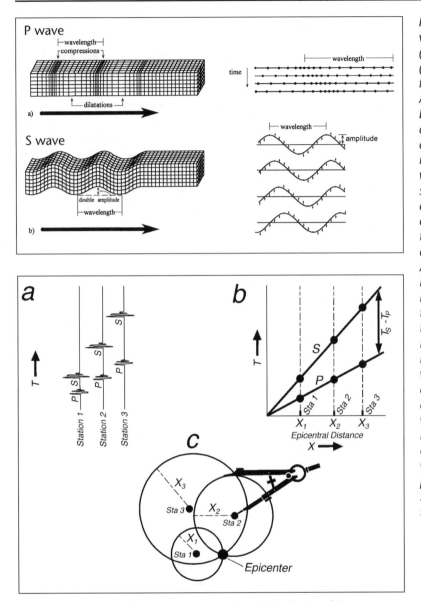

Figure 3-12. Two views of P waves (a) and S waves (b), all moving from left to right. A P wave moves by alternatively compressing and dilating the material through which it passes, somewhat analogous to stop and go traffic on the freeway during rush hour. An S wave moves by shearing the material from side to side, analogous to flipping a rope. Note the illustration of wavelength for P and S waves and amplitude for S waves. The number of complete wavelengths to pass a point in a second is the frequency.

Figure 3-13. How to locate an earthquake. (a) Both P and S waves leave the focus at the same time, but the P wave travels faster. (b) We use the time between the P wave arrival and the S wave arrival to determine the distance the station is from the earthquake, although we still don't know the direction to the earthquake. (c) We plot the distance as the radius of a circle with the seismograph station at its center. With a minimum of three seismograph stations, each with their circles based on the delay between P and S waves, we locate the epicenter, which should be the only point common to all three circles. From R.J. Lillie.

vibrations produced by an earthquake and begin to read and understand the "music of the spheres."

Body waves of large earthquakes travel on a curving path through the Earth for thousands of miles to reach seismographs around the world. I pointed out earlier that only the outermost parts of the Earth are elastic. How can the mantle, which is capable of the slow plastic flow that drives plate tectonics, also behave as an elastic solid when earthquake waves pass through it?

To explain this, I turn to the geologist's favorite toy, Silly Putty. Silly Putty is a soft ball the color of bubble gum that can be stretched out like bubble gum when it is pulled slowly. Hang a piece of Silly Putty over the side of a table, and it will slowly drip to the floor under its own weight, like soft tar (ductile flow). Yet it will bounce like a ball, indicating that it can be elastic. If Silly Putty is stretched out suddenly, it will break, sometimes into several pieces (brittle fracture). The difference is whether the strain is applied suddenly or slowly. When strain is applied quickly, Silly Putty will absorb strain elastically (it will bounce), or it will shatter, depending on whether the strain takes it past its breaking point. If strain is applied slowly, Silly Putty flows. This is the way the asthenosphere and lower crust work. Earthquake waves deform the rock very quickly, and it behaves like an elastic solid. The internal currents that drive the motion of plate tectonics are extremely slow, inches per year or less, and at those slow rates, the rock flows.

Measuring an Earthquake

Magnitude

The chorus of high-frequency and low-frequency seismic waves that radiate out from an earthquake indicates that no single number can characterize an earthquake, just as no single number can be used to describe a Yakima Valley wine or a sunset view of Mt. Rainier or Mt. Hood.

The size of an earthquake was once measured largely on the basis of how much damage was done. This was unsatisfactory to Caltech seismologist Charles Richter, who wanted a more quantitative measure of earthquake size, at least for southern California. Richter established a *magnitude* based on how much a seismograph needle was deflected by a seismic wave generated by an earthquake about 60 miles (100 kilometers) away (Figure 3-14). The particular Wood-Anderson seismograph Richter used

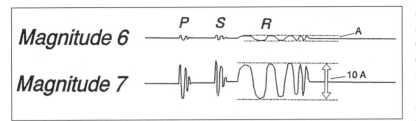

Figure 3-14. Richter's concept of magnitude. The delay between the P wave and the S wave is the same, so the two earthquakes are the same distance away from the seismograph. The larger-magnitude earthquake has a greater amplitude of deflection of the seismogram, in Richter's case, those earthquake waves with a frequency of about five wavelengths per second. In the figure, A is twice the amplitude. From R.J. Lillie.

recorded best those waves that tended to vibrate about five times per second, which is a bit like measuring how loud an orchestra is by how loud the orchestra plays middle C. Nonetheless, it enabled Richter and his colleagues to distinguish large, medium-sized, and small earthquakes, particularly in California, which was all they wanted to do.

Complicating the problem for the lay person is that Richter's scale is logarithmic, which means that a magnitude of, say, 5 would deflect the needle of the seismograph ten times more than a magnitude 4 and that the amplitude of the seismic wave generating an earthquake of magnitude 5 is ten times greater than that for an earthquake of magnitude 4 (Figure 3-14). And an increase of one magnitude unit represents about a thirty-fold increase in release of stored-up seismic strain energy. So a magnitude 7 earthquake might be considered the equivalent of about thirty earthquakes the size of the September 1993 Klamath Falls, Oregon, Earthquake, which was magnitude 6.

Richter never claimed that his magnitude scale, now labeled M_L, was an accurate measure of earthquakes. Nonetheless, the Richter magnitude scale caught on with the media and the general public, and it is still the first thing that a reporter asks a professional about an earthquake: "How big was it on the Richter scale?" Other magnitude scales have been developed, and Richter was chagrined that his own scale, which was the first, continued to have a life of its own. Now, after Richter's death, it is time to fulfill one of his wishes: that the Richter scale be retired to the same museum as the Wood-Anderson seismograph that he used to measure earthquakes.

Some magnitude scales use long-period (low-frequency) waves because they can be recorded at seismographs thousands of miles away from the earthquake. To understand this, think about how heavy metal music is heard a long distance away from its source, a live band or a boom box. Sometimes when my window is open on a summer evening, I can hear a faraway boom box in a passing car, but all I can hear are the very deep, or low-frequency, tones of the bass guitar, which transmit through the air more efficiently than the treble (high-frequency) guitar notes or the voices of the singers. In this same way, low-frequency earthquake waves can be recorded thousands of miles away from the earthquake source. A

Figure 3-15. Intensity map, showing influence of soft sediment northeast of epicenter. Intensity is influenced by earthquake magnitude, distance from the epicenter, and nature of site where recorded: loose soil vs. firm bedrock. From R.J. Lillie.

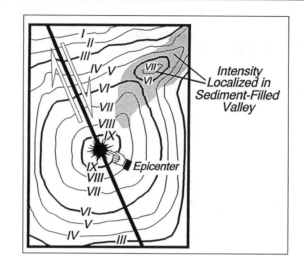

Figure 3-16. Intensity map of the March 25, 1993 Scotts Mills Earthquake. The star marks the epicenter. If you felt this earthquake, find your location on the map, note the intensity, and compare your own observations with those expected with the intensity shown in Table 3-1. (1 km = .62 miles) From Gerald Black, Oregon Department of Geology and Mineral Industries.

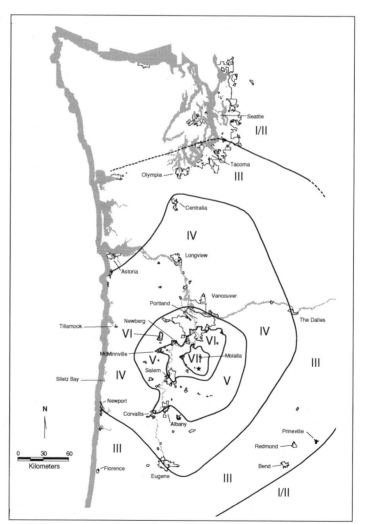

commonly used earthquake scale is the *surface wave magnitude scale,* or M$_S$, which measures the largest deflection of the needle on the seismograph for a surface wave that takes about twenty seconds to pass a point (which is about the same frequency as some ocean waves).

The magnitude scale most useful to professionals is the *moment magnitude scale,* or M$_W$, which comes closest to measuring the true size of an earthquake, particularly a large one. This scale relates magnitude to the area of the fault that ruptures and the amount of slip that takes place on the fault. For large earthquakes, this can be done by measuring the length of the fault that ruptures at the surface and figuring out how deep the brittle rupture is, thereby calculating the area of the rupture. The amount of slip can be measured at the surface as well. The seismologist can also measure M$_W$ by studying the characteristics of low-frequency seismic waves, and the surveyor or geodesist can measure it by remeasuring the location of survey benchmarks to work out the distortion of the ground surface and envisioning a subsurface fault that would produce the observed distortion.

For small- to intermediate-size earthquakes, there is relatively little difference between Richter magnitude, surface-wave magnitude, and moment magnitude. But for very large earthquakes, the difference is dramatic. For example, both the 1906 San Francisco Earthquake and the 1964 Alaska Earthquake had a surface-wave magnitude of 8.3. However, the San Francisco Earthquake had a moment magnitude of only 7.7, whereas the Alaska Earthquake had a moment magnitude of 9.2, which made it the second largest earthquake of the 20th century.

Intensity

Measuring the size of an earthquake by the energy it releases is all well and good, but it is still important to measure how much damage it does at critical places (such as where you or I happen to be when the earthquake strikes). This measurement is called earthquake *intensity,* which is measured by a Roman numeral scale (Table 3-1). Intensity III means no damage, and not everybody feels it. Intensity VII or VIII involves moderate damage, particularly to poorly constructed buildings. Intensity XI or XII is characterized by nearly total destruction. The highest recorded intensity in a historical earthquake in the Pacific Northwest was VIII.

Earthquake intensities are based on a post-earthquake survey of a large area; damage is noted, and people are questioned about what they felt (Figure 3-15). An intensity map is a series of concentric lines, irregular rather than circular, in which the highest intensities are generally (but not always) closest to the epicenter of the earthquake. For illustration, an intensity map is shown for the Scotts Mills, Oregon, Earthquake of March 1993 (Figure 3-16). *continued on page 38* ☞

Modified Mercalli Intensity Scale

Table 3-1. Abridged Modified Mercalli (MM) Intensity Scale. Masonry A: good workmanship, mortar, and design; reinforced, especially laterally, and bound together using steel, concrete, etc. Masonry B: good workmanship and mortar, reinforced, but not designed in detail to resist lateral forces. Masonry C: ordinary workmanship and mortar, no extreme weakness like failing to tie in at corners, but neither reinforced nor designed against horizontal forces. Masonry D: weak materials such as adobe; poor mortar, low standards of workmanship, weak horizontally. From Richter (1958).

Intensity	Description
I	Not felt except by a very few under especially favorable circumstances.
II	Felt only by a few persons at rest, especially on upper floors of buildings.
	Delicately suspended objects may swing.
III	Felt quite noticeably indoors, especially on upper floors of buildings, but many people do not recognize it as an earthquake. Standing automobiles may rock slightly. Vibrations like passing of truck.
IV	During the day, felt indoors by many, outdoors by few. At night, some awakened. Dishes, windows, doors disturbed; walls make creaking sound. Sensation like heavy truck striking building. Standing automobiles rocked noticeably. Peak ground acceleration 0.015-0.02g
V	Felt by nearly everyone, many awakened. Some dishes, windows, and so on broken; cracked plaster in a few places; unstable objects overturned. Disturbances of trees, poles, and other tall objects sometimes noticed. Pendulum clocks may stop.Peak ground acceleration 0.03-0.04g
VI	Felt by all, many frightened and run outdoors. Some heavy furniture moved; a few instances of fallen plaster and damaged chimneys. Damage slight; masonry D cracked.Peak ground acceleration 0.06-0.07g
VII	Everybody runs outdoors. Damage negligible in buildings of good design and construction; slight to moderate in well-built ordinary structures; considerable in poorly built or badly designed structures (masonry D); some chimneys broken. Noticed by persons driving cars. Peak ground acceleration 0.10-0.15g

VIII	Damage slight in specially designed structures; no damage to masonry A, some damage to masonry B, considerable damage to masonry C with partial collapse. Panel walls thrown out of frame structures. Fall of chimneys, factory stacks, columns, monuments, walls. Frame houses moved off foundations if not bolted. Heavy furniture overturned. Sand and mud ejected in small amounts. Changes in well water. Persons driving cars disturbed. Peak ground acceleration 0.25-0.30g
IX	Damage considerable in specially designed structures; well-designed frame structures thrown out of plumb; great in substantial buildings, with partial collapse. Masonry B seriously damaged, masonry C heavily damaged, some with partial collapse, masonry D destroyed. Buildings shifted off foundations. Ground cracked conspicuously. Underground pipes broken. Peak ground acceleration 0.50-0.55g
X	Some well-built wooden structures destroyed; most masonry and frame structures destroyed with foundations; ground badly cracked. Rails bent. Landslides considerable from river banks and steep slopes. Shifted sand and mud. Water splashed, slopped over bank. Peak ground acceleration > 0.60
XI	Few, if any, masonry structures remain standing. Bridges destroyed. Broad fissures in ground. Underground pipelines completely out of service. Earth slumps and land slips in soft ground. Rails bent greatly.
XII	Damage total. Waves seen on ground surface. Lines of sight and level distorted. Objects thrown into the air.

Intensity can also be influenced by the characteristics of the ground. Buildings on solid rock tend to fare better (and thus are subjected to lower intensities) than buildings on thick soft soil. This is discussed further in Chapter 8.

Table 3-1 relates earthquake intensity to the maximum amount of ground acceleration (*peak ground acceleration*, or PGA) that is measured with a special seismograph called a strong-motion accelerograph. Acceleration is measured as a percentage of the Earth's gravity. An acceleration of one g would be just enough to lift you (or anything else) off the ground. Obviously, this would have a major impact on damage done by an earthquake at a given site.

As pointed out above, Intensities VII and VIII may result in major damage to poorly contructed buildings whereas well-constructed buildings should ride out an earthquake with much less damage. This points out the importance of earthquake-resistant construction and strong building codes, discussed further in Chapters 12 and 14.

Suggestions for Further Reading

Bolt, B.A. 1993. *Earthquakes*. Newly revised and expanded. New York: W.H. Freeman & Co., 331p.

Lillie, R.J. 1999. *Whole-Earth Geophysics*. Englewood Cliffs, N.J.: Prentice-Hall, 361p.

Richter, C.F. 1958. *Elementary Seismology*. San Francisco: W.H. Freeman and Co., 468p.

Yeats, R.S., K.E. Sieh, and C.R. Allen. 1997. *The Geology of Earthquakes*. New York: Oxford University Press, 568 p. Chapters 2, 3, and 4, pp. 17-87.

The Subduction Zone:
The Big One

*"Then there were lightning flashes, rumblings, and peals of
thunder, and a great earthquake. It was such a violent
earthquake that there has never been one like it since the
human race began on Earth."*
Book of Revelation 16:18.

Discoveries Beneath the Sea

Outside, it is pitch black as pilot Skip Gleason slowly
maneuvers the research submarine *Alvin* up the
barren, heavily gullied slope. It is August 1984, a summer
day in western Oregon, but here at six thousand feet below sea
level the temperature is just above freezing. Inside, Casey Moore
of the University of California at Santa Cruz and Guy Cochrane of
the University of Washington adjust their positions to try to get
comfortable in the cramped quarters of the *Alvin*, in which three
people must operate in a space no more than 6 feet wide. They
peer downward through small portholes at the gray-brown mud
surface passing beneath the sub. The landscape is vast and murky,
and the headlights of the sub penetrate into the gloom no farther
than about 20 feet. Ledges of soft sandstone glide by, festooned
with occasional brittle stars and sea anemones. Skip stares ahead
at particulate matter, suspended in the headlights like snowflakes,
slowly drifting in the current. At this depth and near-freezing
temperature, the sea floor is a moonless desert.

The sub mounts the broad crest of a ridge, and there,
unexpectedly, on a mud flat over partly buried sandstone, is an
oasis! Casey sees a writhing mass of tube worms growing out of a
rocky ledge, looking like a tangle of giant spaghetti or curls of
rope, with the red-brown living organisms extended out beyond
the end of the tubes. Ahead there are lines of huge clams, perhaps
10 inches long, sticking up out of the mud like rows of tilted
tombstones. The sampling arm of the sub tries to pick up one of
these clams, but crushes it instead, and red blood spurts out.

Suddenly there is a flurry of activity in the sub lights. Carnivorous fish and crabs dart in. A crab gorges on the flesh and blood of the broken clam, then silently disappears into the murk. Where did these animals come from? Were they attracted by the smell of blood? Without the lights of the sub, they could not have seen their prey. More important, how could clams and tube worms grow at such depths, without sunlight as an energy source? Similar organisms had been discovered a few years before at high-temperature vents at mid-ocean ridges, where the ocean crust was spreading apart, and where the water temperature could be hundreds of degrees Fahrenheit. But why here, where the water temperature is nearly freezing?

Back in the laboratory, Casey Moore and a co-worker, Vern Kulm of Oregon State University, would learn that the oasis they had found was actually a cold-water seep expelling water a few degrees warmer than the surrounding sea water. The seeps contain methane and hydrogen sulfide gas, the same malodorous emission that comes from a municipal sewage-treatment plant. The clams and tube worms harbor high concentrations of bacteria that oxidize sulfur (which guarantees that they are too stinky to become a popular seafood delicacy). These bacteria manufacture organic materials through a process called *chemosynthesis*, and these materials are transferred to their hosts, the clams and tube worms. Some of the seeps, at least, were formed by water moving up along active faults that are part of the Cascadia Subduction Zone.

Five years later, in August 1989, Chris Goldfinger and Bruce Appelgate, then graduate students at Oregon State University, and electronics technician Kevin Redman of Williamson and Associates, are in the science lab of OSU's research ship *Wecoma*, looking at side-scan sonar imagery taken as the *Wecoma* cruises at the base of the continental slope along the Cascadia Subduction Zone. The ship tows a "fish," an instrument gliding thousands of feet beneath the sea surface and emitting sound signals that echo back from the sea floor to the fish and are then transmitted to the lab aboard ship. On the video screen, these images look like aerial photos, showing the ocean floor in unprecedented clarity and detail. But these "photos" are created from reflected sound waves, not reflected light. The experience is like being in a balloon drifting slowly through the sky, and looking down at a hitherto-unseen landscape.

Suddenly Goldfinger sees a fault. Crossing the screen in a straight line, it cuts through a sea-floor channel and a landslide, and buckles the sea floor into a low hill. The image of the faulted channel on the video screen looks oddly like a man with a guitar, so naturally it became known as "Elvis" (Figure 4-1).

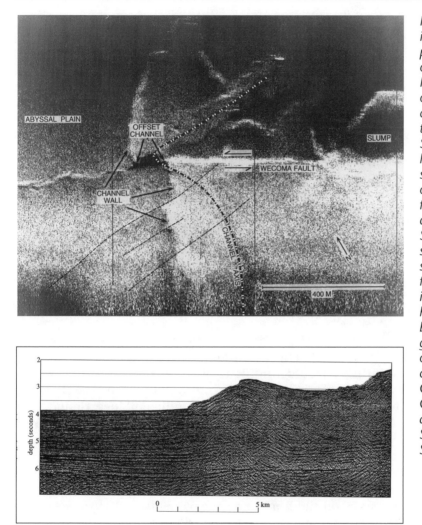

Figure 4-1. Elvis image, marking point of discovery of the Wecoma Fault, which offsets a deep-sea channel more than 300 feet. Slip rate on this left-lateral strike-slip fault is about one inch every four years. Image acquired by SeaMarc 1A side-scan sonar, with sound coming from bottom of image. (Elvis's head and upper body, holding a guitar, are at top of image.) Image courtesy of Chris Goldfinger, College of Oceanic and Atmospheric Sciences, Oregon State University.

Figure 4-2. Seismic-reflection profile of the Cascadia Subduction Zone off central Oregon. West is to the left. Signals from a ship were bounced off the sea floor and off more deeply buried sediment layers, then echoed back to the ship, allowing a profile to be made that shows the geology beneath the sea floor. The flat sea floor on the left is the sediment-covered abyssal plain of the Juan de Fuca Plate. The Cascadia Subduction Zone has thrust highly deformed rocks of the North American Plate over the flat Juan de Fuca Plate. The fault slopes gently to the east. Sediment layers at the left are being forced under the edge of the continent and, in addition, dragged up against the edge of the continent as an accretionary wedge. (1 km = .62 miles) Profile acquired in 1989 by Digicon for the National Science Foundation. Image courtesy of Lisa McNeill and Chris Goldfinger, College of Oceanic and Atmospheric Sciences, Oregon State University.

Figure 4-3. Computer-generated sea-floor image of the central Oregon continental shelf and slope, based on sea floor topographic mapping by the National Oceanic and Atmospheric Administration. Elvis image at the Wecoma Fault (Figure 4-1) is between letters PR and PU. Wecoma Fault (WF) continues up continental slope. Two additional faults B and C are found south of the Wecoma fault. CH at upper right marks location of Cascade Head, north of Lincoln City, Oregon. (1 km = .62 miles) Image courtesy of LaVerne D. Kulm, College of Oceanic and Atmospheric Sciences, Oregon State University.

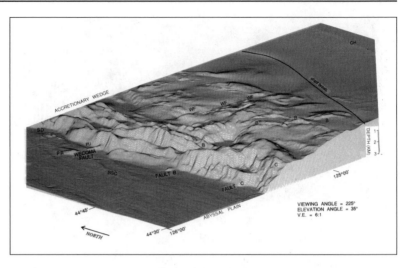

Later, *Alvin* would sample the rocks along the Wecoma Fault, named for the ship that found it. The rocks are strongly sheared, with linear grooves, proof that this is a place where rock grinds against rock.

Using side-scan sonar imagery and topographic mapping by the National Oceanic and Atmospheric Administration (NOAA), Goldfinger would find at least nine of these faults off the Washington and Oregon coast, cutting both the Juan de Fuca Plate and the adjacent North American continental slope. He and Mary MacKay of the University of Hawaii would find active folds buckled up as the Juan de Fuca Plate drives beneath the North American continent (Figure 4-2). Their conclusion: the lower part of the North American continent close to the subduction zone is being crushed and deformed into faults and folds almost everywhere, like snow on the front of a snowplow blade. The source of the destruction: a much larger fault, previously hidden, which slopes gently landward beneath this highly deformed zone.

In ways like this, one of the world's great earthquake faults is slowly coming into view (Figure 4-3), a fault that carries the North American continent on its back as it crushes the deep-sea sediment of the Juan de Fuca Plate beneath it. For three decades after the first discovery that Cascadia is a subduction zone, the fault itself could only be viewed by seismic profiles (Figure 4-2) and by relatively crude depth soundings. With new technology developed by NOAA, the fault can be imaged at the base of the continental slope from Vancouver Island to northern California, near the city of Eureka. On the west side of the fault is the broad sediment-covered plain of the Juan de Fuca Plate, marked only by long, meandering channels carved by sand-laden currents that flow along the sea floor (Figure 4-4). This plain stretches away westward to the Juan de Fuca Ridge, where new oceanic crust is formed by volcanoes at rifts along the ridge axis (Figure 2-5).

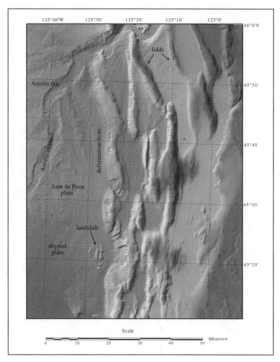

Figure 4-4. Computer-generated sea-floor image of the Oregon continental slope west of Seaside and Cannon Beach, based on sea floor topographic mapping by the National Oceanic and Atmospheric Administration. Elongate hills were formed by folding of sediment when plates collided at the Cascadia Subduction Zone (marked "deformation front"). The seaward end of the Astoria Submarine Canyon and Channel is seen at upper left. (1 km = .62 miles) Image courtesy of Chris Goldfinger and Lisa McNeill, College of Oceanic and Atmospheric Sciences, Oregon State University.

East of the subduction-zone fault, the continental slope rises as a rugged mountain wall, with fold ridges heaved up where the plates converge (Figures 4-3, 4-4). Landslides off southern Oregon, also related to subduction, are tens of miles across. Off Washington, the continental slope is carved into great submarine canyons, including the Astoria Canyon west of the mouth of the Columbia River. North of the Astoria Canyon is another canyon, then another and another, cutting deeply into the slope off Washington. At the top of the slope is the continental shelf, a flat surface carved during lower sea-levels of the Ice Ages. East of that, finally, is the shoreline itself.

These submarine canyons were not eroded by running water, as canyons on land are, because the continental slope was never above sea level. They were cut during the last few hundred thousand years, in the Pleistocene, by slurries of water and sand, brought to the Pacific by the Columbia River, swollen with floodwater from melting ice sheets in central British Columbia, and by other major rivers draining melting glaciers in Puget Sound and flowing west through the present Straits of Juan de Fuca. The muddy and sandy water was heavier than clear seawater, so it churned violently down the continental slope like great snow avalanches, carving the submarine canyons in the process. The avalanches traveled for hundreds of miles, far out onto the Juan de Fuca Abyssal Plain. When the currents finally stopped, the sediment settled out as *turbidites*, sand and mud deposits named for the turbid water that carried them.

*Figure 4-5 .
Coastal features
used as evidence
for great
subduction-zone
earthquakes: (a)
Sudden
subsidence of
coastal forest,
killing trees and
depositing tidal
sediment
containing marine
fossils directly on
the forest litter.
(b) Subsidence
accompanied by a
tsunami (seismic
sea wave, see
Chapter 9),
depositing a layer
of sand on top of
the forest
deposits. (c)
Buried sand may
be liquefied during
earthquake,
erupting onto
surface (see
Chapter 8); this is
rarely seen in the
Cascadia
marshes. Image
courtesy of Brian
Atwater, U.S.
Geological Survey.*

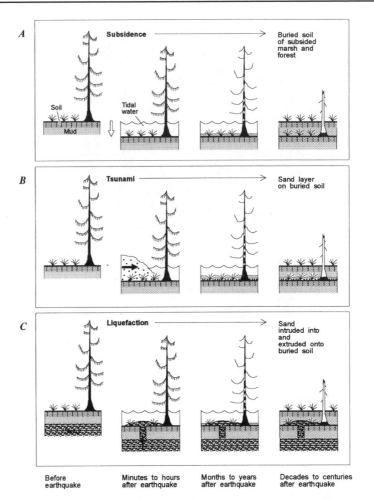

In the 10,000 years since the Pleistocene, the Columbia River floods have been smaller, more like they are today, and the sediment avalanches no longer have the energy to erode the submarine canyons. An ash layer from the cataclysmic eruption of Mt. Mazama, which formed Crater Lake seven thousand years ago, was carried down the Columbia River and deposited within the channels of these great submarine canyons, proof that these canyons are Pleistocene relics, and are not actively eroding today. Since the deposition of the Mazama ash, thinner turbidite layers have been deposited within the channels at irregular time intervals, on the average, about once every five hundred years. These are the same time intervals postulated for great Cascadia Subduction Zone earthquakes. That correlation caused John Adams to suggest that the thin Holocene turbidites, in contrast to the canyon-eroding Pleistocene turbidites related to glacial meltwater, might have been triggered not by Columbia River floods but by great Cascadia Subduction Zone earthquakes.

Figure 4-6. (a) Tree roots from a spruce forest submerged abruptly 1700 years ago in Niawiakum estuary, Willapa Bay, Washington, exposed at very low tide. The tree roots match the forest ecosystem in the distance and document an abrupt subsidence of around 10 feet. The 300-year subsidence event is represented by a soil zone halfway up the cut bank and is better seen in the following illustration. Photo by Robert Yeats. (b) In this close-up view of the Niawiakum exposure, the 300-year soil is marked by the shovel blade. Note the exposed tree root at the right edge of the photo. A marsh similar to the one at the top of the picture was overwhelmed by the ocean, and gray clay with fossils was deposited on top. Photo by Brian Atwater, U.S. Geological Survey.

Earthquakes in the Estuaries

It is in the bays and estuaries along the coastline that the most conclusive evidence for great earthquakes was found by Brian Atwater and his colleagues, as stated in the Introduction (Figures 4-5 through 4-9). From Port Alberni, at the end of a deep fjord on the west coast of Vancouver Island, to Humboldt Bay in northern California, and at many bays and estuaries in between (Figure 4-8), the sediments gave evidence of sudden drops in the land level. The marshes and forests were found to be overlain directly by gray clay with marine microfossils (Figure 4-6), which Atwater could explain only by sudden subsidence of the coastline. Some of these drops appeared to have been accompanied by great waves

Figure 4-7. Dead forest of western red cedar sticking up through a brackish-water tidal marsh at Copalis River on the Washington coast. The forest was killed during rapid subsidence accompanying a Cascadia Subduction Zone earthquake. Tree rings from the dead trees provide evidence that they died sometime after the end of the A.D. 1699 growing season and before the beginning of the A.D. 1700 growing season. This age is consistent with the age based on a Japanese tsunami, discussed below. The forest in the background is above the highest tides. Photo by Brian Atwater, U.S. Geological Survey.

from the sea that deposited sand on the marsh deposits; the last of these waves struck about three hundred years ago. Rick Minor of Heritage Research Associates in Eugene, Oregon, and Wendy Grant of the U.S. Geological Survey found Native American fire pits in the youngest buried marsh soils at the Nehalem and Salmon river estuaries in northern Oregon (Figure 4-9). Atwater's explanation was the catastrophic explanation: great earthquakes on the subduction zone.

Geologists from Japan, England, and New Zealand, including specialists in the ecology of marshes and estuaries, have critically scrutinized this evidence to look for defects in Atwater's earthquake hypothesis and to search for another, less apocalyptic, explanation. They were unable to find support for a non-seismic explanation for any of seven marsh soils buried at Grays Harbor in southwest Washington. For some of the buried marsh deposits, however, the evidence is ambiguous. These could have other origins such as gigantic Pacific storms or changes in the configuration of the estuary itself. But all agree that the burial of marshes that took place three hundred and seventeen hundred years ago, at least, was caused by sudden submergences of the coast at the time of two great Cascadia earthquakes. The average difference in age of successive marsh and forest burials was found to be five hundred years, although the age difference for some was as small as one hundred fifty years or as large as a thousand years.

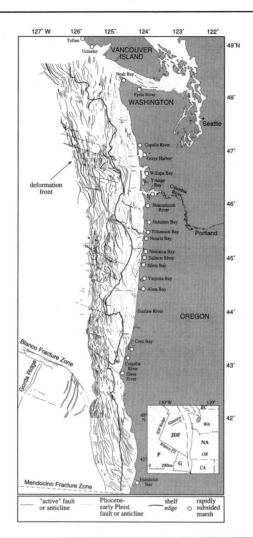

Figure 4-8. Map of the Pacific Northwest coast locating sites of coseismic subsidence on the coast from Vancouver Island to northern California (open circles). Active faults and folds of the Cascadia Subduction Zone are also shown. Heavy line is the edge of the continental shelf. Illustration courtesy of Lisa McNeill, Oregon State University.

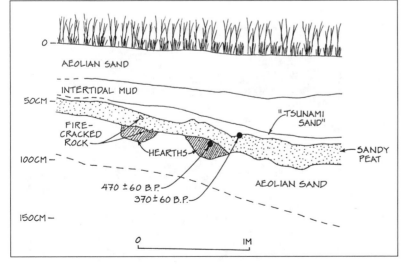

Figure 4-9. Schematic cross section of buried Native American campsite (hearths, fire-cracked rock) overlain by a soil zone submerged by the A.D. 1700 Cascadia Subduction Zone Earthquake and covered by a tsunami deposit. From Minor and Grant (1996); drawing courtesy of Rick Minor, Heritage Research Associates, Eugene, Oregon.

Tree Stumps in the Surf

Like most geologists who live on the Oregon coast, Roger Hart is a beachcomber. But he was not prepared for what he saw on the beach near his house south of Newport: huge tree stumps with root systems up to 15 feet across. One of the effects of the El Niño winters of 1973-74, 1982-83, 1994-95, and 1997-98 had been to sweep the beach sand out to sea, exposing the stumps of an ancient forest, including western hemlock and Sitka spruce, rooted in the rocks in the surf zone (Figure 4-10). And the stumps were at other places, too: hundreds of them, from Neskowin north of Lincoln City to Sunset Bay southwest of Coos Bay. Some of the stumps had the original forest duff preserved around them, and the forest soil could be traced up a low rise to a grassy flat above the beach. Radiocarbon dating showed that the trees were late Holocene, although none were found younger than one thousand years.

How could you have mature trees in the surf zone where salt water would prevent any tree from growing? Only one idea made sense to Hart (Figure 4-11). Clearly, the surf had been there first, eroding away the beach cliffs to a flat surface, a marine wave-cut platform. But then, somehow, the marine surface had risen out of the water, high enough and for a long enough time for a mature forest to grow and become rooted in the surface. Then, the surface, now covered by forest, dropped back into the sea, and the trees died, leaving only their stumps. The waves resumed their attack on the beach cliffs.

Figure 4-10. Rooted tree stump in surf zone at Moore Creek on central Oregon coast, exposed by El Niño currents of 1997-98 winter, which removed much of sand cover. Dashed line marks formerly forested slope leading up to a higher marine terrace on which houses are constructed. A lower marine terrace platform is also present at right. Photo by Roger A. Hart, College of Oceanic and Atmospheric Sciences, Oregon State University.

The uplift and subsidence resemble Atwater's evidence from the marshes and estuaries, except that the evidence for uplift was more clearly displayed by the tree stumps on the beach. Uplift occurred during the interseismic interval between earthquakes as the crust rebounded after the last great event. Subsidence

Forest Soil

Uplifted Platform

Rooted Stump in Surf Zone

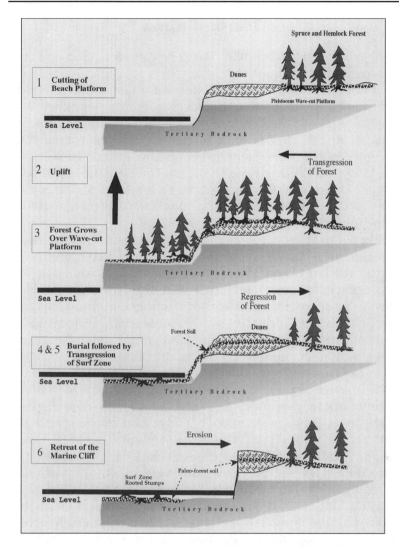

1 Cutting of
   Beach Platform

2 Uplift

3 Forest Grows
   Over Wave-cut
   Platform

4 & 5 Burial followed by
       Transgression
       of Surf Zone

6 Retreat of the
   Marine Cliff

Spruce and Hemlock Forest

Dunes

Pleistocene Wave-cut Platform

Sea Level

Tertiary Bedrock

Transgression
of Forest

Sea Level

Tertiary Bedrock

Regression
of Forest

Forest Soil   Dunes

Sea Level

Tertiary Bedrock

Erosion

Surf Zone
Rooted Stumps   Paleo-forest soil

Sea Level

Tertiary Bedrock

Figure 4-11. Diagrams illustrating formation of trees the stumps of which are now preserved in the surf zone. (1) Marine platform is cut into beach cliff. (2) Uplift takes place, possibly in the interseismic interval between earthquakes. (3) Former marine platform is covered by coastal forest. (4, 5) Forested marine platform is dropped back down, possibly by an earthquake, killing the trees but preserving their roots, which are subsequently covered by beach sand. (6) Waves cut once again into the beach cliff. Diagram by Roger A. Hart, College of Oceanic and Atmospheric Sciences, Oregon State University.

accompanied a subduction-zone earthquake, just as it did in the marshes elsewhere along the coast. Without evidence from the marshes, Hart would not have been able to tell that the subsidence had been abrupt; he only saw the stumps. However, if subsidence had taken place slowly, the stumps might not have been preserved at all.

No tree trunks have been found that have been dated as three hundred years old, which would mark their subsidence as accompanying the last great earthquake. But only a very few of the stumps have been dated, and some may be that young. One of the stumps is more than four thousand years old. Was it uplifted and downdropped several times during several earthquakes, and if so, why was it preserved? There are many questions, but only a few answers. Maybe when we have fifty radiocarbon dates, one of the stumps might turn out to be three hundred years old.

The Bad News

How did the Cascadia Subduction Zone gain its reputation as the source of great earthquakes?

It was not always so. Most subduction zones around the world are shaken by frequent earthquakes, some of magnitude 9 or greater. But not Cascadia, which has been as seismically quiet as Kansas. At first, it was thought that the apparent absence of recorded earthquakes might be because the Juan de Fuca Plate is no longer subducting beneath North America. The eruption of Mt. St. Helens on May 18, 1980, was a dramatic demonstration that subduction is still going on, and another explanation needed to be found.

Then it was suggested that the absence of recorded earthquakes is due to the relatively few seismographs in the Pacific Northwest. But in the last twenty years, the University of Washington, the U.S. Geological Survey, and the Geological Survey of Canada have developed an extensive network of seismographs throughout the region. This sophisticated network recorded many earthquakes in the continental crust and in the subducting Juan de Fuca Plate, but almost none precisely on the subduction zone itself.

In the past few years, the U. S. Navy has opened access to the hydrophone arrays it had established to monitor enemy submarines by recording the sound waves from their engines. These hydrophone arrays record not only submarine-engine noise, but also record whale calls—and earthquakes. They reveal unprecedented details about the seismicity of the Juan de Fuca spreading ridge and other sea floor features. But even at those listening levels, the subduction zone remains quiet. Why?

For a long time, it was thought (perhaps "hoped" is a better word) that the absence of earthquakes meant that the subduction zone slides smoothly beneath the continent. Subduction without earthquakes was still being suggested in a paper in a major scientific journal as recently as 1979. But in 1980, Jim Savage of the U. S. Geological Survey and his colleagues began repeated measurements of networks of surveying benchmarks around Seattle, in Olympic National Park, and at the Hanford Nuclear Reservation. Their conclusion: these networks show that the crust is being slowly deformed in a way that is best explained by elastic strain building up in the crust, as illustrated in Figures 3-2 and 3-3. The obvious source of this strain: the Cascadia Subduction Zone. The reason that there have been no earthquakes on the subduction zone is an ominous one: the subduction zone is locked. *Completely locked.* If this is the case, then strain must ultimately build up along the subduction-zone fault, inexorably, at 1.6 inches per year, until eventually the subduction zone will rupture in a massive earthquake.

At about the same time (as already reported in the Introduction), John Adams, then of Cornell University, was studying the re-surveys of highway benchmarks and discovering that the coastal regions of Oregon and Washington are being slowly tilted eastward. A few years later, Heaton and Kanamori showed that the geophysical setting of Cascadia is like that of southern Chile, where the largest earthquake of the 20th century struck in 1960. A short time after that, in 1986, Brian Atwater paddled up the Niawiakum River estuary in his kayak and discovered the submerged marshes and forests of Willapa Bay (located in Figure 4-8).

For about ten years, starting in the late 1970s, the argument raged among scientists about whether or not the Cascadia Subduction Zone poses an earthquake threat, triggered by a major economic and political issue: was it safe to build and operate nuclear power plants in western Washington and Oregon and northern California? Proponents of the big-earthquake hypothesis were led by scientists of the U.S. Geological Survey, influenced by geodesists such as Jim Savage who were re-surveying benchmarks, and later by geologists like Brian Atwater. As described in the Introduction, it was only in 1987 that the controversy was finally resolved at the Oregon Academy of Sciences meeting in Monmouth, Oregon, where it was recognized that the paradigm change had occurred. Most of the leading Cascadia earthquake researchers agreed at this meeting that the Cascadia Subduction Zone does indeed pose a major earthquake threat. When a paradigm change takes place, particularly for a topic that has such an impact on society, scientists take on a new mission: to inform the general public of the consequences and implications of this new understanding.

Even though there was general agreement that there would be huge earthquakes on the Cascadia Subduction Zone, a new debate began over how big the expected earthquake would be. Would it be of magnitude 8 or magnitude 9? This debate is still going on. At this point, it is useful to state what scientists agree on and what they do not, and to show what the social implications of a magnitude 8 or magnitude 9 event would be. It is not, as some have suggested, analogous to being struck by a tractor-trailer or a compact car!

Instant of Catastrophe
or Decade of Terror?

After Atwater's discovery at Neah Bay and Willapa Bay, other scientists found evidence of marshes buried by sudden subsidence accompanying earthquakes in Humboldt Bay in northern California, at South Slough near Coos Bay in southern Oregon, at Salmon River near Lincoln City, Oregon, at Nehalem Bay and Netarts Bay in northern Oregon, at the mouth of the Copalis River in Washington, and at Port Alberni on the Pacific coast of Vancouver Island (Figure 4-8). Carbon from buried soils and from drowned tree trunks was sent to radiocarbon labs for dating. The result: the youngest marsh burial occurred about three hundred years ago at nearly all sites along the Cascadia Subduction Zone from British Columbia to northern California. If this was caused by a single earthquake, as the similarity in radiocarbon ages would suggest, that earthquake would have a moment magnitude (M_w) of 9, close to the size of the great Alaskan earthquake of 1964. It would rank among the largest earthquakes ever recorded.

A common saying among geologists is that *what has happened, can happen*. If the earthquake three hundred years ago was a magnitude 9, the next subduction-zone earthquake could also be a 9. If this were to happen, what would be the impact on our society?

All of western Washington and Oregon, southwesternmost British Columbia, and north coastal California would be devastated by a magnitude 9 earthquake, so that emergency response teams would have to come from inland cities or from central and southern California. Intense shaking from a magnitude 9 event would last two to three minutes; a magnitude 8 event would have strong shaking for about half that time. A building might survive strong shaking lasting a minute, but not twice or three times as long. For comparison, the strong shaking for the Kobe and Northridge earthquakes each lasted less than thirty seconds. Some of the shaking during these smaller earthquakes was as strong as that expected for a great subduction zone earthquake; it just didn't last as long.

This shaking would trigger landslides throughout the Coast Range, Olympic Mountains, and Vancouver Island, in Puget Sound and the Willamette Valley, and even on the continental slope, where landslides could trigger tsunamis. For even a magnitude 8 event, large sand bars like those at Long Beach, Washington, or at the mouth of Siletz Bay, Oregon, could become unstable, as would low-lying islands in the tidal reaches of the lower Columbia River. The Pacific coastline would drop permanently, as shown in Figure 4-5, as much as 2 to 4 feet, inundating low-lying areas such as Coos Bay, Siletz Bay, Tillamook Bay, Cannon Beach, and Seaside.

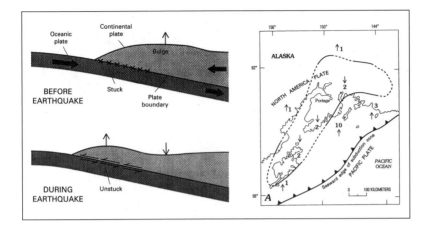

Figure 4-12. (Left) Cross section showing elastic strain buildup in edge of continental plate before earth-quake, then sudden release (elastic rebound) during earthquake, causing part to go up and part to go down. The Pacific Northwest coast should go down. Modified from Brian Atwater, U.S. Geological Survey. (Right) Map of part of southern Alaska, showing the crust that went down in the great 1964 earthquake (M_w 9.2) and the crust that went up. Numbers show subsidence or uplift in meters. Uplift and subsidence accompanying this earthquake were used to model uplift and subsidence accompanying a Cascadia Subduction Zone earthquake. (100 km = 62 miles) Modified from George Plafker, U.S. Geological Survey.

Seismic sea waves, or tsunamis, could be as high as 30 to 40 feet with a magnitude 9 earthquake, but less than half that with an 8. Fifteen to thirty minutes after the mainshock had died away, the first of several tsunamis would strike. In some cases, the water would first rush out to sea, exposing sea floor never before seen as dry land, but a short time later, a wall of water would rush inland, sweeping the sand from barrier bars inland, overwhelming beach houses and bayfront boutiques and restaurants as far as several blocks away from the sea. These destructive waves would be repeated several times.

The mainshock would be followed by aftershocks, some with magnitudes greater than 7, large earthquakes in their own right. These aftershocks would continue at a diminishing rate for many years. For a magnitude 8 earthquake, these would affect a limited part of the Pacific Northwest perhaps two to three hundred miles long, but for a magnitude 9 event, the entire Northwest from Vancouver Island to northern California would be affected.

Because a magnitude 9 earthquake would devastate such a large area, it would have catastrophic and perhaps disastrous effects on the economy of the Northwest, the ability of government to serve the people, and the ability of insurance companies to pay their claims. The economic effects of a magnitude 8 event would be great, but not as cataclysmic as those of a magnitude 9 because a much smaller area would be affected. If a magnitude 8 earthquake originated west of the mouth of the Columbia River, it would severely damage the Portland metropolitan area, but not the cities of Puget Sound or the southern Willamette Valley. Emergency response teams from those areas could come to the aid of Portland and adjacent communities in Oregon and Washington. There would be less damage, fewer insurance claims, less destructive effects on the overall economy of the United States and Canada than a magnitude 9 earthquake.

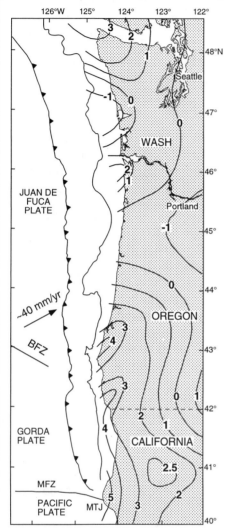
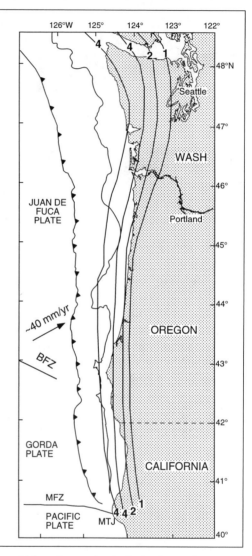

Figure 4-13. Map of the Cascadia Subduction Zone showing contours of uplift in the past fifty years in millimeters, from Mitchell and Weldon, University of Oregon (left) and from Hyndman and Wang, Pacific Geoscience Centre (right). Mitchell and Weldon showed the complexities of the data as they observed it releveling highways in western Oregon and Washington, supporting a smaller maximum earthquake on the subduction zone. Hyndman and Wang, on the other hand, smoothed out the data to fit their idea that the maximum earthquake could be of magnitude 9. Faults and folds crossing the subduction zone and adjacent North American plate led McCaffrey and Goldfinger to suggest that the maximum earthquake would be much smaller than a 9. (But the Japanese tsunami evidence favors a 9!). BFZ, Blanco Fracture Zone; MFZ, Mendocino Fracture Zone. Arrow shows direction and amount of plate convergence in millimeters per year. Image courtesy of Chris Goldfinger, College of Oceanic and Atmospheric Sciences, Oregon State University.

A diagram illustrating the buildup and release of strain in the next great Cascadia earthquake is shown in Figure 4-12.

How do we learn whether the last earthquake was a magnitude 8 or a 9? Radiocarbon dates can provide accuracy to within a few decades, which is not proof that all the marshes and estuaries were buried at the same time from Vancouver Island to northern California. In southwest Japan, the Nankai Subduction Zone broke in two magnitude 8 earthquakes, one in 1944, while Japan was in the throes of World War II, and one in 1946, when the country was trying to rebuild after the end of the war. If these earthquakes had not been recorded historically, radiocarbon dating could not have provided evidence that these were two different earthquakes; the numbers would appear to document one great earthquake rather than the two that actually occurred. Gary Carver of Humboldt State University points out the dilemma: one gigantic earthquake ("instant of catastrophe") versus a series of smaller ones (a "decade of terror") about three hundred years ago.

Tree-ring dating can get closer to a true date than radiocarbon dating can. Gordon Jacoby of Columbia University and Dave Yamaguchi of the University of Washington have compared the pattern of growth rings of trees killed in several estuaries in southwest Washington. Variations in the growth patterns of trees from year to year, related to unusual wet seasons or drought years, allowed these scientists to conclude that trees in four of these estuaries were inundated some time between August 1699 and May 1700, strong evidence that the estuaries were downdropped at the same time by an earthquake of magnitude greater than 8. However, these correlations have not been extended north to Vancouver Island or south to northern California, which would strengthen the case for a single magnitude 9 earthquake.

Clifton Mitchell and Ray Weldon of the University of Oregon studied re-levelings of U. S. Highway 101 along the coast from Crescent City, California, to Neah Bay, Washington, taking advantage of a more accurate leveling survey carried out after John Adams had published his results. They found that over the past fifty years, southern Oregon, the mouth of the Columbia River, and northwest Washington have been rising at about an inch or more every ten years (Figure 4-13). But the central Oregon coast around Newport and the area around Grays Harbor, Washington, are not uplifting at all. This suggests that only some parts of the Cascadia Subduction Zone are building up elastic strain. Imagine irregular hang-ups or strong points (called *asperities*) along the subduction zone that concentrate all the strain and localize the uplift, separated by other regions where strain is not accumulating. The zones of no strain around Newport and Grays Harbor could have terminated the rupture, preventing it from shearing off the next asperity to the north or south. This line of reasoning adds support to the "decade of terror" hypothesis of several smaller earthquakes rather than one humongous one.

Rob McCaffrey of Rensselaer Polytechnic Institute in New York has determined the largest earthquakes observed on various subduction zones around the world, including those with a longer recorded history than Cascadia. He finds that the largest earthquakes, the magnitude 9s, strike subduction zones where the upper plate acts like a rigid slab and is not internally deformed, as shown in the diagram on the upper left side of Figure 4-12. The evidence of small faults and folds near the subduction zone found by Chris Goldfinger shows that the upper plate at Cascadia is not a rigid slab, but is strongly deformed internally. McCaffrey and Goldfinger therefore have suggested that the largest earthquake on Cascadia would be in the range of magnitude 8 to 8.3. This idea is consistent with a comparison of subduction zones around the world a decade earlier by Tom Heaton and Hiroo Kanamori of Caltech, leading to an estimate of maximum earthquake size at Cascadia of magnitude 8 to 8.5.

But Roy Hyndman and Kelin Wang of the Pacific Geoscience Centre at Sidney, B.C., argue that the earthquake is more likely to be a 9 rather than an 8. Using temperature estimates in the crust on Vancouver Island and offshore, they calculated which parts of the subduction zone would be stuck and which parts would slide freely due to higher temperature at greater depth. They also measured the changes in leveling lines across Vancouver Island and the Straits of Georgia. They compared their leveling data with uplift of the land with respect to sea level, taking advantage of the fact that they could use three coastlines: both sides of Vancouver Island and the mainland coast northwest of Vancouver.

Hyndman and Wang's model predicts that the next great earthquake would rupture the entire subduction zone from Canada to California, a magnitude 9 rather than an 8. But their model does not take into account the north-south variation in uplift found by Mitchell and Weldon, in particular the absence of uplift of highway markers along Oregon Highway 101 from Newport to Tillamook (Figure 4-13). In addition, their idea is contrary to the maximum size of subduction zones elsewhere around the Pacific Rim, in which the largest earthquakes occur only on those subduction zones where there is little or no deformation of the upper plate.

A Japanese Tsunami and Native American Legends: A Detective Story

The difficulty in figuring out the maximum size of a Cascadia earthquake, of course, is the lack of local historical records at the time the last great subduction-zone earthquake struck the Pacific Northwest. But there is one last chance. Suppose the earthquake generated a tsunami that was recorded somewhere else around the Pacific Rim where people *were* keeping records. This leads us to Japan, the first country on the Pacific Rim of Fire to develop a civilization that kept written records.

In May 1960, an earthquake of moment magnitude 9.5, the greatest earthquake of the 20th century, struck the coast of southern Chile. This earthquake generated a large tsunami that traveled northwestward across the Pacific Ocean and struck Japan twenty-four hours later, causing one hundred forty deaths and great amounts of damage (Figure 4-14). Cascadia is closer to Japan than Chile, and if a magnitude 9 earthquake ruptured the Cascadia Subduction Zone, a resulting tsunami could have been recorded in Japan. The height of the tsunami wave could give evidence about whether the magnitude was 9 or only 8.

The southwestern part of Japan, closer to the ancient civilization of China, developed first, and the first local subduction-zone earthquake in southwestern Japan was recorded in A.D. 684. Records of earthquakes, tsunamis (*tsunami* is a Japanese word meaning "harbor wave"), and volcanic eruptions were kept at temples and villages, principally in southwest Japan until A.D. 1192, when the government was moved to the fishing village of Kamakura on Tokyo Bay, leaving the emperor in isolated splendor far to the west, in Kyoto. In A.D. 1603, the Tokugawa rulers moved the administrative capital farther north to Edo, another small outpost which would become the modern capital of Tokyo. By this time, the entire Pacific coast of Honshu, which faces Cascadia, had been settled, and written records were being kept.

At the time, the Japanese did not necessarily make a connection between earthquakes and tsunamis, but compilation of these ancient records by Japanese scientists and historians in recent years shows that most of the tsunamis recorded from the earliest times were related to the great subduction-zone earthquakes that frequently struck the Japanese Home Islands. But a few tsunamis did *not* accompany a local earthquake. Japanese investigators were able to correlate most of these "exotic" tsunamis to subduction-zone earthquakes in South America, where local records were kept. Earthquakes in Peru in A.D. 1586 and 1687, before the Cascadia earthquake, and in Chile in A.D. 1730 and 1751, after the event, produced tsunamis that were recorded in Japan.

*Figure 4-14. (Top)
Wave fronts of
tsunami
accompanying the
1960 Chilean
Earthquake (M$_w$
9.5) in hours, as
tsunami crossed
Pacific. (Below)
Tide gauge record
of 1960 tsunami
recorded at
Miyako, Japan, in
hours. From K.
Satake, Geological
Survey of Japan.*

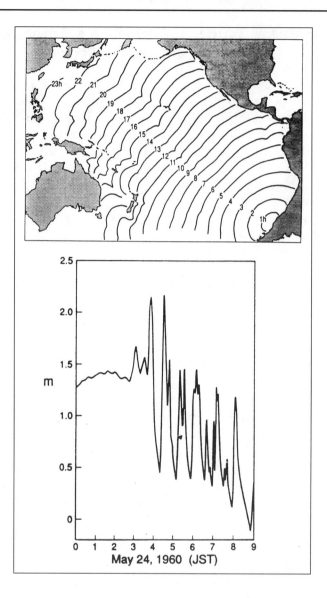

But Kenji Satake, then of the University of Michigan and now
of the Geological Survey of Japan, found records for one tsunami
that could not be correlated to a local Japanese earthquake and
had no apparent source in other subduction zones around the
Pacific where records were kept, including South and Central
America and the Kamchatka Peninsula off Siberia. On January 27
and 28, A.D. 1700, this tsunami produced waves as high as 9 feet
that were recorded at five different coastal sites on the main island
of Honshu from the far north, near Hokkaido, to the Kii Peninsula
south of Kyoto, still the imperial capital of Japan. Houses were
damaged, and rice paddies and storehouses were flooded. The
distribution of recording sites along most of the Pacific coast of

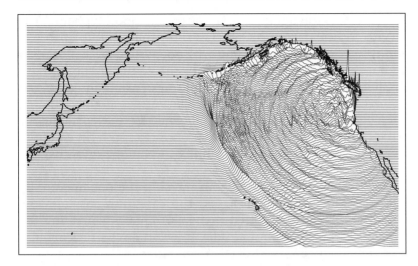

Figure 4-15.
Computer model
of the tsunami
resulting from a
great earthquake
on the Cascadia
Subduction Zone
on January 26,
A.D. 1700. The
tsunami has
already reached
southern Alaska,
and the first wave
has just reached
the Hawaiian
Islands. Japan is
at far left. Note
how far individual
waves are
separated from
one another, and
how high the
waves are due
west of Cascadia,
in the direction of
seismic wave
propagation,
compared to
waves off Baja
California, at
lower right. From
K. Satake,
Geological Survey
of Japan.

Honshu ruled out a local source of the tsunami, such as a submarine landslide or volcanic eruption.

At a meeting on earthquakes held at Marshall, California, in September 1994, Alan Nelson of the U.S. Geological Survey was having lunch with Satake and his colleague Kunihiko Shimazaki of the University of Tokyo. Nelson had been studying the buried marshes at Coos Bay, Oregon, and considering whether these marshes had been downdropped by earthquakes or by some other means. He explained to the two Japanese seismologists that an earthquake-induced subsidence event or events along the Northwest coast from Canada to California had produced radiocarbon dates indicating that all the subsidence events took place about three hundred years ago. These dates could not be pinned down closer than a few decades around A.D. 1700. Could the Japanese tsunami of that year have been the result of a great Cascadia earthquake?

First, Satake and Shimazaki had to exclude all other subduction zones around the Pacific Rim that, like Cascadia, were not settled by people keeping records in A.D. 1700, for example, Alaska and the Aleutian Islands. But the great 1964 Alaska Earthquake of M 9.2, the second largest earthquake of the 20th century, had generated only a very small tsunami in Japan, although, as will be seen in Chapter 9, it produced a destructive tsunami in the Pacific Northwest. This was due to the orientation of the Aleutian Subduction Zone, which is parallel to Japan rather than perpendicular to it, so that the largest tsunamis were propelled to the south and southeast, away from Japan. The Kamchatka-Kurile Subduction Zone was another possibility, but explorers and traders were arriving there as early as the 1680s, and again, the orientation of the subduction zone was parallel to Japan. By process of elimination, this left Cascadia.

Could the tsunami have been caused by a local typhoon? The records for the day of the tsunami show that central Japan had sunny or cloudy weather and was not visited by a storm. In addition, even a gigantic "storm of the century" should have produced a more localized distribution of tsunamis than was observed. A monster typhoon could have struck all the recording sites, but not all at the same time. It would have swept along the coast from south to north, or from north to south. In addition, most typhoons in Japan strike during the summer months, and would be most unusual in January.

Satake knew how fast tsunamis travel in the open ocean. By backtracking the tsunami across the Pacific to the Cascadia coastline, he calculated that if the earthquake generating the tsunami had come from Cascadia, it would have struck about 9 p.m. on January 26, 1700. Satake's computer model of a Cascadia tsunami on its way to Japan is shown as Figure 4-15.

Could there be confirmation in the oral traditions of Native Americans living along the coast at that time? Garry Rogers of the Pacific Geoscience Centre in Sidney, B.C., found in the provincial archives at Victoria a tradition that an earthquake had struck Pachena Bay on the west side of Vancouver Island during a winter night; the following morning, it was discovered that the village at the head of the bay had disappeared. This is consistent with Satake's calculated time of the earthquake based on the Japanese tsunami. Traditions of the Chinook included references to ground shaking. The Makah, Tillamook, and Coos tribes have stories of the inundation of coastal settlements by "tidal waves" or tsunamis. Deborah Carver of Trinidad, California, has collected stories recorded in the early part of the 20th century from Wiyot, Yurok, Tolowa, and Chetco living on the coast of northern California and southern Oregon. Many of these stories tell of strong shaking from a great earthquake along at least 200 miles of coastline, followed by many aftershocks, liquefaction of sediments, subsidence of coastal regions, and tsunamis that lasted for several hours. Six of these stories indicated that the earthquake struck at night. The earthquake and tsunami destroyed many villages and drowned many people living there. Carver reported that one purpose of the Yurok "Jumping Dance" was to repair or re-level the Earth after an earthquake.

The story that follows is from an interview recorded by A.L. Kroeber in his book *Yurok Myths*:

And from there [Earthquake and Thunder] went south—
They went south first and sank the ground—Every little
while there would be an earthquake, then another
earthquake, and another earthquake—And then the water
would fill those [depressed] places—"That is what human

beings will thrive on," said Earthquake. "For they would have no subsistence if there were nothing for the creatures [of the sea] to live in. For that is where they will obtain what they will subsist on, when this prairie has become water, this stretch that was prairie: there will be ocean there."—"Yes, that is true. That is true. That is how they will subsist," said Thunder. "Now go north." Then they went north together and did the same: they kept sinking the ground. The earth would quake and quake and quake again. And the water was flowing all over.

This story spoke of land that sank into the ocean during an earthquake—exactly what Brian Atwater, Alan Nelson, and Deborah's husband, Gary, had concluded from their study of marsh deposits on the Pacific coast. In addition, Gary Carver studied a subsidence site in northern California and concluded that the subsidence occurred after the leaves had fallen and before new growth appeared on the trees; that is, probably during the winter.

Rick Minor suggested that Cascadia Subduction Zone earthquakes might explain an oddity of Native American archeology along the coast. Sea level rose rapidly from twelve thousand to five thousand years ago, as glacial ice sheets melted, and then stabilized close to the present level four to five thousand years ago. But there is very little archeological evidence for Native American settlement along the coast prior to about two thousand years ago. Could the lag in settlement be a result of abrupt coastal subsidence and great tsunamis accompanying past subduction-zone earthquakes? Were Native Americans more concerned about earthquake and tsunami hazards than we are today?

M 8 or M 9? Where Do We Stand?

Satake developed a set of computer models that showed the size of the tsunami that would be generated from earthquakes of different moment magnitude. His computer model (Figure 4-15) suggested that the 9-foot waves recorded in Japan must be produced by an earthquake of M 9; a tsunami from an earthquake of M 8 in Cascadia would produce a much smaller tsunami, probably too small to be recorded. In addition, the tsunami record in Japan provided evidence for only one Cascadia earthquake ("instant of catastrophe") and not a series of earthquakes over several years ("decade of terror").

Satake's evidence has not stilled the controversy over whether there was a magnitude 8 or 9 earthquake. A subduction-zone earthquake near the island of Biak in eastern Indonesia in 1996 produced a tsunami in Japan; this region, like Cascadia, also had no written records in A.D. 1700. There are other subduction zones off the coast of Papua New Guinea and farther east in the islands of the southwest Pacific. Could an earthquake south of Japan have produced the A.D. 1700 tsunami? Satake's computer models are more sensitive to the amount of slip along the subduction-zone fault, which could be as much as 65 feet, and less sensitive to the length of the subduction zone from north to south. However, he was following the prevailing view that very long faults (600 miles or more) could produce greater slip than shorter ones (200 miles or less).

If Gordon Jacoby and Dave Yamaguchi could extend their tree-ring correlations north and south to include most of the Cascadia subduction zone, the argument for a magnitude 9 earthquake would be greatly strengthened. McCaffrey's and Hyndman's conflicting models need to be tested; much research needs to be done. Until we know more, we need to take a "wait and see" attitude. This means that we should plan for an earthquake of M 9 while hoping that it will be smaller, "only" M 8.

Suggestions for Further Reading

Atwater, B.F., and others. 1995. Summary of coastal geologic evidence for past great earthquakes at the Cascadia subduction zone. *Earthquake Spectra*, vol. 11, pp. 1-18.

Clague, J.J. 1997. Evidence for large earthquakes at the Cascadia subduction zone. *Reviews of Geophysics*, vol. 35, pp. 439-60.

Gore, R., and J. Richardson. 1998. Cascadia: Living on Fire. *National Geographic* vol. 193, no. 5, pp. 6-37.

Hart, R., and C. Peterson. 1997. Episodically buried forests in the Oregon surf zone. *Oregon Geology*, vol. 59, pp. 131- 44.

Hyndman, R.D. 1995. Giant earthquakes of the Pacific Northwest. *Scientific American*, vol. 273, no. 6, pp. 50-57.

Satake, K., K. Shimazaki, Y. Tsuji, and K. Ueda. 1996. Time and size of a giant earthquake in Cascadia inferred from Japanese tsunami records of January 1700. *Nature*, vol. 379, pp. 246-49.

Earthquakes in the
Juan de Fuca Plate

Commotion in the Ocean

Thirty million years ago, the oceanic crust west of North America formed part of the Farallon Plate, not the Pacific Plate (Figure 5-1). The Farallon and Pacific plates were separated by the East Pacific Rise, part of the world-encircling mountain system that marks where new oceanic crust is formed and spreads away (Figure 2-3). But sea-floor spreading on the Mid-Atlantic Ridge forced North America westward, away from Europe and toward the East Pacific Rise. The Farallon Plate was slowly subducted beneath North America, and the Pacific Plate was brought into contact with the North American Plate along the San Andreas Fault. Now the Farallon Plate is largely gone, and its only remnants are the Rivera and Cocos plates off Mexico and Central America and the Juan de Fuca Plate off the Pacific Northwest. Subduction still continues today along the Rivera, Cocos, and Juan de Fuca plates.

Visualization of these examples of plate tectonics stretches the imagination until we recall that this has taken thirty million years, a length of time that overwhelms our ability to understand it. We are forced to put our imagination of natural processes into ultra-high speed, such that lifetimes flash by in a couple of seconds, and we would get a plate-boundary subduction-zone earthquake at Cascadia every fifteen seconds. Even at that rate, the disappearance of the Farallon Plate would seem extraordinarily slow.

The Juan de Fuca Plate is entirely oceanic, with thin crust made up of basalt. No part of it is above sea level. The crust is nowhere more than a few tens of millions of years old, which means that it is relatively shallow, weak, and hot. Its weakness means that it is subject to internal deformation where it interacts with the continental edge of North America. At its northern and southern ends, where the spreading center is closest to the base of the continent, and the oceanic crust is youngest, the weak oceanic plate is being actively deformed internally, deformation that is

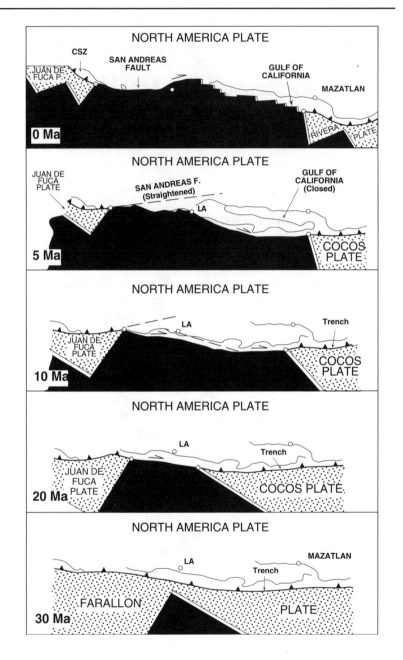

Figure 5-1. Thirty million years of plate tectonics off western North America. Formerly, the Farallon Plate was subducting under the North American Plate. The Pacific Plate, moving northwest, contacted North America, forming the San Andreas Transform Fault, and breaking the Farallon Plate into the Cocos and Rivera plates off Mexico and the Juan de Fuca Plate off the Pacific Northwest.

marked by high seismicity. These seismically active regions are generally referred to as separate plates, the Explorer Plate off Vancouver Island and the Gorda Plate off northern California (Figure 5-2). The Juan de Fuca Plate between its northern and southern ends has few earthquakes, indicating that internal deformation is less important there.

The fact that the Juan de Fuca Plate is completely oceanic means that we are not able to measure its displacement rates directly but instead must rely on indirect geophysical evidence. All permanent seismic stations are onshore, resulting in considerable inaccuracy in locating earthquakes on the plate. However, in recent years, the declassification of the U.S. Navy's hydrophone detection system has allowed scientists of the National Oceanic and Atmospheric Administration in Newport, Oregon, to study earthquakes using seismic waves (*T-phase waves*) that are transmitted through ocean water rather than through the crust beneath the ocean. They have been able to improve greatly the accuracy and detection threshold for earthquakes far from the coast.

Mapping of the distribution of earthquakes shows that the spreading centers, the Juan de Fuca, Gorda, and Explorer ridges, generate low-level seismicity related to the movement of magma that rises to the surface and forms new oceanic crust. These

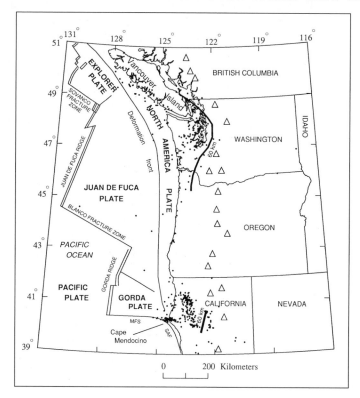

Figure 5-2. Distribution of earthquakes deeper than about 16 miles in the Pacific Northwest. Nearly all of these are intraplate earthquakes in the downgoing Juan de Fuca Plate. Oddly, these earthquakes are not distributed evenly but are concentrated in Puget Sound, coastal Vancouver Island, and northwestern California. Triangles are active Cascade volcanoes. (100 km = 62 miles) From U.S. Geological Survey Professional Paper 1560.

earthquakes are small, most of them too small to be detected by ordinary seismographs onshore. On the other hand, the deforming Explorer and Gorda plates are struck by a large number of earthquakes, especially the Gorda Plate off the northern California coast, which sustained an earthquake of M 7.2 on November 8, 1980. This earthquake, 30 miles west of Trinidad, California, destroyed a bridge and caused $1.75 million in damages and six injuries. The Gorda Plate has accounted for more historical seismicity in northern California than any other source, including the Cascadia Subduction Zone and the overlying North American plate. However, it is unlikely to generate earthquakes in the M 8 range, as expected on the subduction zone and on the San Andreas Fault.

Offshore Transform Faults: The Northwest's Answer to the San Andreas Fault

In Chapter 2, we considered two types of plate boundaries: *ocean ridges* or *spreading centers*, where new oceanic lithosphere is created as plates move away from each other, and *subduction zones*, where oceanic lithosphere is recycled back into the interior of the Earth as plates move toward each other. The Juan de Fuca and Gorda ridges are examples of spreading centers, and the Cascadia Subduction Zone is an example of the convergence of two plates (Figure 2-5). We also considered a third type of plate boundary where plates neither converge nor diverge but instead move past each other without destroying or creating lithosphere. These are called *transform faults* because they transfer plate motion between two spreading centers. They involve the entire lithosphere and not just the Earth's upper crust.

The San Andreas Fault is a transform fault in which continental rocks of the North American Plate move past continental rocks of the Pacific Plate. Transform faults in the Pacific Northwest, on the other hand, are found on the deep ocean floor, where they form linear topographic features called *fracture zones*. The Blanco Fracture Zone separates the Juan de Fuca and the Gorda ridges, and the Sovanco Fracture Zone separates the Juan de Fuca and the Explorer ridges (Figure 5-2). These are typical transform faults. The grinding of one plate past the other causes many earthquakes on these fracture zones. In fact, the fracture zones have the highest instrumental seismicity in the Pacific Northwest, onshore or offshore. Large earthquakes on the Blanco Fracture Zone are felt frequently every year in southern Oregon and northern California.

At first glance, the Blanco Fracture Zone resembles a left-lateral strike-slip fault because of the apparent left offset of the Juan de Fuca and the Gorda ridges. But this apparent left offset would only be true if these ridges had once been a continuous unbroken ridge that was later separated along the Blanco Fracture Zone. This is not the case. Remember that the Juan de Fuca Plate is moving away from the Pacific Plate at these spreading centers. Imagine yourself standing on the Pacific Plate looking northward across the Blanco Fracture Zone at the Juan de Fuca Plate. The Juan de Fuca Plate moves from left to right along the Blanco Fracture Zone with respect to your position on the Pacific Plate. This means that the transform fault on the Blanco Fracture Zone is a *right*-lateral, not *left*-lateral, fault.

As another thought experiment, imagine two jigsaw puzzle pieces that lock together by a tab that projects from one piece into the other. Now pull the pieces slowly apart. They are difficult to separate because the sides of the tab resist being pulled apart. In the same way, the Pacific and Juan de Fuca plates are being pulled apart, with magma welling up along the spreading centers as the plates are separated. Along the Blanco Transform Fault, the crustal plates push past each other, generating friction and producing earthquakes. These earthquakes could be as large as magnitude 7 or even larger, but probably not 8. The crust is too warm and therefore too weak to generate such large earthquakes. Accordingly, despite the high instrumental seismicity on the Blanco Transform Fault, including many earthquakes felt onshore, it does not constitute a major hazard to communities along the coast, in part because the earthquakes are many miles offshore, and in part because these offshore earthquakes are not large enough.

Like the Blanco, the San Andreas Fault is also a transform fault, separating the Gorda Plate from a spreading center in the Gulf of California of northwest Mexico (Figure 5-1). The Blanco differs from the San Andreas in involving relatively hot oceanic crust and mantle, whereas the San Andreas cuts across colder continental crust for most of its length. For this reason, the San Andreas generates significantly larger earthquakes than does the Blanco. So, fortunately for the Pacific Northwest, the Blanco is the weaker relative; it generates many earthquakes, but no giant ones.

Two transform faults lie off the coast of Vancouver Island: the Sovanco Fracture Zone that separates the Explorer Plate and the Pacific Plate, and the Nootka Fracture Zone that separates the Explorer Plate and the Juan de Fuca Plate (Figures 2-4, 5-2). Like the Blanco, these fracture zones are characterized by high seismicity, but are not believed to generate very large earthquakes. Later in the chapter, we will consider the possible relation between the oceanic Nootka Fracture Zone and two large historical earthquakes in continental crust of central Vancouver Island.

Earthquakes in the Juan de Fuca Plate Beneath the Continent

The greatest amount of seismicity generated by the Juan de Fuca Plate itself (not including the Explorer and the Gorda plates) is beneath western Washington, where it is being subducted beneath North America (Figure 5-2). Oddly, this lower-plate seismicity does not extend very far south into Oregon (Figures 5-2, 5-3). If subduction is taking place all along Cascadia, why should seismicity be concentrated only in Washington?

To answer this question, we look at the contours of the subducting Juan de Fuca Plate, and we observe that the plate has an eastward-convex bend in Washington, curving from a north trend in Oregon to a northwest trend in southwest British Columbia (Figure 5-4). This arch in the subduction zone may explain why the Olympic Mountains are so much higher than the Coast Range of Oregon or the hills of southwest Washington. The Olympic Mountains are arched up where the subduction zone bends the most, in map view.

Figure 5-3. Epicenters of earthquakes of M 6 and larger. The 1872, 1936, and 1993 earthquakes were crustal; all others were in the Juan de Fuca Plate. Larger circles indicate larger-magnitude earthquakes. (100 km = 62 miles) From U.S. Geological Survey Professional Paper 1560.

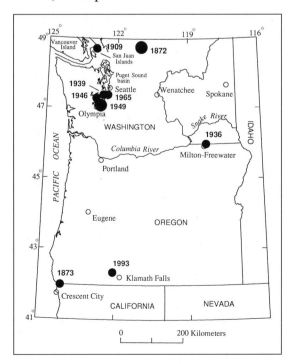

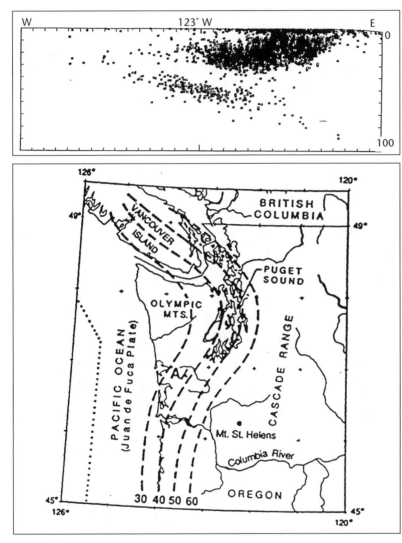

Figure 5-4. (Top). Seismicity cross section across the Puget Sound region showing crustal earthquakes, Juan de Fuca Plate (slab) earthquakes, and the plate boundary between, with no earthquakes. (Below). The distribution of slab earthquakes helps determine the contours of the top of the Juan de Fuca Plate, in kilometers below sea level. Notice that these contours are convex to the east, causing compression within the slab as it subducts beneath North America, analogous to the folds in a tablecloth at the corner of a table. Cross section and map from Robert Crosson, University of Washington.

To imagine the effect of this eastward-convex arch, consider a tablecloth hanging over the corner of a table. The tablecloth is straight along the sides of the table, but it makes a fold at the corner. Now suppose that instead of a tablecloth, the table is covered by a sheet of hard plastic, the edges of which stick out over the side of the table. You want to bend the plastic down the side of the table, like the tablecloth, but you find that it won't bend at the corner unless you make a cut in the plastic so that the two sides fit together down the sides. This is the same difficulty I have in gift-wrapping a present in a box. The wrapping folds neatly down the sides of the box, but in order to make the corners neat, I have to make a fold in the wrapping paper where it goes around the corner. I do not excel at this, and so I generally have the present gift-wrapped at the store or by my wife.

This is the problem the Juan de Fuca Plate has when it is forced to bend beneath North America. The plate can bend easily beneath Oregon or beneath southwest British Columbia, where the subduction zone is straight, but in trying to bend beneath the curved arch beneath Washington, internal stresses are built up that generate earthquakes. These earthquakes are 30 to 40 miles beneath the surface, deeper than the others we have been considering in the preceding chapter and will consider in the following chapter. We call these events *slab earthquakes*, named for the great slab of Juan de Fuca oceanic crust and mantle that is being subducted beneath North America (Figure 5-4).

This "corner problem" explains the distribution of slab earthquakes beneath Puget Sound, but not in southwest British Columbia. Slab earthquakes occur there in two zones, even though the downgoing Juan de Fuca Plate is north of the Washington "corner" and is relatively straight. One zone is a northward continuation of the Puget Sound deep zone on the mainland west coast, near Vancouver, and the other zone is beneath the west coast of Vancouver Island (Figure 5-2). Why should the slab have earthquakes beneath the straight subduction zone in British Columbia, but not the straight subduction zone in Oregon?

Seismologists at the Pacific Geoscience Centre in Sidney, B.C., are quick to say that "we really don't know." But the deeper zone of high seismicity appears to correspond to a downward increase in the dip of the subducting slab beneath Vancouver Island and the mainland coast, producing a bend in the slab (Figure 5-5). The zone beneath the west coast of Vancouver Island may correspond to a shallower bend, but here the correlation is much less clear.

Another problem posed by slab earthquakes is that the continental crust above the seismically active slab is also seismically active. The crustal seismicity is high beneath Puget Sound where the slab seismicity is high. In Northern California, both the Gorda Plate and the overlying and adjacent continental crust are characterized by frequent earthquakes. On Vancouver Island, the largest crustal earthquakes occurred on the onshore projection of the Nootka Transform Fault, and they were characterized by left-lateral strike-slip faulting, just as earthquakes on the Nootka Fault are.

If our speculations about a bending origin for the localization of seismicity are correct, there should be no obvious relationship between earthquakes in the slab and earthquakes in the crust. Yet they appear to be somehow coupled, even though the seismicity zones in the North American crust and in the Juan de Fuca Plate are generally separated by lower crust that is too hot and ductile to produce earthquakes. These questions, now being addressed

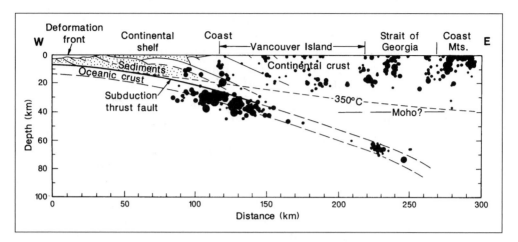

by seismologists in Canada and the United States, are of practical importance because they bear on estimates of hazards for major cities in the Pacific Northwest.

Two Big Ones Beneath Puget Sound

The largest known historical events to strike either Washington or Oregon were slab earthquakes (Figure 5-3). The first of these, on April 13, 1949, really should have been no great surprise. The southwesternmost Puget Sound region had been struck by earthquakes on November 13, 1939 (M 5.8), and on February 15, 1946 (M 6.3). Both were slab earthquakes, and both had produced intensities as high as VII, which meant minor damage and collapse of chimneys (Figure 5-3). In addition, Vancouver Island had been struck by an even larger earthquake of M 7.3 on June 23, 1946, although this was a crustal earthquake, not a slab earthquake.

The 1949 earthquake struck the southern Puget Sound region just before noon on April 13. Strong shaking lasted about thirty seconds. Most people were at work, getting ready to go to lunch. Most schools were on vacation, which turned out to be a blessing because of the collapse of many unreinforced brick school buildings. The epicenter was between Olympia and Fort Lewis, and the high-intensity damage zone extended from Rainier, Oregon, on the Columbia River, north to Seattle (Figures 5-6 to 5-8). The earthquake was felt from Vancouver, B.C., to Klamath Falls and Roseburg, Oregon. A sidewalk clock outside a jewelry store at 1323 Third Avenue in Seattle stopped at the moment of the earthquake: 11:56.

In Washington, 11-year-old Marvin Klegman was killed, and two other children were injured by falling bricks as they played outside the Lowell School in Tacoma. Jack Roller was killed when

Figure 5-5. Cross section of the Cascadia Subduction Zone across southern Vancouver Island showing crustal structure based on surface geology, a deep seismic-reflection profile, the distribution of earthquakes located by seismographs (solid circles; size proportional to magnitude), and temperature based on geothermal measurements onshore and offshore. (100 km = 62 miles) From Garry Rogers and Roy Hyndman, Pacific Geoscience Centre, Sidney, B.C.

part of the Castle Rock School building collapsed on him. Five students and two teachers were injured at Adna School 10 miles west of Centralia. One little girl was critically injured as she left her second-grade classroom. Tons of bricks fell from the Lafayette School building in Seattle, but school was not in session, and children were playing in the schoolyard far from the building. The auditorium collapsed at Puyallup High School (Figure 5-6), but no one was in it at the time. Part of the Boys Training School at Chehalis crumpled and fell, injuring two boys.

There were many narrow escapes. Freda Leaf, 71, jumped into the Duwamish River but was rescued by a neighbor, D.V. Heacock. Part of the roof of the Busy Bee Restaurant on Second Avenue in Seattle fell in, and the patrons headed for the exit. The proprietor, George Pappas, immediately saw the danger and ordered the bartender, a big man named Bill Given, to block the exit. Moments later, tons of bricks cascaded onto the sidewalk in front of the restaurant. Water spilled out of an old water tower at the reservoir at Roosevelt Way and East 86th Street; a few minutes before, painters working at the tower had knocked off for lunch. At the Tacoma Narrows Bridge, under repair at the time, a 23-ton steel saddle mounted to hold up a suspension cable, dislodged and plunged off the bridge and through a scow on the water below, injuring two people. In Olympia, the Old Capitol Building (Figure

Figure 5-6. Puyallup High School damaged in 1949 earthquake. Unanchored roof and ceiling beams over the stage of the auditorium slid off supporting walls and crashed to the floor. From Thorsen (1986); illustration from collection of Washington Division of Geology and Earth Resources.

Figure 5-7. Damage to Old State Building, Olympia, Washington, in 1949 earthquake. From Thorsen (1986); illustration from collection of Washington Division of Geology and Earth Resources.

5-7) and the State Insurance Building were the worst hit. Governor Arthur Langlie and his assistant, Dick Everest, were in their offices in Olympia and were showered with falling plaster.

At the Blue Mouse Theater in Tacoma, people were watching the earthquake scene from *The Last Days of Pompeii* as the earthquake struck. In a bizarre coincidence, a crucifixion scene with accompanying earthquakes was being shown at the time of the earthquake at the nearby Roxy Theater. At Second and Occidental in Seattle, a man was seen walking rapidly down the street after the earthquake, clad only in underwear, sports coat, and shoes.

In Oregon, broken water pipes flooded the basements of two stores in Astoria, plaster cracked in Florence, and dishes crashed from their shelves in Newport. Chimneys crashed at Reed College in Portland, and office workers on the twelfth floor of the new Equitable Building were knocked to the floor.

Fortunately, perhaps amazingly, only seven lives were lost, and damage was only $15 million, even though the magnitude was 7.1. In today's dollars, the losses would be perhaps twenty times that, of course, but they were still remarkably low. Probably the main reason, aside from school being out of session, was that the focal depth of the earthquake was about 35 miles below the surface, meaning that the shock waves had 35 miles in which to weaken in amplitude before reaching the surface. Because it was such a

Figure 5-8. Yesler Way, downtown Seattle, showing damage in 1949 earthquake from falling parapets and brick ornamentation and a collapsed fire escape, shown at left. Photo by George Cankonen, Seattle Times, from collection of Washington Division of Geology and Earth Resources.

deep earthquake, the Intensity VIII zone was very large, but there were no areas of Intensity IX or X, as there might have been with a crustal earthquake of the same magnitude.

On April 29, 1965, a second large slab earthquake struck at 8:29 in the morning, with magnitude 6.5. Its epicenter was between Kent and Des Moines, south of Sea-Tac Airport between Seattle and Tacoma. Like the 1949 earthquake, its focus was greater than 30 miles beneath the surface (Figures 5-9, 5-10).

Adolphus Lewis, 75, a retired laborer, was on his way from his hotel room to have breakfast when he was killed by falling debris (Figure 5-9). Raymond Haughton, 52, was killed, and Eugene Gould, 50, critically injured when a 50,000-gallon wooden water tank on a 200-foot tower collapsed at the Fisher Flouring Mills. In total, six people were killed, including those suffering heart attacks, and property damage was estimated as $12,500,000. As in 1949, there was considerable damage to school buildings. In Seattle, parts of Broadview Elementary School collapsed, and there was damage to the Ballard High School auditorium. The greatest damage seemed to be to Alki Elementary School, where a chimney fell into the boiler room, narrowly missing the custodian. Unlike 1949, no pupils were injured.

The 8:15 mass at St. James Cathedral was interrupted when low-hanging chandeliers began to swing violently. Two hundred parishioners fled the cathedral, but returned for the remainder of the service when the tremors subsided. At the Rainier Brewing Company, two thousand-barrel aging tanks were knocked off their platforms. One split open, spilling enough beer for fifteen thousand cases. Engineer John Strey found himself wading hip deep through the foamy beer. The restaurant at the top of the Space Needle was full of customers when it began to sway, "like riding the top of a flagpole." No one ran for the elevators, and all finished breakfast after the violent shaking had ceased.

In summary, the two slab earthquakes were characterized by very large areas of intensity VII, but only the 1949 earthquake had a very large area of intensity VIII. There were no areas of higher intensity, such as one would expect for crustal earthquakes of the same magnitude, probably due to the greater distance from the source to the ground surface. Unlike crustal earthquakes, these events, together with the 1939 and 1946 Puget Sound earthquakes, lacked significant aftershocks, as is characteristic of deep slab earthquakes. A deep earthquake off the west coast of Vancouver Island on December 16, 1957, with M 6.3, had only one aftershock, and intensities recorded were not much higher than III.

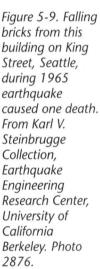

Figure 5-9. Falling bricks from this building on King Street, Seattle, during 1965 earthquake caused one death. From Karl V. Steinbrugge Collection, Earthquake Engineering Research Center, University of California Berkeley. Photo 2876.

Figure 5-10. Failure of brick veneer over wood frame at 60th Avenue, Alki Point, Seattle. From Karl V. Steinbrugge Collection, Earthquake Engineering Research Center, University of California Berkeley. Photo 2844.

Why do these slab earthquakes occur so much deeper than the crustal earthquakes? At depths below 30 miles, crustal rocks, including granite and basalt, would be at temperatures high enough to make them too weak to store enough elastic strain energy to generate earthquakes (Figure 2-1). In contrast, the downgoing Juan de Fuca Plate would be composed of mantle peridotite with a thin cover of oceanic crust. The peridotite would still be brittle at those depths. The slab would be young enough that it would not be as thick as slabs of much older lithosphere that are subducting beneath the western Pacific. Accordingly, it is generally believed that the Juan de Fuca Plate beneath the edge of the North American continent is not capable of storing enough strain energy to produce earthquakes much larger than the M 7.1 event of April, 1949 beneath Puget Sound.

Suggestions for Further Reading

Rogers, A.M., T.J. Walsh, W.J. Kockelman, and G.R. Priest,eds. 1996. Assessing earthquake hazards and reducing risk in the Pacific Northwest. U.S. Geological Survey Professional Paper 1560, 306p.

Thorsen, G.W., compiler. 1986. The Puget Lowland earthquakes of 1949 and 1965. Washington Division of Geology and Earth Resources, Information Circular 81, 113p.

Earthquakes in the Crust:
Closer to Home

Introduction

We have heard the bad news regarding the next great subduction-zone earthquake, but there is one small bit of good news. The epicenter is likely to be offshore: 100 miles from Portland, 120 miles from Seattle, and 140 miles from Vancouver. This means that seismic body waves will be considerably smaller when they reach the major population centers than they will be offshore or along the coast.

But there is still more bad news. The continental crust directly beneath the major cities of the Pacific Northwest has its own earthquake problem. Earthquakes within the crust would be a lot smaller, to be sure. The largest historical crustal earthquake, of magnitude 7.3, struck a thinly populated area on central Vancouver Island in 1946. Three earthquakes in Oregon in 1993 served as wake-up calls: the Scotts Mills "Spring Break Quake" of M 5.5 near Salem, and two earthquakes west of Klamath Falls of M 5.9 and 6.0. The Scotts Mills Earthquake resulted in more than $28 million in losses, including damage to the rotunda at the State Capitol in Salem.

Figure 6-1 shows the large earthquakes recorded in the Pacific Northwest from 1833 through 1993, all of which ruptured either the continental crust, the oceanic crust of the Juan de Fuca Plate to the west, or the oceanic crust of the Juan de Fuca Plate beneath the edge of the continent.

Our historical earthquakes have been troublesome, particularly to the communities affected, but they have not been catastrophes like the Northridge or Kobe earthquakes. But evidence has been found for another, more ominous, prehistoric earthquake that, if it happened today, would result in catastrophic losses to the Pacific Northwest. Our search for this earthquake takes us to Seattle and a detective story leading to this earthquake that took place one thousand years ago, about the time of the Norman Conquest of Britain. The detectives uncovering evidence of this earthquake were paleoseismologists, practicing their new field of identifying

*Figure 6-1.
Epicenter map
showing the
larger
earthquakes in
the Pacific
Northwest for the
period 1833
through
December 1993,
based largely on
data from the
University of
Washington
seismic network.
The size of the
epicenter dot is
proportional to
the magnitude of
the earthquake.
Largest circle, M
equal to or
greater than 7;
next smaller, M 6
to 7; next smaller,
M 5 to 6; points,
M less than 5.
Triangles show
active Cascade
volcanoes. (100
km = 62 miles)
From U.S.
Geological Survey
Professional Paper
1560.*

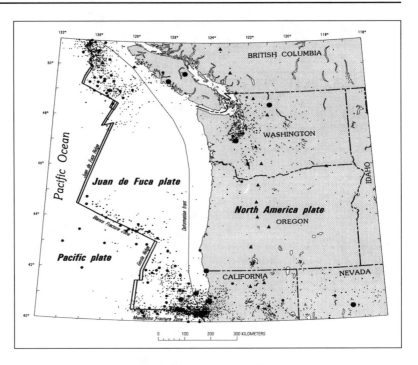

earthquakes by their geologic signature. The fault they discovered extends east-west through downtown Seattle.

Ghost Forests, Raised Shorelines, and the Seattle Fault

When the level of Lake Washington was lowered in 1916 to accommodate the Lake Washington Ship Canal, boaters began to notice something strange beneath the surface of the lake. Dead trees! In growth position, underwater, like silent phantoms (Figure 6-2). In 1919, more than 175 of them, primarily Douglas fir, were removed as navigational hazards. But there were still enough of them left that in 1991 salvage logging was attempted, using a barge and crane to raise the tree trunks from the floor of the lake (Figure 6-3). The wood was found to be in surprisingly good shape.

Careful surveying with side-scan sonar revealed three sunken forests: one northwest of Kirkland near the eastern shore of the lake, and two others off the southeast and southwest shores of Mercer Island. How did the forests get there? The surveys of the lake floor, together with observations by divers, showed that the forests slid into the lake as parts of giant landslides. The rings on some of the tree trunks that were hauled up for logging extended all the way out to the bark (Figure 6-4), which enabled Gordon Jacoby of Columbia University to show that all the trees died in

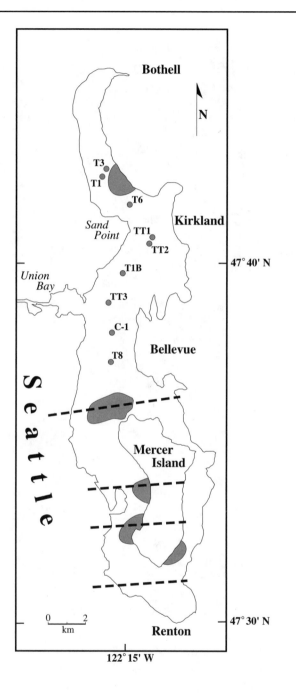

Figure 6-2. Map of Lake Washington, east side of Seattle, locating sunken forests and major submarine landslides (heavy stipple). Circles locate sediment cores shown in Figure 6-5. Dashed lines extending across southern half of lake are possible fault traces, correlated to the Seattle Fault. From Robert Karlin, University of Nevada Reno, and Sally Abella, University of Washington.

Figure 6-3. Tree trunk dredged from Lake Washington and dated as 1100 years old. Photo courtesy of Pat Williams, Lawrence Berkeley Laboratory.

Figure 6-4. Tree rings from a 1100-year-old tree dredged up from the bottom of Lake Washington. Dark zone at top is the bark. Each pair of light and dark rings represents annual growth of one year. Photo by Gordon Jacoby, Columbia University.

the fall, winter, or early spring of the same year, about a thousand years ago. More landslides were found south of Union Bay and at the north end of Mercer Island. But what triggered the landslides?

Why did all these trees slide into Lake Washington at the same time? To answer this question, Bob Karlin of the University of Nevada-Reno and Sally Abella of the University of Washington took core samples of sediments that have been accumulating at the bottom of the lake for more than thirteen thousand years, following the melting of a great Pleistocene ice cap that covered Puget Sound as far south as Olympia. An ash layer in many of the

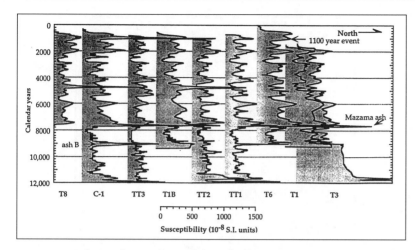

Figure 6-5. Correlation of sediment cores in Lake Washington based on their magnetic properties. These cores provide a record of geological events for more than ten thousand years. Mazama ash is from the eruption of Mt. Mazama, forming Crater Lake, 6850 years ago. 1100 year event is a turbidity current deposit dated as 1100 years ago that is correlated to a major earthquake on the Seattle Fault. From Robert Karlin, University of Nevada Reno, and Sally Abella, University of Washington.

cores came from the catastrophic volcanic eruption at Crater Lake that is known to have taken place 6,850 years ago. The sediment cores contain fossil pollen, providing information about changing conditions on land surrounding the lake as well as changing climate since the Ice Age (Figure 6-5). Starting in the 1880s, the pollen changes abruptly from Douglas fir to alder, evidence of systematic logging and the steady deforestation of western Washington starting about that time. This sediment also provides evidence for the lowering of the lake level when the Ship Canal opened in 1916.

Karlin and Abella also found an unusually conspicuous sediment layer between the Crater Lake ash bed and the flood of alder pollen as logging of the forests began (Figure 6-5). This layer was deposited by a flow of turbid sediment, a small-scale version of the late Pleistocene sediment flows that carved and subsequently partly filled the great submarine canyons off the Columbia River. By correlating the magnetic properties of sediments from core to core (Figure 6-5), Karlin and Abella determined that this sediment layer was deposited about eleven hundred years ago, about the same time that the landslides carried the forests to the floor of Lake Washington. Could the sediment layer and the landslides have the same origin?

The next clue in the detective story came from the shore of Puget Sound, near the lighthouse at West Point, in Discovery Park in the Magnolia District of Seattle. Workers there were excavating for a sewer line when they found something unusual: an ancient beach where early inhabitants had built fires and thrown away shells. The beach deposit was overlain by a salt-grass marsh deposit, which was itself overlain by a sand layer containing a Douglas fir driftwood log (Figure 6-6). Brian Atwater of the U.S. Geological Survey was called in, and he concluded that the sand was deposited by a great wave, or tsunami. The marsh deposit could have been

Figure 6-6. (top) Map of West Point area of Magnolia Bluff, Seattle, locating excavation described at right. (1 km = .62 miles) (below) Excavation for sewer line showing sand sheet deposited by tsunami and overlying tidal-marsh deposits and an ancient beach where inhabitants had built fires and thrown away shells (midden). The tsunami deposit is overlain by mud and sand and another saltgrass marsh deposit. Numbers are radiocarbon dates in years. (4 meters = just over 13 feet; 30 meters = just under 98 feet 6 inches) From Brian Atwater, U.S. Geological Survey.

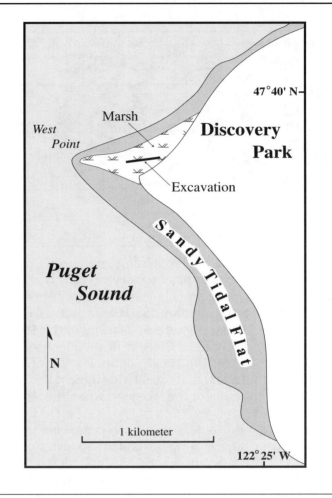

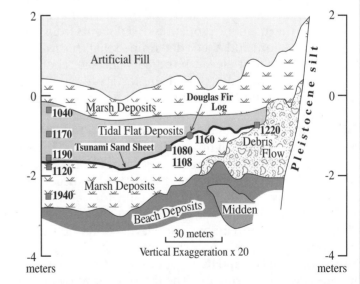

suddenly downdropped by an earthquake, like the marsh deposits he had been studying on the Washington coast. Another tsunami sand deposit was uncovered to the north at Cultus Bay, at the southern end of Whidbey Island. The sand deposits were dated and found to have been deposited by a tsunami one thousand to eleven hundred years ago—about the same time as the landslides and the sediment layer in Lake Washington.

Atwater asked Gordon Jacoby to look at tree rings on the driftwood log from the sewer excavation at West Point. Jacoby found that the tree-ring pattern was a perfect match with the tree rings from the sunken forests of Lake Washington: *the same season of the same year!* That meant that the tsunami in Puget Sound and the landslides in Lake Washington happened at the same time. What could cause both events? The most logical explanation: both were triggered by a single large earthquake. But a subduction-zone earthquake was ruled out: these features were too far to the east.

Meanwhile, Bob Schuster of the U.S. Geological Survey was working in the southeast Olympic Peninsula, looking at dead trees that had been drowned in mountain lakes dammed by rockslides (Figure 6-7). Radiocarbon dates of these drowned trees indicated that three or four out of six rockslides that he studied could have been deposited at the same time, between one thousand and thirteen hundred years ago. No rockslides of this magnitude have happened in historic time, not even during the slab earthquake of magnitude 7.1 that struck Puget Sound in 1949. Schuster concluded that the rockslides may have been triggered by shaking accompanying a large earthquake, perhaps larger than the 1949 earthquake, or at least of much higher intensity.

Farther west, Brian Atwater was studying the sediment at the mouth of the Copalis River, north of Grays Harbor on the southwest side of the Olympic Peninsula. This was part of his work on Pacific coastal marshes overwhelmed by subsidence accompanying subduction-zone earthquakes. Sure enough, just as he had found in other coastal marshes, the buried soils were consistent with sudden subsidence—except for one, which showed no evidence for subsidence and was unique in that it was accompanied by sand erupted from a fissure several hundred feet long. The soil was older than the buried marshes related to the last subduction-zone earthquake; between nine and thirteen hundred years rather than three hundred years. Perhaps the vented sand could have accompanied an earthquake in the crust.

Were all of these features formed by the same earthquake about a thousand years ago? If they were, could the fault producing the earthquake be identified? Bob Bucknam of the U.S. Geological Survey came up with a candidate fault, based on evidence he found at Restoration Point, which juts into Puget Sound at the south

Figure 6-7. Drowned snags breaking the surface of Jefferson Lake in southeastern Olympic Peninsula at low-water level. The rock avalanche dam, partially covered by a modern forest, forms the far shore of the lake. Note the large boulders at the toe of the rock avalanche on the lake shore at the right. Photo by Robert L. Schuster, U.S. Geological Survey.

end of Bainbridge Island, within sight of the tall office buildings of downtown Seattle (Figure 6-8). Above the present tide pools on the modern marine platform is an older marine platform, sloping seaward, which had been raised suddenly as much as 21 feet some time between five and seventeen hundred years ago, based on radiocarbon dating. A few miles to the north, near the ferry landing at Winslow, sediment of the same age showed evidence of subsidence. Could the difference in uplift be signs that a fault lies between Restoration Point and Winslow, uplifting the first site and downdropping the second?

Across Puget Sound in West Seattle, there is another uplifted platform at Alki Point very similar to the one at Restoration Point, but harder to work out due to the presence of houses. And to the north at West Point in the Magnolia District, where the tsunami deposit and driftwood log were found in Discovery Park, the sediment had subsided (Figure 6-6). If the same fault passed between Alki Point and West Point, it would trend east, crossing downtown Seattle beneath the Alaskan Way Viaduct and crossing beneath Lake Washington north of the Floating Bridge. Bucknam called this structure the Seattle Fault (Figure 6-8).

The bedrock geology provides support for such an east-trending structure. Bedrock is found at the surface in the southern part of Seattle, including Alki Point, Rainier Valley, Beacon Hill, and the Newcastle Hills between Renton and Issaquah, east of Lake Washington. But to the north, including West Point, where subsidence was documented, bedrock is buried to depths of 2,000 to 3,000 feet. This indicated that the long-term subsidence over hundreds of thousands of years was in the same direction as the subsidence across Bucknam's Seattle Fault on both sides of Puget Sound.

For a more detailed look at the structure beneath the surface of the ground, Bucknam and his colleague, Sam Johnson, also of the U.S. Geological Survey, obtained seismic-reflection profiles acquired by the petroleum industry in the search for oil and gas in the Puget Sound area. These seismic profiles confirmed that an east-trending fault crosses this area about where Bucknam predicted it should do so. Unfortunately for our earthquake search, there is no fault at the surface. Bucknam and Johnson concluded that this fault was "blind," that is, it *never* made it to the Earth's surface. In this respect, it was like a blind fault beneath the San Fernando Valley, California, that ruptured during the 1994 Northridge Earthquake.

The evidence indicates that the Seattle Fault was the source of an earthquake around one thousand to eleven hundred years ago. This fault extends from Bainbridge Island across downtown Seattle to Lake Washington and Lake Sammamish, where another sunken forest has recently been found. Shaking accompanying the earthquake caused forested regions next to Lake Washington and Lake Sammamish to slide into the lakes, and large rockfalls on the Olympic Peninsula to block several mountain valleys, producing lakes. The earthquake caused the land to rise up at Restoration Point and Alki Point and to subside farther north. Uplift of the seafloor generated a great sea wave that struck the coastline at Magnolia and at the south end of Whidbey Island. The amount

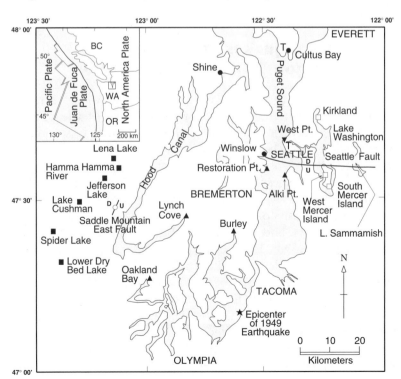

Figure 6-8. The Seattle Fault. U (beside fault lines) means upthrown side, D means downthrown side. Filled upright triangle: uplifted tidal platform; filled upside-down triangle: subsided tidal-marsh deposit; filled circle: tidal-marsh deposit showing no evidence of subsidence; T: tsunami deposit; filled square: rock avalanche; open square: submarine landslide in Lake Washington. Numbers are radiocarbon dates. (10 km = 6.2 miles) From Robert Bucknam, U.S. Geological Survey.

of uplift at Restoration Point suggests an earthquake with a magnitude of at least 7.

Were this earthquake to repeat today, the losses would be catastrophic: the fault extends beneath the most expensive real estate in the Pacific Northwest in an area inhabited by hundreds of thousands of people. Unlike the earthquake of magnitude 7.1 that struck Olympia in 1949, that originated at depths greater than 30 miles, this earthquake would have its focus within 10 to 15 miles of the surface, so that shaking would be much more intense.

When will the next earthquake strike the Seattle Fault? The answer to this question is unknown. Recurrence intervals of earthquakes on the Seattle Fault could be many thousands of years.

Does all the paleoseismologic evidence point to just one earthquake? There is no reason to assume that the sand vented to the surface at Copalis River, on the Pacific coast, at the same time as the earthquake on the Seattle Fault. Other sites showing evidence of uplift at the head of Hood Canal and along the shore of Puget Sound near Tacoma and Olympia may have been related to a different earthquake, or possibly not to an earthquake at all. Vented sand found by Steve Obermeier of the U.S. Geological Survey in overbank deposits of rivers near Centralia, Washington appear to be related to a different crustal earthquake far to the south of Puget Sound.

Earthquakes at the End of the Oregon Trail: Willamette Valley

Fifty million years ago, northwest Oregon was a low coastal plain, with the shoreline close to the western edge of the present Willamette Valley, extending northwestward toward Astoria into what would one day become the Coast Range. East of the shoreline, rivers deposited clean sand, and in their floodplains were broad swamps and marshes, perhaps like the tropical Pacific coast of Guatemala today. Over the next few million years, the sand and the organic deposits of the swamps were slowly buried beneath younger deposits, and the organic materials began to turn into coal and generate gas. The rock layers containing the coal and the sand were tilted, folded, and faulted. North of the Columbia River, the buried swamp deposits of this ancient tropical coast would form the major resource for a coal-mining industry in western Washington. South of the Columbia, the economic potential of the deposits was still unrealized.

Near the backwoods village of Mist, Oregon, Chuck Newell had a dream. As a geologist for Shell Oil Company and later as an independent consultant, Newell had slogged up the brushy creeks and barren clearcuts of the northern Coast Range, and slowly pieced together an idea about the hidden geologic structure. Maybe the gas from the swamp deposits had migrated into the river sand, now hardened into sandstone. Maybe there was a gas field beneath an *anticline*, a broad uparched fold that Newell had mapped beneath the alder and devil's club jungle of the Coast Range.

This seemed a far-fetched idea because no one had ever discovered commercial quantities of oil or gas in Oregon or Washington, despite nearly a century of exploration. However, Newell convinced Wes Bruer, his former classmate at Oregon State University and a geologic consultant for Reichhold Chemical Company, that the Mist Anticline might contain commercial quantities of gas. Reichhold had purchased the Phillips urea plant at St. Helens, Oregon, and the plant required about 9 million cubic feet of gas per day as raw material feedstock for the production of urea. Accordingly, Reichhold was persuaded to drill a well, and the Mist gas field was discovered. Overnight, Oregon had a local source of natural gas, the first in the Pacific Northwest.

As soon as the word was out, lease brokers fanned out across the Willamette Valley talking to grass-seed farmers and timber owners. Geophysical trucks laid cable and geophones along country roads and through pastures for seismic surveys. Wildcat wells were drilled from Hillsboro to Salem and as far south as Eugene.

Alas, there were no more Mist gas fields, and the oil and gas boom crashed as quickly as it had started. But left behind were all the seismic profiles and wildcat well logs, which illuminated for the first time the complex geology beneath the orchards and vineyards of the Willamette Valley. There were folds and there were faults, including a fault extending along the northern foot of the Waldo Hills east of Salem, and another passing beneath the Benedictine abbey at Mount Angel (Figures 6-9 and 6-10). These faults had been discovered in the search for oil and gas. Could they be an earthquake hazard?

Ken Werner, a graduate student at Oregon State University, collected the seismic surveys and well logs and mapped a subsurface fault extending from the Waldo Hills northwest beneath Mount Angel to the city of Woodburn near Interstate 5. In 1990, while Werner was working on his thesis research, seismologists John Nábělek of Oregon State University and Steve Malone of the University of Washington told him about a flurry of small earthquakes they had just recorded beneath Woodburn. Werner concluded that these earthquakes were related to the subsurface Mount Angel Fault (Figure 6-11). In September 1992, Werner and his colleagues published a paper in *Oregon Geology*, a journal published by the Oregon Department of Geology and Mineral

Figure 6-9. Tectonic map of the northern Willamette Valley, showing faults and folds (anticlines, synclines, monoclines) mapped based on seismic-reflection profiles and exploratory wells drilled in the search for oil and gas. MAF is the Mount Angel Fault. Although the Mount Angel Fault later was blamed for the 1993 Scotts Mills Earthquake, it is not clear whether or not the other faults or any of the folds are active. Portland is just to the north of the figure. (10 km = 6.2 miles) From Yeats et al. (1996), mapping by Ken Werner.

Figure 6-10. Tectonic map of the southern Willamette Valley, using a data set similar to that used for Figure 6-9. (10 km = 6.2 miles) From Yeats et al. (1996), mapping by Erik Graven.

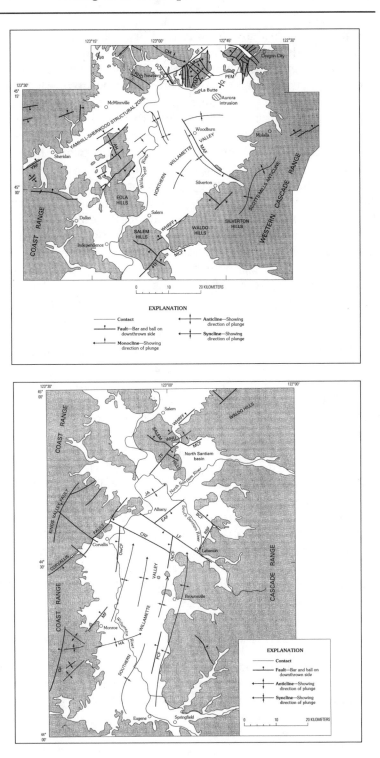

Industries, with a map of the fault and a discussion of the Woodburn earthquake swarm. Unknown to Werner, strain had been building up on the Mount Angel Fault beneath the Waldo Hills southeast of Woodburn and was already near the breaking point.

The break came without warning six months later, at 5:34 a.m. on March 25, 1993, 10 miles beneath the soft green hills east of the village of Scotts Mills, at the east edge of the Willamette Valley (Figure 6-9). In Molalla, 8 miles north of the epicenter, José Alberto Nuñez felt the powerful rumbling and watched as his kitchen cabinets blew open, scattering glassware and dishes onto the kitchen floor. To the night crew at the Safeway store in Woodburn, 15 miles northwest of the epicenter, the earthquake was a ground wave rolling beneath the floor, spilling out merchandise aisle by aisle. Ricky Bowers was driving across a bridge on State Highway 18 over the Yamhill River at Dayton, 25 miles away, when the bridge jumped off its supports, causing him to slam into the exposed concrete slab, blowing out all four of his tires.

Students were on spring break at Molalla Union High School, an unreinforced brick building constructed in 1925, where two gables on the exterior facade collapsed. The timing of the earthquake prevented serious injury to students, and school officials had only to worry about where classes would be held the following week. A block away from the school, Philip Fontaine ran out into his front yard, carrying his young son. "The children were all screaming. Everything was just shaking and not stopping."

At Mount Angel, 10 miles to the west, there was major damage to the Benedictine convent and training center, the Benedictine abbey, and St. Mary's church and school.

Commercial buildings in the historic downtown district of Woodburn were hit hard. Sharon Walsh, caretaker of the 102-year-old Settlemier Mansion, cowered as the house creaked and heaved, cracked and twisted, and she braced herself for a collapse. José Nuñez made it to his office at the Salud Medical Center in Woodburn only to find it in a shambles, with a gaping hole in the ceiling. In the town of Newberg, 28 miles northwest of the epicenter, at least 90 buildings were damaged.

Prior to the earthquake, the State Capitol building in Salem, 21 miles away, had been declared vulnerable to an earthquake, with a price tag for seismic reinforcement of four million dollars. The legislature chose not to act. The earthquake produced cracks inside the rotunda, causing it to be closed indefinitely. Concrete fireproofing on the steel I-beams supporting the ceiling of the legislative chambers was also damaged. High atop the Capitol, the ten-ton statue of the Golden Pioneer rocked and lurched, rotating a sixteenth of an inch, but miraculously did not fall from its perch.

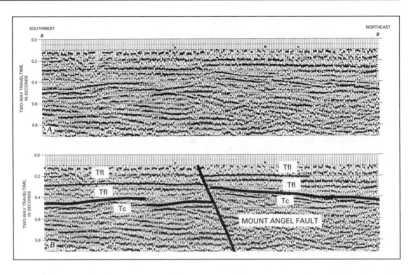

Figure 6-11. Seismic-reflection profile obtained in the search for oil and gas in the Willamette Valley. The horizontal lines are layers of rock beneath the surface that have been offset by the Mount Angel Fault. The bottom diagram is identical to the top one except it contains a geologic interpretation. Tc = Columbia River Basalt; Tfl = younger sediment filling the northern Willamette Valley. Photo by Ken Werner, Oregon State University, from Yeats et al. (1996).

Damage was estimated at more than $28,000,000, with $4,500,000 to the State Capitol alone. (The ultimate cost of retrofitting the Capitol has been estimated at more than $67,000,000!) Surprisingly, there were no deaths. Injuries were limited to those from falling glass and bricks and to some of the employees of a large Wal-Mart store overcome by fumes from bottles and cans of garden chemicals that had crashed to the floor. Unreinforced masonry buildings suffered a disproportionate share of the damage. The timing of the earthquake was fortunate: early in the morning during the week of spring vacation, preventing deaths at the unreinforced Molalla High School building. Losses would have been much higher if the earthquake had struck one of the larger communities of the Willamette Valley rather than a rural area in the foothills of the Cascades.

Former Senator Ron Cease of Portland, a member of the legislature at the time, may have said it best: not being able to walk beneath the rotunda on their way to work had a bracing effect on Oregon's legislators!

As shown in Figure 6-9 and 6-10, there are other faults in the Willamette Valley and, at the northern end of the valley, downtown Portland is next to the Portland Hills Fault extending along the foot of the Portland Hills. The Corvallis Fault is mapped on the northwest side of the city of Corvallis in low hills slated for urban development. Despite considerable efforts, none of these faults can be shown to displace Holocene deposits (younger than ten thousand years). Accordingly, we cannot state that these faults are active. The faults can be marked on the maps of areas being considered for urban development, and developers, local government, and potential buyers can make up their own minds about the potential for fault rupture.

Southwest British Columbia

Northern Vancouver Island just doesn't seem like Earthquake Country. The highway from Victoria runs past small towns along the east coast of the island; it is lined with firs, with breathtaking views of the Straits of Georgia, the Gulf Islands, and on a clear day, the snow peaks of the Coast Mountains. The road passes through Courtenay to Campbell River, past fishing villages and logging camps, and one branch of the road crosses the Forbidden Plateau and Strathcona Provincial Park on its way to a lonely, storm-swept fjord below Gold River, on the Pacific Ocean side of the island.

This thinly populated region was the location of the largest crustal earthquakes in the short recorded history of the Pacific Northwest, an event of M 7.3 on June 23, 1946, and an earlier earthquake of M 7.0 on December 6, 1918 (large black dots in Figure 6-1).

The 1946 earthquake produced extensive chimney damage in Campbell River, Courtenay, and Comox, and there were many landslides in the mountains and much liquefaction and slumping of coastal sediment. Despite extensive areas of intensity VIII from Campbell River to Courtenay, only one person was killed when his boat at Deep Bay was swamped by a wave, possibly generated by slumping of sediment into the water.

The 1918 earthquake struck along the desolate west coast of Vancouver Island, damaging the lighthouse at Estevan Point, south of Nootka Sound. The area of highest intensity was thinly populated, with widely scattered fishing villages accessible only by boat, and damage was slight. The focus of the earthquake was about 10 miles deep, and intensities up to VI were recorded. It was felt as far away as Seattle and the community of Kelowna in the Okanagan Valley east of the Cascades.

The seismograms of both earthquakes, as recorded at distant stations, showed that the motion was consistent with left-lateral strike slip on a crustal fault (or faults) striking northeasterly. This is the same strike as the Nootka Fault, a major left-lateral strike-slip transform fault on the deep ocean floor west of the continental slope, a fault that forms the boundary between the Juan de Fuca Plate and the Explorer Plate (Figure 2-5). However, the earthquakes are not located directly on the landward projection of the Nootka Fault but are offset about 40 miles to the east. The more heavily populated regions of Vancouver and Victoria experience quite a few small earthquakes, indicating that the region is a northern continuation of the seismically active crust beneath Puget Sound. This poses a dilemma for seismologists such as Garry Rogers of the Pacific Geoscience Centre in Sidney, B.C., concerned about estimates of seismic hazards in these areas. Should Rogers and his colleagues consider that earthquakes as large as the 1946 event, M 7.3, are possible in Vancouver or Victoria, or anywhere else in the shallow continental crust of southwestern British Columbia? Or should they conclude that the large crustal earthquakes in central Vancouver Island are part of a zone that has an unusually high seismic hazard because of its proximity to the offshore Nootka Fault, thereby reducing the perception of hazard to Vancouver and Victoria? The answers to those questions are not yet at hand.

Do Small Earthquakes West of the Cascades Mean Bigger Ones in the Future?

The financial cost of the Scotts Mills Earthquake was the highest of any earthquake in the history of the Pacific Northwest, but this was due to its location, in a region of moderate population in the Willamette Valley. But it was not the only earthquake in western Oregon with magnitude greater than 5. Portland was struck by earthquakes of magnitude 5.5 on November 5, 1962, and magnitude 5.2 on October 12, 1877. Near Mt. St. Helens, the Elk Lake Earthquake of magnitude 5.5 ruptured the north-northwest-trending Mt. St. Helens Fault Zone, defined on seismicity maps by a linear zone of minor earthquakes (Figure 6-1). This fault zone, together with another near Mt. Rainier, seems to be similar in geologic structural type to the Mount Angel Fault. Marvin Beeson of Portland State University has described a fourth fault of this type along the foot of the Portland Hills in downtown Portland, extending southeast to the Clackamas River. However, unlike the Seattle Fault, Beeson has found no evidence that this fault is active.

Crustal earthquakes of M 7 and higher have been recorded historically only on Vancouver Island, where special tectonic circumstances may apply. Or they may not.

The prehistoric earthquake on the Seattle fault had a magnitude of at least 7. A poorly located earthquake in 1872, somewhere in northern Washington, either west or east of the Cascades, may have had a magnitude of 7.4. On May 2, 1996, a magnitude 5.3 earthquake struck a few miles east of the small town of Duvall, in the foothills of the Cascades northeast of Seattle. It resulted in only minor damage, and its main claim to fame was that it caused the evacuation of the Kingdome during a Seattle Mariners baseball game. The previous year, on January 28, a magnitude 5 earthquake struck the southern Puget Sound region north of Tacoma.

Earthquakes such as these are likely to occur anywhere west of the Cascades, although they are more likely in the Puget Sound region. They rate a newspaper story for a day or so, a story which usually gives off a whiff of impending doom, but earthquakes like these do little damage. It is difficult to assign most of them to a specific fault (the Scotts Mills Earthquake being the exception), although faults have been mapped throughout the region. It has not even been possible to assign the large earthquakes of central Vancouver Island to a specific fault.

Most of the faults in western Washington and all of them in western Oregon, including the Mount Angel Fault, cannot be shown by geologists to be active because they do not offset latest Pleistocene or Holocene sediments. Accordingly, in assessing the probability of damaging crustal earthquakes, it is better to say that the entire area is seismically active without trying to pinpoint a specific fault. In a later chapter, we will learn how to use the frequency of earthquakes of various magnitudes to forecast the probability of earthquakes of larger magnitudes, say magnitudes 6 or 7, somewhere in a given *region* like the Willamette Valley, Puget Sound, or the Fraser River Delta of southwestern British Columbia, rather than on a specific *fault*.

Basin and Range: The Klamath Falls Earthquakes of 1993

Vacations in their native Oregon were a tradition with Ken and Phyllis Campbell. They came late in the year to avoid the hottest part of the summer at their home in Phoenix, Arizona. Their 1993 excursion had been a grand trip, visiting old high-school friends and taking a cruise ship up the Inside Passage to Alaska. But it was getting late, and Phyllis was anxious to reach their destination, a bed and breakfast in Klamath Falls, a city where she had gone to first grade. Ken was already looking forward to getting back to Phoenix, where he was constructing a workshop to restore classic cars and build toys for his grandchildren. Driving south on U.S. Highway 97 toward Klamath Falls, Phyllis watched the deer along the side of the road.

As they approached Modoc Point, a steep cliff beside the road, it occurred to Phyllis that she wouldn't see any deer on the left side of the highway because the cliff came right down to the road, and there was no shoulder. Suddenly she saw a blinding flash of light, then another one, and she thought for an instant that it must have been transformers exploding from a power surge.

At that instant, there was a loud crack, and Phyllis heard Ken cry out, "No!" A 14-foot boulder smashed down onto their pickup, killing Ken instantly. The windshield collapsed inward, and the truck spun out of control. When the spinning stopped, Phyllis found that she could unhitch her seat belt, but could not unhitch Ken's. Nothing worked: she couldn't get the electric windows to open or the electric locks on the door to work, even though the engine was racing. She tried to turn off the ignition, but the key came off in her hand. She knew that Ken had to be dead, but she did not know how to get out of the truck. Then there was a man at the window, and she was pulled to safety. The deadly boulder and the breached highway barrier are shown in Figure 6-12.

At 8:28 p.m., September 20, 1993, Ken Campbell had become the first fatality due to an earthquake in Oregon. An 82-year-old woman, Anna Marion Horton of Chiloquin, died of a heart attack because she was frightened by the violent shaking of her house. At the Classico Italian restaurant in downtown Klamath Falls, bricks fell and blocked the sidewalk, and diners left their pasta uneaten and fled the building.

More than a thousand buildings were damaged (you can see some of this damage on the cover), with a total loss of more than $7.5 million. The Klamath County Courthouse, built in 1924, and the Courthouse Addition suffered damage of more than $3 million. Unreinforced masonry buildings suffered the worst; well-built wood-frame houses that were bolted to their foundations fared relatively well.

There had been a warning twelve minutes before: a foreshock of magnitude 3.9. However, this part of Oregon was poorly covered by the existing network of seismographs, and there was no system in place to evaluate the foreshock and issue a warning. Then, more than two hours after the first shock of magnitude 5.9, an even larger earthquake of magnitude 6 struck the region. The depth of

Figure 6-12. Boulder at Modoc Point, alongside U.S. Highway 97, that breached a roadside barrier and took the life of Ken Campbell during the September 20, 1993 Klamath Falls Earthquake. Boulder has been pushed back behind barrier. Photo by David Sherrod, U.S. Geological Survey.

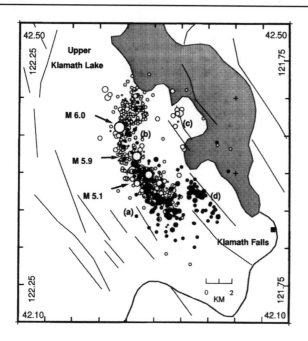

Figure 6-13. Earthquakes and aftershocks of the Klamath Falls Earthquake sequence, September-December 1993. Size of circles proportional to magnitude with the largest M 6.0. Open circles show earthquakes from September 20 to the time of an aftershock of M 5.1 on December 4. Solid circles show aftershocks from December 4 to 16. Second sequence is closer to Klamath Falls but is still west of Upper Klamath Lake. Note the absence of earthquakes in the city of Klamath Falls itself. Thin solid lines are faults; note that faults east of lake did not have earthquakes in 1993. (1 km = 0.62 miles) From U.S. Geological Survey.

the earthquakes was about 6 miles, much shallower than the Scotts Mills Earthquake. They were located west of Upper Klamath Lake beneath the Mountain Lakes Wilderness, between 15 and 20 miles west-northwest of Klamath Falls (Figure 6-13). Starting in early December, a new swarm of earthquakes began east of the first group, close to the western shore of the lake, closer to Klamath Falls (Figure 6-13). After the first of the year, the aftershocks slowly began to die away.

Unlike the country west of the Cascades, the stark, arid landscape of southeastern Oregon leaves little of its geology to the imagination. Dave Sherrod of the U.S. Geological Survey had been mapping the faults of the Klamath Falls region for several years, and early in 1993, before the earthquake, he had met with Klamath Falls officials to discuss the potential hazard.

The basin containing Upper Klamath Lake and Klamath Falls is a *graben*, downdropped between faults that dip downward toward and beneath the lake. These are called *normal faults*, and they result when the crust is pulled apart (Figure 6-14). Modoc Point, where Ken Camphell met his death, is part of a fault block. Over hundreds of thousands of years, the countryside east of Highway 97 has been uplifted, and the lowland to the west downdropped along west-dipping faults, so that it now lies beneath the lake. Farther south, other normal faults extend through the main part of Klamath Falls.

West of Upper Klamath Lake are other less prominent normal faults at the west edge of Howard Bay, in the Mountain Lakes Wilderness, and extending beneath Lake of the Woods (Figure 6-

Figure 6-14. Structure of the Basin and Range Province of eastern Oregon. Because the crust is extending east-west, normal faults form. The basin formed between two opposing normal faults is called a graben. Upper Klamath Lake (see Figure 6-13) occupies a graben. From U.S. Geological Survey.

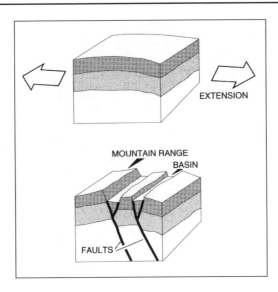

13). These faults, which dip east, were activated by the 1993 earthquakes, although there was no evidence that any of them ruptured all the way to the surface.

Fortunately for Klamath Falls, the faults on the *west* side of the graben ruptured rather than the faults on the *east* side, which extend directly through the city. If the eastside faults had ruptured with earthquakes of comparable magnitudes, the damage to Klamath Falls, with its unreinforced masonry buildings, would have been a major disaster.

Eastward from the Cascades from Bend and Klamath Falls to the Owyhee River country stretch the block-fault mountains and the dry-lake grabens that make up the Oregon Basin and Range: Green Ridge and Walker Rim, Summer Lake and Winter Ridge, Lake Abert and Abert Rim, and finally, higher than all the rest, and with evidence of Pleistocene glaciers, Steens Mountain, followed by the Alvord Desert (Figure 6-15).

Mark Hemphill-Haley, then with Woodward-Clyde Consultants, found a fault at the base of the Steens, snaking along the west edge of the Alvord Desert Graben. Unlike the faults west of the Cascades, the Steens Mountain Fault shows geological evidence of a Holocene earthquake within the last ten thousand years, based on trench excavations. Hemphill-Haley could then conclude on the basis of geologic evidence alone that the fault at the foot of the Steens is *active* in the legal sense of the word, which means that special precautions should be taken to guard any major structures against seismic shaking. Fortunately, there are only a few ranches and herds of livestock, and they would probably survive a magnitude 7 quake without much problem.

Hemphill-Haley had the answer to why Steens Mountain is there in the first place. It has been gradually raised up from the

Figure 6-15. Steens Mountain in southeastern Oregon. An active fault with evidence for Holocene displacement is found at the base of Steens Mountain, separating it from the Alvord Desert in the foreground. Steens Mountain has been uplifted along the normal fault at its base accompanied by earthquakes over several million years. Photo by Robert Yeats.

desert floor along its range-front fault, accompanied by literally thousands of earthquakes over a period of millions of years, each seismic elevation just a few feet. The cumulative effect of all these individual uplifts is the massive, rugged fault-block mountain we see today, snow capped much of the year, towering over the playa flats of the Alvord Desert to the east (Figure 6-15)

West of Steens Mountain, a swarm of earthquakes struck the small town of Adel, in Warner Valley, in 1968, with the largest of magnitude 5.1 (Figure 6-16). Silvio Pezzopane and Ray Weldon of the University of Oregon found other active faults in the desert west of Abert Rim, and they applied the new science of paleoseismology to find evidence of prehistoric earthquakes in backhoe trenches across fault scarps. Faults that are considered active on the basis of offset of Holocene deposits were found in Paulina Marsh, at the west edge of Summer Lake near Winter Rim, and along the west boundary of Abert Rim.

The Oregon Basin and Range is the northern continuation of the Basin and Range of Nevada (Figure 6-17), including the Central Nevada Seismic Zone, which was rocked repeatedly by a series of seven earthquakes, starting in 1915 and ending in 1954, the largest of magnitude 7.5. Fault scarps that formed during several of these earthquakes are magnificently preserved in the desert climate (Figure 3-7) and can be seen by driving a back road south of Winnemucca, Nevada, through Pleasant Valley at the western foot of the Sonoma and Tobin ranges, over the Sou Hills, down Dixie Valley east of the Stillwater Range, to U.S. Highway 50, itself broken by a surface rupture accompanying an earthquake of magnitude 7.2 on December 16, 1954. Like the Steens country, the Central Nevada Seismic Zone is thinly populated, and although the earthquakes were felt over large areas, the losses were small.

Figure 6-16. Map showing locations of recent earthquake swarms in southern Oregon and northern California, including the Warner Valley, Oregon, earthquakes of 1968. From the U.S Geological Survey.

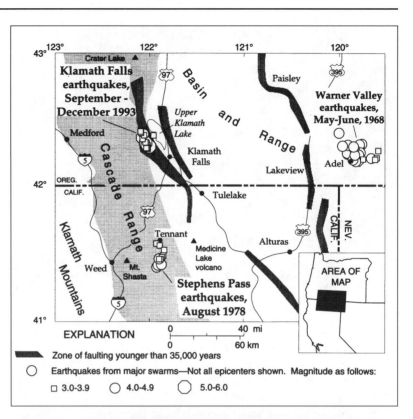

Figure 6-17. A computer-generated topographic map of the Basin and Range Province. The linear pattern is formed by block-fault mountain ranges bounded by normal faults and separated by valleys that are grabens. From the U.S. Geological Survey.

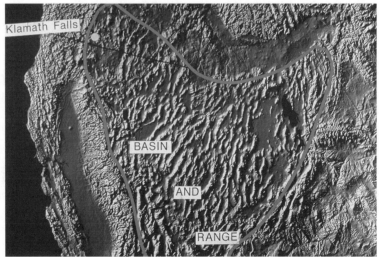

Despite the intense seismic activity in this century, long-term slip rates on faults in the Central Nevada Seismic Zone are extremely slow, comparable to slip rates on faults in the Oregon Basin and Range. Paleoseismology shows that prior to the 20th century earthquakes occurred in this seismic zone many thousands of years ago. We refer to the Nevada earthquakes as an *earthquake cluster*, characterized by intense activity over a short period of time separated by thousands of years of quiet. The Oregon Basin and Range is similar to the Central Nevada Seismic Zone, but its seismic silence shows that it is in a quiet period. We know that this quiet period will end someday, but unfortunately, we do not know when—tomorrow or two thousand years from now. Again, the ponderous certainties of forecasts made in terms of many thousands of years do not answer the societal questions about timing (next year or ten years from now?) that are of interest to you and me and those around us.

The Pasco Basin: Nuclear Wastes and Earthquakes

The military aircraft droned over the bleak December landscape of eastern Washington, and its lone passenger took note of what he saw through the window. As he gazed down at the sagebrush-covered Hanford Reach passing beneath the plane, with the broad ribbon of the Columbia River curving away in the distance, Lt. Col. Franklin Matthias knew that he had the site he wanted: raw desert, virtually unpopulated, but with a dependable water source, the Columbia, close at hand. The nearest large city, Spokane, was nearly 120 miles away. Matthias would report back to his superior, General Leslie Groves, military overseer for the top-secret Manhattan Project, that Hanford was suitable for a large super-secret government project related to the war effort. The year was 1942.

Soon after, in 1943, the few Indians and farmers who had been scratching out a living in the Hanford Reach were hustled out, and the government took over for a crash project to manufacture plutonium for an atomic bomb, the first of which would be dropped three years later on Nagasaki, Japan, to bring an end to World War II. Then came the Cold War, and Hanford continued to expand, still in secrecy, bringing jobs and prosperity to the Pasco Basin and the Tri-Cities of Richland, Pasco, and Kennewick. In addition to manufacturing plutonium, atomic reactors produced energy for the Bonneville power grid, and nuclear wastes began to be stored on the Hanford Reach.

In the 1980s, the site was proposed as a national nuclear waste dump, the Basalt Waste Isolation Project. By this time, though, serious reservations had been expressed about nuclear waste disposal in general and the Hanford site in particular. The Hanford N Reactor and the plutonium manufacturing facilities were shut down, and later, the proposed waste disposal site was shifted to Nevada.

But still the legacy of nuclear wastes already stored at Hanford hangs over the Tri-Cities, and so it is useful now to look at the geologic setting and consider Hanford's hazard from earthquakes. Clearly, geology and earthquakes were not considered at all in Col. Matthias's report to General Groves. Now, however, a nuclear reactor is considered to be a *critical facility,* meaning that it is necessary to conduct exhaustive site studies to determine its long-term stability to hazards, even those that may be very unlikely, including earthquakes. Are the reactors and the plutonium manufacturing plants able to withstand earthquake shaking? Would highly toxic radioactive waste stored in subterranean tunnels leak out following a major earthquake? To answer these questions, we look for evidence of past earthquakes in the geology around the site, especially in the long ridges of basalt known as the Yakima Folds.

Betweeen Wenatchee and Hanford, the Columbia River turns southeast through a sagebrush-covered black-rock wasteland, away from the ocean, to cut a succession of gorges through basalt ridges on its way to the last canyon, Wallula Gap, where it turns sharply back on itself and heads west to Portland (Figure 6-18). These basalt ridges, Frenchman Hills, Saddle Mountain, and Rattlesnake Mountain, are anticlinal folds in the Columbia River Basalt, crumpled like a heavy carpet after a sofa has been pushed over it (Figure 6-19). The Columbia has eroded through these anticlines as they formed. The anticlines are best seen in the canyon of the Yakima River between the towns of Ellensburg and Yakima—not from Interstate 82, which soars high over the gorge, but on lonely State Highway 821, which twists along the banks of the Yakima as the river lazes across broad synclines and churns through anticlinal cliffs of basalt.

Geologic catastrophes are not new to this dark land. Sixteen million years ago, great floods of basaltic lava issued from crustal fractures in easternmost Washington and Oregon and western Idaho and poured across the Columbia Plateau in a broad front, hemmed in only by the Cascades, through which the lava burst in a fiery river more than 20 miles across to enter the northern Willamette Valley and finally to flow into the sea (inset, Figure 6-18). These lava eruptions have no counterpart in human history. One cannot imagine looking toward an advancing front of molten

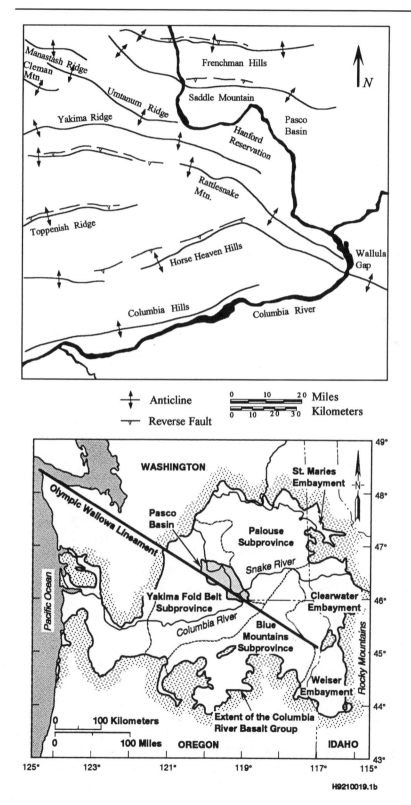

Anticline

Reverse Fault

0 10 20 Miles
0 10 20 30 Kilometers

Figure 6-18 (top) Tectonic map of Yakima Fold Belt, including the Hanford Reservation. Anticlines are upfolded ridges of Columbia River Basalt that may be underlain by blind faults that could be the sources of earthquakes. (below) Regional map showing location of Yakima Fold Belt and the Olympic-Wallowa Lineament and the distribution of the Columbia River Basalt. Olympic-Wallowa Lineament may have been formed by regional strike-slip faulting that could generate earthquakes.

H9210019.1b

Figure 6-19. Geologic cross section across Yakima Fold Belt west of Hanford Reservation. Folds in basalt are interpreted as being forced up by compressional faults in rigid crust beneath the basalt; these faults may be earthquake sources. (10 km = 6.2 miles; 100 m = 328 feet)

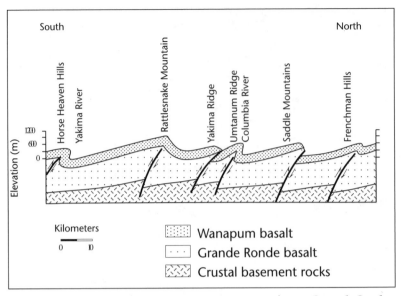

basalt extending from horizon to horizon, from Grand Coulee south to northern Oregon, flowing faster than one could ride a horse, almost like water. This happened not just once but dozens of times over several million years.

Long after the basalt lava had frozen into stone, less than a hundred thousand years ago, there was a different kind of catastrophe in the Pleistocene. At that time, the interior of British Columbia was covered by a vast ice cap, like Greenland today, and glaciers had advanced southward as far as Spokane, damming the Columbia River and its tributaries at Spokane to form a huge body of fresh water, Glacial Lake Missoula, that extended across Idaho into Montana, almost to the Continental Divide. At the end of the Pleistocene, the glaciers slowly began to melt and retreat, and the ice dam at Spokane suddenly ruptured. The lake drained first beneath the ice, then floated the ice roof and caused it to collapse; the resulting iceberg-strewn deluge, lasting at least a week, drained Lake Missoula, carrying more water than all the streams on Earth do today.

Nothing else on Earth matched this apocalyptic flood. The great volume of water was too much for the valley of the Columbia River, and water rushed across the Columbia Plateau, carrying away the rich Palouse soil and eroding down to the bare basalt, forming a broad wasteland called the Channeled Scablands. The thundering torrents carved out the Grand Coulee and Dry Falls and deposited giant sand bars on the Columbia River below Wenatchee, so large that they can be seen from space. Like its basaltic predecessor millions of years before, the water flowed out across a broad front. The doomsday scenario repeated itself many times as the ice cap retreated, then advanced, then retreated, over and over again. The last time was about twelve thousand years ago.

These catastrophes are silent now, and we have no expectations of new flows of basalt or new gigantic floods of water. The great lava flows and flood deposits form only an apocalyptic backdrop for the present landscape. But now a new specter of catastrophe has arisen at Hanford—the fear of earthquakes.

Like the Puget Sound region, the Pasco Basin experiences many small earthquakes. But Pasco has something more—the great anticlinal ridges of basalt through which the Columbia and Yakima rivers have chiseled their dark gorges (Figure 6-19). Geologists working at the Hanford Nuclear Reservation tended to downplay the role earthquakes may have had in forming these ridges, perhaps from wishful thinking, perhaps because they did not want to answer questions they had not been asked. One theory was that the anticlines formed during or soon after the eruption of basalt and were no longer active or an earthquake risk.

In fairness to the geologists at Hanford, anticlines were not considered as harbingers of earthquakes until 1983, when an earthquake of M 6.7 trashed the downtown section of Coalinga, California, a small town on the west side of the San Joaquin Valley. There was no active fault at the surface at Coalinga, but the forces accompanying the earthquake were shown to add to the folding of an anticline at the surface. The implication of active folding is that the fold is underlain by a blind reverse fault or *blind thrust*, one that does not reach the surface, but tends to force one block over another: faulting at depth, but only bending at the surface (Figures 3-10, 6-19). The 1994 Northridge Earthquake was caused by rupture on a blind thrust.

I once saw a Volkswagen bus that had been in a highway accident. There had been a carpet on the floor, as if its owner had been camping inside the bus. During the wreck, the flooring was buckled and broken, but the carpet was still continuous over the flooring, although it had a large hump in it over the break in the flooring. I thought about that VW bus as I studied the Northridge Earthquake—the bump in the carpet was the anticline, giving a silent clue to the unseen fault beneath. The same analogy could be made for the basalt ridges in the Pasco Basin.

Two college teachers, Bob Bentley of Central Washington University in Ellensburg and Newell Campbell of Yakima Valley College, trudged into Indian territory to examine Toppenish Ridge, a narrow anticline south of the city of Yakima (left center, Figure 6-18). They found normal faults on the crest of the anticline and reverse faults on its north flank where the anticline had been thrust northward toward the plowed fields of the Yakima Valley. These structures are not the same age as the Columbia River Basalt; they are much younger, possibly still active. Similar evidence was later found that the east end of the Saddle Mountains Anticline, east of the Columbia and north of Hanford, is also active. As shown in

Figure 6-19, the prominent anticlines overlie and provide evidence for blind reverse faults beneath, faults that themselves could produce large earthquakes at the nuclear reservation.

Another, more subtle structural lineament traverses southeast across the Hanford Reach and across the Yakima folds, a dislocation visible on satellite images and on computer-generated digital topographic maps. This is called the Olympic-Wallowa Lineament (Figure 6-18b), and it can be traced across the Cascades to the Olympic Peninsula and across the Hanford Reservation to the Wallowa Mountains in northeastern Oregon. Geologists have had difficulty in mapping the Olympic-Wallowa Lineament on the ground, even though it can be observed from space. However, geology students from Whitman College at Walla Walla found evidence that a branch of this structure may cut Holocene deposits only a few thousand years old. More needs to be learned.

In summary, as Hanford's nuclear operations wind down, and the Tri-Cities await their fate, an earthquake assessment seems long overdue. The Hanford installation is not the only critical facility in the Pasco Basin; there are also the Wanapum, Priest Rapids, and McNary dams on the Columbia River. Failure of one of these dams could cause a repeat of the catastrophic floods of the Pleistocene, although on a greatly reduced scale. Critical facilities will be considered in a later chapter.

Pacific Coast and Offshore

The Pacific coast of the Northwest is struck on occasion by winter storms of great ferocity, among the most violent in the world. The ocean waves that crash against the rocky headlands and from time to time across Highway 101 are agents of geologic change. They grind down rocky platforms and tide pools and eat into the base of the sea cliffs, occasionally causing beachfront homes and condos built on top of the cliffs to topple into the sea. The boundary between the rocky platform and the sea cliff is called the *shoreline angle* (Figure 6-20), and it is formed at sea level.

Highway 101 and many of the resort cities and fishing villages of the coast rest on older, higher sand-covered marine platforms that were eroded during the late Pleistocene. A marine platform 125,000 years old marks a time when sea level was as much as 20 feet higher than it is today. At places like Cape Arago, Oregon, several of these platforms of different ages lie at different elevations, like giant stair steps, the oldest more than 200,000 years old. The shoreline angles of these old marine platforms indicate the position

Figure 6-20. View south from Cape Foulweather along the central Oregon coast. The Inn at Otter Crest is in foreground, and Otter Rock village and Devil's Punchbowl are behind. Within the surf are outcrops of basalt that have been planed off by wave erosion to a flat platform. The angle between the eroded platform and the beach cliff is called the shoreline angle and is at sea level. The Inn at Otter Crest and Otter Rock are built on an older marine erosion platform that may be eighty thousand years old (note horizontal layer in sea cliff). It, too, has a shoreline angle marking sea level in late Pleistocene time. Photo by Alan Niem, Dept. of Geosciences, Oregon State University.

of ancient Pleistocene sea levels. Careful surveying by Harvey Kelsey of Humboldt State University in Arcata, California, and his colleagues and students shows that these shoreline angles are not horizontal, like the modern one is, but they rise and fall, and in some places are cut by faults (Figures 6-21). Because the shoreline angles reflect ancient sea levels, meaning that they were once horizontal, their deformation allowed Kelsey to measure tectonic crustal deformation along the Pacific coast.

The seismicity of the coastal regions north of California is relatively low, and there is no direct evidence that the formerly horizontal shoreline angles were deformed by earthquakes. But Lisa McNeill of Oregon State University found that some of the downwarps along the coast, such as South Slough near Coos Bay, Oregon, and the mouth of the Queets River in Washington, correspond to active folds offshore, and these structural lows contain peat deposits that were downdropped suddenly by great earthquakes. A fault may cut the late Pleistocene terraces at Newport, Oregon. Even Willapa Bay, the site of Atwater's discovery of buried marshes in Niawiakum Estuary, is the location of an active syncline offshore. The low seismicity suggests that deformation of these shoreline angles and downdropping of the structural depressions may be secondary crustal responses to past great earthquakes on the Cascadia Subduction Zone. Alternatively, they may be related to earthquakes in the crust that were not associated with movement on the subduction zone.

Offshore on the continental shelf and slope, active deformation is more intense. The continental shelf itself, very

Figure 6-21. (top) Map of Cape Arago-Coos Bay region, southwest Oregon, showing marine terrace platforms and active faults. (below) Cross section along the coast from Cape Arago to Coos Bay showing tilting and faulting of Whiskey Run marine terrace and platform, eighty thousand years old. One cross section shows the vertical scale exaggerated ten times the horizontal scale, the other shows the cross section without vertical exaggeration. (1 km = .62 miles; 100 m = 328 ft) From G. McInelly and H. Kelsey, Humboldt State University.

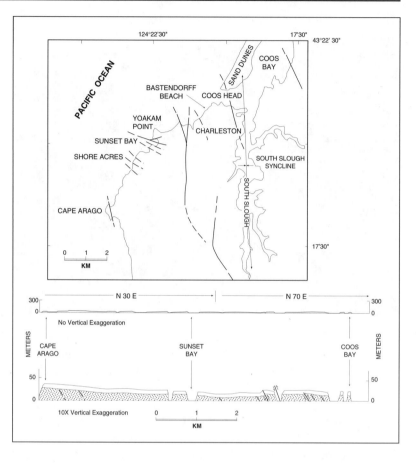

broad off Washington, narrow off southern Oregon and northern California, was eroded to a flat surface during times of Pleistocene glacial advance, when great expanses of ice had taken up water that otherwise would have returned to the sea. During these times of ice advance, sea level was almost 400 feet lower than it is today, and the continental shelf was dry land.

Chris Goldfinger and I asked ourselves if the coastline at the time of maximum ice advance twenty-one thousand years ago, when sea level was 400 feet lower, shows the same evidence of erosion as the modern coast does. To answer this question, we surveyed the edges of Nehalem Bank, Heceta Bank, and Coquille Bank on the Oregon continental shelf, using side-scan sonar and *Delta*, a two-person submersible. What we discovered was truly remarkable: another Oregon coast, drowned beneath the sea at the edge of the shelf, complete with rocky headlands, estuaries, and barrier-island sand bars (Figure 6-22). *Delta* cruised along this Pleistocene beach, now covered by soft mud, and we observed holes at the base of the cliff rather like the holes made by organisms at the base of modern sea cliffs. The rise of sea level approximately fourteen thousand years ago had been so rapid, more than an inch per year, that these shoreline features were preserved, like the wreck of the *Titanic*, rather than being destroyed by wave erosion.

But unlike the present shoreline angle, which is at sea level and is horizontal, these shoreline angles rise and fall, like the shoreline angles of the raised Pleistocene beaches along the coast. The continental shelf had been warped and tilted, possibly during earthquakes.

One of our most memorable discoveries was during our survey of Stonewall Bank southwest of Newport, Oregon, an area known to local fishermen as "the rock pile." Our side-scan sonar imagery showed that Stonewall Bank is a rocky ridge split by a broad former river channel, the seaward extension of the Yaquina River when

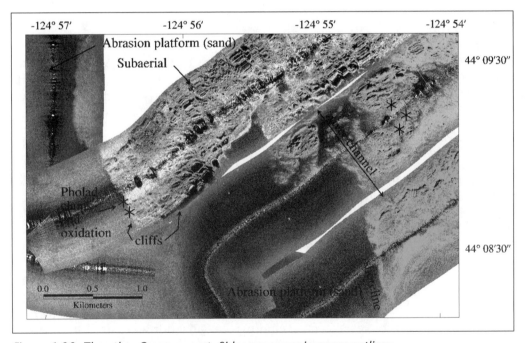

Figure 6-22. The other Oregon coast. Sidescan sonar imagery outlines a shoreline angle developed at the maximum Pleistocene ice advance twenty-one thousand years ago on the west side of Heceta Bank west of Florence, now covered with 400 feet of sea water. Visible are rocky cliffs (like the present coastline north of Otter Rock) and the mouth of a Pleistocene river. Some of the rocks at the base of the cliffs have been bored by marine organisms. The dark gray region in the lower left half of the picture is the former marine erosion platform, now covered with Holocene mud. The Heceta Bank shoreline angle is warped and deformed, evidence of deformation of the Oregon continental shelf. (1 km = .62 miles) Image courtesy of Chris Goldfinger, College of Oceanic and Atmospheric Sciences, and Charles Hutto, Dept. of Geosciences, Oregon State University.

Figure 6-23. Sidescan sonar image of a river channel crossing Stonewall Bank, southwest of Newport, now covered with 200 feet of sea water. The channel, marking the seaward continuation of the Yaquina River, is now tilted eastward, evidence of deformation of the Oregon continental shelf in the last twelve thousand years. (100 m = 328 ft) Image courtesy of Chris Goldfinger, College of Oceanic and Atmospheric Sciences, Oregon State University; see also Yeats et al. (1998).

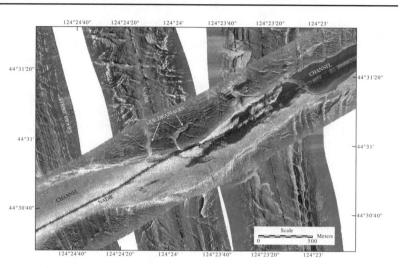

sea level was lower than it is today (Figure 6-23). Surprisingly, the river channel now slopes about 25 feet *eastward* toward Newport. Since water must have run downhill toward the west, we concluded that the river channel was tilted back toward its source during the last twelve thousand years. We had discovered the eastern flank of a broad anticline beneath Stonewall Bank, an anticline formed by a blind reverse fault like the fault that ruptured during the Northridge Earthquake and the faults that may underlie the folded basalt ridges of the Pasco Basin (Figure 6-19).

North of California, the instrumental seismicity of the coast and continental shelf is low, and it is unclear what sort of earthquake hazard is represented by the deformed coastal terraces and drowned shorelines of the continental shelf. South of Crescent City, California, however, the northern California coastal and offshore region is highly seismic, accounting for about 25 percent of the seismic energy released throughout California in the past fifty years, even including the San Andreas Fault System. More than sixty earthquakes have produced damage in the region since records were first kept in the mid-1800s, starting with an earthquake in 1873 that wrecked part of Crescent City, and continuing through the Petrolia Earthquake of April 25, 1992 of M 7.1. The Petrolia Earthquake heavily damaged the small towns of Fortuna and Scotia, south of Eureka, and was accompanied by permanent uplift of the rocky wave-cut platform for a distance of about 15 miles, killing off the marine organisms living in tide pools and attached to the rocks (Figure 6-24).

The Petrolia Earthquake ruptured the Cascadia Subduction Zone plate boundary, the only historical earthquake known to have done so. Does this mean that subduction-zone earthquakes are

Figure 6-24. Marine platform uplifted by the 1992 Petrolia Earthquake on the Cascadia Subduction Zone. The platform is covered with bleached algae and shellfish killed by uplift of the platform. Note that in northern California, where the Cascadia Subduction Zone is close to the coast, coseismic deformation is by uplift, whereas north of Coos Bay, coseismic deformation is by subsidence. Gary Carver included for scale. Photo by T. Dunklin, courtesy of Lori Dengler, Humboldt State University.

likely to be only in the magnitude 7 range rather than magnitude 8 or 9, as has been proposed? Probably not, because the southern end of the Cascadia Subduction Zone in northern California is significantly different from the subduction zone farther north. In fact, the subduction zone almost comes ashore between Trinidad, north of Arcata, and Cape Mendocino, south of Eureka (Figure 6-25), where it has been studied by Gary Carver and his colleagues and students at Humboldt State University, situated at Arcata, a region characterized by active folding and faulting. This means that the Cascadia Subduction Zone here involves continental crust, whereas farther north it involves oceanic crust being forced under the western edge of the continent.

Several reverse faults and folds cross the shoreline obliquely, including the Mad River Fault between Trinidad and Arcata (Figure 6-26), and the Little Salmon Fault south of Eureka. These structures account for more than half an inch of shortening per year, much higher than any deformation rates known in onshore western Oregon or Washington. Backhoe trenches across these fault zones provide paleoseismologic evidence that for several thousand years the shortening has taken place through large earthquakes, larger than the shocks that the region has experienced in the past century and a half. The largest of these historical crustal earthquakes was northeast of Arcata, a M 6.5 event on December 21, 1954 that caused $2.1 million in damage and one death.

Paleoseismology also shows that the most recent subsidence of marshes in Humboldt Bay took place three hundred years ago, which makes it the same age as subsidence farther north all the way to Vancouver Island. Carver and Sam Clarke of the U.S. Geological Survey have used this synchroneity of dates to argue

Figure 6-25 The Cascadia Subduction Zone comes ashore in northern California, where active folds and thrust faults have been studied in detail by Gary Carver and his associates. The subduction zone ends at the Mendocino Transform Fault, which turns southeast to become the San Andreas Fault. The Gorda Plate and spreading center are also shown; the plate is being internally deformed along the Cascadia Subduction Zone and the Mendocino Transform Fault. (10 km = 6.2 miles) Based on a drawing and cross section by Gary Carver, Humboldt State University.

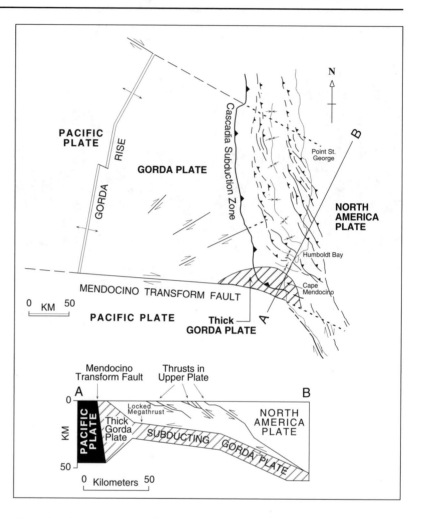

that the last rupture of the subduction zone continued all the way south to Humboldt Bay in an earthquake as large as M 9.

Curiously, under a new California insurance plan discussed in Chapter 10, the Eureka region will be charged earthquake insurance rates that are among California's lowest, despite accounting for a quarter of the state's seismicity!

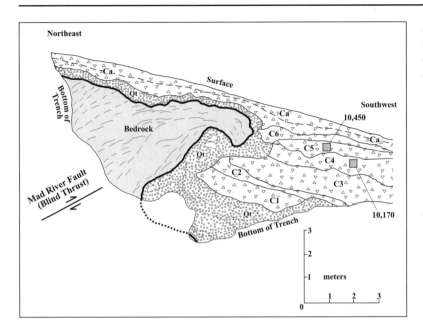

Figure 6-26. Paleoseismological evidence for earthquakes on the Mad River thrust fault at McKinleyville, California, based on a backhoe excavation. Bedrock has been thrust over sediments that are radiocarbon dated as ten thousand years. The marine terrace platform (heavy solid line) has been folded, indicating that the Mad River Fault is blind at this locality. (1 m = just over 3 ft 3 in) From Gary Carver, Humboldt State University.

Suggestions for Further Reading

Allen, J.E., M. Burns, and S.C. Sargent. 1986. *Cataclysms on the Columbia*. Portland: Timber Press, 211p.

Bott, J.D.J., and I.G. Wong. 1993. Historical earthquakes in and around Portland, Oregon. *Oregon Geology*, vol. 55, no. 6, pp. 116-22.

Campbell, N.P., and R.D. Bentley. 1981. Late Quaternary deformation of the Toppenish Ridge uplift in south-central Washington. *Geology*, vol. 9, pp. 519-24.

Cassidy, J.F., R.M. Ellis, and G.C. Rogers. 1988. The 1918 and 1957 Vancouver Island earthquakes. *Seismological Society of America Bull.*, vol. 78, pp. 617-35.

D'Antonio, M. 1993. *Atomic harvest: Hanford and the Lethal Toll of America's Nuclear Arsenal*. New York: Crown Publishers, 304p.

Geomatrix Consultants. 1995. Seismic design mapping, State of Oregon. Final report prepared for the Oregon Department of Transportation, Project 2442, Salem, OR.

Humboldt Earthquake Information Center. How to survive earthquakes and tsunamis on the north coast. Humboldt Earthquake Information Center, Humboldt State University, Arcata CA, 23p.

Hyndman, R.D., G.C. Rogers, H. Dragert, K. Wang, J.J. Clague, J. Adams, and P.T. Bobrowski. 1996. Giant earthquakes beneath Canada's west coast. *Geoscience Canada*, vol. 23, no. 2, pp. 63-72.

Kelsey, H.M. 1990. Late Quaternary deformation of marine terraces on the Cascadia Subduction Zone near Cape Blanco, Oregon. *Tectonics*, vol. 9, pp. 983-1014.

Kelsey, H.M., and G.A. Carver. 1988. Late Neogene and Quaternary tectonics associated with northward growth of the San Andreas Transform Fault, northern California. *Journal of Geophysical Research*, vol. 93, pp. 4797-819.

Kelsey, H.M., R.L. Ticknor, J.G. Bockheim, and C.E. Mitchell. 1996. Quaternary upper plate deformation in coastal Oregon. *Geological Society of America Bulletin*, vol. 108, pp. 843-60.

Komar, P.D. 1997. *The Pacific Northwest Coast: Living with the Shores of Oregon and Washington*. Durham, N.C.: Duke University Press, 195p.

Madin, I.P., and others. 1993. March 25, 1993, Scotts Mills earthquake—western Oregon's wake-up call. DOGAMI, *Oregon Geology*, vol. 44, no. 3, pp. 51-57.

Pezzopane, S.V., and R.J. Weldon. 1993. Tectonic role of active faulting in central Oregon. *Tectonics*, vol. 12, pp. 1140-69.

Stein, R.S., and R.S. Yeats. 1989. Hidden earthquakes. *Scientific American*, vol. 260, no. 6, pp. 48-57. A discussion of blind faults and earthquakes

Wiley, T.J., and others. 1993. Klamath Falls earthquakes, September 20, 1993—including the strongest quake ever measured in Oregon. DOGAMI, *Oregon Geology*, vol. 55, no. 6, pp. 127-36.

Wong, I.G., and J.D.J. Bott. 1995. A look back at Oregon's earthquake history, 1841-1994. DOGAMI, *Oregon Geology*, vol. 57, no. 6, pp. 125-39.

Yeats, R.S., E.P. Graven, K.S. Werner, C. Goldfinger, and T.A. Popowski. 1996. Tectonics of the Willamette Valley, Oregon. U.S. Geological Survey Professional Paper 1560. pp. 183-222; map, 1:100,000 scale.

Yeats, R.S., L.D. Kulm, C. Goldfinger, and L.C. McNeill. 1998. Stonewall anticline: An active fold on the Oregon continental shelf. *Geological Society of America Bulletin*, vol. 110, pp. 572-87.

$\backsim 7 \backsim$

Memories of the Future:
The Uncertain Art of
Earthquake Forecasting

"What's past is prologue."

William Shakespeare, *The Tempest,* Act II

"Since my first attachment to seismology, I have had a horror of predictions and of predictors. Journalists and the general public rush to any suggestion of earthquake prediction like hogs toward a full trough."

Charles Richter, *Bulletin of the Seismological Society of America,* 1977

A Mix of Science and Astrology

Predicting the future does not sit well with most earthquake scientists, including Charles Richter, quoted above. Prediction bears a whiff of sorcery and black magic, of ladies with long dangling earrings in darkly lit tents reading the palm of your hand. Geologists and seismologists involved in earthquake prediction research find themselves sharing the media spotlight with trendy astrologers, some with business cards, armed with maps and star charts. I heard about one woman on the Oregon coast who claims to become so ill before natural disasters—that have included major California earthquakes and the eruption of Mt. St. Helens—that she has to be hospitalized. After the disaster, she recovers dramatically.

Some of these people claim that their predictions have been ignored by those in authority, especially the U.S. Geological Survey. They go directly to the media, and the media see a big story. One forecast of a disastrous earthquake at the small town of New Madrid, Missouri, on December 3, 1990, by a self-styled climatologist named Iben Browning was taken seriously by the media, even after a panel of experts had concluded in October of that year that the prediction had no scientific basis (Spence et al., 1993). If anything, the nay-saying scientists added interest to the story. Browning, who held a PhD degree in zoology from the

University of Texas, based his prediction on a supposed 179-year tidal cycle that would reach its culmination on December 3, exactly 179 years after a series of earthquakes with magnitudes greater than 8 had struck the region. His prediction had been made in a business newsletter that he published with his daughter and in lectures to business groups around the country. Needless to say, he sold lots of newsletters.

Despite the rejection of his prediction by the seismological establishment, Browning got plenty of attention, including an interview on *Good Morning America*. As the time for the predicted earthquake approached, more than thirty television and radio vans with reporting crews converged on New Madrid, school was let out, and the annual Christmas parade was canceled. Earthquake T-shirts sold well, and the Sandywood Baptist Church in Sikeston, Mo., announced an Earthquake Survival Revival.

The date of the earthquake came and went. Nothing happened. The media packed up and left, and the residents of New Madrid were left to pick up the pieces of their lives. Browning instantly changed from earthquake expert to earthquake quack. He died a few months later.

In the 1970s, the U.S. Geological Survey once funded a project to evaluate every nonscientific forecast it could find, including strange behavior of animals before earthquakes, to check out the possibility that some people or animals could sense a premonitory change not measured by existing instruments. Preliminary findings indicated no statistical correlation whatsoever between forecasts and actual events. The project was aborted for fear that it might earn the Golden Fleece Award of then-Senator William Proxmire of Wisconsin for the month's most ridiculous government waste of taxpayers' money.

Earthquake Forecasting by Scientists

Most of the so-called predictors, even those who have been interviewed on national television, will claim that an earthquake prediction is successful if an earthquake of *any* magnitude occurs in the region. Let's say that I predict that an earthquake will occur in the Puget Sound region within a two-week period of June of this year. An earthquake occurs, but it is of M 3, not "large" by anyone's definition. Enough M 3 earthquakes occur randomly beneath Puget Sound that a person predicting an earthquake of unspecified magnitude in the area is likely to be correct. Or say that a person predicts that a large earthquake will occur somewhere in the world in the middle of this year. It is quite likely that an earthquake of at least moderate size will occur *somewhere* on the appointed day. Ordinarily, this earthquake would not be reported in the media, except that the predictor would point to it as a successful prediction ignored by the scientific establishment.

To issue a legitimate prediction, a scientist, or anyone else, for that matter, must provide an approximate *location*, *time*, and *magnitude*, and the prediction must be made in such a way that its legitimacy can be checked. The prediction could be placed in a sealed envelope entrusted to a respected individual or group, which would avoid frightening the public in case the prediction was wrong. Of course, for a prediction to be of value to society, it *must* be made public, but until prediction becomes routine (if it ever does), one must consider the negative impact on the public of a prediction that fails.

Prediction was one of the major goals of the federal earthquake program when it was established in the United States (see Chapter 13), and at one time it looked as if that goal might be achieved sooner than expected. After the 1971 Sylmar Earthquake in the San Fernando Valley of California, a team of seismologists at Columbia University suggested that the speed of earthquake waves that passed through the Earth's crust beneath the San Fernando Valley had become slower a few months before the earthquake, then increased to normal just before the event. Similar changes in speed of earthquake waves had also been noted before small earthquakes in the Adirondacks of New York State and in Soviet Central Asia.

Then in 1975, a senior research fellow at Caltech claimed that he could detect the same thing happening again near the aftershock zone of the Sylmar Earthquake: a slowdown of earthquake waves, presumably to be followed by a return to normal speed and another earthquake. Other seismologists disagreed. Nonetheless, he issued a "forecast": not his term, for he characterized it as "a test of a hypothesis." If the changes in the speed of earthquake waves were significant, then there should be another earthquake of magnitude 5.5 to 6.5 in an area adjacent to the Sylmar shock within the next twelve months. He became an overnight celebrity and appeared in *People* magazine. An irate Los Angeles city councilman threatened to sue both the scientist and Caltech. He achieved his fifteen minutes of fame, but his predicted time for the earthquake ran out, with no earthquake. Meanwhile, other scientists tested the Columbia University theory and found a relatively poor correlation between the variation in speed of earthquake waves in the crust and future earthquakes. (Maybe the Caltech scientist was right in location but off on the time and magnitude. The Northridge Earthquake struck the San Fernando Valley 23 years after the Sylmar event, and its magnitude was 6.7, larger than had been predicted.)

At about the same time as the San Fernando "test of a hypothesis," a prediction was made by Brian Brady, a geophysicist with the U.S. Bureau of Mines, who worked in the field of mine safety (Olson, 1989). Between 1974 and 1976, Brady published a series of papers in an international peer-reviewed scientific journal, *Pure and Applied Geophysics,* in which he argued that characteristics of rock failure leading to wall collapses in underground mines were generally applicable to earthquakes. These papers combined rock physics and mathematical models to provide what Brady claimed to be an earthquake "clock" that would provide the precise time, place, and magnitude of a forthcoming earthquake. Brady noted that earthquakes in 1974 and 1975 near Lima, Peru, had occurred in a region where there had been no earthquakes for a long time, and forecast a much larger earthquake off the coast of central Peru. Brady's work received support from William Spence, a respected geophysicist with the U.S. Geological Survey.

His prediction received little attention at first, but gradually it became public, first in Peru, where the impact to Lima, a city of five million people, would be enormous, later in the United States, where various federal agencies grappled with the responsibility of endorsing or denying a prediction that had very little support among mainstream earthquake scientists. The prediction received major media attention when it was announced that the expected magnitude would be greater than 9, and the preferred date for the event was June 28, 1981. Finally, in January 1981, a meeting was convened of the National Earthquake Prediction Evaluation Council (NEPEC), a select panel of respected earthquake scientists organized to review critically any earthquake prediction. The panel of experts considered the Brady and Spence prediction and rejected it.

However, the NEPEC meeting did not make the controversy go away, nor did it convince Brady that his prediction had no scientific basis. An interview of Brady by Charles Osgood of *CBS News* shortly after the January NEPEC meeting was not broadcast until June 1981, close to the predicted arrival time of the earthquake. Officials of the Office of Foreign Disaster Assistance took up Brady's cause, and the NEPEC meeting was described as a "trial and execution." The NEPEC panel of experts was labeled a partisan group ready to destroy the career of a dedicated scientist rather than endorse his earthquake prediction.

John Filson, an official with the U.S. Geological Survey, made a point of being in Lima on the appointed day to reassure the Peruvian public. The earthquake did not keep Brady's appointment with Lima, Peru. It has not arrived to this day.

A more sophisticated but more modest forecast was made by the U.S. Geological Survey seismological establishment for the

San Andreas Fault at Parkfield, California, a backcountry village in the California Coast Ranges. Before proceeding further, we must distinguish between the term *prediction*, in which it is proposed that an earthquake of a specified magnitude will strike a specific region in a restricted time window (hours, days, or weeks), and the term *forecast*, in which a specific area is identified as having a higher statistical chance of an earthquake in a time window measured in months or years.

Parkfield had been struck by earthquakes of M 5.5 to 6 in 1901, 1922, 1934, and 1966, and newspaper reports suggested earlier earthquakes in the same vicinity in 1857 and 1881. These earthquakes came with surprising regularity every twenty-two years, give or take a couple of years, except for 1934, which struck ten years early. The 1966 earthquake arrived not twenty-two but thirty-two years later, resuming the schedule followed by the 1922 and earlier earthquakes. The proximity of Parkfield to seismographs that had been operated for many years by the University of California, Berkeley, permitted the interpretation that the last three earthquake epicenters were in nearly the same spot. Furthermore, foreshocks prior to the 1966 event were similar in pattern to foreshocks recorded before the 1934 earthquake.

Accordingly, a forecast was issued in 1984 that there was a 95 percent chance, or probability, that an earthquake of magnitude similar to the earlier ones would strike Parkfield sometime in the period 1987 to 1993. Parkfield was instrumented heavily to detect very small earthquakes, changes in crustal strain, changes of water level in nearby monitored wells, and changes in the Earth's magnetic and electrical fields. The strategy was that detection of these subtle changes in the Earth's crust might lead to a short-term forecast and also might aid in forecasting larger earthquakes in more heavily populated regions. A system of alerts was established whereby civil authorities would be notified in advance of an earthquake.

The year 1988, the twenty-second anniversary of the 1966 shock, came and went with no earthquake. The next five years passed; still no earthquake. By January 1993, when the earthquake had still not occurred, the forecast was rated by most people as a failure.

One scientist compared the forecast experiment to a man waiting for a bus, which is due at noon. Noon comes and goes, then ten minutes past noon, then twenty past. No bus. The man figures that the bus will arrive any minute. He stands up and looks down the street. The longer he waits, the more likely the bus will show up. In earthquake forecasting, this is called a *time-predictable model*: the earthquake will follow a schedule, like the bus.

But there is another view: that the longer the man waits, the *less* likely the bus will arrive. Why? The bus has had an accident, or a bridge collapsed somewhere on the bus route. The "accident" for Parkfield may have been an earthquake of M 6.7 in 1983, east of Parkfield, away from the San Andreas Fault, near the oil-field town of Coalinga in the San Joaquin Valley. The Coalinga Earthquake may have redistributed the stresses building up on the San Andreas Fault to disrupt the twenty-two-year earthquake schedule at Parkfield.

Another idea of the 1970s was the *seismic gap theory*, designed for subduction zones around the Pacific Rim, but applicable also to the San Andreas Fault. According to theories of plate tectonics, there should be about the same amount of slip over thousands of years along all parts of a subduction zone like the Aleutians or Central America (or central Peru, for that matter, leading Brady toward his prediction). Most of the slip on these subduction zones should be released as great earthquakes. But segments of each subduction zone have been seismically quiet a lot longer than adjacent segments, indicating that those segments that have gone the longest without an earthquake are the most likely to be struck by a future earthquake. This is a variation of the time-predictable model, of waiting for the bus. The longer you wait, the more likely the bus will show up.

But Yan Kagan and Dave Jackson, two geophysicists at the University of California at Los Angeles, compared the statistical prediction in 1979 of where earthquakes should fill seismic gaps with the actual experience in the following ten years. If the seismic gap theory worked, then the earthquakes of the 1980s should neatly fill the earthquake-free gaps in subduction zones identified in the 1970s. But the statistical correlation between seismic gaps and earthquakes of the next decade was found to be poor. Some seismic gaps had been filled, of course, but earthquakes also struck where they had not been expected, and some seismic gaps remain unfilled to this day.

The Japanese became entranced by the possibility of predicting earthquakes at about the same time as a federal earthquake-research program was established in the United States. However, in contrast to the broad-based program initiated in the U.S., the Japanese focused on prediction, with their major efforts targeting the Tokai area along the Nankai Subduction Zone southwest of Tokyo. Like the San Andreas Fault at Parkfield, the Nankai Subduction Zone appeared to rupture periodically, with major M 8 earthquakes in 1707, 1854, and a pair of earthquakes in 1944 and 1946. But the Tokai area, at the east end of the Nankai Subduction Zone, did not rupture in the 1944 earthquake, although it had ruptured in the previous earthquakes. Like Parkfield, the Tokai Seismic Gap was heavily instrumented by the Japanese in search of short-term precursors to an earthquake.

Unlike Parkfield, Tokai is a heavily populated area, and the societal benefits of a successful earthquake warning there would be very great.

According to some leading Japanese seismologists, there are enough geologic differences between the Tokai segment of the Nankai Subduction Zone and the rest of the zone that ruptured in 1944 and 1946 to explain the absence of an earthquake at Tokai in the 1940s. The biggest criticism was that the Japanese were putting too many of their eggs in one basket: concentrating their research on the Tokai experiment at the expense of a broader-based study throughout the country. The folly of this decision became apparent in January 1995, when the Kobe Earthquake ruptured a relatively minor strike-slip fault far away from Tokai. The Kobe fault had been identified by Japanese scientists as one of twelve "precautionary faults" in a late stage of their seismic cycle, but no official action had been taken.

After the Kobe Earthquake, the massive Japanese prediction program was subjected to an intensive critical review. In 1997, the Japanese concluded at a meeting that their prediction experiment was not working—but they elected to continue supporting it anyway! Similarly, research dollars are still being invested at Parkfield, but the experiment is now called an attempt to "capture" an earthquake or to record it with the network of instruments set up in the mid-1980s, rather than forecast an earthquake.

Have the Chinese Found the Way to Predict Earthquakes?

Should we write off the possibility of predicting earthquakes as simply wishful thinking? Before we do so, we must first look carefully at earthquake predictions in China, a nation wracked by earthquakes repeatedly throughout its long history. More than eight hundred thousand people lost their lives in an earthquake in north-central China in 1556, and another one hundred eighty thousand died in an earthquake in 1920.

During the Zhou Dynasty, in the first millenium B.C., the Chinese came to believe that heaven gives wise and virtuous leaders a mandate to rule, and removes this mandate if the leaders are evil or corrupt. This became incorporated into the Taoist view that heaven expresses its disapproval of bad rule through natural disasters such as floods, plagues, or earthquakes. In March 1966, the Xingtai Earthquake of M 7.2 struck the densely populated

North China Plain 200 miles southwest of the capital city of Beijing, causing more than eight thousand deaths (Ma et al., 1990). It may have been his concern about the mandate from heaven that led Premier Zhou Enlai to make the following statement:

> There have been numerous records of earthquake disasters preserved in ancient China, but the experiences are insufficient. It is hoped that you can summarize such experiences and will be able to solve this problem during this generation.

This call for action may be compared to President Kennedy's call to put a man on the Moon by the end of the 1960s. Zhou had been impressed by the earthquake-foreshock stories told by survivors of the Xingtai event, including a M 6.8 event fourteen days before the mainshock, fluctuations in groundwater levels, and strange behavior of animals. He urged a prediction program "applying both indigenous and modern methods and relying on the broad masses of the people." Thus, in addition to developing technical expertise in earthquake science, China would also involve thousands of peasants who would monitor water wells and observe strange behavior of animals. Zhou was distrustful of the existing scientific establishment, including the Academia Sinica and the universities, and he created an independent government agency, the State Seismological Bureau (SSB), in 1970.

Following an earthquake east of Beijing in the Gulf of Bohai in 1969, it was suggested that earthquakes after the Xingtai Earthquake were migrating northeast toward Beijing, the Gulf of Bohai, and Manchuria. Seismicity increased, the Earth's magnetic field underwent fluctuations, and the ground south of the city of Haicheng in southern Manchuria rose at an anomalously high rate. This led to a long-range forecast that an earthquake of moderate magnitude might strike the region in the next two years. Monitoring was intensified, earthquake information was distributed, and thousands of amateur observation posts were established to monitor various phenomena. On December 22, 1974, a swarm of more than one hundred earthquakes struck the area of the Qinwo Reservoir near the city of Liaoyang, the largest of M 4.8. At a national meeting held in January 1975, an earthquake of M 6 was anticipated somewhere within a broad region of southern Manchuria.

As January passed into February, anomalous activity became concentrated in the vicinity of the city of Haicheng. Early on February 4, more than five hundred small earthquakes were recorded at Haicheng. This caused the government of Liaoning Province to issue a short-term earthquake alert. The people of Haicheng and nearby towns were urged to move outdoors on the unusually warm night of February 4. The large number of foreshocks made this order easy to enforce. Not only did the people move outside into temporary shelters, they also moved their animals and vehicles outside as well. So when the M 7.3 earthquake arrived at 7:36 p.m., casualties were greatly reduced, even though in parts of the area more than 90 percent of the houses collapsed. Despite a population in the epicentral area of several million people, only about one thousand people died. Without the warning, most people would have been indoors, and loss of life surely would have been many times larger. China had issued the world's first successful earthquake prediction.

However, in the following year, despite the intense monitoring that had preceded the Haicheng Earthquake, the industrial city of Tangshan, 220 miles southwest of Haicheng, was struck without warning by an earthquake of M 7.6, resulting in the deaths of about two hundred fifty thousand people. Unlike Haicheng, there were no foreshocks. And there was no general warning.

What about the mandate from heaven? The Tangshan Earthquake struck on July 28, 1976. The preceding March had seen major demonstrations in Tiananmen Square by people laying wreaths to the recently deceased pragmatist Zhou Enlai and giving speeches critical of the Gang of Four, radicals who had ousted the pragmatists, including Deng Xiaoping, who would subsequently lead the country. These demonstrations were brutally put down by the military (as they would be again in 1989), and Deng was exiled. The Gang of Four had the upper hand. But after the Tangshan Earthquake, Chairman Mao Zedong died and was succeeded by Hua Guofeng. The Gang of Four, including Mao's wife, opposed Hua, but Hua had them all arrested on October 6. Deng Xiaoping returned to power in 1977. One could say that the mandate from heaven had been carried out!

Was the Haicheng prediction a fluke? In August 1976, the month following the Tangshan disaster, the Songpan Earthquake of M 7.2 was successfully predicted by the local State Seismological Bureau. And in May 1995, a large earthquake struck where it was predicted in southwestern China. Both predictions resulted in a great reduction of casualties. As at Haicheng, both earthquakes were preceded by foreshocks.

Why have the Chinese succeeded where the rest of the world has failed? For one thing, Premier Zhou's call for action led to a national commitment to earthquake research unmatched by any other country. Earthquake studies are concentrated in the SSB, with a central facility in Beijing, and offices in every province. The SSB employs thousands of workers, and seismic networks cover the entire country. Earthquake preparedness and precursor monitoring are carried out at all levels of government.

Even so, perhaps most of it is luck. All of the successful forecasts have included many foreshocks, and at Haicheng the foreshocks were so insistent that it would have taken a major government effort for the people *not* to take action. No major earthquake in recent history in the United States or Japan is known to have been preceded by a large number of foreshocks. Also, despite the few successful predictions in China, many predictions have been false alarms, probably more than would have been acceptable in a Western country.

A Strange Experience in Greece

On a pleasant Saturday morning in May 1995, the townspeople of Kozáni and Grevena in northwestern Greece were rattled by a series of small earthquakes that caused people to rush out of their houses. While everyone was outside, enjoying the spring weather, an earthquake of M 6.6 struck the region. Damage was more than $500 million dollars, but no one was killed. Just as at Haicheng, the foreshocks alarmed people and caused them to go outside. The saving of lives was not due to any official warning; the people in the area simply did what they thought would protect themselves.

No official warning? Into the breach stepped Panayiotis Varotsos, a solid-state physicist from the University of Athens. For more than fifteen years, Varotsos and his colleagues Kessar Alexopoulos and Konstantine Nomicos, have been making earthquake predictions based on electrical signals they have measured in the Earth using a technique called VAN, after the last names of its three originators. Varotsos claimed that his group had predicted an earthquake in this part of Greece some days or weeks before the Kozáni-Grevena Earthquake, and after the earthquake, he took credit for a successful prediction. In fact, Varotsos had sent faxes a month earlier to scientific institutes abroad noting signals indicating that an earthquake would occur in this area. But the actual epicenter was well to the north of either of two predicted locations, and the predicted magnitude was variously about 5 or between 5 and 6, depending on location. The uncertainties of his magnitude predictions amounted to a factor of 1,000 in energy release.

Although his prediction methodology has changed greatly over this period, he still claims to be able to predict earthquakes of magnitude greater than M 5 one or two months in advance. As a result, Varotsos' group at Athens has received about 40 percent of all the earthquake-related research funds in Greece, all without review by his scientific colleagues. His method has been widely publicized in Japan, where the press has implied that if the VAN method had been used, the Kobe Earthquake would have been predicted. He has been heavily criticized by earthquake scientists internationally, in part because most of his results have been presented not in scientifically reviewed journals but in newspapers and magazines, on television, and even in Japanese comic books.

This section on prediction concludes with two quotations from eminent seismologists separated by more than fifty years.

In 1946, James Macelwane wrote in the *Seismological Society of America Bulletin*: "The problem of earthquake forecasting [he used the word *forecasting* as we have used *prediction*] has been under intensive investigation in California and elsewhere for some forty years, and we seem to be no nearer a solution of the problem than we were in the beginning. In fact the outlook is much less hopeful."

In 1997 Robert Geller of Tokyo University wrote in *Astronomy & Geophysics,* the Journal of the Royal Astronomical Society: "The idea that the Earth telegraphs its punches, i.e., that large earthquakes are preceded by observable and identifiable precursors—isn't backed up by the facts."

Reducing our Expectations:
Forecasts Rather than Predictions

Our lack of success in predicting earthquakes has caused earthquake program managers to cut back on prediction research and focus on the effects of earthquakes and on the faults that are the sources of earthquakes. Yet in a more limited way, we can say something about the future; indeed, we must, because land-use planning, building codes, and insurance underwriting depend on it. We do this by adopting the strategy of weather forecasting—20 percent chance of rain tonight, 40 percent tomorrow.

Earthquake forecasting, a more modest approach than earthquake prediction, seems to have much more relevance to public policy and our own expectations about what we can tell about future earthquakes. The difference between an earthquake prediction and an earthquake forecast has already been examined: a prediction specifies time, place, and magnitude of a forthcoming earthquake, whereas a forecast is much less definite.

We consider two types of forecasts: *deterministic* and *probabilistic.* A deterministic forecast estimates the largest earthquake imaginable on a particular fault or in a given region. A probabilistic forecast deals with the likelihood of an earthquake of a given size striking a particular fault or region within a future time interval of interest to society. An analogy may be made with hurricanes. The National Weather Service can forecast how likely it is that southern Florida may be struck by a hurricane as large as Hurricane Andrew in the next five years; this is probabilistic. It could also forecast how large a hurricane could possibly be: 200 mile per hour winds near the eye of the storm, for example. This is deterministic.

The Deterministic Method

Our debate in Chapter 4—about whether the next (or any future) Cascadia Subduction Zone earthquake will be of magnitude 8 or 9—was essentially a deterministic discussion. We made no claim about *when* the earthquake will strike, other than to say that such an earthquake is possible, or credible; we attempted to define the *maximum credible earthquake*, or MCE.

How do we do this? In Chapter 3, we learned that the moment magnitude (M_w) of an earthquake could be estimated from the area (length times depth) of the fault that ruptures and the amount of slip on that fault. The length of a potential earthquake rupture on a fault can be measured even if the fault has not ruptured in historic time; the slip per earthquake can be worked out from paleoseismological excavations along a fault scarp. These values can be compared with a data set of hundreds of earthquakes around the world that relate M_w to fault length and slip per earthquake.

We know the length of the Cascadia Subduction Zone, and based on slip estimated from other subduction zones worldwide and on our own paleoseismic estimates of the greatest amount of subsidence of coastal marshes during an earthquake ("what has happened can happen"), we can estimate a maximum moment magnitude, assuming that the entire subduction zone from Vancouver Island to northern California ruptures in a single earthquake (Figure 7-1). As stated earlier, we assign a magnitude 9 for the largest earthquake on the Cascadia Subduction Zone, even though many scientists believe that the largest expected earthquake would only rupture part of the subduction zone with a maximum magnitude of only 8.2 to 8.4. While the debate on maximum earthquake size continues, we go with the larger number, particularly for critical facilities like power plants and dams.

Some probability is built into a deterministic assessment. A nuclear power plant should be designed for a maximum credible earthquake even if the recurrence time for it is measured in tens of thousands of years. The result of an earthquake-induced failure of the core reactor would be catastrophic, even if the possibility is very small. Yet there is a limit. The possibility that the Earth might be struck by a comet or asteroid, producing a version of nuclear winter and mass extinction of organisms (including ourselves), is real but is so remote, measured in tens of millions of years, that we do not incorporate it into our preparedness planning.

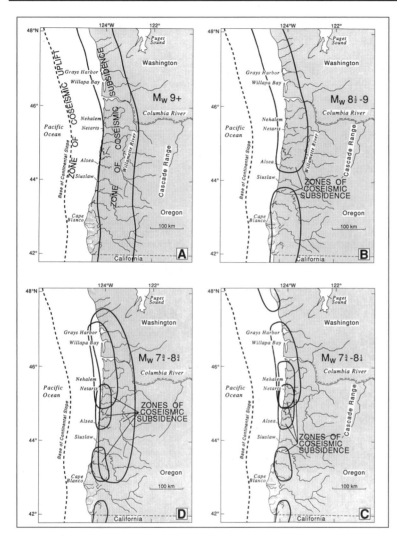

Figure 7-1. The deterministic choices for the maximum magnitude earthquake on the Cascadia Subduction Zone. (A) The entire subduction zone ruptures at the same time, resulting in an earthquake of M$_w$ 9+. (B) through (D). Segments of the subduction zone of various sizes rupture independently, resulting in smaller earthquakes. From Alan Nelson and Stephen Personius, U.S. Geological Survey.

A second deterministic estimate must be considered in the Pacific Northwest: that of a local crustal earthquake on, say, the Seattle Fault or the Portland Hills Fault. Its magnitude would be smaller than even the lower deterministic estimates of the magnitude of an earthquake on the Cascadia Subduction Zone, but because the crustal earthquake is closer to the Earth's surface and may strike directly beneath a major city, it needs separate treatment.

It is difficult to estimate the effects of crustal faults in the Pacific Northwest, because there are no through-going crustal faults in the region comparable to the San Andreas Fault, and most of the crustal faults that were described in Chapter 6 cannot be demonstrated to be active based on geologic evidence for offset of Holocene sediments or on instrumental seismicity. A moment magnitude of 7.1 is generally used, based on the estimated length of the Seattle Fault, which ruptured one thousand years ago, as described in Chapter 6.

Probabilistic Forecasting

We turn now to *probabilistic methods*. Examples of probability are: (1) the chance of your winning the lottery, (2) the chance of your being struck in a head-on collision on Interstate 5, or (3) the chance your house will be destroyed by fire. Even though you don't know if you will win the lottery or have your house burn down, the probability or likelihood of these outcomes is sufficiently well known that lotteries and gambling casinos can operate at a profit. You can buy insurance against a head-on collision or a house fire at a low enough rate that it is within your means, and the insurance company can show a profit (see Chapter 10).

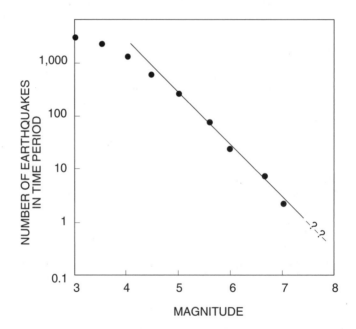

Figure 7-2. Illustration of the Gutenberg-Richter (G-R) relationship for thirty years of seismicity data for the Imperial Valley of southern California. Shown are the number of earthquakes of a given magnitude for the time period. Note that both scales are logarithmic, that is, each unit is ten times larger than the preceding one, as earlier discussed for magnitude. For this reason, the straight line may be somewhat misleading. The drop-off in seismicity for lower magnitudes is generally related to the sensitivity of the seismic network; it does not record all the smaller events. Projecting the straight line downward, G-R predicts 0.4 earthquakes of M 8 in the thirty-year time period, or one M 8 earthquake every 75 years. This prediction is questionable, as is the timing of still larger earthquakes. From C.R. Allen, Caltech, in Yeats et al., 1997.

In the probabilistic forecasting of earthquakes, we use geology, paleoseismology, and seismicity to consider the likelihood of a large earthquake in a given region or on a particular fault some time in the future. A time frame of thirty years is commonly selected, because that is likely to be within the attention span of political leaders and the general public. A one-year time frame would yield a probability too low to be noteworthy to a legislative body or to a state governor, whereas a one hundred-year time frame, longer than most life spans, might not be taken seriously, even though the probability would be much higher.

In 1954, Beno Gutenberg and Charles Richter of Caltech studied the instrumental seismicity of different regions around the world and observed a systematic relationship between earthquake magnitude and earthquake recurrence. Earthquakes of a given magnitude interval are about ten times more frequent than those of the next higher magnitude (Figure 7-2). The departure of the curve from a straight line at low magnitudes is explained by the detection threshold of seismographs to measure very small events. These small events would only be detected when they are close to a seismograph; others that are farther away would be missed. So Gutenberg and Richter assumed that if the seismographs could measure all the events, they would fall on the same straight line as the larger events that are sure to be detected, no matter where they occur in the region of interest.

This is known as the *Gutenberg-Richter (G-R) relationship* for a given area. If the curve is a straight line, then only a few years of observation of earthquakes of low magnitude could be extrapolated to forecast the recurrence frequency for earthquakes of larger magnitudes not covered by the data set.

Clarence Allen and his colleagues at Caltech showed that thirty years of earthquakes in all of southern California and adjacent northern Baja California, Mexico, seemed to predict the recurrence of larger events within the entire region, at least up to a point. But for smaller regions and for individual faults, the Gutenberg-Richter relationship did not hold up.

A flaw in the assumptions built into the relationship is that the line would continue to be straight for earthquakes larger than the data set. For example, if the Gutenberg-Richter curve predicted one M 7 earthquake in ten years for the region (not far from the curve shown in Figure 7-2), this would imply one M 8 per one hundred years, one M 9 per one thousand years, and one M 10 per ten thousand years! Clearly this cannot be so, because no earthquake larger than M 9.5 is known to have occurred. Allen has pointed out that if a single fault ruptured all the way around the Earth, an impossible assumption, the magnitude would be only 10.6. So the Gutenberg-Richter relationship fails us where

Figure 7-3. Seismicity of central California, 1980-86, to compare the seismicity of that part of the San Andreas Fault that ruptured in 1857 (southeast or lower right corner), which does not image the fault at all, to the seismicity of that part of the San Andreas Fault that ruptures frequently, as at Parkfield, or creeps accompanied by very small earthquakes, which images the fault very well. That part of the fault in the northwest or upper left corner of the map ruptured in 1906, but is not well imaged by microearthquakes. (100 km = 62 miles) From U.S. Geological Survey.

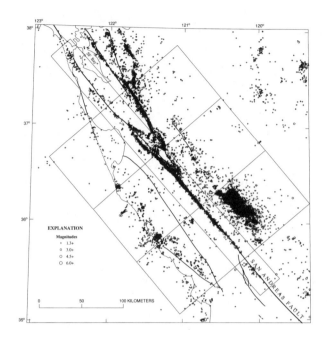

we need it the most, in forecasting the frequency of large earthquakes that are most devastating to society.

The Gutenberg-Richter relationship contains another questionable assumption: the more earthquakes are recorded on seismographs, the greater the likelihood of much larger earthquakes in the future. Suppose your region had more earthquakes of magnitudes below 7 than the curve shown in Figure 7-2. This would imply a larger number of big earthquakes and a greater hazard. At first, this seems logical. If you feel the effects of small earthquakes from time to time, you are more likely to worry about bigger ones.

Yet our study of Cascadia leads us to exactly the opposite conclusion. North of California, the Cascadia Subduction Zone fault has essentially *zero instrumental seismicity*, at least for the past few decades of high-quality observation, so that a Gutenberg-Richter estimate of the recurrence of M 9 earthquakes would be extremely long. But the study of subsided marshes along the coast tells us that large earthquakes of at least M 8 should recur every five hundred years or so.

To illustrate this point further, those parts of the San Andreas Fault that ruptured in large earthquakes in 1857 and 1906 are very quiet seismically today. This is illustrated in Figure 7-3, a seismicity map of central California, with the San Francisco Bay area in its northwest corner. The San Andreas Fault extends from the upper left to the lower right corner of this map. Those parts of the San Andreas Fault that release moderate-size earthquakes frequently, like Parkfield and the area northwest of Parkfield, stand out on the seismicity map. The fault is weakest in this area, and it is unlikely to store enough strain energy to release an earthquake of magnitude 7. However, the fault in the northwest corner of the map (part of the 1906 rupture) has relatively low instrumental seismicity, and the fault in the southeast corner (part of the 1857 rupture) is not marked by earthquakes at all. The segments of the fault with the lowest instrumental seismicity have the potential for the largest earthquake, almost a magnitude 8.

The flaw in the extrapolation of the Gutenberg-Richter curve to higher magnitudes is that seismicity, which measures the release of stored elastic strain energy, depends on the strength of the crust being studied. A relatively weak crust would have many small earthquakes, because the crust could not store enough strain to release a large one. A strong crust would release few or no earthquakes until strain had built up enough to rupture the crust in a very large earthquake.

Paleoseismicity leads to still another criticism of the Gutenberg-Richter relationship. Dave Schwartz and Kevin Coppersmith, then of Woodward-Clyde Consultants in San Francisco, were able to identify individual earthquakes in backhoe trench excavations of active faults in Utah and California based on fault offset of sediment in the trenches. They found that fault offsets tend to be about the same for different earthquakes in the same backhoe trench, indicating that the earthquakes producing the fault offsets tend to be about the same magnitude. This led them to the concept of *characteristic earthquakes*: a given segment of fault tends to produce the same size earthquake each time it ruptures. This would allow us to dig backhoe trenches across a suspect fault, determine the slip on the last earthquake rupture (preferably on more than one rupture event), and forecast the size of the next earthquake. When compared with the Gutenberg-Richter curve for the same fault, which is based on instrumental seismicity, the characteristic earthquake, when combined with its recurrence interval, tends to be bigger than the curve would predict (Figure 7-4). Furthermore, the Gutenberg-Richter curve cannot be used to extrapolate to earthquake sizes larger than the characteristic earthquake. The characteristic earthquake is as big as it ever gets on that particular fault.

These two examples suggest that no meaningful link may exist between the Gutenberg-Richter relationship for small events and the recurrence and size of large events, unless the period of instrumental observation is very long. Unfortunately, we have not had seismographs running long enough.

The characteristic earthquake concept has been shown to work for many faults around the world, but not for some others.

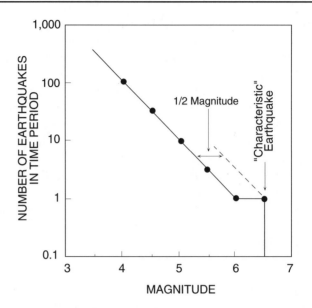

Figure 7-4. Comparison of the Gutenberg-Richter (G-R) relationship with the characteristic earthquake model, derived from geological studies that suggest that the largest earthquake for a particular segment of a fault will be a similar size, event after event. When earthquake recurrence intervals are taken into consideration, G-R underpredicts the size of the characteristic earthquake and does not allow for extrapolation to higher magnitudes. From Kevin Coppersmith and Robert Youngs, Geomatrix Consultants, San Francisco.

Paleoseismologic information from some backhoe trenches across the San Andreas Fault in central California suggests that individual segments of the fault have produced earthquakes ranging in size from M 7 to nearly M 8. Those parts of the fault do not rupture as characteristic earthquakes.

Before considering a probabilistic analysis for a region in northern California, we introduce the *principle of uncertainty*. There is virtually no uncertainty in the prediction of high and low tides, solar or lunar eclipses, or even the return period of Halley's Comet. These events are based on well-understood orbits of planetary bodies. However, the recurrence interval of earthquakes is controlled by many variables, as we learned at Parkfield. The strength of the fault may change from earthquake to earthquake. Other earthquakes may perturb the buildup of strain on the fault, as the 1983 Coalinga Earthquake may have done for the predicted Parkfield Earthquake. Why does one tree in a forest fall today, but its neighbor of the same age and same growth environment takes another hundred years to fall? That is the kind of uncertainty we face with earthquake forecasting.

How do we handle this uncertainty? Figure 7-5 shows a *probability curve* for the recurrence of the next earthquake in a given area or along a given fault. Time in years advances from left to right, starting at zero at the time of the previous earthquake. The probability of an earthquake at a particular time since the last earthquake increases upward at first. The curve is at its highest when we think the earthquake is most likely to happen, and then the curve slopes down to the right. We feel confident that the earthquake will surely have occurred by the time the curve drops to near zero on the right side of the curve. Another way of saying this is that we are 100 per cent sure that the earthquake will happen at some time when the curve is higher than zero.

The graph in Figure 7-5 has a darker band, which represents the time frame of interest in our probability forecast. The left side of the dark band is today, and the right side is the end of our time frame, commonly thirty years from now. There is a certain probability that the earthquake will occur during the time frame we have selected.

This shows the similarity to weather forecasting, except we are talking about a thirty-year forecast rather than a five-day forecast. If the meteorologist on the six-o'clock news says there is a 70 percent chance of rain tomorrow, this also means that there is a 30 percent chance that it will *not* rain tomorrow. The weather forecaster is often wrong, and the earthquake forecaster has a strong chance of being wrong as well.

Imagine turning on the television and getting the thirty-year earthquake forecast: "There is a 10 percent chance of an earthquake of magnitude 6 in our region in the next thirty years." That might not affect our vacation plans, but it could affect our building codes and insurance rates.

How do we draw our probability curve? We take into account all that we know: frequency of earthquakes based on historical records and geologic evidence, the long-term geologic rate at which a fault moves, and so on. Generally, a panel of experts is convened to debate the various lines of evidence and arrive at a consensus about probabilities. The debate is often heated, and agreement may not be reached in some cases.

Our probability curve has the shape that it does because we have some knowledge about when the next earthquake will occur, based on previous earthquake history, fault slip rates, and so on. But suppose that we had no knowledge at all of when the next

Figure 7-5. The probability for the recurrence of large earthquakes on a given fault or in a given region. Time increases from left to right, and the higher the curve, the greater the likelihood of an earthquake. The previous earthquake happened at time 0. The dark gray band is the time of interest for the probability calculation, commonly thirty years. The left side of the dark band is today. According to this probability, the earthquake will surely have happened by the time the probability curve returns to zero at the right side of the curve.

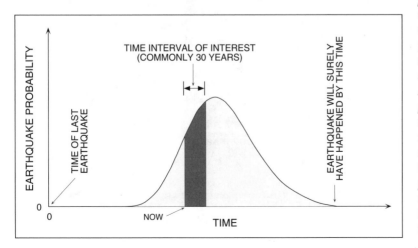

earthquake would occur; that is to say, our data set had no "memory" of the last earthquake to guide us. Then the probability curve would be a straight horizontal line. The earthquake would be just as likely to strike one year as the next. This is the same probability that controls your chance of flipping a coin and having it turn up heads: 50 percent. You could then flip the coin and get heads the next five times, but the sixth time, the probability of getting heads would be the same as when you started: 50 percent.

However, our probability curve is bell shaped; it "remembers" that there has been an earthquake on the same fault or in the same region previously. We know that another earthquake will occur, but we don't know well the displacement per event or the long-term slip rate, and nature builds in an intrinsic uncertainty. The broadness of this curve builds in all these uncertainties.

Viewed probabilistically, the Parkfield forecast was not really a failure; the next earthquake is somewhere on the right side of the curve. We are sure that there *will* be another Parkfield Earthquake, but we don't know when the right side of the curve will drop down to near zero. Time 0 is 1966, the year of the last Parkfield Earthquake. The left side of the dark band is today. Prior to 1988, when the next Parkfield Earthquake was expected, the high point on the probability curve would have been in 1988. That time is long past, but we expect the earthquake very soon. (Perhaps it will have happened by the time you read this.)

The time represented by the curve above zero would be the longest recurrence interval known for Parkfield, which was thirty-

Figure 7-6. Thirty-year probabilities (P) of large earthquakes (M equal to or greater than 7) in the San Francisco Bay region. From Working Group on California Earthquake Probabilities (1990).

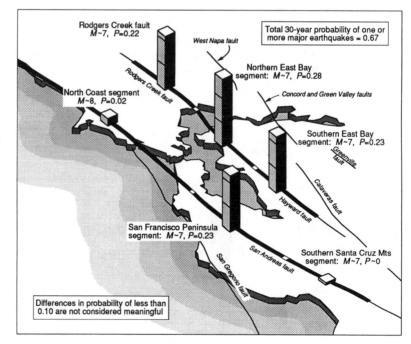

two years (between the 1934 and 1966 events). However, since we are already approaching that date, we will have to extend that time to greater than thirty-two years. The historical sample of earthquake recurrences at Parkfield, although more complete than for most faults, was insufficient.

How about the next Cascadia Subduction Zone earthquake? Time 0 is the year 1700, when the last earthquake occurred. The left edge of the dark band is today. Let's take the width of the dark band as thity years, as we have before. We would still be to the left of the high point in the probability curve. Our average recurrence interval based on paleoseismology is five hundred years, and it has only been three hundred years since the last earthquake. What should be the time when the curve is at zero again? Not five hundred years after 1700, because we expect a great variability in the recurrence interval. The earthquake could strike tomorrow, or it could occur one thousand years after 1700, or 2700 A.D.

We now consider the thirty-year probabilistic forecast for the San Francisco Bay area (Figure 7-6), based on a consensus of experts, in this case, the Working Group on California Earthquake Probabilities. The study was done in 1990, one year after the M 7.2 Loma Prieta Earthquake on the Southern Santa Cruz Mountains Segment of the San Andreas Fault, which, accordingly, now has a low probability of an earthquake of M greater than 7 in the next thirty years. The North Coast Segment of the San Andreas Fault also has a low probability, even though at the time of the forecast, it had been eighty-four years since the great 1906 earthquake on that segment. The mean recurrence interval on this segment is long, and it is still fairly early in its cycle. On the other hand, probabilities on the Rodgers Creek-Hayward Fault are much higher, almost 30 percent in the next thirty years for the northern East Bay segment of the Hayward Fault, which includes the cities of Berkeley and Oakland. The mean recurrence interval from paleoseismology and historical records (the fault last ruptured in 1868) is fairly short, and so the probability is high. The probability that an earthquake with M greater than 7 will occur on one of these faults is much higher than it is on any one fault. It is 67 percent, or two chances in three in the next thirty years, a sobering thought for residents of the East Bay area.

How good is this probabilistic forecast? Figure 7-6 updates an earlier probabilistic forecast made prior to the 1989 Loma Prieta Earthquake. In the earlier forecast, the Southern Santa Cruz Mountains Segment of the San Andreas Fault was identified as an area of high probability for an earthquake in the next few decades. Some scientists stated that this was the most likely segment to rupture, after Parkfield. This segment had slipped much less than segments to the northwest in the great 1906 San Francisco

Earthquake, yet it had relatively low seismicity compared to weak creeping segments of the fault still farther to the southeast (as shown by high instrumental seismicity on Figure 7-3). The available information indicated that this segment of the fault was locked. It was proposed that the southern Santa Cruz Mountains should be heavily instrumented to detect faint precursors of the expected earthquake, but this was not done. As a result, the earthquake community got zapped by Loma Prieta while it concentrated its instrumentation efforts at Parkfield, farther to the southeast. It was a lost chance, except that the probability method successfully identified the fault segment that ultimately did rupture in the Loma Prieta event..

So how good is the post-Loma Prieta forecast shown in Figure 7-6? It may underestimate the hazard for the *region*, as opposed to the sum of the *individual faults* studied because it takes no account of earthquakes on other known active faults for which recurrence intervals are relatively unknown, such as the San Gregorio and Calaveras faults. These faults did not contain enough relevant geologic data to be included in the forecast, so their hazard was not estimated. In addition, the Working Group had considerable disagreement among its members. Would the next earthquake (or set of earthquakes) follow the predicted periodic recurrence, or would they cluster in time, like the 20th-century earthquakes in the Central Nevada Seismic Zone? Would only a single segment rupture, or might more than one segment of a fault (or more than one fault, as happened in the 1992 Landers Earthquake in the Mojave Desert of California) rupture in the same earthquake?

Why Do We Bother With All This?

By now, you are probably suitably unimpressed by how refined our earthquake forecasting techniques are. Yet we continue in our attempts, because insurance underwriters need this kind of statistical information to establish risks and premium rates. Furthermore, government agencies need to know if the chances of an earthquake are high enough to require stricter building codes, thereby increasing the cost of construction. I began this chapter with a discussion of earthquake *prediction* in terms of yes or no, but probabilistic *forecasting* allows us to quantify the "maybes" and to say something about the uncertainties.

Why is the outlook for scientifically reliable earthquake forecasting not more optimistic? The answer may lie in our appraisal in Chapter 2 of the structural integrity of the Earth's crust—not well designed, not up to code. Some scientists believe that the Earth's crust is in a state of critical failure—almost, but not quite, ready to rupture. In this view, the Earth is not like a strong well-constructed building which you can predict with reasonable certainty will not collapse. The crust is more like a row of old tenement shacks, poorly built in the first place with shoddy workmanship and materials, and now affected by rot and old age. These shacks will probably collapse some day, but which one will collapse first? Will the next shack collapse the next day or ten years from then? This is the dilemma of the earthquake forecaster.

But society demands that we try.

Suggestions for Further Reading

Geller, R.J. 1997. Predictable publicity. *Seismological Research Letters,* vol. 68, pp. 477-80.

Lomnitz, C. 1994. *Fundamentals of Earthquake Prediction.* New York: John Wiley & Sons, 326p.

Ma Z., Z. Fu., Y. Zhang, C. Wang, G. Zhang, and D. Liu. 1990. *Earthquake Prediction: Nine Major Earthquakes in China (1966-1976).* Beijing: Seismological Press, and Berlin, Springer-Verlag, 332p.

Olson, R.S. 1989. *The Politics of Earthquake Prediction.* Princeton, N.J.: Princeton University Press, 187p.

Scholz, C.H., 1997, Whatever happened to earthquake prediction? *Geotimes,* vol. 42, no. 3, pp. 16-19.

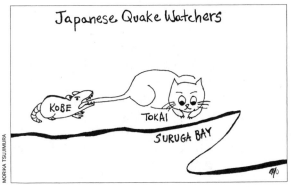

Cartoons illustrating American and Japanese forecasting strategies. From Scholz (1997), with permission from Morika Tsujimura.

ᘐ Part III ᘐ
Shaky Ground and Big Waves

Introduction

U p to this point, we have discussed *earthquake sources*: where earthquakes are likely to strike, how large they might be, and how often they might be expected. From the preceding chapter, you might well conclude that we are not very far along in our ability to forecast the time when an earthquake might occur, although we have devised some fairly elaborate statistical procedures to describe our uncertainty (probabilistic forecasting).

It is also important to describe the geologic setting *at the Earth's surface*, in particular the response of the ground to an earthquake. Most of us are concerned less about the strength of the earthquake itself than we are about its effects where we are at the time, or where we live, or own property, or work. That is to say, earthquake *intensity* is more important to us than earthquake *magnitude*. As has been said about politics, all earthquakes are local.

I am continually amazed at the apparently random damage of a major earthquake. After the 1994 Northridge Earthquake, I visited the Fashion Square Mall at Northridge, in which several major stores and a large parking garage were demolished. Nearby, other shopping malls had hardly been damaged at all. A new parking structure at California State University at Northridge was so badly damaged that it had to be taken down, yet directly across the street from it were small single-family homes that suffered only minimal damage. This was not necessarily due to the distance from the epicenter of the earthquake. Interstate 10, the major east-west artery between Santa Monica and downtown Los Angeles, on the south side of the Santa Monica Mountains and far from the epicenter, suffered severe damage, including the collapse of a major interchange. But condominiums and houses perched high in the Santa Monica Mountains, closer to the epicenter, were not severely damaged.

In recent years, we have come to recognize certain geologic settings where built structures are likely to suffer much more earthquake damage than others. The Oregon Department of

Geology and Mineral Industries has published maps of Portland and Salem that locate the more hazardous environments with respect to construction. Similar maps have been prepared for Victoria, B. C. Although no two earthquakes will produce the same damage pattern in a given region, certain sites can be recognized as hazardous in advance of decisions to develop them.

Some of the greatest losses of life and property come not directly from the shaking but from the dislodging of great masses of earth as landslides and rockfalls. These are not the normal mudslides that plague the Pacific Northwest in a rainy winter. They are generally much larger masses of rock and soil that would not move even during very heavy rainfall. For example, a M 7.9 earthquake on the subduction zone off the coast of Peru on May 31, 1970, caused a slab of rock and ice hundreds of feet across to break off a near-vertical cliff high on Mt. Huascarán, the highest mountain in Peru. The mass of rock and ice fell several thousand feet, disintegrated, slid across a glacier, then overtopped low ridges below the glacier and became airborne. After falling back to the ground, the rock mass swept down the valley of the Shacsha River, entraining the water of the river as it did so. This flow of mixed debris and water reached velocities of 120 miles per hour. Seven miles from its source, this rapidly moving mass separated into two streams of debris, one of which rode over a ridge and buried the town of Yungay. The other stream of debris obliterated the city of Ranrahirca. Nearly twenty-five thousand people lost their lives in this single landslide. Most of the residents of these overwhelmed cities died instantly, without warning. The entire time from the first collapse high on Huascarán to destruction of these cities was less than four minutes!

But landslide danger is not limited to steep slopes. Nearly flat areas underlain by clean, water-saturated sand may fail by liquefaction of the sand, which bursts to the surface as fountains and causes the land itself to move like a gigantic snowboard, snapping utility lines. During the Northridge Earthquake, a mass of land along Balboa Boulevard slid along a very gentle slope, rupturing a buried water line and a gas line. Escaping gas led to a fire that destroyed many homes in the vicinity. Television newscasts showed the odd combination of flames leaping above the roadway combined with torrents of water.

People living on the coast face another hazard: seismic sea waves, or *tsunamis*. Tsunamis have produced catastrophic losses of life numbering in the tens of thousands. The earthquake generating a deadly tsunami may be thousands of miles away, across the ocean. The Pacific Northwest had its own deadly tsunami on Easter weekend, 1964, after the great earthquake in southern Alaska.

One of the main reasons our risk is increasing is that we are building in increasingly unstable and dangerous areas. The demand for housing has caused urban development to expand onto river floodplains, steep hillslopes, and sand bars such as Siletz Spit at Lincoln City on the Oregon coast. These environments pose hazards other than earthquakes, as shown in the drowned-out homes in the floods of February 1996, and in the recent mudslides of Portland and Puget Sound, all unrelated to earthquakes.

I was astounded to read an Associated Press article on December 23, 1996, stating that the demand for building sites in the Portland metropolitan area is so strong that builders have hired professional scouts to look for owners of undeveloped land or farm land who might be persuaded to sell, if not now, perhaps two or three years in the future. Land hunters may call up a title company and request information on any land parcel two acres or larger in a particular area. Armed with that information, they start calling landowners. Some land in Washington County, Oregon, is reported to be selling for $150,000 an acre.

No mention was made in the article of the known fact that some of these building sites around Portland, as well as Seattle and other cities in the Pacific Northwest, are dangerously flawed by their geology, with possibilities of landslides, flooding, earthquake shaking, and liquefaction. I know of no automatic legal provision that a potential homeowner in these newly developed subdivisions (as well as in neighborhoods long since built up) must be fully informed of these geologic hazards before purchasing a lot or a home. I recall the Keizer, Oregon, homeowner who had lived in his new house only a few months when he was flooded out by the Willamette River in February 1996. Said he on the TV evening news: "The county said it was OK." Neither the landowner, who may get more than $100,000 an acre for the family farm, nor the developer wants to be the one to enlighten the unwary buyer.

California now has legislation that requires inspection of building sites with respect to earthquake hazards as well as other geologic hazards. Protection of this sort is available in Washington and Oregon only in a few communities where grading ordinances have been passed. (See Chapter 14, pages 259-62 for a definition and discussion of grading ordinances.)

In all these cases, it is possible to assess the geologic hazards to construction and, in most cases, to "engineer" around them, although strengthening a building site against earthquakes increases the cost of development. The person considering building on a particular site (or moving to an already-built house on such a site) must weigh the risk of an unlikely but potentially catastrophic earthquake against the possibility that the house could remain safe for a lifetime.

In the two chapters that follow, I consider these hazards and conclude that, indeed, we know quite a lot about predicting *how* a particular site will respond, even though we do not know *when* the earthquake will strike that will put the site and the people living and working there at risk. We know enough, in fact, that we could put teeth into laws requiring that a buyer be made aware of geologic hazards before investing in a piece of property. We could make sure that local grading ordinances require inspection of building sites against possible geologic hazards, in addition to inspection of the building itself. I will return to such ordinances in Chapter 14.

↬ 8 ↫

Solid Rock and Bowls of Jello

*"Anyone who hears my words and puts them into practice
is like the wise man who built his house on rock. When the
rainy season set in, the torrents came and the winds blew
and buffeted his house. It did not collapse; it had been
solidly set on rock. Anyone who hears my words but does
not put them into practice is like the foolish man who built
his house on sandy ground. The rains fell, the torrents
came, the winds blew and lashed against his house. It
collapsed under all this and was completely ruined."*
Matthew 7:24-27

Introduction

We live in earthquake country, but we don't want
to leave the Pacific Northwest. Fortunately, we
know how to improve our chances for survival simply
by making intelligent decisions about where we live or work. The
technology is at hand to evaluate the geologic setting of a building
site with respect to earthquake hazard.

Three different earthquake problems are associated with surface
sites: (1) amplification of seismic waves by soft surficial deposits,
(2) liquefaction of near-surface sediments, and (3) landslides. I
will consider each of these in turn.

Amplification of Seismic Waves by Soft Surficial Deposits

It is a short stroll from Fort Mason, west of Ghirardelli Square and
Fisherman's Wharf in San Francisco, to the fashionable townhouses
of the upscale Marina District, yet the intensity of ground motion
of these two areas during the earthquake of October 17, 1989, was
dramatically different. The Marina District experienced intensities
as high as IX, higher even than at the epicenter itself, more than
60 miles away. Fort Mason and Fisherman's Wharf experienced
intensities of only VII. The difference was the foundation material.

The Marina District was constructed in part of fine sand fill from San Francisco Bay that was hydraulically emplaced after the 1906 earthquake, together with rubble from buildings destroyed by that earthquake. This material was pushed together to make a building site for an international exposition in 1915 that said to the world, "San Francisco is back!" Yes, San Francisco was back, all right, but the sand and rubble contained a time bomb: the foundation was too poorly consolidated to hold up well during the next earthquake. In October 1989, the bomb went off.

Figure 8-1 shows seismograms of an aftershock of magnitude 4.6 on October 21 recorded at Fort Mason (MAS), where the seismograph was established on bedrock, and two sites in the Marina District, one (PUC) on dune sand from an ancient beach, and the other (LMS) on the artificial fill emplaced after the 1906 earthquake. Notice that the seismic waves were much stronger at PUC and LMS that at MAS, an indication of more violent seismic shaking, leading to more damage. The waves were also of much lower frequency. Engineers call a station like MAS a *rock site*, and stations like PUC and LMS *soil sites*.

An analogy is commonly made between these two types of site and a bowl of jello on a table, an experiment that can be done at home. Stack two or three children's blocks on top of one another on the table top, then stack some more blocks on top of the jello. Then push the table suddenly. The blocks on the jello will fall over, whereas the blocks directly on the table top may remain standing. The shaking of the blocks on the table illustrates the effect of a seismic wave passing through bedrock. When the shaking reaches the bowl of jello, however, the waves are amplified so that the top of the jello jiggles and causes the blocks to topple.

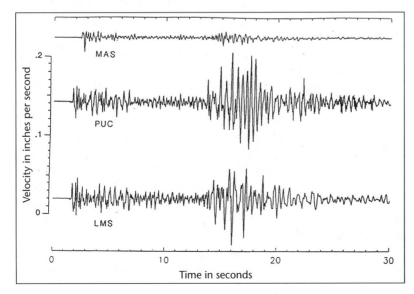

Figure 8-1. Seismograms of a magnitude 4.6 aftershock of the Loma Prieta Earthquake on October 21, 1989 at three temporary stations at the north end of San Francisco Peninsula, showing amplification of ground motion in two soil sites in the Marina district (PUC, LMS) compared to a bedrock site at Fort Mason (MAS). From U.S. Geological Survey.

In a similar fashion, the soft foundation materials at a soil site will amplify the seismic waves, which results in much more vigorous shaking than would be expected at a rock site.

A tragic illustration of this phenomenon was provided by the magnitude 7.9 Mexico City Earthquake of 1985. Actually, the epicenter of the earthquake was in the Pacific Ocean on a subduction zone, hundreds of miles from Mexico City. It is called the Mexico City Earthquake because of the terrible losses suffered by that city. More than fifteen million people live in Mexico City, many in substandard housing, which was one reason why so many lives were lost. But more important is the geologic foundation: Mexico City is built on the former lake bed of Lake Texcoco. The clay, silt, and sand of this ancient lake, in part saturated with water, greatly amplified the seismic waves traveling through the crust from the subduction zone. More than five hundred buildings fell down, and more than eight thousand people were killed. The floor of Lake Texcoco truly acted like the bowl of jello resting on the table top that is the Earth's crust beneath the lake deposits.

The Mexico City Earthquake provided a lesson for the major cities of the Willamette Valley, Puget Sound, and southwestern British Columbia. Much of the foundation of these cities is soft sediment: deltaic deposits of the Fraser River, glacial deposits in Puget Sound, and alluvial deposits of the Willamette and Columbia rivers. Even though a subduction-zone earthquake would be far away, near the coast or offshore (as it was for Mexico City), these soft sediments would be expected to amplify the seismic waves and cause more damage than if the cities were built on bedrock. Fortunately for the people of the Pacific Northwest, building standards here are higher than those in Mexico City, so we would not expect as high a loss of life. In addition, geotechnical experience with many earthquakes around the world permits a forecast of the effects of near-surface geology on seismic waves from various earthquake sources. In other words, this is a problem we can do something about.

These techniques are illustrated by a study done by Woodward-Clyde Federal Services and the Oregon Department of Geology and Mineral Industries for the City of Portland (Wong et al., 1993). Because no two earthquake sources are alike, Wong and his colleagues programmed computer simulations based on a Cascadia Subduction Zone earthquake of M_w 8.5 and crustal earthquakes of M_w 6 and M_w 6.5. Because the surface effects are strongly influenced by the distance of a site from the epicenter, they used distances from the crustal source to the site of 5, 10, and 15 kilometers.

What property of a seismic wave is best for determining the hazard to buildings? Wong's group chose *peak horizontal acceleration,* expressed in *percentage of gravity (percent g)*. Acceleration is the rate of increase in speed of an object. If you step off a cliff and fall through space, your speed will accelerate from zero at a rate of 32 feet (9.8 meters) per second every second, due to the gravitational attraction of the Earth. We call this an acceleration of 1 g. When an earthquake has a vertical acceleration greater than 1 g, objects such as stones or clods of earth are thrown into the air, as first observed during a great earthquake in India in 1897. During the 1971 San Fernando, California, Earthquake, vertical accelerations greater than 1 g were recorded, with the result that a fire truck with its brakes set was tossed about the Lopez Canyon Fire Station, leaving tire marks on the garage door frame 3 feet above the floor.

Horizontal accelerations may be measured as well. A car accelerating at a rate of 1 g would travel 100 yards from a stationary position in slightly more than 4 seconds. As we will see later, horizontal accelerations are particularly critical, because many older buildings constructed without consideration of earthquakes are designed to withstand vertical loads, such as the weight of the building itself, whereas an earthquake may cause a building to shake from side to side, accelerating horizontally. A higher peak acceleration will lead to a higher earthquake intensity at a given site.

Strong shaking is measured by a special type of seismograph called a *strong-motion accelerometer.* These instruments are designed to deal with the problem that an ordinary continuous-recording seismograph may go off scale during a strong earthquake. The strong-motion instrument does not record continuously, but is triggered to start recording when the first earthquake wave arrives, and it stops recording when the waves diminish to a low level. These instruments record the acceleration in percent g. They are of particular use to structural engineers, who use the recordings to determine how buildings vibrate during an earthquake. Several instruments may be placed in a single tall building, one in the basement and others on upper floors, showing very different response to shaking of different levels of the building. It would be prudent to install strong-motion accelerometers in all major structures such as dams or skyscrapers. The installation cost is very small compared to the cost of the building, and the information revealed during an earthquake is invaluable in future engineering design.

Another consideration is the period of the earthquake waves that are potentially damaging. *Period* is the length of time it takes one wave length to pass a given point (Figure 3-12). We have already encountered *frequency,* the number of wave lengths to pass a point in a second. Frequency is equal to 1 divided by the period.

As we saw in Chapter 3, earthquakes, like symphony orchestras, produce waves of short period (piccolos and violins) and long period (tubas and bass violins).

Wong and his colleagues considered the effects on four sites in Portland, Oregon, of a spectrum of waves from high frequency with periods of 0.02 seconds to low frequency with periods of 10 seconds (Figure 8-2). The information they used to construct their models included the slip on the assumed earthquake fault and the near-surface geology. They drilled several boreholes and measured the density (weight per given volume) of the various sedimentary layers they encountered as well as the speed of sound waves passing through the sediments. Soft sediment such as sand or clay tends to be low in density, whereas bedrock such as basalt has a high density. Sound waves (and earthquake waves) pass slowly through soft sediment, and much more rapidly through bedrock.

As the seismic waves pass from bedrock to soft sediment, they slow down and increase in amplitude. The increase in amplitude causes greater acceleration of the ground at a particular site, which leads to more intensive shaking. For these reasons, the thickness and density of the soft sediment layers directly beneath the surface are critical to the calculation of shaking and potential damage.

Figure 8-2 shows an example of some of their calculations, in this case for a Cascadia Subduction Zone earthquake. These are logarithmic curves; each division has a value ten times that of the previous one. The curves show that the greatest accelerations are expected for seismic waves with periods ranging from 0.4 to 2 seconds. Different sets of curves were obtained for the crustal earthquakes. There is considerable difference in the curves among

Figure 8-2. Acceleration in percent gravity (g) of seismic waves of different periods from a postulated Cascadia Subduction Zone earthquake at four soil sites in Portland. Earthquake is 120 km from Portland. From Wong et al. (1993).

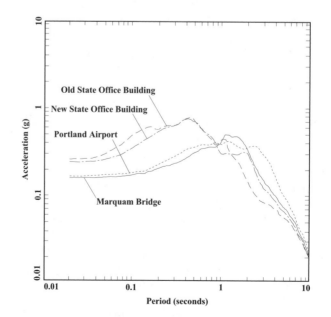

the four sites, emphasizing the importance of understanding the near-surface geology.

Another factor important in constructing these curves is the *attenuation* of seismic waves as they leave the earthquake focus and reach the site in question. Attenuation is affected by the strength and rigidity of the crust through which the seismic wave must pass. Imagine putting your ear against the cut surface of a long log which is struck on the other end by a hammer. If the log is made of sound wood, the vibration of the log caused by the hammer may be enough to hurt your ear. The attenuation of the wave in the log is low. However, if the log is made of rotten wood, you may hear a dull "thunk," indicating that the attenuation is high. In the crust, high attenuation means that the strength of the earthquake wave falls off fairly rapidly with distance from the focus.

In the discussion above, we have been concerned about the effect on earthquake shaking of the geology at or near the surface of the ground. Recent research in California has shown that the *path* traveled by an earthquake from the source to the surface also can have a dramatic effect on shaking. Kim Olsen and Ralph Archuleta of the University of California at Santa Barbara constructed elaborate computer models of the effects of a M 7.75 earthquake on the San Andreas Fault on shaking in the Los Angeles Basin, 30-40 miles away. The Los Angeles Basin is filled to depths of 4 to 6 miles with sedimentary rocks that have a much lower density than crustal rocks beneath the basin or in the adjacent mountain ranges. Olsen and Archuleta showed that their simulated earthquake would generate surface waves that would slow down and increase dramatically in amplitude as they entered the thick sedimentary rocks of the Los Angeles Basin. In addition, the surface waves would echo off the base and the steep sides of the sedimentary basin, so that strong shaking would last much longer than it would at the source of the earthquake.

This effect could also be felt in sedimentary basins that are much shallower than the Los Angeles Basin. For example, the Tualatin Basin in Oregon, including the cities of Beaverton, Hillsboro, and Forest Grove, contains up to 1,500 feet of sediment with a low density compared to that of the basalt underlying the Chehalem Mountains to the south and the Portland Hills to the northeast. Seismic waves could be amplified and the duration of strong shaking lengthened in this basin. Other basins with such a potential hazard include the Portland-Vancouver Basin in Oregon and Washington between downtown Portland and Troutdale and the Everett Basin in Washington between downtown Seattle and Everett.

Figure 8-3. Map of the Pacific Northwest and adjacent southwestern Canada with contours showing a 10 percent probability that a given maximum (peak) acceleration will be equaled or exceeded in the next fifty years. Numbers are in percent gravity. The highest numbers, greater than 32 percent gravity, are in coastal southwest Oregon and northwest California, leading to an upgrade of seismic building codes in that area. From the Geological Survey of Canada and the U.S. Geological Survey.

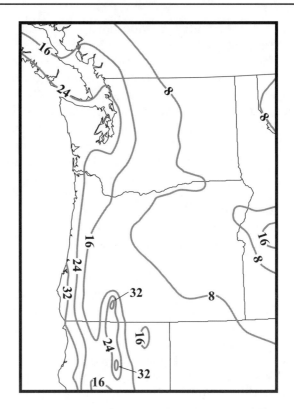

This idea was tested in the Fraser River Delta around Vancouver, B. C., by studying several strong-motion accelerometers that were triggered by a M 5.3 earthquake at Duvall, Washington, in 1996. The shaking recorded by accelerometers in the delta was stronger than those on bedrock sites, as expected. Interestingly, the strongest shaking was found near the edge of the basin underlying the delta, perhaps due to focusing of seismic energy.

This behavior, related to the path the earthquake wave takes from the source to the site, could be considered a very large-scale example of the bowl of jello. In both cases, surface waves are amplified, but in the examples of Los Angeles and the Fraser River Delta, the shaking is related to the path of the earthquake wave through a thick sedimentary basin, analogous to focusing of light through a lens. Path effects have only recently been recognized, and no research has yet been done about path effects relative to basins beneath major cities of the northwestern United States.

The U.S. Geological Survey and the Geological Survey of Canada have combined all of these factors to produce maps showing peak horizontal accelerations over the next fifty years. One of these maps is shown as Figure 8-3. The highest accelerations are forecast along the coast, closest to the subduction zone. However, other structures, particularly those that have ruptured historically, also affect the estimated accelerations.

Liquefaction:
When the Earth Turns to Soup

Soft, unconsolidated sand deposits saturated with water may, under certain conditions, change from a solid to a liquid when shaken. This property may be observed in wet beach sand. Just tap-tap-tap your foot on the saturated sand at the water's edge. The sand will first start to bubble and eject a mixture of sand and water. Then, if there is a very slight slope, the saturated sand from which the bubbles are emanating will flow downslope toward the sea.

Liquefaction is defined as "the act or process transforming any substance into a liquid." If you have the misfortune of building a house on liquefiable sediment, and an earthquake strikes, your house may sink into the ground at a crazy angle as the sediment liquefies. Liquefaction is especially common in clean loose sand or gravelly sand, saturated with water. Most sand layers with liquefaction potential are Holocene in age (less than ten thousand years old), and are unconsolidated. The liquefaction susceptibility of sand can be determined by standard geotechnical engineering tests such as the Standard Penetration Test. During this test, a sampling tube is driven into the ground by dropping a 140-lb weight from a height of 30 inches (okay, it's not rocket science, but it works). The penetration resistance is the number of blows (number of times the weight is dropped) that it takes to drive the sampler one foot into the soil. A low penetration resistance would be less than ten blows per foot; a high resistance would be greater than thirty blows per foot. Liquefiable sands have a very low penetration resistance; it is very easy to drive the sampling tube into the sand.

Sands that are subject to liquefaction are almost always buried to depths less than 30 feet. At greater depths, the overburden pressure is high enough to prevent liquefaction from taking place, unless the shaking is extremely strong. When earthquake waves shake the sand, the pressure of the waves deforms and compresses the sand for an instant, raising the water pressure in the pore spaces between sand grains, thereby turning the sand-water mixture into a liquid. This temporary overpressuring (*cyclic shear stress* or *cyclic loading*) is repeated as long as strong shaking takes place. Such sand is generally overlain by a more cohesive material, such as clay, which serves to confine the compressed water in the sand. If the sediment layer is on a slight slope, it will move downslope *en masse*; this is called a *lateral spread*.

Perhaps the most spectacular expressions of liquefaction occur when watery sand vents to the surface through a clay cap, where it may spout up in the air like a fountain or geyser for minutes to hours after the mainshock, leaving a low crater or mound (*sand boil)* after the fountain has died down (Figures 8-4, 8-5). Excavation of sand boils by a backhoe or bulldozer may reveal a vertical filling of sand within the clay cap, called a *sand dike*. The sand dike marks the place where sand at depth has vented to the surface.

Much of the severe damage in the Marina District of San Francisco during the 1989 earthquake was due to liquefaction of the artificial fill that had been emplaced after the 1906 earthquake. Sand boils erupted into townhouse basements, streets, yards, and parks. Lateral displacement of the ground surface broke underground utility lines, leaving about a thousand homes without gas or water. The broken gas lines caused large fires to break out.

Liquefaction of beach deposits during the same earthquake severely damaged the San Jose State University Marine Laboratory at Moss Landing (Figure 8-6).

A more severe case of liquefaction during the Good Friday Earthquake of 1964 in Alaska destroyed part of the new Turnagain Heights subdivision of Anchorage, situated on a 30-foot bluff overlooking Cook Inlet. Earthquake waves liquefied a layer of sand and clay, causing part of the subdivision to break up and slide toward the bay. Homes, patios, streets, and trees tilted at crazy angles, and gaping chasms opened, swallowing up and burying alive two small children. One house slid more than 1,200 feet toward the sea, destroying itself as it did so (Figure 8-7). The instability of the water-saturated layer, known as the Bootlegger Cove Clay, had been pointed out in a 1959 report by the U.S. Geological Survey five years before the earthquake, but this information apparently had no influence on development plans for Turnagain Heights.

Figure 8-4. Vertical cross section through a sand boil, showing the liquefied sand layer (H_2), the overlying nonliquefiable clay cap (H_1), and the sand dike transmitting the liquefied sand to the surface, forming a sand boil or sand volcano. From Steve Obermeier, U.S. Geological Survey.

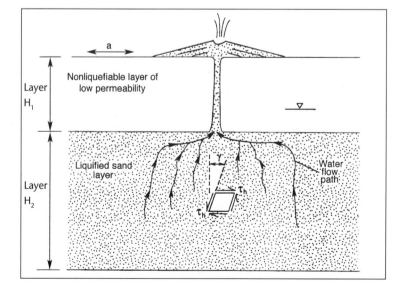

Figure 8-5. Liquefaction at Chehalis, Washington, during the 1949 Puget Sound Earthquake. Photo courtesy of Washington Division of Geology and Earth Resources.

Liquefaction can be triggered by earthquake accelerations as low as 0.1g. It has been observed with earthquakes with magnitudes as low as 5, and it becomes relatively common with magnitudes of 5.5 to 6. Liquefaction is more extensive with a longer duration of shaking, which is itself related to moment magnitude: very large earthquakes may have strong shaking lasting for more than a minute. A lateral spread can move down a slope as low as 0.2 percent, which would hardly appear as a slope at all.

During the Puget Sound Earthquakes of 1949 and 1965, 25 percent of the damage may have been caused by liquefaction (Figure 8-5). Drawbridges across the Duwamish Waterway in Seattle were disabled during both earthquakes. The distance between the piers in the main span of the Spokane Street Bridge was shortened by 6 to 8 inches due to a lateral spread, jamming the drawbridge in the closed position. Geysers of sandy water were reported in 1949 at Longview, Centralia, Puyallup, and Seattle, and sand blows were observed along roadways in Olympia during the 1965 earthquake. A large part of a sandy spit jutting into Puget Sound north of Olympia disappeared in 1949, probably due to liquefaction of the sand.

One of the arguments raised against a seismic origin of the buried marsh deposits on the Pacific coast is the absence of liquefaction features such as sand dikes. However, it should be pointed out that many, if not all, of these marshes are not underlain by clean sand. Pleistocene beach sand may underlie the Holocene

Figure 8-6. Tilted buildings at San Jose State University Marine Laboratory at Moss Landing, California, due to liquefaction of beach deposits during the October 1989 Loma Prieta Earthquake. Photo by G.W. Wilson, U.S. Geological Survey.

Figure 8-7. Destruction of part of Turnagain Heights subdivision of the City of Anchorage by liquefaction of a sand layer in the Bootlegger Clay accompanying the Good Friday 1964 Earthquake in the Gulf of Alaska. The ground and the houses were disrupted; note the tilted trees. Photo by George Plafker, U.S. Geological Survey.

marsh sequences, but if so, it is probably too consolidated and too deeply buried to undergo liquefaction.

On the other hand, liquefaction features are common on low islands in the tidal reaches of the Columbia River between Astoria, Oregon, and Kalama, Washington. These islands are flat, poorly drained, and swampy, and large parts of them are submerged during very high tides. Steve Obermeier of the U.S. Geological Survey examined steep banks sculpted by the river and found that the islands are composed mainly of soft clay-rich silt, locally containing volcanic ash layers from Mt. St. Helens. Radiocarbon dating and correlation of the ash to a dated Mt. St. Helens ash indicate that the silt is less than one thousand years old.

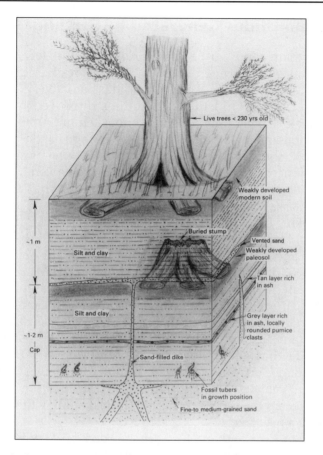

Figure 8-8. Block diagram showing field relations at liquefaction sites on islands in the lower Columbia River. Sand-filled dike cuts through silt and clay with a poorly developed soil at top. Dike connects to thin sand sheet on top of soil that may be remains of sand boil. Tubers have radiocarbon ages of six hundred to one thousand years. Silt and clay on top of sand sheet is younger than dike emplacement; oldest living trees are less than 230 years old. (1 m = just over 3 ft 3 in) From Steve Obermeier, U.S. Geological Survey.

The silt layers are cut by hundreds of sand dikes (Figure 8-8), widest on islands near Astoria, and progressively narrower on islands upriver. These sand dikes were emplaced prior to the oldest trees now found on the islands, which are less than 230 years old. For this reason, Obermeier suggests that the dikes were probably emplaced during the great Cascadia Subduction Zone Earthquake of A.D. 1700. The dikes are present in the islands of the Columbia River because a source of river sand may lie just below the silt layer.

Curt Peterson of Portland State University has found that the late Pleistocene marine terrace deposits of the coast between central Washington and northern California contain abundant dikes, some as thick as 3 feet, that provide evidence for strong earthquake shaking. The source for these dikes is the beach sand marking the base of the terrace. As stated earlier, nearly all examples of liquefaction during historical and late Holocene times involve sand sources that are Holocene in age, not Pleistocene. The sand dikes in the Pleistocene terrace deposits must have been generated by Pleistocene subduction-zone earthquakes, slightly younger than the terrace material in which they are found.

Landslides Generated by Earthquakes

Liquefaction tends to be most pronounced in low flat areas underlain by Holocene deposits. Lateral spreads, a product of liquefaction, generally occur in lowlands with a very low slope. However, most landslides, including those accompanying earthquakes, affect hilly or mountainous terrain. Although most of the thousands of landslides generated during a major earthquake are small, some are very large, as described previously for the landslide accompanying the 1970 earthquake in Peru.

On July 10, 1958, an earthquake of M 7.9 on the Fairweather Fault, Alaska, triggered a landslide on the side of a mountain overlooking Lituya Bay, in Glacier Bay National Park. A great mass of soil and rock swept down the mountainside into the bay, crossed the bay, and had enough momentum to ride up the opposite side to a height of 900 feet, denuding the forest cover as it did so. The slide created a huge water wave 100 feet high that swept seaward, carrying three fishing boats over the sand spit at the mouth of the bay into the ocean. An earthquake of M 7.6 on August 18, 1959, in Montana, just north of Yellowstone National Park, generated a landslide that swept down a mountainside and through a campground, burying a number of campers together with their tents and vehicles. The landslide crossed the Madison River and continued up the other side of the valley, damming the river and creating a new lake.

Earthquakes less than M 5.5 generate dozens of landslides, and earthquakes greater than M 8 generate thousands. The area affected by earthquake-generated landslides increases with increasing magnitude. Some of the commonest landslide types are rockfalls and rockslides. Although rockfalls can have a nonseismic origin, Bob Schuster of the U.S. Geological Survey found that large rockfalls damming lakes on the eastern Olympic Peninsula were most likely formed during a large earthquake. No rockfalls as large as these are known from this area in historic time, which included the 1949 and 1965 earthquakes as well as many severe winter storms.

Anyone who has hiked in the mountains has observed that many rocky talus slopes appear to be quite precarious, and seismic shaking can set these slopes in motion. John Muir, who experienced the 1872 Owens Valley Earthquake (M 7.6) in Yosemite Valley, described it best:

> At half-past two o'clock of a moonlit morning in March, I was awakened by a tremendous earthquake, and though I had never before enjoyed a storm of this sort, the strange thrilling motion could not be mistaken, and I ran out of my cabin, both glad and frightened, shouting, "A noble

earthquake! A noble earthquake!" feeling sure I was going to learn something. The shocks were so violent and varied, and succeeding one another so closely, that I had to balance myself carefully in walking as if on the deck of a ship among waves, and it seemed impossible that the high cliffs of the Valley could escape being shattered. In particular, I feared that the sheer-fronted Sentinel Rock, towering above my cabin, would be shaken down, and I took shelter back of a large yellow pine, hoping that it might protect me from at least the smaller outbounding boulders. For a minute or two the shocks became more and more violent—flashing horizontal thrusts mixed with a few twists and battering, explosive, upheaving jolts,—as if Nature were wrecking her Yosemite temple, and getting ready to build a still better one.

I was now convinced before a single boulder had fallen that earthquakes were the talus-makers and positive proof soon came. It was a calm moonlight night, and no sound was heard for the first minute or so, save low, muffled, underground, bubbling rumblings, and the whispering and rustling of the agitated trees, as if Nature were holding her breath. Then , suddenly, out of the strange silence and strange motion there came a tremendous roar. The Eagle Rock on the south wall, about a half a mile up the Valley, gave way and I saw it falling in thousands of the great boulders I had so long been studying, pouring to the Valley floor in a free curve luminous from friction, making a terribly sublime spectacle—an arc of glowing, passionate fire, fifteen hundred feet span, as true in form and as serene in beauty as a rainbow in the midst of the stupendous, roaring rock-storm. The sound was so tremendously deep and broad and earnest, the whole earth like a living creature seemed to have at last found a voice and to be calling to her sister planets. In trying to tell something of the size of this awful sound it seems to me that if all the thunder of all the storms I had ever heard were condensed into one roar it would not equal this rock-roar at the birth of a mountain talus.

The great landslides of Peru, Madison River, and Lituya Bay described above were rock avalanches, generally triggered by rockfalls at the time of the earthquake. Nearly all rockfalls are small, although locally damaging or deadly, and many have nonseismic origins. However, the great rock avalanches described above seem to be unique to earthquakes, or earthquakes combined with volcanism, as in the case of the huge avalanche that crashed

into Spirit Lake and blocked the Toutle River during the Mt. St. Helens eruption of May 18, 1980. The avalanche was triggered by an earthquake of M 5.2, but both the avalanche and the earthquake may have been an effect of the eruption, which blew out the north side of the mountain.

The Klamath Falls Earthquake of 1993 was accompanied by many landslides, principally rockfalls and rock slides. The largest number of rockfalls was on the southwest side of Upper Klamath Lake, where slopes are locally steeper than 45°. The upper part of the ridge adjoining the lake consists of basalt lava flows underlain by talus and slope material, including many large boulders. During the earthquake, several large boulders as large as 12 feet in diameter were dislodged and fell or rolled down the hillside. The largest rock slide observed during the earthquake was the one at Modoc Point that killed Ken Campbell (Figure 6-12).

The Puget Sound earthquakes of 1949 and 1965 triggered many landslides, including one that dislodged a railroad track near Tumwater, Washington (Figure 8-9).

Landslides on the sea floor are an increasingly recognized phenomenon, principally because of the availability of side-scan sonar and new methods to map the topography of the sea floor. The continental slope off southern Oregon is largely composed of huge landslides, including the one illustrated in Figure 8-10 off Florence, Oregon. Chris Goldfinger has mapped a landslide at the base of the continental slope off central Washington in which individual mountain-size blocks rode down onto the abyssal plain, leaving skid marks on the sea floor in their wake. These landslides are so large that it seems likely that they would have generated huge sea waves, or tsunamis, as similar landslides have been shown to do on Hawaii.

The Coast Range, Olympic Mountains, and the Cascades bear the scars of thousands of landslides that have been mapped by

Figure 8-10. Large landslide at the base of the continental slope west of Florence, Oregon. Slide is 5 miles across; debris has been transported across the deformation front onto the Juan de Fuca abyssal plain. The active Heceta South fault marks part of the northern side of the slide. Image created by Chris Goldfinger at Oregon State University from SeaBeam bathymetric maps of the National Oceanic and Atmospheric Agency and digitized land topographic maps from the U.S. Geological Survey.

geologists. It cannot be conclusively demonstrated that these landslides have an earthquake origin, but certainly many of them do. Some of the smaller ones are slides or flows of soil material, which tend to be tongue shaped or teardrop shaped and to travel down gullies and steep canyons. Many of these form during a wet winter and are unrelated to earthquakes. David Keefer and Randy Jibson of the U.S. Geological Survey summarize geotechnical evidence that suggests that some slides would not have been generated by wet weather during winter storms alone but would require seismic shaking to be triggered. Geotechnical tests, such as the Standard Penetration Test, can be done in any geotechnical evaluation of a building site on a hillside. Other geotechnical tests include measuring the shear strength of soils under both static (nonearthquake) and dynamic (earthquake) conditions.

Two large Pacific Northwest landslides may not have had an earthquake origin. The Hope, B. C., landslide of 1965 was associated with an earthquake, but some people believe that the earthquake may have accompanied initial rupture of the shear surface marking the base of the landslide, and was not the cause of the slide. A spectacular rock slide at Ribbon Cliffs, on the Columbia River north of Wenatchee, Washington, has been attributed to a large crustal earthquake in the North Cascades in 1872, but the location of the epicenter of this earthquake is controversial. These landslides demonstrate the difficulty of

Figure 8-11. Map of the Bonneville landslide (shaded) in the Columbia River Gorge at Cascade Locks. Arrows show direction of flow of landslide material. Bedrock formations shown in clear pattern. Volcanic rocks of the Cascade Range underlie the slide on the Washington side of the Columbia River; Columbia River Basalt is found on the Oregon side.

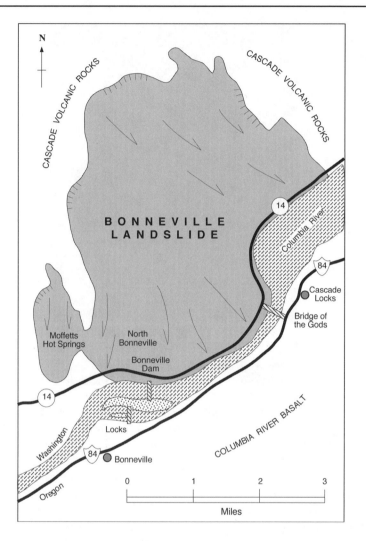

correlating large landslides in mountainous terrain to any earthquake, even when the earthquake occurred in historic time.

I close this section with a discussion of perhaps the most famous landslide in the Pacific Northwest, the Bonneville Landslide on the Columbia River (Figure 8-11). Volcanic rocks have been transported downslope on a thin sticky clay soil formed on top of one of the volcanic formations, forcing the Columbia River to its south bank and narrowing its width by half. The landslide has an area of at least 13 square miles. It may have given rise to a Native American legend concerning the origin of the Bridge of the Gods (right center margin, Figure 8-11). According to legend, the Bridge of the Gods was built by the Great Spirit to allow passage from one side of the river to the other. It was destroyed as a result of a great struggle between warriors now frozen in stone and ice as Mt. Klickitat (Mt. Adams) and Mt. Wyeast (Mt. Hood). A catastrophic landslide in prehistoric times could have dammed the Columbia and allowed people to walk from one side to the other until the river overtopped and cut out the dam. This landslide could have been generated by a great earthquake, as others of similar size in Peru and Alaska have been.

However, there is no evidence for an earthquake origin of the slide, and no evidence that the slide came down all at once. Some of the slides coming down to the river from the Washington side are still active today. The Bonneville Landslide and the Bridge of the Gods remain a geologic enigma.

As stated in a previous section, landslides are not strictly an earthquake-related phenomenon; they are a common side effect of winter storms as well. In evaluating a site for its landslide potential, Scott Burns of Portland State University uses a three-strike rule. Strike 1 is unstable soil, and strike 2 is a steep slope. Strike 3 may be either an earthquake or a heavy winter rainstorm that saturates the ground. By careful selection of building sites, Strikes 1 and 2 can be avoided, so that neither rainfall nor earthquake will cause a landslide.

Much of the loss of life related to an earthquake is caused by landslides. In some cases, the slide mass moves slowly enough that people can get out of its way, but in rockfalls and rock avalanches, such as the large slides in Alaska, Peru, and Montana discussed in a previous section, the motion of the rock and soil mass is so quick that people are overwhelmed before they have an opportunity to get out of the way.

Earthquake Hazard Maps of Metropolitan Areas

Historically, state agencies dealing with geology have focused on resources, figuring that a better understanding of mineral and fossil fuel potential will add to the economy of the state. Until recently, this has been true for the Oregon Department of Geology and Mineral Industries; it has published maps and reports of the state's geology as a guide toward discovering new minerals and fuels and to regulate the extraction of these deposits. This is why "mineral industries" is part of the name of the agency.

In recent years, the department has received a new mission: a better understanding of the natural hazards facing the state. As part of this mission, it has prepared maps of the Portland and Salem metropolitan areas at a scale of one inch equals 2,000 feet that classify the area into earthquake hazard zones. The information discussed earlier in this chapter has been used to make the maps: the bedrock geology, the thickness, density, and seismic shear-wave (S-wave) velocity of near surface sediment, the steepness of slope in hillside areas, and the degree of susceptibility of those slopes to landsliding. The hazards measured are the amount of seismic wave amplification, the potential for liquefaction, and the tendency of hillslopes to fail in landslides.

The maps divide the area underlain by Quaternary sediment into three (for Portland) to five (for Salem) hazard categories of ground-shaking amplification based on sediment thickness and S-wave velocity. Areas underlain by bedrock do not amplify seismic waves. Similarly, there are three to five categories of liquefaction potential of surficial sediment, with no liquefaction potential for areas underlain by bedrock. Classification of slope stability is based on steepness of slope ranging from no hazard where the land is flat to a high hazard where the slope exceeds 22°, with a special category for hillsides already marked by landslides.

Maps of individual hazards (seismic shaking, liquefaction, and slope stability against landsliding) are combined, using a computer model, to subdivide each area into four earthquake hazard zones, with A marking the highest hazard zone and D the lowest. The A ranking generally means that the area has ranked high in at least two of the three hazards described (seismic shaking, liquefaction, slope stability). An area could rank very high in one category and low in all others and receive a B ranking. The map can be used to state that a broad area such as Portland International Airport has a particular level of hazard (Zone B). The Oregon State Capitol and Willamette University are ranked Zone C. The maps are detailed enough that you could get an idea of the earthquake hazard category for your own home, if you live in one of the areas covered by the maps.

The maps are designed for general planning purposes for designing earthquake hazard mitigation programs for Oregon's major cities. Damage estimates for lifeline services and disaster-response planning could effectively be based on these maps. However, they are not a substitute for site-specific evaluations of a building site based on borings and trenches, although they could be used for feasibility studies and for design.

Although there is no province-wide program for earthquake hazard maps in British Columbia, a demonstration project for the city of Victoria has been completed, in part funded by the city itself. The maps are similar to those described for Portland and Salem. Similar maps are being constructed by the California Division of Mines and Geology for urban areas in southern California. In Washington, the Division of Geology and Earth Resources is preparing maps showing liquefaction potential in lowland areas of the Puget Sound region because of the extensive liquefaction accompanying the earthquakes in 1949 and 1965.

Suggestions for Further Reading

Burns, S. 1998. Landslide hazards in Oregon, in Burns, S., ed., *Groundwater and Engineering Geology Applications from Oregon.* Belmont, CA: Star Publishing Co., Association of Engineering Geologists Special Pub. 11, pp. 303-15.

Burns, S. 1998. Landslides in the Portland area resulting from the storm of February, 1996, in Burns, S., ed., Environmental, Groundwater and Engineering Geology Applications from Oregon. Belmont, CA: Star Publishing Co., Association of Engineering Geologists Special Pub. 11, pp. 353-65.

Burns, S., and L. Palmer. 1996. Homeowner's landslide guide. Oregon Emergency Management, Federal Emergency Management Agency Region 10, and Oregon Department of Geology and Mineral Industries, 10p. (free).

Dragovich, J.D., and P.T. Pringle. 1995. Liquefaction susceptibility map of the Sumner 7.5-minute quadrangle, Washington, with a section on liquefaction analysis by Palmer, S.P. Washington Division of Geology and Earth Resources Geologic Map GM-44, 1 sheet, 1:24,000, text 26p.

Gerstel, W.J., M.J. Brunengo, W.S. Lingley, Jr., R.L. Logan, H. Shipman, and T.J. Walsh. 1997. Puget Sound bluffs: The where, why, and when of landslides following the holiday 1996/97 storms. *Washington Geology*, vol. 25, no. 1, pp. 17-31.

Jibson, R.W. 1996. Using landslides for paleoseismic analysis, in McCalpin, J.P., ed., *Paleoseismology*. San Diego, CA: Academic Press, pp. 397-438.

Keefer, D.K. 1984. Landslides caused by earthquakes. *Geological Society of America Bulletin,* vol. 95, pp. 406-71.

Keller, E.A. 1988. *Environmental Geology*, Fifth Edition. Columbus, OH: Merrill Publishing Co., 540p.

Kramer, S.L. 1996. *Geotechnical Earthquake Engineering.* Englewood Cliffs, N.J.: Prentice-Hall.

Monahan, P.A., V.M. Levson, E.J. McQuarrie, S.M. Bean, P. Henderson, and A. Sy. In press, Earthquake hazard map of Greater Victoria showing areas susceptible to amplification of ground motion, liquefaction and earthquake-induced slope instability. British Columbia Geological Survey, Open-File Report.

Muir, J. 1912. *The Yosemite*. The Century Company, republished by Doubleday and Co., Inc., New York.

Obermeier, S.F. 1996. Using liquefaction-induced features for paleoseismic analysis, in McCalpin, J.P., ed., *Paleoseismology*. San Diego, CA: Academic Press, pp. 331-96.

Oregon Department of Geology and Mineral Industries. Landslides in Oregon. Free circular.

Oregon Department of Geology and Mineral Industries. 1991-1996. Earthquake hazards maps of Portland and Salem metropolitan areas: GMS 79, 89-92, 104-105.

Oregon Department of Geology and Mineral Industries. 1997. Relative earthquake hazard map of the Portland Metro Region, Clackamas, Multnomah, and Washington Counties, Oregon: Interpretive Map Series IMS-1.

Palmer, S.P., H.W. Schasse, and D.K. Norman. 1994. Liquefaction susceptibility for the Des Moines and Renton 7.5-minute quadrangles, Washington. Washington Division of Geology and Earth Resources Geologic Map GM-41, 2 sheets, scale 1:24,000, text 15p.

Palmer, S.P., T.J. Walsh, R.L. Logan, and W.J. Gerstel. Liquefaction susceptibility for the Auburn and Poverty Bay 7.5-minute quadrangles, Washington. Washington Division of Geology and Earth Resources Geologic Map GM-43, 2 sheets, scale 1:24,000, text 15p.

Tsunami!

"Shortly after the shock, a great wave was seen from the distance of three or four miles, approaching in the middle of the bay with a smooth outline; but along the shore it tore up cottages and trees, as it swept onwards with irresistible force. At the head of the bay it broke in a fearful line of white breakers, which rushed up to a height of 23 vertical feet above the highest spring tides. Their force must have been prodigious; for at the Fort a cannon with its carriage, estimated at four tons in weight, was moved 15 feet inwards. A schooner was left in the midst of the ruins, 200 yards from the beach. The first wave was followed by two others, which in their retreat carried off a vast wreck of floating objects. In one part of the bay, a ship was pitched high and dry on shore, was carried off, again driven on shore, and again carried off."

Charles Darwin, *Voyage of the Beagle,* describing a tsunami in southern Chile on February 20, 1835.

The Easter Weekend Tsunami of 1964

The warning about a cataclysmic earthquake on the Cascadia Subduction Zone some time in the indefinable future has a mythical cast to it, as if in actual fact the Earth could not shudder and gyrate in the way scientists have stated that it would. But this doomsday scenario is based on an actual earthquake that wracked southern Alaska without warning on Good Friday, March 27, 1964. Alaska is not a heavily populated state, of course, and it had even fewer people in 1964, so the human toll was less than, say, the Kobe Earthquake in Japan, which was more than a hundred times smaller. But the area of destruction was enormous, stretching for great distances, devastating the city of Anchorage and small towns hundreds of miles away.

The instantaneous effects on the landscape were of a scale seen only once before in this century, in southern Chile in May 1960. Parts of Montague Island in the Gulf of Alaska rose more than 30 feet into the air. A region 500 miles long and almost 100 miles

Figure 9-1. Permanent flooding of the village of Portage, Alaska, at the head of Turnagain Arm of Cook Inlet, as a result of 6 feet of tectonic subsidence during the 1964 Good Friday Earthquake. After the earthquake, the shoreline was as much as 2 miles inland from the pre-earthquake shore line. Photo courtesy of U.S. Geological Survey.

across, extending from Kodiak Island to the Kenai Peninsula and Anchorage and the mountains beyond (Figure 4-12), sank as much as 8 feet, so that sea water drowned coastal marshes and forests permanently, just as the last great Cascadia Earthquake had drowned the Pacific Northwest coastline three hundred years ago (Figure 9-1).

The sudden change in elevation of the land had its equivalent on the sea floor, causing perhaps 50,000 square miles of ocean floor to be abruptly heaved up or dropped down. This produced an effect entirely separate from the earthquake waves that radiated outward through the crust to lay waste the communities of southern Alaska. The depression and elevation of the sea floor generated an unseen wave in the sea itself that rushed out in all directions. Fifteen minutes after the first earthquake waves had permanently dropped the coastline, a monstrous ocean wave 20 to 30 feet high raced up Resurrection Bay toward the burning ravaged city of Seward, carrying ahead of it flaming wreckage, including a diesel locomotive that rode the wave like a surfboard. Residents living near the Seward Airport climbed onto their roofs as the first wave smashed through the trees into the houses, carrying some of them away. Then came a second wave, as strong as the first. Similar scenes were played out in the coastal communities of Cordova and Valdez. At Valdez, the wave was reported to be more than 200 feet high!

These were the waves that headed to the nearby Alaskan shore. But other waves rolled silently southward into the Pacific Ocean at hundreds of miles per hour (Figure 9-2). A ship on the high seas might encounter these long-period waves, and its crew would not be aware of them; there would just be an imperceptible lifting of

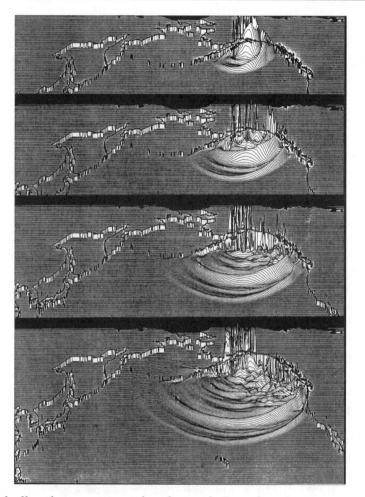

Figure 9-2. Computer simulation of tsunami following Good Friday 1964 Earthquake in the Gulf of Alaska. Top image shows waves one hour after the earthquake; successive images show waves at two, three, and four hours after the earthquake. Japan at left; west coast of United States on right; Hawaii at bottom center of lower image. Tsunami has reached Vancouver Island in third image and is about to strike Crescent City, California, in bottom image. Note that waves approaching Japan are much smaller than those approaching the United States; also note how waves turn toward the coast as they slow down. From Kenji Satake, Geological Survey of Japan.

the hull as the waves passed underneath. But when a wave entered the shallows, the water moved by the energy of the wave gripped the sea bottom, causing the wave to slow down and gain in height until it towered above the shoreline in its path. The movement of the sea floor that had triggered the tsunami had a directivity to it, preferentially southeast rather than south toward Hawaii or southwest toward Japan. The Alaska Tsunami was like a torpedo fired directly at the coast of Vancouver Island, Washington, Oregon, and California.

An hour and twenty-six minutes later, the tsunami warning service in Honolulu, Hawaii, issued a tsunami advisory, indicating that a sea wave could have been generated by the earthquake. None had yet been confirmed, despite the damage to towns along the Alaska coastline, mainly as a result of the loss of communications between Alaska and Hawaii. The main concern in Honolulu was for a tsunami in Hawaii, similar to previous destructive tsunamis in 1946, 1952, and 1957. The warning service issued an expected arrival time of the tsunami in Hawaii.

Fifty-three minutes after the tsunami advisory was issued, a report from Kodiak Island, Alaska, told of seismic sea waves 10 to 12 feet above normal. Thirty-five minutes later, a second report was received from Kodiak, and based on those two reports, a tsunami warning was issued by Honolulu. At almost the same moment, nearly three hours after the earthquake, the tsunami made landfall on Vancouver Island.

First to be struck was Hot Springs Cove, an Indian village near the northern tip of the island, where eighteen houses were damaged. Then the wave passed down the west coast of the island, deeply indented with fjords carved out by glaciers during the Pleistocene. The fjords concentrated the force of the tsunami like air scoops, with the effect that towns at the landward end felt the worst effects of the waves. The tsunami swung left past Cape Scott into Quatsino Sound and bore down on Port Alice, ripping away boat ramps and seaplane moorings, flooding buildings, floating twelve houses off their foundations, and tumbling thousands of feet of logs along the waterfront like jackstraws.

Farther south, the wave turned inland past Ucluelet into Barclay Sound, past Bamfield Lighthouse and a group of fifty startled teenagers on Pachena Beach. The lighthouse raised the alarm, which gave ten minutes notice to the twenty-five thousand residents of Port Alberni, at the head of the fjord nearly two-thirds of the way across Vancouver Island. Larry Reynolds, 18, raced from his house on high ground to watch after the first wave had hit. As the second wave surged into the street, Reynolds could hear people screaming and could see men running in front of the wave as it crashed into the town. He watched as two large two-story houses were lifted from their foundations; they floated serenely out into the Somass River, where they broke up and sank. Six tourist cabins in a row along the river bank bowed gracefully as they rose up simultaneously, but then they came down separately as the wave passed. The Japanese freighter *Meishusan Maru* broke away from its moorings and rode the wave like a giant surfboard, landing on the mudflats. The captain and crew, perhaps wise in the ways of tsunamis, simply waited for the next wave, which refloated the ship, and they were able to regain the harbor.

Southward the wave rolled, past the southern end of Vancouver Island, and it was recorded by the tide gauge at Neah Bay. Logs were scattered in Quilcene Bay near Hood Canal in Puget Sound. But the main tsunami continued on past Cape Flattery and the wild uninhabited coastline of Olympic National Park. Incredibly, there still had been no loss of life on Vancouver Island or the Washington side of the Straits of Juan de Fuca.

By this time, warnings of the oncoming tsunami were being broadcast throughout the Pacific Northwest. Hearing the warning was Mrs. C.M. Shaw, whose daughter and son-in-law, Mr. and Mrs. Henry Kane, were spending the weekend at Kalaloch Resort in Olympic National Park with their daughter, Patty, another couple, Mr. and Mrs. Charles W. Elicker, and the Elickers' son Drew. Mrs. Shaw phoned the resort, and an employee found Charles Elicker. Horror-struck, Elicker raced for the beach, where the two children, both 11, had been given permission to camp for the night. Elicker routed them from their sleeping bags, and Drew raced for a 40-foot embankment of clay with a sparse cover of salmonberry. But Patty wanted to collect her pup tent and sleeping bag. Elicker realized that there was no time. In the moonlight, he could see the great wave coming, a churning wall of water jumbled with logs and driftwood. He grabbed Patty's hand, and they raced toward the embankment and safety.

But Elicker was losing the race with the tsunami; there was not enough time. Gripping Patty's hand, he scrambled up the embankment, grasping at brush, and finally managing to cling to a spindly tree as the wave drenched them up to hip level. As the wave retreated, Elicker decided to climb higher, where another wave hit them at leg level. But they were safe. The next day, they found Patty's pup tent and sleeping bag a half mile down the beach.

On came the wave down the coast, refracting to the east and heading for shore at a low oblique angle. It struck the Quinault Indian Reservation, routing four Tacoma men from their tent on the beach at Taholah, south of Pt. Grenville. On to the tiny community of Copalis Beach, where the firehouse siren in the shopping area began to wail its alarm. Leonard Hurlbert dashed out of the Surf and Sand Restaurant, where his wife worked in the kitchen, to race home and check on their sleeping children. He was driving close to 50 miles an hour when he reached the bridge across the Copalis River. A few seconds earlier and he would have made it. But he reached the bridge at the same time as a wall of water from the sea. The bridge began to buck and heave, and over it went, casting Hurlbert, still in his car, into the river (Figure 9-3). Trapped underwater, he forced open the door on the driver's side against the pressure of the water. But as he was escaping, he found his leg pinned between the top of the door and the roof of the car. With the desperate force of a man who knew he must be drowning, Hurlbert somehow freed his leg and hurled himself toward air, severely damaging the ligaments in his left arm as he did so.

A half mile north of Copalis Beach, Mr. and Mrs. David Mansfield and their children Robert, 20, Linda, 14, and David, 7, were camped on the beach in their trailer. They had been up until eleven o'clock, walking on the beach in the moonlight. Shortly after they turned out the light, their trailer began to rock, and as

they looked outside their window, they saw their car floating away. The trailer began to roll, with the Mansfields still inside, and they suddenly found themselves tumbling outside the trailer, under water. They swam toward land, but as they tried to reach a place where they could stand, they were battered by a huge log, 3 feet across, that threatened to crush them. Linda was drifting away, but Robert grabbed her by the arm, and finally, miraculously, they all reached firm ground. The force of the waves had torn off most of their clothes; all Mrs. Mansfield had on was a T-shirt when they wandered into a tavern looking for help.

And still the giant waves rolled relentlessly south, past four Renton boys driven from their tent at Long Beach, past Cape Disappointment to the Oregon coast, where the tsunami turned deadly. At Seaside, the waves pushed the Necanicum River back up its bed, overflowing and drowning out a trailer park. Mary Eva Deis, 50, died of a heart attack when the waves struck her house. Farther south at Cannon Beach, a wharf was swept away, carrying several small boats out to sea, and several houses were ripped from their foundations.

At Beverly Beach, north of Newport, a Boeing engineer from Seattle, Monte McKenzie, his wife Rita, and their four children, Louis, 8, Bobby, 7, Ricky, 6, and Tammy, 3, had come to spend the Easter weekend camping. On Friday, they were following a trail along the coast when they found a driftwood shelter. What an experience to camp directly on the beach on such a beautiful spring weekend! They got permission from the caretaker of Beverly Beach State Park to camp there and settled in for the night, when a small wave caught them in the shelter. They had time to grab the kids, and they were running for the beach cliff when the first of the great waves struck. Rita was a senior Red Cross lifesaver, and she had taught all her children to swim. She gripped two of them by the hands, but great, shifting logs knocked her unconscious. Monte was thrown against the cliff, where he climbed up and vainly tried to flag down cars on Highway 101. He ran to the caretaker's house, and police were called, but it was too late. Rita was found on the beach 400 yards away from their campsite, battered but alive. But the kids were gone. They found Ricky's body, but the other three were never recovered.

The tsunami swept down the Oregon coast, tearing out docks at Gold Beach and smashing small boats at the mouth of the Rogue River, and on into California, trapping Stuart Harrington and Donald McClure, two Air Force sergeants eel fishing at the mouth of the Klamath River. A wall of water, choked with driftwood, picked them up and carried them a half-mile up the river. They scrambled through the driftwood to the surface, and McClure helped Harrington climb up on a larger log that appeared to offer protection. They heard a response to their cries for help. Then the water and floating logs began to rush back toward the sea, and both men slipped into the water to swim for shore. McClure had helped Harrington remove his jacket and shirt to make it easier for him to swim. Harrington swam through the maelstrom to the shore, below the boat docks, where he found to his horror that McClure, who had saved his life, had not made it.

The tsunami swept inexorably south. The small logging town of Crescent City, California, lay in its path.

The California Disaster Office issued an emergency bulletin at 11:08 p.m. to emergency response officials and the California Highway Patrol in all coastal counties that a tsunami was possible. This bulletin was received at the Del Norte County Sheriff's headquarters, and by 11:20, the civil defense director and the sheriff had arrived at headquarters. At 11:50, the California Civil Defense Office estimated the arrival time of the tsunami at midnight. By the time a second bulletin had arrived at 11:50, sheriff's deputies had been sent to low-lying areas to warn people of a possible sea wave. However, they did not order an evacuation.

The first wave arrived on schedule at 11:59 p.m. on March 27, after the warning had been repeated by both radio stations. But the first wave was fairly small, reaching across the beach only to Front Street and doing little damage other than depositing some debris. Civil Defense authorities had received a report from Neah Bay, Washington, that the tsunami had done no damage there. People began to relax. The next wave at 12:40 a.m. on March 28 was larger, but still not too bad. The sea waves were behaving like previous tsunamis to hit Crescent City. The worst appeared to be over, and some people headed for their homes or to the waterfront to survey the damage to their businesses and begin to clean up. The sheriff's office still had not issued a general alarm.

Then, at 1:20 a.m. came the first giant wave, a wall of water 15 feet high that breached a jetty, smashed into the fishing fleet at Citizens Dock at Elk Creek, and roared across Highway 101 south of town. Jack McKellar and Ray Thompson had gone down to the harbor earlier to check on Thompson's boat, the *Ea*. As they loosened the moorings, the wave spun the *Ea* around like a top, and it shot out of the harbor into the open sea. They were carried so far from shore that they were spared the worst effects of the tsunami.

The wave caved in the west wall of the Long Branch Tavern at Elk Creek, terrifying the patrons when the lights went out. People jumped up on the bar and juke box, with scarcely any headroom for breathing. Everyone climbed up onto the roof, and Gary Clawson and Mack McGuire swam out to get a boat. When they returned, seven people, including Clawson and his parents, got into a rowboat. The water was smooth, and they headed across Elk Creek toward Front Street. They were only a few boat lengths away from the stream bank when the water began to pull the boat sideways toward the Elk Creek bridge. Bruce Garden lunged forward and grabbed the bridge, which kept him from going under. The other six were slammed against a steel grating on the other side of the bridge, choked with debris. Clawson, a strong swimmer, came up for air, and as the water receded, he tried to revive the others. But the other five passengers drowned in the darkness.

The next great wave at 1:45 a.m., largest of all, crested at nearly 21 feet. Peggy Sullivan, six months pregnant, saw the waves from the front door of her room at Van's Motel. She told her son Gary, 9, to dress, and threw a quilt around her 23-month-old daughter Yevonne. As they stepped outside with Yevonne's bottle, she saw a wall of water coming toward them, carrying houses like matchboxes. Gary was carried off in one direction, and Sullivan and the baby in the other; Sullivan's shoes and the baby's quilt were torn away at the same time. She was swept down the driveway and became jammed against a sports car, driftwood piled at her back, but still held onto Yevonne and her bottle. Gary had been swept into the back of a garage, where he was rescued by a stranger. Severely injured, Sullivan was taken to the hospital. Although she and her two children survived, she lost her unborn child.

The first of the huge waves swept into downtown Crescent City, tearing out a 25-ton tetrapod used in the construction of the seawall. Stores along Front Street crumbled. At first, boats were washed four blocks inland, then they and the wreckage of buildings were carried out to sea by the suction as the water retreated (Figures 9-4 and 9-5). The Texaco oil tank farm burst into flames, and the tanks exploded, causing fires that burned out of control for more than ten hours.

Figure 9-4. Aerial view of Crescent City, California, after the tsunami accompanying the 1964 Good Friday Earthquake in southern Alaska. Harbor is toward the viewer. Photo courtesy of Lori Dengler, Humboldt State University.

Wally Griffin described the scene from the sheriff's office when the lights went out: "There was a continuous crashing and crunching sound as the buildings gave way and splintered into rubble, and there were flashes from high powered electrical lines shorting out that resembled an electrical storm approaching from the east, except some of the flashes were blue. Added to the display were two explosions that could have been mistaken for thunder without the normal rolling sound."

A big log crashed through the walls of the post office, and, as reported by Griffin, "when the water receded, it sucked the letters out like a vacuum cleaner," and they were later found festooning the parking lot and nearby hedges. Adolph Arrigoni, 70, drowned in his house on B Street, and James Park, 60, drowned when the wave floated his trailer off its foundation.

Peggy Coons, curator of the Crescent City Lighthouse, had gotten up before midnight to go to the bathroom when she noticed in the moonlight that all the rocks around the island on which the lighthouse stood had disappeared. She and her husband dressed and went outside, where they saw a huge, debris-choked wave, high above the outer breakwater, bearing down on the town. Then the water roared back past them at high speed, leaving the beach strewn with debris. The second wave passed them, and they saw lights blinking out along the shoreline. Again the water drained back past them to the sea.

The third wave started fires in the town, and sparks flew. When the water drained out this time, three-quarters of a mile from the

Figure 9-5. Damage from the 1964 tsunami in Crescent City, California. Photo courtesy of Washington Division of Geology and Earth Resources.

normal shoreline, it revealed the sea bottom, a "mystic labyrinth of caves, canyons, basins and pits, undreamed of in even the wildest fantasy" (Peggy Coons in Griffin 1984).

In the distance Coons could see a massive black wall of water, with boiling and seething whitecaps glistening in the moonlight. A Coast Guard cutter and several smaller boats 2 miles offshore appeared to be riding high above the wall. The water struck with great force and split around the island, picking up driftwood logs as it struck the mainland. They saw bundles of lumber at Dutton's Lumber Yard fly into the air as others sailed gracefully away. There was a great roar, and buildings, cars, boats, and lumber were moving and shifting. Then the return wave came past them, carrying mattresses, beds, furniture, television sets, and clothing. Coons saw more waves, but they were smaller. The damage had been done.

The waves destroyed twenty-nine blocks and left one hundred fifty businesses a total loss. Eleven people had died. Governor Edmund G. Brown asked the president to declare Crescent City a disaster area.

And still the tsunami sped south. The wave was still 3 feet high near the Golden Gate Bridge. At Sausalito, the mooring cables of the 66-year-old ferryboat *Berkeley* snapped, causing the ferry to list and damage the pier. Altogether, the damage to boats in San Francisco Bay amounted to nearly a million dollars. Ten-foot waves struck Catalina Island off the southern California coast. An alarm was raised on the west coast of Mexico, but the tsunami, finally, was spent. Tide gauges recorded the tsunami all around the Pacific Ocean; it was recorded in Peru nearly 10 hours after the fourth wave struck Crescent City and nearly 16 hours after the earthquake.

What was learned? First, the loss of life was entirely preventable, because there was plenty of time to evacuate low-lying coastal areas even as far north as Vancouver Island. The first two waves at Crescent City were no larger than previous tsunamis, convincing local authorities that the worst was over, and no evacuation order was necessary. For warnings to be heeded, people would have had to have their radios or television sets on; a siren would have been more effective, combined with emergency-service personnel noisily alerting people to the danger.

A quarter-century would pass before Kenji Satake would develop computer models showing the directivity effects of tsunamis, the pointed gun of the Alaska Earthquake aimed directly at the Pacific Northwest coast. And there were many low-lying coastal areas that were *not* hard hit, indicating that the wave was strongly controlled by the bottom topography of the sea floor that channeled and accentuated the tsunami as it headed for shore.

Some Facts About Tsunamis

First, a tsunami is *not* a tidal wave. Tides are affected by the attraction between the Moon and Earth, and tsunamis are completely unrelated. If a tsunami arrived at the same time as a high tide, as it did at Crescent City, its effects might be worse than if it arrived at low tide, because the wave could travel farther onto the land. Another term is *seismic sea wave*. This is correct for most tsunamis, but not all, for tsunamis can also be generated by submarine volcanic eruptions or submarine landslides. The cataclysmic eruption in 1883 of Krakatau, a volcanic island in Indonesia, was followed by a sudden collapse of the central volcano and an inrush of water, generating a tsunami that, together with the eruption, killed more than thirty-six thousand people. We use the Japanese word *tsunami*, which means harbor wave, in light of the fact that a tsunami increases in height as it enters a harbor, as it did at Port Alberni and Crescent City.

During the Alaska Earthquake of 1964, a section of sea floor more than 400 miles long and 100 miles across suddenly uplifted, forcing the overlying water upward and outward as if the sea floor were a giant paddle (Figures 4-12, 9-6). Although this happened almost instantaneously, it was not the *speed* of the uplift but the sheer *volume* of the water displaced that produced the powerful tsunami. A tsunami generated by a sudden change in the sea floor has a very long wave length, and the wave front extends from the sea surface to the sea floor, miles below. The wave travels at great speed, as much as 500 miles an hour, depending on the depth of water.

Figure 9-6. (a) Formation of a tsunami by sudden offset on the sea floor. Wave has a low amplitude as it travels in the deep sea. (b) Wave amplitude grows as tsunami enters shallow water and approaches the land. From R.J. Lillie.

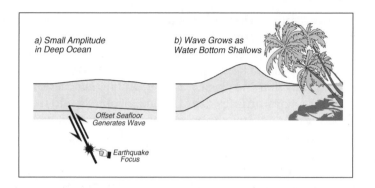

The wave travels fastest through the deep ocean and slows down as it approaches the land, as can be observed in the computer simulation in Figure 9-2. The waves traveling down the coast are slower than those in the open sea, so that the wave front makes a sweeping turn to the left and attacks the coast almost head on.

Tsunamis are also unusual in having very long wave periods. (Figure 3-12 illustrates wave amplitude and wavelength; the period is the length of time it takes a full wavelength to pass a point.) An ordinary ocean wave breaking on the beach has a period of 5 to 15 seconds, but a tsunami has wave periods ranging from 7 minutes to nearly an hour, depending on the origin of the tsunami. It was the long period of 25 to 40 minutes that caused so much loss of life at Crescent City and elsewhere. The wave rushes onshore and causes a lot of damage, then recedes. Observers assume that the tsunami differs from an ordinary ocean wave only in size: if the next wave does not arrive in the next few minutes, they assume that the danger is past. They return to the shore, out of curiosity or out of a desire to help in rescue operations or in cleaning up the damage. Then, perhaps as much as an hour later, another giant wave strikes. The loss of life from the follow-up wave, which may be bigger than the first one, is commonly larger than that from the initial wave.

A tsunami has essentially no expression on the ocean surface. (Here Figure 9-2 is misleading, because it gives the impression that great wave heights are found in the deep ocean as well as along coastlines.) The height of a tsunami on the open ocean is typically only a few feet, less than the normal surface waves observed on the ocean. Ships at sea cannot give warning, because people on board a ship are unable to detect the passage of the tsunami. During a deadly tsunami that struck Hilo, Hawaii, in 1946, the crew of a freighter anchored less than a mile offshore was surprised to see huge waves breaking over buildings and trees onshore, because they were not strongly affected by the wave as it passed their ship.

As a tsunami enters shallow water, it slows down and its tremendous energy is focused on a wave front of decreasing area.

This causes it to convert to a gigantic surface wave (Figure 9-7). The way in which this happens is of critical importance in tsunami hazard analysis. It depends on the direction and energy of the approaching tsunami, of course, but it is very much influenced by the configuration of the sea floor. Hilo Harbor is particularly susceptible to tsunamis because the bottom of the harbor is funnel shaped, concentrating the energy of the wave into a smaller area. In a similar fashion, the Vancouver Island fjords funneled the wave energy of the 1964 tsunami as a great bore, smashing against the communities at the heads of the fjords. Crescent City has a similar problem. Because the tsunami is controlled by water depth, even in deep water, the configuration of offshore banks and submarine canyons has an influence on the size of a tsunami.

Much of the seafloor topography off the coast of Washington has been mapped in great detail, but the information is classified secret by the U.S. Navy, unavailable to the general public. For this reason, Washington coastal communities are less able to evaluate fully their danger from tsunamis than communities on the Oregon coast, where seafloor topography has been made public. However, less detailed topographic maps of the entire Pacific Northwest offshore region are available from the U.S. National Oceanic and Atmospheric Administration (NOAA).

In the 1964 earthquake, the sea floor was suddenly pushed upward and outward to the southeast, so that the first evidence of the tsunami on the Pacific Northwest shoreline was the huge wave that crashed on the beach and entered the harbors. But at Seward, Alaska, on the north side of the uplift, the great force of the earthquake propagated *away* from the town. People at Seward could see a huge wave approaching them, but as they looked at the small-boat harbor, they saw that it had been magically drained of water. This was part of the tsunami, too, but the sea had rushed away from land rather than toward it, immediately followed by the first wave to drive into the port and town.

Seward, and Cook Inlet behind it to the northwest, abruptly subsided during the earthquake, just as the coastal marshes of the Pacific Northwest had subsided during the great Cascadia Earthquake of A.D. 1700, and previous earthquakes as well. If the next Cascadia earthquake behaves like the illustration in Figure 4-12, then the first evidence of the accompanying tsunami might be a sudden outrushing of water, followed by a great wave. Coastal areas would see exposed parts of the sea floor that people living there had never before seen exposed, even at the lowest tides. There would be a great temptation to go to the beach to see this phenomenon, which could be fatal, because there would not be enough time to get back to high ground before the first wave struck.

Figure 9-7. Tsunami in 1946 striking the beachfront area at the Puumaile Tuberculosis Hospital east of Hilo on the Island of Hawaii, 3,800 km from the earthquake source in the Aleutian Islands to the north. (1 km = 0.62 mile.) Waves here were over 20 feet high, topping the breakwater and causing flooding at the hospital. Photo by Mrs. Harry A. Simms, Sr., courtesy of the National Oceanic and Atmospheric Administration.

Tsunami Warning Systems

The tsunami at Crescent City struck more than four hours after the earthquake. Loss of communication with Alaska delayed the issuance of a tsunami advisory for nearly an hour and a half after the earthquake, and the advisory was not upgraded to a warning until two hours and twenty minutes after the earthquake, about the time the first wave was striking the north end of Vancouver Island.

The warning system in place at that time, the Pacific Tsunami Warning System, was established in Honolulu, Hawaii, after a disastrous tsunami in Hawaii in 1946 triggered by an earthquake on the Aleutian Subduction Zone of Alaska. Problems with the warning system in 1964 led to the establishment of a second warning center, the West Coast/Alaska Tsunami Warning Center in Palmer, Alaska. Both are operated by NOAA. The Alaska center is responsible for tsunami warnings to Alaska, British Columbia, Washington, Oregon, and California.

In 1968, these tsunami warning services were integrated with those of other Pacific nations into the International Coordination Group for the Tsunami Warning System in the Pacific, which has established the International Tsunami Information Center.

Seismographs and tide gauges around the Pacific Rim report immediately to Honolulu and Palmer, and tsunami arrival times are estimated for shorelines around the Pacific. A pressure gauge has been designed to be emplaced on the deep ocean floor, permitting tracking of tsunamis in the deep sea, which has never been possible before. NOAA, aided by funds from the Department of Defense, has set up two of these deep-sea tsunami detectors, one off the Aleutian Islands, and one off Oregon.

When a subduction-zone earthquake strikes anywhere around the Pacific Ocean, a *tsunami watch* is established. As soon as the epicenter of the earthquake is located, commonly within a few minutes, the travel time of a potential tsunami is determined, and stations near the epicenter are alerted. As soon as the existence of tsunami waves is confirmed, then a *tsunami warning* is issued around the entire Pacific. For the Pacific Northwest, the tsunami warning would come from Palmer, Alaska. As the tsunami advances, its progress is monitored, and the warning is updated with new projected arrival times of waves and possible wave heights. This gives time for local authorities to order evacuation of low-lying areas.

Modeling of tsunamis gives more confidence to the warnings, because models can take into account the strong directivity of tsunamis. Thus it is important to learn not only the location of the epicenter and the magnitude of an earthquake, but also the direction of motion of the ocean floor, which can be determined by studying the wave forms of seismograms of the mainshock recorded at many seismograph stations. Armed with such information, the warning of the 1964 Alaska Tsunami could have been more strongly directed to the Pacific Northwest and less toward Japan, which recorded the tsunami, but did not suffer damage.

A tsunami wave has been compared to the waves in a pond radiating out from a pebble that is thrown into the pond; the pebble represents the earthquake. The directivity of a tsunami leads to a better analogy. It is more like rolling a log into the water; the waves in front of the log are much higher than the waves at the ends.

Tsunami warning systems work well for distant tsunamis that travel great distances, such as the 1960 Chile tsunami that traveled from Chile to Japan, and the 1964 Alaska tsunami that did damage as far as southern California. But a more severe problem is warning people in coastal areas when the earthquake occurs on a subduction zone that is just offshore. Tsunami warnings were of no use to towns in southern Alaska inundated by the 1964 tsunami. How about earthquakes on the Cascadia Subduction Zone?

The first problem is that there is not much time, perhaps no more than five to fifteen minutes before the first wave reaches the coast. A tsunami struck the northwest coast of Japan only seven minutes after a large offshore earthquake, killing schoolchildren on the beach. The best advice now is to get to high ground immediately when the shaking from a great earthquake stops long enough to allow one to move. Don't wait for a tsunami alert.

Another problem, which may or may not be important in the Pacific Northwest, is the existence of so-called *slow earthquakes*, earthquakes which are quite large, but the wave motion of which is so slow that not much shaking damage is done. A slow

Figure 9-8. Map of Newport, Oregon, showing areas subject to tsunami runup. From the Oregon Department of Geology and Mineral Industries and the Center for Tsunami Inundation Mapping Effects (TIME), part of the National Oceanic and Atmospheric Administration.

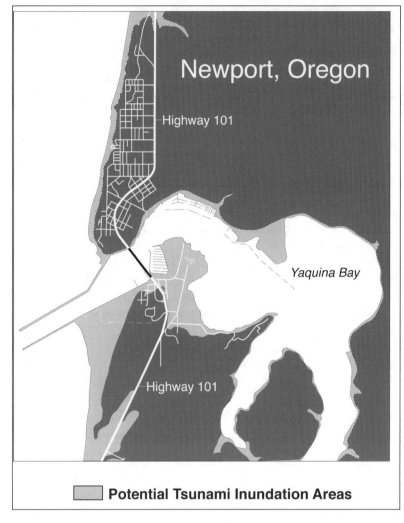

Highway 101

Newport, Oregon

Yaquina Bay

Highway 101

▨ **Potential Tsunami Inundation Areas**

earthquake in Nicaragua on September 2, 1992, produced a tsunami that killed hundreds of coastal villagers. The tsunami was unusually large for the amount of shaking that was recorded. If such an event struck the Northwest, people might not take the earthquake seriously until it was too late. Again, as soon as the shaking stops, move to high ground.

Finally, as was shown in the 1964 tsunami, a warning system needs more than notification by radio. A siren system would wake people up if the tsunami struck at night, as it did in 1964. The siren at Copalis Beach probably saved lives there.

Tsunami Hazard Maps in Oregon

In 1995, the Oregon legislature passed a bill which limits construction of new essential facilities and special occupancy structures in tsunami flooding zones. Directed by this new law, the Department of Geology and Mineral Industries (DOGAMI) prepared a series of tsunami hazard maps at a scale of 1 inch to 2,000 feet of the entire Oregon coast, available as Open-File Reports O-95-09 through O-95-66, and explained in O-95-67, which also contains an index map of the individual tsunami warning maps. Figure 9-8 is a map of Newport, Oregon, showing areas subjected to tsunami runup.

These maps were created using computer models of the earthquake source on the Cascadia Subduction Zone as well as the configuration of the continental slope and shelf and the detailed configuration of coastal bays, harbors, and estuaries. The tsunami maps show where tsunamis are likely to be focused, such as they were at Hilo, Hawaii, and Crescent City, California. The towns of Seaside and Cannon Beach, Oregon, are shown to be at great risk from tsunamis.

During their tsunami study, DOGAMI designed a tsunami warning logo that is now being posted in Oregon beach communities. This logo (Figure 9-9) now has been adopted by the other Western states.

Were there giant tsunamis in the Pacific Northwest in the past? Paleoseismic evidence indicates that there were. The buried peat deposits of Willapa Bay and other regions are directly overlain by a thin layer of laminated sand that shows evidence of being derived from the sea. Sand thickness and grain size diminish away from the sea (Figure 9-10). In southern Oregon, some of the coastal lakes that have formed behind sand bars show evidence of giant waves sweeping across the sand bars. Thus it seems likely that the next Cascadia Subduction Zone earthquake will be accompanied by a tsunami.

Figure 9-9. Tsunami warning logo designed by the Oregon Department of Geology and Mineral Industries and adopted by all Pacific Coast states.

Figure 9-10. Exposure at low tide of sediments below the modern tidal marsh at Willapa Bay, southwest Washington. The shovel blade is at the top of the dark soil layer marking a former marsh that subsided abruptly in A.D. 1700 during the last Cascadia Subduction Zone earthquake. The strongly layered sediments just above the soil layer are sands deposited by a tsunami that immediately followed the subsidence. Photo by Brian Atwater, U.S. Geological Survey.

Suggestions for Further Reading

Bernard, E.N., et al. 1991. *Tsunami Hazard: A Practical Guide for Tsunami Hazard Reduction.* Dordrecht, The Netherlands: Kluwer Academic Publishers.

Dudley, W.C., and M. Lee. 1988. *Tsunami!* Honolulu: University of Hawaii Press.

Griffin, W. 1984. *Crescent City's Dark Disaster.* Crescent City, CA.: Crescent City Printing Co., 188p.

Nance, J.J. 1988. *On Shaky Ground.* New York: William Morrow and Co., 416 p. Description of the 1964 Alaska Tsunami in Alaska.

Oregon Department of Geology and Mineral Industries. 1997. Tsunami hazard map of the Yaquina Bay area, Lincoln County, Oregon. Publication IMS-2.

Priest, G.R. 1995. Explanation of mapping methods and use of the tsunami hazard maps of the Oregon coast. Oregon Department of Geology and Mineral Industries Open-File Report O-95-67.

Priest, G.R. 1995. Explanation of mapping methods and use of the tsunami hazard map of the Siletz Bay area, Lincoln County, Oregon:.Oregon Department of Geology and Mineral Industries Geological Map Series Report.

Satake, K. 1992. Tsunamis, in *Encyclopedia of Earth System Science,* vol. 4, pp. 389-97. Academic Press.

Toppozada, T., G. Borchardt, W. Haydon, M. Peterson, R. Olson, H. Lagorio, and T. Anvik, T. 1995. Planning scenario in Humboldt and Del Norte Counties, California, for a great earthquake on the Cascadia Subduction Zone. California Division of Mines and Geology, Special Publ. 115, 157p.

～ Part IV ～
Prevention and Countermeasures

I t is one thing to be convinced that earthquakes are a threat. We face dangers from ground shaking, landslides, liquefaction, tsunamis, possibly even surface rupture. But what can we do about it?

The chapters that follow describe the human response to earthquakes at all scales, from the national government to the individual. Should we purchase earthquake insurance? If so, it may be useful to learn about the problem from an insurance company's point of view, which means we need to learn about risk. The cost of your insurance may be influenced by what actions you take as a homeowner (or even as a renter) to make your house more secure against earthquakes. These actions may also save your life or prevent serious injury during an earthquake. How about the safety of the building where you work, or the bridge you must cross on the way to work, or the dam upstream from your home?

The government is involved at all levels, federal, state, and (in some cases) local. Research on earthquakes and on earthquake engineering is funded in the United States by the federal government, and we turn to the federal government for help in a disaster. The state government may help as well, although this is more likely in California, where earthquakes have raised more havoc in the past. Building codes and grading ordinances, where they are in effect, give us some security that the structure we live or work in will not collapse during an earthquake, or that the ground on which that structure is built will remain stable during an earthquake. But builders and developers may resist such ordinances, because they may increase their cost of doing business.

Finally, what should each of us do to plan against an earthquake?

~ 10 ~

Earthquake Insurance: Hazards, Perils, Risks, and Losses

"What would happen if someone discovered how to predict earthquakes? No more earthquake insurance."
   Richard J. Roth, Jr., State of California Department of Insurance, 1997

Some Philosophical Issues

Should you buy earthquake insurance for your house? For your business? Before addressing these questions directly, let's take a look at insurance in general and then at the particular problems raised in insuring against earthquakes.

You own a house, and you don't want to lose it in a fire, a flood, a landslide, or an earthquake. You may take chances on the little things in life, but not your home—there's too much at stake. Fortunately, you are contacted by a company that offers to take the risk for you—for a price. The company is gambling that it can assume the risk of the loss of your house, and the houses of a lot of other people, and the price it gets for doing so will allow it to make money. The company is not offering you charity, but a business deal in which it expects to earn a profit. This doesn't bother you if the insurance is affordable, because you figure that the price you have paid is worth not having to worry about losing your home.

The company that takes the risk is an `insurance company` and the price you have paid is called the `premium`. The danger you are insuring against—fire or hurricane or earthquake—is called a `peril`. An earthquake is often referred to in other contexts as a `hazard`, but the insurance industry defines "hazard" as something that makes your danger worse, like failing to reinforce your house against an earthquake, or allowing dense brush to grow against your house so that it is more vulnerable to summer brush fires. You can do something about the hazard, but you can't do much about the peril.

The company sells you fire insurance or automobile insurance, gambling that your house won't burn down or you won't wreck your car, so that the company can keep your premium and make money. The company wins its gamble when your house doesn't burn down and you don't wreck your car. You read about house fires almost every day in the newspaper, and there are plenty of auto accidents, but enough people pay fire and auto insurance premiums that the insurance company can pay the losses and still make money.

Insurance is a competitive business, so the company wants to charge you a premium low enough to get your business, but high enough that it can make money after paying off its claims. It can do this because it calculates approximately how many house fires and auto accidents it is likely to have to pay off during the premium period. These payouts, plus its own operating expenses and a small profit, determine what it charges you for a premium.

But suppose that an evil spirit casts a spell on automobile drivers so that instead of the usual number of auto accidents, there are hundreds of times more. Or an army of arsonists goes around setting houses on fire. The claims on the insurance company would be many times more costly than the number the company had figured on when it calculated premiums, and it would lose money. It could even go broke.

In a way, this is what an insurance company faces in a large urban earthquake, and indeed, in any natural catastrophe, such as Hurricane Andrew. The difference is that the insurance company is dealing not with claims from a large number of individual automobile accidents or house fires, but from a single gigantic "accident" such as an earthquake or a hurricane. The losses due to the 1994 Northridge Earthquake were $20 billion, and those due to the Kobe Earthquake may have been as high as $200 billion.

A large destructive earthquake is an extremely rare event in any given place, and nearly all the time, the insurance company collects your premium and makes money. But when an earthquake finally strikes a big city, the losses could be so great as to bankrupt the company. If earthquake scientists could finally get it right and make accurate probabilistic forecasts of when, where, and how large an earthquake will be, then the company could charge a premium high enough to keep it from bankruptcy, even from a rare catastrophic event, but low enough to sign you up. But unlike fire and auto insurance, the insurance industry does not have sufficient reliable information on which to base its premium. In addition, the losses from an earthquake might be so high that the premium would be very expensive, discouraging homeowners from purchasing earthquake insurance.

Consider the earthquake losses from the great San Francisco Earthquake of 1906. (The dollar figures are small, but so was the size of the insurance industry at that time.) The Fireman's Fund

Insurance Company found that it was unable to meet its loss liabilities of $11,500,000, and it closed down to be reformed as a new company, paying off claims with 56.5 percent cash and 50 percent stock in the new company. Four American and two British companies paid their liabilities in full, but forty-three American and sixteen foreign companies did not, spending months and years in legal battles to avoid paying off their claims. Four German companies immediately stopped doing business in North America to avoid paying anything. Another offered to pay only a fraction of its losses.

The problem was that the insurance industry had underestimated its potential losses in a catastrophic earthquake. The premium was not *cost-based*.

This is why the scientific controversy about whether the next Cascadia earthquake will be a magnitude 8 or 9 is being followed with nervous fascination by the insurance industry. Insurance companies have no problem with a Scotts Mills Earthquake, not even with several Scotts Mills Earthquakes. It can probably even handle, say, a magnitude 8 earthquake that damages Portland but does not extend to Eugene or Tacoma. But a magnitude 9, frankly, gives insurance underwriters fits. Jeff Fletcher of Northern Pacific Insurance Company in Portland, Oregon, told me that his objective was simply to still be in business after the big earthquake.

A Brief Primer on Insurance

Insurance is our social and economic way of spreading the losses of a few across the greater population. We are pretty sure our house won't burn down, but we buy fire insurance for the peace of mind that comes from knowing that on the odd chance that it *does* burn down, our investment would be protected. Our insurance premium is our contribution to setting things right for those few people whose houses do burn down, since the house that burns down could be ours.

Insurance is a business, but it is also a product. There is a consumer's market, insurance has value, and there is a price for the product, called the premium. But insurance differs from other products in that its cost to the company is determined only after it *is sold*. For this reason, the company tries as hard as it can to estimate in advance what that cost is likely to be.

For an insurance company to stay in business, it must be able to (1) predict what its potential losses are likely to be, (2) calculate the cost of premiums that would permit it to pay off its losses and still make a profit, (3) collect the premium, and (4) pay off its claims as required in the insurance contract. The larger the number of contracts it writes, the more likely it is that the actual results will follow the predicted results based on an infinite number of contracts, a statistical relationship known as the *Law of Large Numbers.*

An insurance company is made up of many parts: the executive department that determines overall corporate direction (including the basic decision about whether or not the company wants to be in the earthquake business at all), the department that sends out your statement, the department that settles your claim, and the department that worries about risk so that the price of the premium fits the risk exposure of the company. This process is called *rating.* To determine a rating for earthquake insurance for your house, the insurer may take into account the quality of its construction, its proximity to a known active fault, and the ground conditions. *Underwriting* is the determination of whether or not to insure you at all. For example, if you are an alcoholic and have had several moving automobile violations, including accidents that were your fault, the underwriter may refuse you automobile insurance at any price.

An insurance company has *reserves,* money for the payment of claims that have already been presented, but have not yet been settled, probably because the repair work has not yet been completed, or the claim is in litigation. Reserves are not available for future losses; these losses show as a liability on the company's books. A *policyholder surplus,* or *net worth capital, or retained earnings* are funds that represent the value of the company after all the liabilities (claims) have been settled. This is the money available to pay for future losses.

It turns out that the insurance company, too, wants to hedge its bets against the future. Fortunately, there are insurance companies that insure other companies, a process called *reinsurance.* Let's say that the original company insures a multimillion-dollar structure, but wants to spread the risk. So it finds another company to share the risk, and that company, a reinsurance company, then receives part of the premium. It may well be the reinsurance industry that is most interested in the results of scientists and engineers in earthquake probability forecasting and in assessing ground response to earthquake shaking. Some say that even the reinsurance industry would be unable to pay all claims arising from a catastrophic earthquake, and only the federal government, with its large cash reserves, can serve as the reinsurer of last resort. I return to this question later in the chapter.

We start with that which insurance does best: insure against noncatastrophic *losses* such as auto accidents, fires, and loss of life. These are called *insurable risks.* The loss must be *definite,* it must be *accidental*, it must be large, it must be *calculable*, and it must be *affordable*. Enough policies need to be written so that the Law of Large Numbers kicks in. The *principle of indemnity* (which excludes life insurance, of course) is to return the insured person or business to the condition that existed prior to the loss. This means replacing or repairing the property or paying out its value as established in the insurance contract. The contract may include both direct coverage, replacing the property that was damaged or destroyed, and indirect coverage, taking care of the loss of income in a business or loss of use of the property. There may be a protection against liability. The contract may contain a *deductible clause*, which states that the insurance company will pay only those losses exceeding an agreed-upon amount. The higher the deductible, the lower the premium. This reduces the risk exposure for the company and reduces the number of small claims that are submitted.

The underwriter has calculated the exposure risk using the Law of Large Numbers. A lot of historical information about fire and auto accident losses is available, so that the risk exposure is calculable; the underwriter can recommend premium levels and types of coverage with considerable confidence that the company will be able to offer affordable coverage and still make a profit. The underwriter also looks for favorable factors that might reduce the risk. For fire insurance, a metal roof and vinyl siding would present less risk than a shake roof and wood siding. Auto insurance may include discounts for nondrinkers or for students with a grade-point average of B or better. The underwriter also looks for general trends, like the effect of the elimination of the 55 mph speed limit on auto accident risk (probably increasing risk exposure), or of laws requiring seat belts and child restraints in automobiles (probably reducing risk exposure).

Catastrophic Insurance

Insurance against natural catastrophes is much more complex and more poorly understood, and the underwriting department of a large company may employ engineers, geologists, and seismologists to help it calculate the odds. The insurance market in California changed drastically after the 1989 Loma Prieta and 1994 Northridge earthquakes. The insurance market in the Pacific Northwest is now changing as a result of increased awareness of the possibility of a great subduction-zone earthquake and losses resulting from the two moderate-sized earthquakes in Oregon in 1993. If a magnitude 9 earthquake struck the Cascadia Subduction Zone, the devastation would spread across a large geographic area, including many cities and towns. As a result, an insurance company would have a large number of insured customers suffering losses in a single incident, thereby defeating the Law of Large Numbers. Insurance losses after a major earthquake would have an effect on *insurance capacity.*

Insurance capacity is in part controlled by the fact that all the insurance companies in a region can write only so much insurance, controlled by their financial ability to pay the claims. (This is not the same as *insurance surplus,* which is simply assets minus liabilities.) Part of the role of the executive department of an insurance company is to decide how to distribute its surplus among different kinds of losses. For example, an insurance company might be so concerned about the uncertainties in writing earthquake insurance that it is only willing to risk, say, 10 percent of its surplus, which then defines its capacity for earthquake insurance. It could lose big, but still risk a small enough percentage of its business that it would not go out of business. In making its decision about capacity, the company estimates its *probable maximum loss (PML)* exposure to earthquakes, meaning the highest loss that it is likely to endure. If the company finds that its estimated PML is too high, it reduces its capacity for earthquake insurance in favor of noncatastrophic insurance, thereby reducing its PML exposure. The company might decide to get out of the earthquake insurance business altogether. Insurance capacity was reduced after the losses following the 1994 Northridge Earthquake; there was too much uncertainty in figuring out the risk.

The capacity becomes reduced after a major earthquake at the same time that the demand for earthquake insurance increases. This creates a seller's market for the underwriter, who can set conditions more favorable to the company. Among these conditions may be those affecting the stability of the building site, the proximity to active faults, and the structural upgrading of the building to survive higher earthquake accelerations. If you are a building owner, your attention to these problems can have an economic payoff in lower earthquake insurance rates, just as a good driving record can lower your automobile insurance premium.

Just as health insurers prefer to insure only healthy people, earthquake insurers prefer to insure properties that are more likely to survive an earthquake. Your insurance premium will be higher (or you may be uninsurable) if your house is next to the San Andreas Fault. If your building is constructed on soft sediment of the Willamette River or on beach deposits along the coast, which might liquefy or fail by landsliding, your premium may be higher than if you have built on a solid rock foundation.

Maps of the Portland metropolitan area showing regions susceptible to liquefaction, landsliding, and strong ground motion from earthquakes were designed to highlight those areas in which the danger from earthquakes might be much greater than other areas. However, an Oregon insurance executive told me that after examining the earthquake hazard map of suburban Beaverton, he elected *not* to show the map to his underwriters. The areas subject to strong ground motion and liquefaction in Beaverton were so large that the underwriters might have decided not to offer earthquake insurance in Beaverton at any price. Rather than do that, he decided to ignore the map and offer the insurance anyway! Time will tell if this decision was a wise gamble or not.

Insurance underwriters are very much aware that the principal damage in an earthquake is to buildings that predate the upgrading of building codes. They know that buildings that are constructed under higher standards are more likely to ride out the earthquake with minimum damage. Therefore, your premium will be lower (or your building may be insurable) if you agree to first retrofit such a building against earthquakes, thereby reducing the risk to the company as well as to yourself. From an insurance standpoint, building codes may be regarded as a set of minimum standards, and these standards are designed for *life safety* rather than *property safety.* The building code is said to have worked if everybody gets out of the building alive, even if the building itself is a total loss. If your structure has been engineered to standards much higher than those required by the code, so that not only the people inside, but also the property itself survives, your insurance premium could be significantly lower. You would need to determine whether or not the reduced premium more than offsets the increased construction costs or retrofit costs necessary to ensure that your building rides out the earthquake.

Another way for the insurance company to reduce its PML exposure is to establish a high deductible. A common practice is to express the deductible as a percentage of the value of the covered property at the time of loss. For example, your house is insured for $200,000, and your deductible is 10 percent of the value of the house at the time of loss. An earthquake strikes, and damage is estimated at $50,000. Ten percent of $200,000 is $20,000, so the insurance company pays you $30,000, the difference between the deductible and the estimated damage.

Now we get into some gray areas. First, liability insurance. Suppose the owner of the building where you work or rent your apartment has been told that the building is not up to earthquake code but chooses not to retrofit. An earthquake destroys the building, and you are severely injured. Do you have a negligence claim against the building owner that his insurance would be required to pay off?

Or suppose that a geologist has told the city council that an active fault runs through some undeveloped property next to the city. The city ignores this advice and approves a high-density subdivision across the fault line. Under pressure from the developer and landowner, the city requires only minimal engineering and geological surveys prior to approving the subdivision, so that the fault is not located with respect to specific building sites. An earthquake strikes the city, accompanied by strong shaking and rupture along the fault, destroying two hundred houses and killing a hundred people. Are the city and developer (and the bank lending the money for the development) liable for damages, inasmuch as they chose to ignore professional advice about the hazard?

Another gray area is government intervention. A major catastrophe like the Northridge Earthquake brings immediate assistance from the Federal Emergency Management Agency (FEMA), including low-interest loans and direct assistance. The high profile of any great natural catastrophe, a hurricane as well as an earthquake, makes it likely that the president of the United States, together with the director of FEMA (or, in British Columbia, the prime minister) will show up on your doorstep. Billions of dollars of federal assistance will be forthcoming; this is generally a one-shot deal, aid that is nonrecurring. The net effect of this aid is to compensate for the large losses in the affected region, although not necessarily the losses of insurance companies. This aid follows the insurance principle that losses are spread across a larger population, in this case, the citizens of the United States or Canada. However, the aid focuses on *relief* rather than *recovery*.

Government Intervention

State governments have already intervened in the insurance business. A state insurance commissioner must approve the rates charged by an insurance company within the state. A natural distrust of insurance companies is spurred by consumer advocacy groups. Citizens see the gleaming downtown office buildings owned by insurance companies at the same time that they see their own insurance premiums going up, and they conclude that they are being cheated. The state department of insurance may respond to this distrust by developing an adversarial relationship with the insurance industry within the state. Insurance premiums have become a political issue in California, first, health insurance premiums, and more recently, following Northridge, earthquake insurance premiums.

This adversarial relationship can be a particular problem in insuring against catastrophes. The insurance industry has developed computer models to estimate its losses in a major catastrophe, models that suggest that premiums are not high enough, are not *cost based*. But these models are proprietary, meaning that an insurance company may not want to release the details of the model and lose its competitive advantage. Accordingly, state departments of insurance may not accept or trust these models, or they may regard them as biased in favor of the industry. This problem should diminish in future years as such computer models become more sophisticated and more widely accepted by the public.

Government intervention could be taken to an extreme: the government could take over catastrophic insurance altogether, rather than merely regulating insurance at the state level. The United States government is already involved in flood insurance; a federal insurance program is administered by the Federal Insurance Administration, part of FEMA. There is also a federal crop insurance program. However, there is no federal program of earthquake insurance.

In 1987, a group of insurance-industry trade associations and some insurance companies organized a study group called the Earthquake Project to consider the effects of a great earthquake on the U.S. economy in general and the insurance industry in particular. This group, renamed the Natural Disaster Coalition after the multibillion dollar losses from Hurricane Andrew, concluded that the probable maximum losses from a major disaster would exceed by far the insurance industry's capacity to respond, and that a federal insurance partnership was necessary. The study group proposed legislation to establish a primary federal earthquake insurance program for residences and a reinsurance program for commercial properties. However, the proposal was criticized as an insurance-industry bailout, and no action was taken. A revised proposal attracted more congressional support, but the potential federal liability in case of a great disaster doomed this proposal as well. In 1996, the Natural Disaster Coalition proposed a more modest plan that would reduce federal involvement and establish a national commission to consider ways to reduce the costs of catastrophic insurance. This failed to win sufficient administration support for adoption, but it will be considered by a future Congress.

Another proposed solution is to allow insurance companies to accumulate tax-free reserves to be available to pay claims in the event of a catastrophe, a system now in effect in New Zealand, as explained below. Let's say that a catastrophe with losses of $100 million will occur once every ten years, far in excess of the premiums expected in the year the catastrophe struck. If the insurance industry collected and accumulated $10 million annually for ten years, then it could meet its claims in the year of the catastrophe. However, under present accounting regulations, the $10 million collected during a year in which no catastrophe occurs must be taxed as income. For this reason, the insurance company must pay off its $100 million losses with the $10 million in premiums that it collected that year plus income collected earlier on which it has already paid taxes. The proposal to accumulate tax-free reserves against a catastrophe has met with enough congressional resistance to prevent it from being passed into law. A similar proposal is under consideration in Canada.

Government *has* become directly involved in earthquake insurance in California, where the state has orchestrated the establishment of a privately financed earthquake authority, and New Zealand, where the government has gotten into the insurance business directly.

In California, earthquake insurance has been offered since before the 1906 San Francisco Earthquake, with major problems paying claims from that disaster, as we have seen. But for the most part, earthquake insurance has been profitable for the insurance industry, up until the 1989 Loma Prieta Earthquake followed by the 1994 Northridge Earthquake. For most of the period since the 1906 San Francisco Earthquake, claims and payments were far less than premiums, even including three large earthquakes (1971 Sylmar, 1983 Coalinga, 1987 Whittier Narrows), two of which struck densely populated areas. But the claims and payments rose dramatically from less than $3 million for the Sylmar Earthquake to about $1 billion for earthquake shaking damage after the Loma Prieta Earthquake. In 1989, as a result of the Loma Prieta Earthquake, claims and payments exceeded premiums for the first time since 1906.

But the 1994 Northridge Earthquake really broke the bank: about $12 billion against about $1 billion in premiums for 1994-95. One insurance company severely underestimated its potential for losses from the Northridge Earthquake; it would have gone out of business except for a buyout from another carrier. Not all of the $12 billion paid out was earthquake insurance, which covers damage from shaking. About 20 percent of the loss was paid from other types of insurance, including insurance against fire, property damage and liability, commercial and private vehicle losses, loss of life, disability, medical payments, and so on.

These figures point out another trend in the earthquake insurance market: the sharp rise in insurance premiums and claims after California began to require in 1985 that a company offering homeowners' insurance must also offer earthquake insurance, although the homeowner was not required to buy it. Because the Northridge Earthquake broke the Law of Large Numbers, the insurance industry was faced with a problem larger than simply earthquake insurance—the much larger market for homeowners' insurance that had become legally linked to earthquake insurance.

As a result, the industry severely restricted capacity for not only earthquake insurance but homeowners' insurance as well, with some companies getting out of the homeowners' insurance business altogether. Demand greatly outstripped supply, and homeowners' insurance premiums skyrocketed. In response to complaints about the high premiums, companies pointed to studies that suggested that future losses could exceed $100 billion, losses that would bankrupt many companies. Losses of $200 billion from the Kobe Earthquake of 1995 in Japan solidified that view, although only a small fraction of the Kobe Earthquake loss was covered by insurance. Insurance companies and homeowners took their concerns to the California legislature in Sacramento.

The result was the California Earthquake Authority (CEA), signed into law by Governor Pete Wilson in September 1996. Insurance companies representing more than 70 percent of the residential property insurance market agreed to participate. The CEA is managed by the state insurance commissioner, but it is financed privately. Insurance premiums have more than doubled, and payouts are expected to be lower. One estimate for residential claims if the CEA had been in operation at the time of the Northridge Earthquake: $4 billion less than the amount actually paid out.

The CEA has been described as a "mini-earthquake policy." Structural damage to residences is covered, with a deductible of 15 percent of the value rather than 10 percent. The policy covers damage to certain contents up to $5,000 and emergency living expenses up to $1,500. However, swimming pools, fences, driveways, outbuildings, and landscaping are not covered at all. The $10.5 billion fund, capped by the legislature, is provided by premiums and cash advances by insurance and reinsurance companies. Claims are processed by individual insurance companies and paid by the state. If the CEA ran out of money, policyholders would get only partial payment of claims, and there could be a surcharge up to 20 percent on their policy if claims exceeded $6 billion.

The three largest insurers, State Farm, Allstate, and Farmers, are committed to the CEA, as are some midsize carriers. But many smaller carriers have stayed out. This means that the CEA will be able to pay out only about $7.5 billion instead of the $10.5 billion estimated with 100 percent participation. Some insurance underwriters believe that the premiums are still too low to protect against catastrophic losses; that is, CEA is still not cost based. The higher cost has been criticized by consumer advocates; it has driven many homeowners away from obtaining or renewing earthquake coverage. At present, no more than 25 percent of California homeowners have earthquake insurance.

Under the CEA, insurance premiums vary from region to region, divided by California's 2,100 ZIP codes. Much of the San Fernando Valley, which suffered two damaging earthquakes in less than twenty-five years, is paying 40 percent more than most of the rest of the Los Angeles metropolitan area. But the city of Palmdale, in the Mojave Desert adjacent to that part of the San Andreas Fault that ruptured in 1857 in an earthquake of M 7.9, pays significantly lower rates than much of Los Angeles! San Francisco Bay Area residents are paying rates 4 $1/2$ times higher than residents of Eureka, on the northern California coast. This coast was struck by a M 7.1 earthquake in 1992 and is at risk from an earthquake on the Cascadia Subduction Zone, yet the region has rates that are among California's lowest. Perhaps the lesson to be learned here is that if your area has recently had an earthquake, you will be overcharged for earthquake insurance, but if not, earthquake insurance may be a bargain.

Controversy over the great disparity in earthquake insurance rates from region to region has led to a review of the CEA's probabilitistic hazard model by the California Division of Mines and Geology under contract to the state Department of Insurance.

The age and type of home also affect rates. The owner of a $200,000 wood-frame house in Hollywood or Westwood in Los Angeles would pay $540 in earthquake insurance if the house was built in 1979 or later, $660 if the home was built between 1960 and 1978, and $700 if the house was built before 1960, a recognition of higher construction standards in recent years. But if the house was *not* of wood-frame construction, the premiums would be $960 in Hollywood. The new insurance rates recognize the value of well-constructed houses in which earthquake risks have been taken into consideration.

New Zealand, like the Pacific Northwest, is a land of great natural beauty in which the spectacular mountains and volcanoes are related to natural hazards, especially earthquakes and volcanic eruptions. Written records have been kept for about the same length of time as in our region, but unlike the Northwest, New Zealand has suffered great earthquakes during that time, in 1848, 1855, 1888, 1929, and 1931. The country was thinly populated during most of the historical period, and losses, although locally severe, did not threaten the economy of the nation.

In June and August 1942, the capital city of Wellington and the nearby Wairarapa Valley were struck by earthquakes which severely damaged thousands of homes. It was the darkest period of World War II, with the war being waged in Pacific islands not far away to the north. Because of the war, there was little money for reconstruction after the earthquakes, and two years later, much of the rubble in the Wairarapa Valley had not even been cleared. Something had to be done.

In 1944, while the war still raged to the north, the government collected a surcharge from all holders of fire insurance policies and established the Earthquake and War Damage Commission to collect the premiums and pay out damage claims on residential property from war or earthquakes. Later, coverage against other natural disasters was added: tsunamis, volcanic eruptions, and landslides. In 1993, Parliament passed the Earthquake Commission Act, changing the name of the administering agency to the Earthquake Commission. Under the new act, the insurance automatically covers all residential properties that are insured against fire. It provides full replacement of a dwelling up to a value of $112,500 (in New Zealand dollars) and contents up to $22,500. Only residential property is covered. The commission took on additional roles in disaster prevention and public education as a means to reduce its potential losses.

The arrangement has worked well since 1944, in large part because New Zealand has not suffered a disastrous earthquake in an urban area since the commission was established. Earthquake premiums have continued to accumulate at a rate of about $150 million per year in those years when there are few claims, and the fund now has $2.5 billion to cover earthquake losses. The damages paid out as a result of the 1987 Edgecumbe Earthquake (M 6.6) were nearly $136 million, as compared to $2.4 million after the much larger 1968 Inangahua Earthquake (M 7.1) nearly twenty years earlier. The sharp increase in losses, even after earthquakes of moderate size in rural areas, suggests that there may be rough times ahead for the Earthquake Commission.

It is generally recognized that the entire $2.5 billion in the Earthquake Fund might cover only half the losses of a major earthquake in Wellington, where an active fault runs through the center of the city. The New Zealand government guarantees that it will cover all claims in excess of the fund in case of a major catastrophic earthquake. The problem then would be that after the fund had been exhausted by an earthquake, the government would have to step in and cover even small claims until the fund had built up its assets once more. For this guarantee, the government has taken two steps: (1) purchasing reinsurance, and (2) charging an Earthquake Commission tax, which brings in an additional $20 million per year to pay for reinsurance. Still, the financial outcome of an earthquake in Wellington as large as those in 1848 and 1855 is unclear.

Summary Statement and Policy Issues

Insurance against earthquakes is a high-stakes game involving insurance companies, policyholders, and in some cases, governments. Because earthquakes occur rarely at a given location (in a human time frame, at least), consumers tend to underestimate their need for catastrophic coverage. In most places in the U.S., the percentage of property owners with earthquake insurance is much lower than the 25 percent in California.

The demand for earthquake insurance shoots up after a catastrophic earthquake at the same time the capacity of insurance companies to offer such insurance sharply decreases. Insurance is, after all, a business, and for the business to succeed, it must make money.

Insurance companies may underestimate the premiums they should charge in a region like the Pacific Northwest, where a catastrophic earthquake has not occurred in the 175 years of record keeping. But premiums may be priced too high in places that have recently suffered major losses, like the San Fernando Valley or the San Francisco Bay Area. The quality of construction, particularly measures taken to mitigate against earthquake shaking, will have an increasing impact on premium costs.

The Institute of Building and Home Safety (IBHS), an association of insurance companies, has an Earthquake Peril Committee which has as its goal the reduction of potential losses. This includes discouraging developers from building in areas at risk from earthquakes and other natural disasters. If a project is awarded an IBHS Seal of Approval, it may be eligible for hazard reduction benefits, including lower premiums.

The federal governments of the United States and Canada have still not determined what their roles should be. Should earthquake insurance be mandatory? Should it be subsidized by the government, particularly for low-income homeowners who are not likely to be able to afford the premiums if they are truly cost based? The small percentage of properties that are insured raises a potential problem for the finance industry; uninsured homeowners may simply walk away from their mortgages and declare bankruptcy if their uninsured homes are destroyed by an earthquake. Should FEMA's efforts include recovery and not simply relief?

Problems such as these tend to be ignored by the public and by government except in the time immediately following an earthquake. There is a narrow time window (teachable moment) for the adoption of mitigation measures and the consideration of ways to deal with catastrophic losses.

Should you have earthquake insurance if you live in the Northwest? I would say yes! It's a terrific bargain, even in those parts of California adjacent to the Cascadia Subduction Zone. Why? The Pacific Northwest has not yet had a great earthquake in its historical period, so that few people have the insurance. This reduces the probable maximum loss exposure of insurance companies, allowing them to offer earthquake insurance at a rate below its true, long-term cost.

Suggestions for Further Reading

California Department of Conservation. 1990. Seismic Hazard Information Needs of the Insurance Industry, Local Government, and Property Owners of California. California Department of Conservation Special Publication 108.

Insurance Service Office, Inc. 1996. Homeowners insurance: Threats from without, weakness within. ISO Insurance Issues Series, 62p.

Palm, R., M. Hodgson, R.D. Blanchard, and D. Lyons. 1990. *Earthquake Insurance in California: Environmental Policy and Individual Decision Making.*   Boulder, CO: Westview Press.

Roth, R.J., Jr. 1997. Earthquake basics: insurance: What are the principles of insuring natural disasters? Oakland, CA: Earthquake Engineering Research Institute.

11

Is Your Home Ready for an Earthquake?

*"If a builder builds a house for a man and does not make
its construction firm and the house collapses and causes the
death of the owner of the house—that builder shall be put
to death."*
    The Code of Hammurabi, ca. 2250 B.C.

Introduction: How Safe is Safe Enough?

Chances are two out of three that you will be at home when the next big earthquake strikes, and one out of three that you will be in bed. Therefore, the ability of your home to withstand an earthquake affects not only your pocketbook but also your life and the lives of those who live with you. If you are an owner, and even if you are a renter, you can take steps to make your home safer against the next earthquake.

But first you need to make some decisions. Sure, you want to be safe, but how much are you willing to spend to make your home environment safer? Is it your goal that your *house* survives the earthquake, or only that *you and those around you* walk away from your house without serious injury? This would be an easier decision if scientists could tell you when the next earthquake will strike. But they can't. You could be spending a lot of money protecting against an earthquake that might not strike during your lifetime.

This chapter reviews the steps you can take to protect your home, your valuables, and yourself from earthquake shaking, and it presents those steps in order of importance. The chapter does not consider house damage from liquefaction, landslides, surface rupture, subsidence, or tsunamis. It assumes that the site of your house will be shaken but not permanently deformed by the earthquake.

It is most important to keep your house from collapsing or from catching on fire, so those preventive steps are presented first. This is followed by discussion of other, less critical prevention measures.

Then you can make the decision about how much protection is enough for you.

Some Fundamentals: Inertia, Loads, and Ductility

Imagine for a moment that your house is sitting on a flatcar on a train that is transporting the house to another state. Suddenly the train collides with another train, and the flatcar stops abruptly. What happens to your house? If your house was anchored to the flatcar and was wood-frame, as most houses in the Pacific Northwest are, it probably would not collapse, although your brick chimney might topple over. If your entire house was made of brick or concrete block, unreinforced by steel rebar, then the entire house might collapse.

This analogy introduces an important concept. The jolt to your house during the train wreck is analogous to the shocks the house might receive during a large earthquake, except that the earthquake jolts would be more complicated. The motion may be sharply back and forth for tens of seconds, combined with ups and downs and sideways motions. The response of the house and its contents (including you) to these jolts follows the *principle of inertia*.

The principle of inertia states that a stationary object will remain stationary, or an object traveling at a certain speed in a certain direction will continue traveling at that speed and in that direction, unless acted on by some outside force. Because of inertia, your body is pulled to the right when you turn your car sharply left. It is inertia that makes seat belts necessary. If your car hits a tree, and you are not wearing a seat belt, the inertia of your body keeps you moving forward at the same rate as the car before it was hit, propelling you through the windshield.

Stack some blocks on a towel on a table. Then suddenly pull the towel out from under the blocks and toward you. The blocks will seem to fall *away* from you, as if they were being propelled by some force acting in a direction away from you. This force is called an *inertial force*. The inertia of the blocks tends to make them stay where they are, which means that they must fall away from you when you pull the towel toward you.

I saw a graphic illustration of inertia at the Olive View County Hospital which was destroyed by the Sylmar Earthquake, in California, in February 1971. The hospital, only three months old when the earthquake struck, consisted of several stories that seemed to weather the earthquake without damage. (In fact, glasses of water on the bedside tables of some of the patients on the top floor weren't even spilled.) But the walls on the ground floor, which had much more open space and, therefore, was much weaker than the upper floors, like a garage beneath a house, were tilted in one direction. The ground beneath the hospital had moved suddenly in a horizontal direction, but the inertia of the hospital building caused it to appear to move in the opposite direction (Figure 12-10). The inertial forces were absorbed in the weaker ground floor. (For an illustration of inertial forces damaging a garage, see Figure 11-5.)

Engineers refer to the forces acting on a building as *loads*. The weight of the building itself is called a *dead load*. Other forces, such as the weight of the contents of the building, including people, or snow on the roof, or wind coming out of the Columbia Gorge, or earthquakes, are called *live loads*. The building must be designed to support its own weight, and this is standard practice. It also must be designed to support the weight of its contents, and this is also standard practice, although occasionally the news media report the collapse of a gymnasium roof due to a load of snow and ice.

Except for wind whistling down the Columbia Gorge, all the loads mentioned above are *vertical loads,* and they are commonly accounted for in engineering design. The wind load, however, is a *horizontal load*, and in designing buildings in downtown (and sometimes windy) Portland, horizontal wind loads are indeed taken into account. Earthquake loads are both vertical and horizontal. They are very complex, and in contrast to wind loads, they are applied suddenly, with high *acceleration.*

I have already discussed acceleration as a percentage of the attraction of the Earth due to its gravity, or g. During a space shuttle launch, astronauts are subjected to accelerations of several g when they rocket into space. A downhill ride on a roller-coaster temporarily counteracts the Earth's gravity to produce zero g, and this accounts for the thrill (and sometimes queasy feeling) we experience. Acceleration during an earthquake is the Earth's answer to a roller-coaster ride. If the shaking is enough to throw objects into the air, the acceleration is said to be greater than 1 g. High accelerations, particularly high horizontal accelerations, are more damaging than low accelerations.

The dead weight of a building and its contents can be calculated fairly accurately and accounted for in engineering design. These loads are called *static loads*; they do not change with time. Wind loads and earthquake loads change suddenly and unpredictably; these are called *dynamic loads*. The engineer must design a structure to withstand dynamic loads that may be highly variable over a very short period of time, a much more difficult task than designing for static loads alone. Unfortunately, awareness of the potential for earthquake loads is so new in the Pacific Northwest that most older buildings have not been designed to stand up against the dynamic loads caused by earthquakes.

In Chapter 2, rocks of the crust were described as either *brittle* or *ductile*. Brittle crust fractures under the accumulated strain of the movement of tectonic plates, to produce earthquakes. The underlying ductile crust is warm and pliable and deforms without producing earthquakes.

Structural engineers use these terms in a similar way to refer to buildings. A building that is *ductile* is able to bend and sway during an earthquake without collapsing. In some cases, the building "bounces back" and is not permanently deformed. Deformation is *elastic*, as I described earlier for rubber bands and diving boards. In other cases, the building deforms permanently, but it still does not collapse, so that people inside can escape, even though the building may be a total loss. Steel-frame buildings tend to be ductile. Wood-frame houses are also ductile. This is fortunate for us, because in the Pacific Northwest most of us live in wood-frame houses.

In contrast, a *brittle* structure is unable to deform during an earthquake without collapsing. Brittle buildings include those made of brick or concrete block joined together with mortar, but not reinforced with steel rebar, or mud-block buildings (adobe), common in underdeveloped countries. In an earthquake in the Pacific Northwest, your wood-frame house may survive, but your chimney, made of brick, may collapse. Your house is ductile, but your chimney is not.

The reinforcing techniques described below are for a house that has already been built; this is called a *retrofit*. These techniques are also applicable to new construction, in which case they are a lot less expensive. This is immediately apparent in shoring up the foundation; it is the difference between working comfortably on a foundation before the house is built on top of it and working in a confined crawl space.

Protecting Your Foundation

If you have a poured-concrete foundation, first check on its quality by hitting it with a hammer. If the hammer makes a dull thud rather than a sharp ping, or if there are throughgoing cracks more than an eighth of an inch wide, or if the concrete is crumbly, you will need to seek professional help.

Let's assume that the concrete is okay. The next job is to see if your house is bolted to the foundation and is adequately braced. Otherwise, horizontal inertial forces may slide the foundation out from under the house, which happened to wood-frame houses in

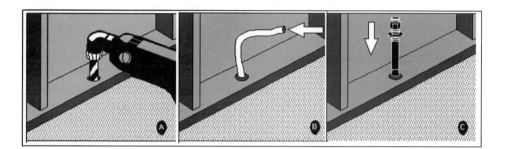

Figure 11-1. Bolt the cripple wall to the foundation through the mudsill, using a sill bolt. (A) Drill hole, using a right-angle drill. (B) Blow powder out of hole, using flexible tubing. (C) Hammer in sill bolt. Tighten nut to expand bolt. From U.S. Geological Survey.

northern California during earthquakes in October 1989 and April 1992.

Some houses are built on a concrete slab, or floor. Others have a concrete foundation around the edge of the house; in these a board is generally found between the house and the foundation called a *mudsill*. Houses built before 1940, and even many houses built after that time in the Pacific Northwest, were not required to be bolted to the foundation through the mudsill. In 1974, the Uniform Building Code began to require that walls be anchored to foundations (Figure 11-1). The standard retrofit technique is to drill a hole through the mudsill and into the foundation with a rotary hammer or a right-angle drill, which can be rented, although you should purchase your own drill bit. Next drive a *sill bolt* (also called an *anchor bolt*) into the hole you have just drilled, using a sledge hammer, having first cleaned out the hole and made sure that it is deep enough to accommodate the sill bolt. The sill bolt has a washer on top and an expanding metal sleeve at the base that slides up, spreads, and wedges in the concrete. Bolt sizes range from $1/2$ by 7 inches to $3/4$ by 10 inches; a standard size is $5/8$ by 8 $1/2$ inches. The larger ones give more protection against lateral loads and are preferred if the house has more than one story. If the nut on top of the bolt won't tighten, or the bolt climbs out of the hole as you tighten it, then the concrete may be decomposing. An alternative in that case is to set the bolt with epoxy cement.

In new construction, the sill bolt is set when the foundation is poured, a fairly simple operation.

The spacing of bolts, in both new construction and in retrofits is at least one every 6 feet, and one within 12 inches of the end of any mudsill. Placing the bolts midway between the studs (the vertical members that support the walls) makes it easier to work on them.

The next step is stiffening the *cripple wall*, which is made of short studs and sits between the mudsill and the floor joists of the house itself (Figure 11-2). The cripple wall bounds the crawl space under the house where you are working. The problem here is that if these vertical studs are not braced, they may tilt over like a set

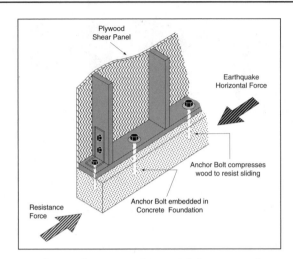

Figure 11-2. Anchor cripple wall to foundation using sill bolts, and to mudsill by hold-down. Cripple wall is further strengthened by plywood shear panel. From Earthquake Engineering Research Institute.

of dominoes due to horizontal inertial forces so that your house collapses on its crawl space and flops down on its foundation.

Since 1973, the Uniform Building Code has required bracing of cripple walls; the bracing requirements were increased in 1991. If your home was built before those critical dates, you may need to brace the cripple wall yourself. The recommended stiffening technique is to use $^1/_2$-inch plywood, $^5/_8$-inch if you use a nail gun (Figure 11-2). The plywood should be treated with a preservative prior to installation to prevent rot. Ideally, you should sheathe the entire cripple wall in plywood, but at a minimum, install 8 linear feet of plywood from each interior corner of the crawl space for one-story houses, 16 feet for two-story houses. Anchor the plywood panels with 8-penny nails 4 inches apart around the edges of each panel and 6 inches apart on each interior stud. (The nailing pattern is important; one of the most memorable sounds of a house breaking up during an earthquake is the wrenching noise of nails being pulled from the walls.) Drill vent holes 1 inch in diameter to prevent moisture buildup. Ideally, this plywood sheeting should be at least twice as long as it is tall. If it is not, the sheeting should be reinforced with anchors and hold-downs (Figure 11-2). These anchors bolt into the foundation and into corner posts of the cripple walls, increasing the bracing.

Another solution, particularly if the cripple wall is very short or if the floor joists of the house rest directly on the foundation, is $^1/_4$-inch structural steel bolted into the foundation with expansion bolts and into the floor joists.

If you are a do-it-yourselfer, plan on spending at least $600 for the materials. However, working in crawl spaces is messy and confined, and you may wish to employ a professional. This will cost you several times as much as doing the job yourself; a contractor may charge as much as $25 per installed bolt. But reinforcing the cripple wall and foundation may be the most

Figure 11-3. This Victorian wood-frame house in Ferndale, California, was built on a post and pier foundation, but was not bolted to its foundation, so that it slid off during the 1992 Petrolia Earthquake. The floor level of the house was at the same height as the front steps. The house moved to the right and down with respect to the steps. Note also the wooden skirting, formerly part of the outside wall, which is now flat on the ground. Photo courtesy of National Oceanic and Atmospheric Administration.

important step you can take to save your house. For examples of cripple-wall failure, see Figures 11-3 and 11-4.

As insurance companies in the Pacific Northwest begin to gauge earthquake-insurance premiums to the details of construction of your house, as they already are doing in California, reinforcement will almost certainly reduce your premium.

Soft-story Buildings

A common failure in California's recent earthquakes was the two- or three-car garage with living space overhead. Many condominiums in the Pacific Northwest have most of the first floor devoted to parking, with apartment space in the upper floors. The large amount of open space at the garage door means less bracing against horizontal forces than in standard walls, so these open areas are the first to fail in an earthquake (Figure 11-5). Similar problems arise, although on a smaller scale, with large picture windows, sliding-glass patio doors, or double doors.

Make sure that the wall around the garage door and the wall in the back of the garage, on the opposite side from the door, are sheathed with $1/2$-inch plywood, just as cripple walls are. Because of the limitations for bracing on the garage door itself, bracing

Figure 11-4. This house south of Petrolia, California, shifted off its foundation during the 1992 Petrolia Earthquake because it was not anchored to the foundation and its cripple wall was not reinforced. The house shifted to the right, as seen by the collapsed wooden skirting. The separation of the house and the small porch is an example of connection failure. Photo courtesy of National Oceanic and Atmospheric Administration.

Figure 11-5. Soft-story failure to three-car garage during 1971 Sylmar, California Earthquake. The large door opening resulted in inadequate shear resistance to horizontal ground motion. Photo by J. Dewey, U.S. Geological Survey.

the back wall, opposite from the door, will increase the overall resistance of the structure to earthquake ground motion sideways to the door.

Plywood sheathing should completely surround any large picture window or set of double doors. The sheathing should be at least as wide as the opening and extend from bottom to top of the opening. Because the interior wall is finished in drywall or plaster, the best time to add sheathing is during initial construction or a remodel of your house.

Utility Lines

One of the greatest dangers in an earthquake is fire. Fire caused much of the loss of life and property in the 1906 San Francisco Earthquake and the 1995 Kobe Earthquake, and large fires destroyed property in the Marina District of San Francisco after the 1989 Loma Prieta Earthquake. The problem is natural gas.

If gas connections are rigid, they are likely to shear during an earthquake, releasing gas that only needs a spark to start a fire. Gas connections should be flexible. In addition, after an earthquake, you need to shut off the main gas supply to the house (Figure 11-6). Learn where the gas supply line is, and ensure that the shut-off valve is not stuck in place by turning it $^1/_8$ turn ($^1/_4$ turn is the closed position). Place the wrench you would use to shut off the gas *near the valve*. Tell all members of the family where the wrench is and how to use it. In the event of a major earthquake, shutting off the gas is a top priority. You won't have time to rummage around a heavily damaged house looking for a wrench.

For $400 to $600, you can have an automatic shutoff valve installed on the gas line. This valve, located between the gas meter and the house, is actuated by earthquake shaking, which knocks a ball or cylinder off a perch inside the valve into a seat, thereby shutting off the gas. Consider an automatic shutoff valve if you are away from home a lot and are not likely to be around to shut off your gas after an earthquake. A disadvantage of the automatic

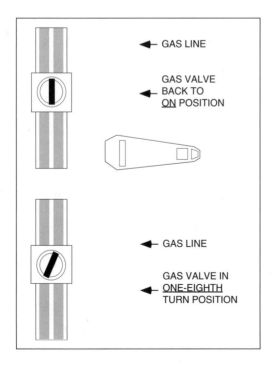

GAS LINE

GAS VALVE BACK TO ON POSITION

GAS LINE

GAS VALVE IN ONE-EIGHTH TURN POSITION

Figure 11-6. Shut-off valve for the main gas supply line to house. Top: valve in "on" position. Bottom: Check to be sure valve is not frozen by turning it $^1/_8$ turn. Specialized wrench available from gas company is also shown.

shutoff valve is that you would not be able to tell easily if you had a gas leak in your house after the valve had shut off the gas. If you are confident that you don't have a gas leak, you should know how to reset the valve yourself, because after a major earthquake, weeks might go by before the gas company or a plumber could get to your house and reset the valve for you. Remember that when the valve is reset, you must immediately relight all the pilot lights in your appliances.

All gas lines and water pipes should be supported at least every 4 feet. Earthquake vibrations may be strongly exaggerated in unsupported pipe in your basement or crawl space. If pipes are not supported, strap them to floor joists or to walls.

If liquefaction occurs, underground utility lines may be severed, even if your house is anchored below the liquefying layer and doesn't fail. Underground gas lines failed due to liquefaction in the Marina District of San Francisco, triggering many fires.

Strapping the Water Heater and Other Heavy Appliances and Furniture

Your water heater is the most unstable appliance in the house. It is heavy, being full of hot water, and it is tall, likely to topple over due to horizontal forces from an earthquake. The water heater should be strapped in place, top and bottom, with strong nylon webbing or with plumber's tape (metal, perforated tape). The tape should be anchored to studs in the wall at both ends (Figure 11-7). Make a complete loop around the water heater before anchoring it to the studs. This precaution is very easy and inexpensive to do and will not reduce the effectiveness of the water heater at all.

If the water heater is right against the wall, brace it against the wall with two-by-fours so that it doesn't bang against the wall during an earthquake. If it is against a concrete wall, install heavy-duty eye screws on both sides of the water heater and run steel cable through the eye screws, again making a complete loop around the heater.

Built-in appliances such as dishwashers, stoves, and ovens may not be braced in place; they may only rest on a trim strip. One homeowner was quoted in *Sunset Magazine* as saying after the October 1989 Loma Prieta Earthquake: "I assumed built-in appliances are fixed in place. NOT SO! Our built-in oven and overhead built-in microwave slid out." Make sure your appliances are securely braced (Figure 11-8). A gas stove may topple over, snapping the gas line and causing a fire. Make sure the refrigerator

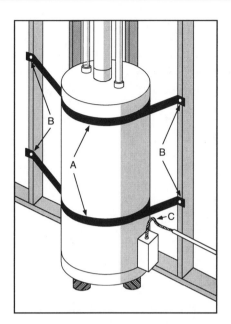

Figure 11-7. Strap water heater, top and bottom, with plumber's tape (A) which is attached to studs (B). If the water is heated by gas, the gas supply line (C) should be flexible. In this example, water heater rests against stud. If water heater is against drywall or plaster wall, brace it with a two-by-four so that it does not bang against the wall.

is secured to the wall. Baby-proof refrigerator door locks are effective in preventing food in the refrigerator from spilling out on the floor.

Look around your house for tall top-heavy furniture, like a china cabinet, tall chest of drawers, or wardrobe. These should be attached to studs in the wall to keep them from falling over. There are two concerns. One is the loss of heirloom china in your china cabinet. The other is the possibility of a heavy piece of furniture falling on you or on a small child. For either of these reasons alone, securing these large pieces of furniture to the wall is a good idea.

Figure 11-8. Damage to contents of the kitchen in a residence in Petrolia, California, as a result of the 1992 Petrolia Earthquake. Appliances shifted several inches away from the wall. All items were shaken off the shelves with considerable glassware breakage. Photo courtesy of National Oceanic and Atmospheric Administration.

Safety Glass

A major problem in an earthquake is shattered glass windows, which may flex and essentially blow out, showering those within range with sharp fragments of glass. An expensive option is to replace glass in large picture windows or sliding doors with tempered or laminated glass. A much cheaper alternative is safety film, which costs about $3 to $4 per square foot, installed. This bonds the glass to a 4-mil thick acrylic sheet; the adhesive strengthens the glass and holds it together if it breaks, like the safety glass in a car windshield. You can do this yourself, but it is hard to prevent air bubbles from being trapped under the film, so consider having it installed professionally.

Cabinets

Figure 11-9. Safety latches for earthquakes. The simple hook and eye (A) is inexpensive and secure, but you may not remember to close it each time you use the cabinet because it takes an extra step to do so. Some latches (B, C) mount on the surface of the door; others (D) mount inside the door, hold the door firmly shut, and are opened by being pushed gently inward. A child-proof latch (E) prevents the door from being opened more than an inch or two. It closes automatically, but is more trouble to open.

Remember José Nuñez of Molalla, who watched his kitchen cabinets blow open during the 1993 Scotts Mills Earthquake, spewing their contents onto the kitchen floor? Magnetic catches often fail. However, babyproof catches, which are inexpensive, will keep cabinet doors closed during an earthquake (Figure 11-9). Heavy spring-loaded latches are advised, especially for cabinets containing valuable dishes.

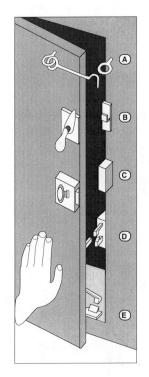

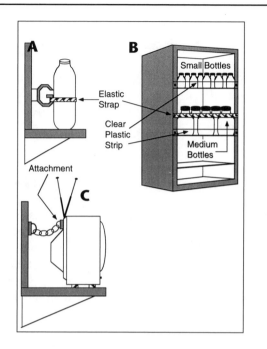

Figure 11-10. Securing items on open shelves: (A) Attach counter-top items to wall with bungee cord. (B) Secure small items with a vertical strip and larger items with a strip and bungee cord. (C) Large items, like a TV set, can be attached to wall with chain.

If small children live in your house, you may already have babyproof catches, but they are probably only on cabinets near the floor, within the child's reach. For earthquake protection, the most important places for babyproof catches are the *highest* cabinets, particularly those containing heavy breakable dishes or fragile glassware. Don't forget the medicine cabinet in the bathroom, where prescription medicine could fall on the floor and mix, producing a toxic combination.

Put layers of foam or paper between heirloom plates that are seldom used but are at great risk during an earthquake. Line your shelves with non-skid shelf padding, available at marine- and recreational-vehicle-supply houses because they are also useful to keep items on the shelf during a heavy sea or when your recreational vehicle is traveling down a bumpy road. In a similar vein, consider a rail around open shelves to keep items from falling off (Figure 11-10). Hold-fast putties are small balls that flatten and stick to the bottom of a large vase to keep it from toppling over; these putties will peel off and leave no residue. Lead weights in old socks can be placed in the bottom of vases or table lamps to keep them in place.

You won't be able to take all these precautions. But, considering that a third of your life is spent in bed, lie down on your bed and look around for those items of furniture that might fall on you during an earthquake. A heavy chest of drawers? A large wall mirror? A ceiling fan? A large headboard? At least secure those items that might endanger your life. Then do the same for the beds where other members of your family sleep, particularly small children. (Maybe it's simpler to move the bed rather than secure the furniture!)

Renters may face a restriction by the landlord against fastening any furniture to the wall. A discussion with the landlord may help, particularly if you are willing to fill the holes in the wall when you move.

Bricks, Stonework, and Other Time Bombs

If you live in an old unreinforced brick house, you are in real danger, and none of the retrofit techniques mentioned above are going to do much good outside of a major costly reinforcing job. Fortunately for the Pacific Northwest, old brick houses are being phased out of the building inventory; most of us live in wood-frame houses. (Legislation to establish a time line to phase out unsafe buildings was introduced in the 1997 Oregon Legislature, but it failed to win much support.)

But one part of your house is still likely to be unreinforced—your masonry chimney (Figure 11-11). Chimneys collapsed by the hundreds during the Puget Sound earthquakes of 1949 and 1965. Most commonly, they snap at the roof line. A tall chimney is likely to be set in motion by the earthquake waves, resulting in collapse. The taller the chimney, the more likely it is to fall through the roof into your house. Some recent building codes require internal and external bracing of chimneys to make them more likely to survive an earthquake. Perhaps the rule of thumb here is how much of a threat to safety your chimney poses. If someone is

Figure 11-11. Brick chimney on this house in Petrolia, California, collapsed during the 1992 Petrolia Earthquake. The fireplace inside the house was also shattered. Photo courtesy of National Oceanic and Atmospheric Administration.

likely to be killed or severely injured by a falling chimney, take it down. Prefabricated metal chimneys can be attached to an existing brick firebox so that no brick projects above the roof line.

Inside, there's the mantel. In some houses, the mantel is field stone, very attractive, but very heavy if it fails, particularly if the mortar has been weakened by a chimney leak. Field stone and brick veneer on the outside of the house may pose a hazard as well. If you want a natural stone appearance, install the lightest weight material you can.

Free-standing wood-burning stoves are popular in the Pacific Northwest. A study done by Humboldt State University found that over half the wood-burning stoves in the area near the epicenter of the April 1992 M 7.1 Petrolia, California, Earthquake moved during the earthquake, and several fell over. Fire codes in some states leave stoves unsupported on all four sides, which may cause them to slide or turn over during an earthquake. If a stove tipped over and separated from its stovepipe, cinders or sparks could easily cause a fire.

The following steps are recommended (Figure 11-12). (1) Anchor a stove resting on a brick hearth, attaching the legs of the stove to the hearth with bolts. Mobile-home-approved stoves have pre-drilled holes in the legs for anchoring to the floor framing. (2) For a stove resting directly on a concrete slab, anchor the stove directly to the concrete. (3) Anchor the stovepipe to the flue, and tie together each of the stovepipe segments.

In the Kobe Earthquake, thousands of people were killed in their beds in wood-frame houses because their roofs were of tile,

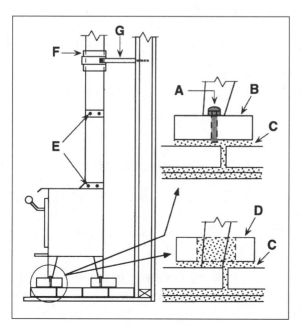

Figure 11-12. For a stove built on a brick hearth, anchor stove with ³/₈-inch diameter bolt (A) through ¹/₂-inch hole to new brick (B). Grout brick to the existing hearth with one inch of new grout (C). As an alternative, build an 8-inch-square brick pad with grout pocket (D) at each leg. There should be at least one inch of grout around each leg; fill pocket completely with grout. Provide sheet metal screws (E) at flue exit and between stovepipe sections. Provide a radiation shield with pipe clamp (F) braced to wall, using tension ties attached to wall stud with ³/₈-inch by 3-inch lag screws. From Humboldt State University.

Figure 11-13. Propane tank. Mount tank on 6-inch-thick concrete pad (A) using four $^1/_2$-inch diameter bolts (B) with 3-inch minimum embedded into concrete. Provide a flexible hose connection (C) between tank and the rigid supply line. From Humboldt State University.

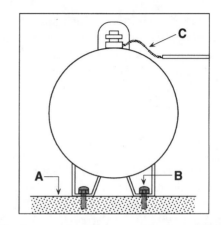

which made the houses top-heavy and more subject to collapse. Clay tile roofs are the heaviest; composition or wood roofs are lighter. If you re-roof your house, add plywood shear panels over the rafters. This is required in much new construction and may be required of you in a remodel. It strengthens the house.

Propane Tanks

Above-ground propane tanks may slide, bounce, or topple during an earthquake, causing a potential fire hazard from a gas leak. You can reduce the fire danger by doing the following (Figure 11-13): (1) Mount the tank on a continuous concrete pad and bolt the four legs of the tank to the pad. (2) Install flexible hose connections between the tank, the supply line, and the entrance to your house. (3) Clear the area around the tank of objects that could fall and rupture the tank or its gas supply line. (4) Keep a wrench tied near the shut-off valve and make sure all family members know where it is and how to use it. For large tanks, such as those used commercially or on a farm, install a seismic shut-off valve.

Connections

One of my most instructive memories of the 1971 Sylmar Earthquake was a split-level house, where earthquake shaking accentuated the split between the garage with a bedroom over it and the rest of the house (Figures 11-14, 11-15). A common sight is a porch that has been torn away, or a fallen deck or balcony. These connections are the potential weak link in the chain that is your home. Make sure that everything is well connected to everything else so that your house behaves as a unit during shaking (see also Figure 11-4).

Figure 11-14. Split-level house in Crestview Tract, San Fernando Valley, showing failure of the connection between the single story (right) and the two-car garage with bedrooms above. Note the difference in height between the front steps and the single story, indicating cripple-wall failure of the single story. Photo by Robert Yeats.

Figure 11-15. Split-level house in Crestview Tract, San Fernando Valley, California in which the connection between the single-story left section of the house sheared with respect to the two-story section with bedrooms over a two-car garage during the 1971 Sylmar Earthquake. Cracks in the corners of the garage door opening are an indication of soft-story failure. Photo by Robert Yeats.

Mobile Homes and Manufactured Houses

Because these houses must be transported to their destination, they are more likely than an ordinary house to behave as a coherent structural unit during an earthquake. Manufactured houses are built on one or more steel I-beams that provide structural support in the direction of the I-beam. However, mobile homes and manufactured houses face a major problem during an earthquake. They are generally not bolted to a foundation, but instead rest on concrete blocks which are likely to collapse during even low horizontal accelerations (Figures 11-16, 11-17). This would cause the house to flop down onto its foundation, as illustrated earlier for cripple-wall failures. A mobile home is likely to undergo less structural damage than an ordinary house, but there is likely to be extensive damage to contents of the house. The house could

Figure 11-16. This manufactured home slipped off its supporting piers during an earthquake. This type of failure can be avoided by bolting the house to its foundation, as is required for other houses in most states. From Karl Steinbrugge Collection, Earthquake Engineering Research Center, University of California Berkeley.

be prevented from sliding off its blocks during an earthquake by replacing the blocks with a cripple wall and securing it as described above for ordinary houses. This would make the house insurable against earthquakes.

A double-wide mobile home must be well connected at the join between the two halves (*marriage line*) so that the two halves do not fail at the join and move independently during strong shaking. In Oregon, these joins are covered by a State of Oregon Manufactured Dwelling Standard. Ridge beams must be attached with $1/2$-inch carriage bolts spaced at a maximum of 48 inches at 90 degrees and $3/8$-inch lag screws, with washers, spaced every 24 inches at 45 degrees maximum angle. Floor connections must be with $3/8$-inch lag screws with washers installed diagonally at 45 degrees or less, with spacing not exceeding 32 inches. Even so, it is likely that a double-wide manufactured home will fail at the marriage line if it slips off its concrete block foundation during an earthquake.

Okay, So What Retrofitting Are You Really Going to Do?

You probably won't take all of these steps in making your home safer against earthquakes. Doing everything would involve a considerable expense, and this may not be reflected in an increased value of your home, unless it successfully rides out an earthquake. You will probably decide to live with some risk.

Consider at least the following minimum improvements: (1) bolt your house to its foundation, (2) increase the strength of

Figure 11-17. Mobile home has slid off its supports during an earthquake. Photo courtesy of California Office of Emergency Services.

your cripple wall, (3) install flexible connections on all your gas appliances and make sure the main shut-off valve can be turned off quickly in an emergency, (4) secure your water heater, and (5) make sure that large pieces of furniture or large ceiling fixtures won't collapse on anyone in bed. This at least protects you against a catastrophic collapse of your house, and against fire.

Suggestions for Further Reading

California Office of Emergency Services. An Ounce of Prevention: Strengthening Your Wood Frame House for Earthquake Safety. Video and booklet.

Humboldt Earthquake Information Center. How to survive earthquakes and tsunamis on the north coast. Arcata, CA: Humboldt Earthquake Information Center, Humboldt State University, 23p.

Lafferty and Associates, Inc. 1989. Earthquake preparedness—for office, home, family and community. La Canada, CA.

Sunset Magazine. 1990. Quake—2-part series in October and November 1990 issues, available as reprints (Sunset Quake '90 Reprints) from Sunset Publishing Company, 80 Willow Road, Menlo Park, CA 94025.

⤳ 12 ⤳
Earthquake Design
of Large Structures

"I don't know. This looks like an unreinforced masonry chimney to me."
    Santa Claus, undated

Introduction

I t is impossible to earthquake-*proof* a building. A look at the intensity scale (Table 3-1) shows that for intensities of X and worse, even well-constructed buildings may fail. However, most earthquakes have maximum intensities less than X, and well-designed buildings should survive these. The highest intensity recorded in a Pacific Northwest earthquake was VIII in the 1949 Puget Sound Earthquake. A Cascadia Subduction Zone earthquake, however, may have much higher intensities.

Building codes should be designed so that a building will resist (1) minor ground motion without damage, (2) a moderate level of earthquake ground shaking without structural damage but possibly with some nonstructural damage, and (3) a major level of ground motion with an intensity equivalent to the *maximum credible earthquake* for the region (as described in Chapter 7) without structural collapse, although possibly with some structural damage. In this last case, the building could be declared a total loss, but it would not collapse, and people inside could escape safely.

But upgrading the building code does not have an immediate effect on the safety of large buildings. Building codes affect *new construction* or *major remodeling* of existing structures; if a building is not remodeled, it will retain the safety standards at the time it was built. It is for this reason that forty-seven of the sixty-four people who died in the 1971 Sylmar, California, Earthquake lost their lives due to the collapse of a single facility, the Veterans Administration Hospital. This was a reinforced concrete structure built in the 1920s, before the upgrading of building standards a

Figure 12-1. Aerial view of the damage to the San Fernando Veterans Administration Hospital campus after the 1971 Sylmar, California, Earthquake. Of the 64 deaths attributed to the earthquake, 47 were a result of the collapse of this structure, built in 1926, before earthquake-resistant building codes were adopted. Adjacent building, constructed after building codes were upgraded after the 1933 Long Beach Earthquake, did not collapse. Photo by E.V. Leyendecker, U.S. Geological Survey.

decade later after the 1933 Long Beach Earthquake. The collapsed buildings were designed to carry only vertical loads. Figure 12-1 is an aerial view of the hospital campus immediately following the earthquake. The building in the photograph that held up well had been reinforced after the 1933 earthquake. Clearly, retrofitting paid off in terms of lives saved.

In the same vein, the greatest losses in Pacific Northwest earthquakes, including the 1949 and 1965 Puget Sound earthquakes (Figures 12-2, 12-3) and the 1993 Scotts Mills and Klamath Falls earthquakes (the latter pictured on the book cover), occurred in old unreinforced masonry buildings, especially schools, which seem to take the longest time to replace.

It is much more expensive to retrofit a building for earthquake safety than it is to build in the same safety protection for a new building. Typically, a simple structure will cost $9-10 per square foot to retrofit. A nonductile concrete-frame structure will be two to three times more expensive. The cost for a historic building could reach $100 per square foot. The owner of the building must consider the possibility that the money spent in upgrading may not be returned in an increased value of the building or increased income received from it. It is for these reasons that it takes so long to upgrade the building inventory of a city. Legislation would speed the process along.

The problem of retrofitting historic buildings was addressed by the Federal Emergency Management Agency (FEMA) in a grant to the Oregon Department of Geology and Mineral Industries to retrofit Weatherford Hall, a historic building on the Oregon State University campus. To many people, the distinctive architecture of Weatherford Hall captures the essence of the OSU tradition. At one time, it was the oldest continuously operating residence hall

Figure 12-2. Parapet damage to Lafayette School in West Seattle due to the 1949 Puget Sound Earthquake. The school was an unreinforced masonry building. Tons of bricks fell into the schoolyard, but fortunately, school was not in session, and no children were injured or killed. Photo courtesy of Washington Division of Geology and Earth Resources.

west of the Mississippi River. But the unreinforced masonry construction made it a time bomb. The cost of retrofitting against the possibility of earthquakes was beyond the university's budget, and so the building closed in 1994. The FEMA grant provides seed money to remodel the building; other funds will be provided by the state and by private funds, including donations from former Weatherford residents. Weatherford will reopen as a residential college.

Seismic Retrofitting

Traditionally, the goal of seismic retrofitting has been to allow people inside the structure to survive the earthquake. Damage control and protection of property are secondary, except for certain historical buildings. Certain types of structures are known to behave poorly during earthquakes; these are characteristically brittle structures. Unreinforced masonry that bears the structural load of a building with poorly tied floor and roof framing tends to fail by wall collapse. Nonductile concrete-frame buildings are subject to shear failure of weak, unconfined columns. Framed structures with large parts of their walls not tied together tend to behave structurally as soft-story structures (like the attached garage

Figure 12-3. Close-up of an entrance to Lafayette School, covered with bricks. Fortunately, the school was not occupied at the time of the earthquake. Photo courtesy of Washington Division of Geology and Earth Resources.

in the San Fernando Valley shown in Figure 11-5). These structures have failed catastrophically, with loss of life, in recent earthquakes.

Strengthening of existing buildings must ensure that the added reinforcing is compatible with the material already there. For example, a diagonal steel brace might be added to a masonry wall. The brace is strong enough, but it would not carry the load during shaking until the masonry had first cracked and distorted. The brace might prevent total collapse, but the building might undergo enough structural damage to be considered a total loss.

Figure 12-4 shows several types of retrofit solutions for old buildings. The walls may be strengthened by infill walls, or by bracing, or by external buttresses (beautifully displayed by medieval Gothic cathedrals in western Europe), or by adding an exterior or interior frame, or by base isolation. The important thing is for the building to behave as a unit during shaking, because the earthquake is likely to produce failure along weak joins.

The term *diaphragm* is used for a horizontal element of the building, such as a floor or a roof, that transfers horizontal forces between vertical elements such as walls (Figure 12-5a). The

Figure 12-4. Possible retrofit strategies for old buildings. (a) Infill walls. (b) Add braces. (c) Add buttresses. (d) Add frames interior or exterior. (e) Completely rebuild. (f) Isolate building. From AIA/ACSA Council on Architectural Research, Washington, D.C.

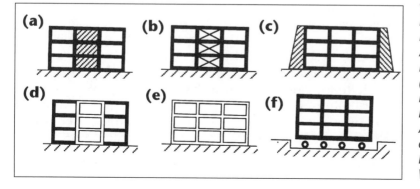

Figure 12-5. A. Horizontal diaphragm. Failure typically occurs at connections to vertical columns. B. Concept of diaphragm as a horizontal I-beam. C, D. Holes in beams or diaphragms for elevator shafts, large doors, etc., interrupt continuity and reduce strength. From AIA/ACSA Council on Architectural Research.

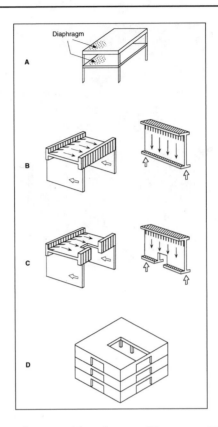

diaphragm can be considered as an I-beam, with the diaphragm itself the web of the beam and its edges the flanges of the beam (Figure 12-5b). In most buildings, holes must be cut in the diaphragm for elevator shafts or skylights (Figure 12-5c). These holes interrupt the continuity and thereby reduce the strength of the diaphragm (Figure 12-5d).

Lateral forces from diaphragms are transmitted to and from the ground through *shear walls*. The forces are shear forces, those tending to distort the shape of the wall, or bending forces for slender structures like a skyscraper (Figure 12-6). Construction may include walls that have higher shear strength or diagonal steel bracing, or both.

Moment-resistant frames are steel-frame structures with rigid welded joints (Figure 12-7). These structures are more flexible than shear-wall structures, which means that they are less likely to undergo major structural damage, but more likely to result in damage to interior walls, partitions, and ceilings. Several steel-frame buildings failed in the 1994 Northridge, California Earthquake, but the failures were in large part due to poor welds at the joints, a failure in design, construction, and inspection.

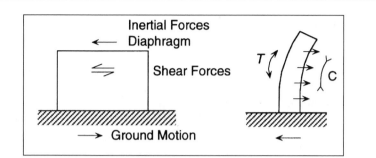

Figure 12-6. Shear walls resist shear stresses transmitted from the ground and bending stresses in slender, tall buildings. From AIA/ACSA Council on Architectural Research.

Figure 12-7. Joint used in a moment-resistant frame.

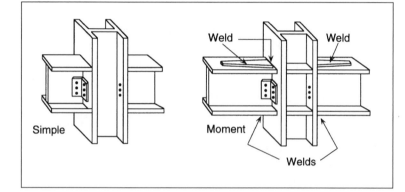

Base Isolation

The normal approach to providing seismic resistance is to attach the structure firmly to the ground. All ground movements are transferred to the structure, which is designed to survive the inertial forces of the ground motion. This is the reason why your house is bolted to its foundation, and the cripple wall is reinforced.

In large buildings, these inertial forces may exceed the strength of *any* structure that has been built within reasonable economic limits. The engineer designs the building to be highly ductile, so that it will deform extensively and absorb these inertial forces without collapsing. Moment-resistant steel-frame structures are good for this purpose, as are special concrete structures with a large amount of steel reinforcing.

These buildings don't collapse, causing death and injury, but, as stated above, they have a major disadvantage. In deforming, they may cause extensive damage to ceilings, partitions, and building contents such as filing cabinets and computers. Equipment, including utilities, will stop operating. High-rise buildings will sway and may cause occupants to become sick and panicky.

The problem with attaching the building firmly to the ground is that the energy of earthquake waves is dissipated by the building itself and its contents, often destructively. Is there a way to dissipate the energy in the foundation *before* it reaches the main floors of the building?

In *base isolation*, the engineer takes the opposite approach; the objective is to keep all the ground motion from being transferred into the building. This is the same objective as in automobile design: to keep the passengers from feeling all the bumps in the road. To accomplish this, the automobile is designed with air-inflated tires, springs, and shock absorbers to keep its passengers comfortable.

One way to do this is to put the building on roller bearings so that as the ground moves horizontally, the building remains stationary (Figure 12-8). A problem with this solution is that roller bearings would still transmit force into the building through friction. In addition, once the building began to roll, its inertia would tend to keep it moving. We need a structure that allows horizontal movement with respect to the ground, but restrains, or dampens, this movement so that as the ground vibrates rapidly, the building vibrates much more slowly.

The solution is to separate the requirement for load bearing (vertical loads) from that for movement (horizontal loads). One way to do this involves a *lead-rubber bearing* (Figure 12-9). This bearing consists of alternating laminations of rubber and steel, which allow for up to 8 inches of horizontal movement without fracturing, but are strong enough to support the building. A cylindrical lead plug is placed in the center of this bearing and serves to dampen the oscillations in the ground produced by an earthquake, just like the shock absorbers in a car. The energy of the earthquake waves is absorbed by the lead plug rather than by

Figure 12-8. Mounting a building on roller bearings so that building remains stationary when the ground moves. The problem: how to stop it from moving. From AIA/ACSA Council on Architectural Research.

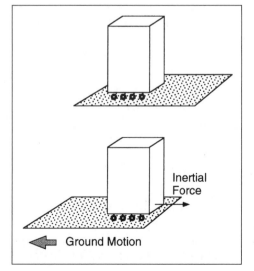

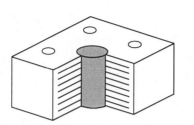

Figure 12-9. Base-isolation bearing. Alternating laminations of rubber and steel with a lead plug in the middle. From AIA/ACSA Council on Architectural Research.

the building itself. The lead plugs do not deform in small earthquakes or high winds; in that respect, they serve as "seismic fuses."

Lead has the advantage of recovering nearly all of its mechanical properties after each deformation from an earthquake. This is analogous to the solid-state ductile deformation of lower crustal rocks without producing earthquakes. The lead-rubber bearings allow the ground under a building to move rapidly, but the building itself moves much more slowly, thereby reducing the accelerations and maximum shear forces applied to the building. The building is allowed to move about 6 inches horizontally. A 6-inch slot around the building is built for this purpose and covered by a replaceable metal grating. The damage to architectural and mechanical components of the building, and the ensuing costly repairs, are greatly reduced and, in some instances, almost eliminated.

Although base isolation adds to the cost of construction, some cost reduction is possible within the building structure itself because so much of the earthquake force is absorbed at the base of the building rather than transmitted into the structure.

Research is underway in Japan and New Zealand, and to a lesser extent in the United States, to design other methods of base isolation. After the 1989 Loma Prieta Earthquake, the California State Legislature passed Senate Bill 920, requiring the state architect to select one new and two existing buildings as demonstration projects for new engineering technologies, including base isolation.

Special Problems

Each large building presents its own set of design problems in surviving earthquake forces, which means that architects must consider earthquake shaking in designing a large structure in a seismically hazardous region like the Pacific Northwest. I consider two problems: soft first stories and the tuning fork problem.

*Figure 12-10.
Damage to the
Los Angeles
County Olive View
Medical Center as
a result of the
1971 Sylmar,
California,
Earthquake. The
first floor, with a
lot of open space,
behaved like a
soft story, causing
the upper floors to
move relatively to
the right, forcing
out the stairwell.
Photo by Robert
Yeats.*

In a building with a *soft first story*, the first floor is weaker than the higher floors. These include buildings in which the first floor is taken up by a parking garage or contains large amounts of open space occupied by a department store or hotel ballroom. Instead of load-bearing walls, these spaces are supported by columns. Building codes commonly limit the height of soft stories to two normal stories, or 30 feet. But the result is that the ground floor is less stiff (has less strength) than the overlying floors. Since earthquake forces enter the building at its base and are strongest there, the soft first story is a stiffness discontinuity that absorbs the force of the earthquake waves. Without a soft first story, the earthquake forces are distributed more equally throughout the entire building. With a soft first story, there is a tremendous concentration of forces on the ground floor and at the connection between the ground floor and the second floor. This may cause collapse or partial collapse of the higher floors, as happened at the Olive View Hospital during the 1971 Sylmar Earthquake (Figures 12-10, 12-11). The problem can be alleviated by adding more columns, stiffening the existing structure.

The second problem may be called the *tuning fork problem*. A large pipe organ has pipes of different lengths so that the organ can play different notes. The deep bass notes are played on long pipes, and the high notes are played on short pipes. A xylophone

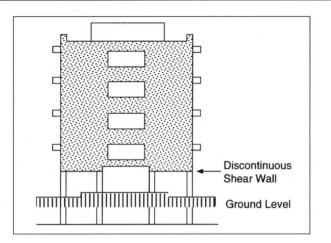

Figure 12-11. Diagrammatic representation of soft story at Olive View Medical Center. From AIA/ ACSA Council on Architectural Research.

works the same way: the high notes are played on short keys, and the low notes are played on long keys. These instruments are designed to take advantage of the *vibrational frequency* of the pipes or keys to make music. A tuning fork works in the same way. Strike the tuning fork and place it tines up on a hard surface. You will hear a specific note, related to the length of the tuning fork, which generates sound waves of a specific frequency, the vibrational frequency of the tuning fork.

Buildings work in the same way. A tall building vibrates at a lower frequency than a short building, just like a tuning fork. The problem comes when the earthquake wave transmitted through the ground has the same frequency as the vibrational frequency of the building. The building *resonates* with the earthquake waves, and the amplitude of the waves is intensified. All other things being the same, a building with the same vibrational frequency as the earthquake waves will suffer more damage than other buildings of different height.

Figure 12-12. Buildings have a vibrational frequency depending on their height. If the vibrational frequency resonates with that of the earthquake waves, shaking will be amplified, and damage will be more severe, as was the case in Mexico City in the 1985 earthquake. From Bolt (1993).

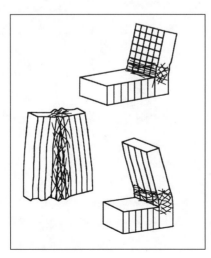

This was demonstrated during the Mexico City Earthquake of 1985. Surface waves with a period of about 2 seconds were amplified by the soft clay underlying most of the city, which also extended the period of strong shaking. Buildings between ten and fourteen stories suffered the greatest damage, because they have a natural vibrational period of 1 to 2 seconds (Figure 12-12). When waves of that characteristic frequency pushed the foundations of those buildings sideways, the natural resonance caused an accentuation of the sideways shaking and great structural damage. In contrast, a thirty-seven-story building built in the 1950s, with a vibrational period of 3.7 seconds, suffered no major structural damage.

Bridges and Overpasses

The most thorough appraisal of the earthquake potential of Oregon was done not by the Department of Geology and Mineral Industries nor by the federal government, but by the Oregon Department of Transportation (ODOT). The television images of people sandwiched in their cars in the collapse of the double-decker Interstate 880 Cypress Viaduct in Oakland, the collapsed span of the Oakland-San Francisco Bay Bridge, and the pancaked freeway interchanges in Los Angeles (Figure 12-13) were not lost on the structural engineers in the Bridge Division, and they traveled to California to see the damage for themselves after the Northridge Earthquake.

Figure 12-13. Damage to the Golden State Freeway (Interstate 5) and Foothills Freeway (Interstate 210) as a result of the 1971 Sylmar, California, Earthquake. Photo by E.V. Leyendecker, U.S. Geological Survey.

The double-decker Cypress Viaduct reminded some of the Marquam Bridge in Portland or the Alaskan Way Viaduct in Seattle. Bridge collapses in Portland could divide the city in two during a major earthquake, creating two cities separated by the Willamette River, with many of the hospitals on the west side of the river. It would take only one collapsed overpass to block Interstate 5 for weeks. In addition, bridge collapses on Highway 101 along the coast could isolate coastal communities for an indefinite period of time.

Five bridges collapsed in the 1994 Northridge Earthquake, one on the Golden State Freeway, two on the Antelope Valley Freeway, one on the Simi Valley Freeway, and one on the Santa Monica Freeway. All of these structures were designed to pre-1974 standards, and none had been retrofitted. The Santa Monica Freeway had been targeted for seismic retrofit, but the earthquake got there first. In some cases, a collapsed bridge was adjacent to a recently retrofitted bridge that suffered little or no damage, even though it had been subjected to earthquake forces similar to those endured by the bridge that collapsed. Clearly, retrofit worked for bridges and overpasses.

The main problem in the older bridges was in the columns supporting the freeway superstructure. There was inadequate column confinement, inadequate reinforcement connections between the columns and the footings on which they rested, and no top reinforcement in the footings themselves. When these problems were overcome in retrofitting, bridges rode through earthquakes reasonably well.

California, through Caltrans, is the nation's leader in the seismic retrofit of bridges. Caltrans estimates that there are about seventeen hundred bridges in the state that require retrofit to prevent collapse during a future strong-motion earthquake, about 10 percent of California's inventory of bridges. Bridges over water, such as the Oakland-San Francisco Bay Bridge, require special consideration, because a collapse could drop a large number of vehicles and passengers into the water. The cost of retrofitting all of these bridges is prohibitive if done in a very short period of time. Strengthening the two Carquinez Strait bridges and approach structures 25 miles northeast of San Francisco, one built in 1927 and one in 1958, would cost nearly $50 million. Decisions on which bridges to retrofit involve establishing priorities based on the potential magnitude of the loss, both directly in damages and lives lost and in economic losses, and then allocating the resources to do the job.

Decisions, Decisions, and Triage

The astronomical cost of retrofitting bridges brings up a major problem faced by society. As you look at the building inventory in your town or the bridge inventory in your state, you soon recognize that in this era of budget cutbacks in government, the money is not available to retrofit everything, or even a sizeable percentage of the inventory. Decades will pass before buildings are retrofitted, with the retrofit decision commonly based on criteria other than earthquake shaking. When faced with scheduling the retrofit of dangerous buildings in Oregon, even over a time frame of many decades, the 1997 Oregon Legislature turned away and did nothing.

The decision on what to retrofit is a form of *triage*. In a major accident involving hundreds of severely injured people, limited medical aid requires decisions to help first those people who are more likely to survive. In earthquake retrofitting, the triage decision would be made to first retrofit those buildings that are most critical to the community, especially in an emergency, or those structures the loss of which would be catastrophic to the population. These structures are called *critical facilities*. Let's consider the second category first.

In Chapter 6, mention was made of the nuclear reactor at the Hanford Reservation in Washington. Catastrophic failure of the reactor could result in the release of lethal amounts of radioactive gases and fluids, endangering the lives of hundreds of thousands of people. Clearly, the nuclear facilities at Hanford are critical facilities; they should be retrofitted to meet the highest seismic design criteria. The large dams along the Columbia River are also critical facilities. If a dam failed during an earthquake, it would release enormous volumes of water from the reservoir impounded behind it. One scenario holds that one dam failure and catastrophic release of water could trigger the next dam failure and the next, like dominoes, all the way to Portland. These dams should be designed to withstand the highest conceivable amount of seismic shaking. The Van Norman Dam in the San Fernando Valley, California, came close to failure during the M 6.7 Sylmar Earthquake (Figure 12-14). Had failure occurred, the waters impounded behind the dam would have overwhelmed many thousands of homes downstream, resulting in the loss of thousands of lives, rather than the small number of lives that were actually lost.

Continuing with our triage dilemma, what facilities in your town must continue to operate after an earthquake? Certainly the command structure of local government must be able to function, because local government leaders will direct rescue efforts

Figure 12-14. Van Norman Dam, San Fernando Valley, California, after the 1971 Sylmar Earthquake. About 800,000 yards of the embankment, including the parapet wall, dam crest, most of the upstream slope, and a portion of the downstream slope, slid into the reservoir, causing a loss of about 30 feet of dam height. Fortunately, the dam was only about half full at the time. Eighty thousand people living downstream from the dam were ordered to evacuate, and steps were taken to lower the water level in the reservoir. Photo by E.V. Leyendecker, U.S. Geological Survey.

and make decisions that could avert some of the spin-off disasters that may accompany an earthquake, such as major fires and tsunamis. So we should include the police and sheriff's departments, the fire department, city hall, and the county building, including the office of county emergency management services.

How about hospitals? Returning again to 1971, several hospitals were severely damaged (Figures 12-1, 12-10), so that injured people had to be transported to other regions not damaged during the earthquake. Schools? Most of the school children of Spitak and Leninakan, Armenia, were in their classrooms when the 1988 Spitak Earthquake struck. The classrooms were in poorly-constructed unreinforced-concrete buildings which collapsed, killing most of the pupils and teachers inside. I am told that there is a missing five- or six-year age gap in those communities in Armenia; most of the young people of that age were killed in the earthquake.

In the Pacific Northwest, school buildings fared badly in the 1949, 1965, and 1993 earthquakes, because so many of them were unreinforced brick buildings (Figures 12-2, 12-3). It was providential that, in all cases, the timing of the earthquakes meant that there were very few people in those buildings. Had the classrooms been full, hundreds of children might have lost their lives. This is a particular problem in Oregon in the wake of Measure 5 and Measure 47, voter-approved initiatives to reduce the role of government. As a result of these initiatives, there is less money to retrofit these buildings or to build new ones. Fortunately, quite a few of them have already been replaced or recycled for reasons other than earthquake hazard, and the problem is much less severe than it was in 1949 or even 1965. Yet many of these time bombs remain.

Suggestions for Further Reading

Earthquake Engineering Research Institute. 1996. Construction quality, education, and seismic safety. Oakland, CA: Earthquake Engineering Research Institute. EERI Endowment Fund White Paper, 68p.

Earthquake Engineering Research Institute. 1996. Public policy and building safety. Oakland, CA: Earthquake Engineering Research Institute. EERI Endowment Fund White Paper, 57p.

Fratessa, P. 1994. *Buildings: Practical Lessons from the Loma Prieta Earthquake.* Washington, D.C.: National Academy Press.

Krinitsky, E., J. Gould, and F. Edinger. 1993. *Fundamentals of Earthquake Resistant Construction.* Wiley Series of Practical Construction Guides. New York: J. Wiley & Sons.

Lagorio, H.J. 1990. *Earthquakes: An Architect's Guide to Nonstructural Seismic Hazards.* New York, J. Wiley & Sons.

Lindeburg, M. Seismic Design of Building Structures, 7th edition. Belmont, CA: Professional Publications.

Manolis, G.D., D.E. Beskos, and C.A. Brabbia. 1996. Earthquake Resistant Engineering Structures. Computational Mechanics, 728p.

Naeim, F., ed. 1989. *The Seismic Design Handbook.* London, Chapman and Hall.

～ 13 ～

The Federal Government and Earthquakes

Introduction

T he study of earthquakes is such a large-scale problem, with so many implications, that it seems impossible for the national government *not* to become involved. The government faces two difficulties: (1) defining the earthquake problem and dedicating the national resources to deal with it, and (2) informing the public about what has been done in such a way that the public can become a partner in reducing the earthquake hazards we face. A third difficulty is convincing the public a long time after the last earthquake that the government ought to be doing anything at all.

Historical Background

For most of recorded history, earthquakes were regarded as unpredictable calamities, acts of God, not subjects for government involvement except for dealing with the consequences. This began to change in 1891, when a killer earthquake devastated a large section of western Japan at the same time that Japan was gearing up its economy to become an equal partner with Western countries. After the 1891 earthquake, the Japanese government authorized a long-term earthquake research program, including the mapping of active faults after a major earthquake, the deployment of seismographs (which were just then being invented), and the re-survey of benchmarks across active faults and along coastlines to look for crustal deformation. The Earthquake Research Institute was established at the University of Tokyo.

As a result of that government focus, Japanese earthquake scientists became world leaders. K. Wadati of Japan invented a magnitude scale before Charles Richter's invention of the one that bears his name; Wadati also was the first to recognize earthquakes hundreds of miles beneath the Earth's surface, outlining what would later be known as subduction zones. Two of the leading seismologists in the United States are transplants from Japan: Hiroo Kanamori of Caltech, and Keiiti Aki, recently retired from the University of Southern California.

In the early 20th century, seismograph observatories were established at Caltech, the University of California at Berkeley, and other places around the world. The Jesuits were important players; a seismograph station was built at Gonzaga College in Spokane, Washington. Seismology developed primarily as an academic pursuit, with earthquake research intertwined with using earthquake waves to image and explore the internal structure of the Earth. At the time of the 1949 Puget Sound Earthquake, the University of Washington had only one recently hired faculty member in seismology who was in the process of building a seismograph station in the sub-basement of the geology building, using state funds. This young man suddenly found himself in the glare of the public eye, trying to answer questions of what, where, and why.

During the first few decades of the 20th century, one of the most important contributions was made by the U.S. Coast and Geodetic Survey (now the National Geodetic Survey). Several scientists followed up on Professor Harry Reid's elastic rebound theory for the 1906 San Francisco Earthquake on the San Andreas Fault (cf. Chapter 3). The Coast and Geodetic Survey re-surveyed many benchmarks in California and confirmed Reid's observation that the area adjacent to the San Andreas Fault was continuing to build up strain, even as it had done before the earthquake.

For the most part, though, major government funding of earthquake research began only after the Soviets successfully tested nuclear weapons following World War II. This funding did not come about because of any concern about earthquake hazards, but because of the Cold War. The United States and its NATO allies wanted to monitor Soviet (and later, Chinese) underground nuclear tests using seismographs. Using seismograph records, it was possible to distinguish between earthquakes and nuclear explosions and also to determine the size of an underground nuclear test, just as seismologists are able to determine the magnitude of an earthquake.

By the early 1960s, the United States, in cooperation with other Western countries, had established a worldwide seismograph network, called WWSSN, to monitor the testing of nuclear weapons, particularly after the signing of the Nuclear Test Ban Treaty in 1963. One of those seismograph stations was located in Corvallis, Oregon. The WWSSN had a spectacular serendipitous scientific payoff. By allowing the world's earthquakes to be located much more accurately than before, the network provided evidence that these earthquakes followed narrow bands that were found to be the boundaries of great tectonic plates. By 1966, the plate tectonics revolution had overturned the prevailing view of how the Earth works, and seismology, because of the WWSSN, had played a major part.

The U.S. Geological Survey (USGS) began to prepare detailed investigations of major earthquakes starting with an earthquake in Alaska in 1899 and continuing with USGS scientists participating in investigations of the 1906 San Francisco Earthquake and the 1959 Hebgen Lake Earthquake near Yellowstone Park. The USGS played a major role in the study of the great 1964 Alaska Earthquake. In carrying out these studies, the USGS was following in the tradition of the Geological Survey of India, which studied in detail great Himalayan earthquakes in 1897, 1905, and 1934. The USGS's involvement continued and accelerated following earthquakes in California in 1968 and 1971.

The study of earthquakes was, in many respects, a new mission for the USGS. Like all government geological surveys around the world, the USGS had been established in the 19th century to map mineral and fuel resources. For the United States, this meant the exploration of the newly acquired territories of the American West. The USGS was given additional responsibilities with topographic mapping of the United States and study of the country's water resources, both missions related to its goal of understanding and developing natural resources. Geological surveys in the states, including those in Washington, Oregon, and California, also had as their major mission the mapping of natural resources. It is because of this tradition that the California state survey is called the Division of Mines and Geology, the Oregon survey the Department of Geology and Mineral Industries, and the Washington survey the Division of Geology and Earth Resources.

With its focus on earthquakes, as well as on other geologic hazards such as landslides and coastal erosion, a field now called *environmental geology*, the USGS took on a new role of advising the public of safe ways to use the land. This led to the establishment in 1977 of the USGS as the lead agency, together with the National Science Foundation (NSF), in a coordinated federal program to evaluate earthquake hazards.

The National Earthquake Hazard Reduction Program (NEHRP)

Two earthquakes in the mid-1970s strongly affected the decision to increase the involvement of the federal government in earthquake studies. The first was the Haicheng, China, Earthquake

in February 1975, which had been predicted by the Chinese early
enough to reduce greatly the loss of life (see Chapter 7). The second
was an earthquake in August 1975, close to the Oroville Dam, in
the foothills of the Sierra Nevada at the headwaters of the
California Aqueduct. That earthquake, together with large
earthquakes in China in 1961 and India in 1967, both of which
had caused great loss of life, suggested that people can actually
cause earthquakes by manipulating the water level of reservoirs
and by the artificial pumping of fluids down boreholes for waste-
water disposal or for improved recovery of oil. These two
earthquakes finally laid to rest the view that earthquakes are acts
of God in which humans play no role. The general public and,
indeed, many people in the scientific community, came to believe
that earthquakes could be predicted and, by understanding the
fluid pressures accompanying filling of reservoirs and pumping
of fluids into or from wells, they even might be controlled.

This led to the passage of the Earthquake Hazards Reduction
Act of 1977 (Public Law 95-124), which directed President Johnson
to establish a National Earthquake Hazards Reduction Program
(NEHRP, pronounced "Neehurp"). Among the objectives written
into law in P.L. 95-124 were (1) retrofitting existing buildings,
especially critical facilities such as nuclear power plants, dams,
hospitals, schools, public utilities, and high-occupancy buildings,
(2) designing a system for predicting earthquakes and for
identifying, evaluating, and characterizing seismic hazards, (3)
upgrading building codes and developing land-use policies to
consider seismic risk, (4) disseminating warnings of an earthquake,
and organizing emergency services after an earthquake, (5)
educating the public, including state and local officials, about the
earthquake threat, including the identification of locations and
buildings that are particularly susceptible to earthquakes, (6)
focusing existing scientific and engineering knowledge to mitigate
earthquake hazards, and considering the social, economic, legal,
and political implications of earthquake prediction, and (7)
developing basic and applied research leading to a better
understanding of control or modification of earthquakes.

Objective (6) contains a word, *mitigate,* which may be unfamiliar
to many, but which appears so often in public statements as well
as legislation that a definition should be presented here. To
mitigate means to moderate, to make milder or less severe. The
earthquake program thus does not take on the job of *eliminating*
the earthquake threat, but rather that of *moderating* the problem—
an important distinction.

Although the 1977 law included several nonresearch objectives
such as public education and upgrading of building codes, the
legislation was primarily pointed toward research. The bill

authorized new appropriations for two agencies, the USGS and the National Science Foundation, to conduct or to fund earthquake-related research through grants and contracts to universities and other nongovernmental organizations. The legislation did not indicate how the nonresearch objectives were to be implemented. Instead, the president was directed to develop a plan for implementation. Furthermore, the legislation left unclear which agency was in charge.

The president's implementation plan, sent to Congress in 1978, gave much of the responsibility for implementation of Public Law 95-124 to a lead agency, but, as in the law itself, the lead agency was not specified. A multiagency task force was designated to develop design standards for federal projects. In the following year, Executive Order 12148, dated July 20, 1979, designated the newly created Federal Emergency Management Agency (FEMA) as the lead agency. This decision was included in 1980 in the first reauthorization legislation for the earthquake program, Public Law 96-472. This legislation included a fourth agency, the National Bureau of Standards, later to be renamed the National Institute of Standards and Technology (NIST), as an integral, although only a small, part of NEHRP.

NEHRP was reauthorized five more times without significant change in the scope of the program. But by 1990 it was clear that Congress intended to make some changes. During the 1980s, it became apparent that the goal of earthquake prediction was not going to be achieved in the immediate future, as described in Chapter 7. The 1987 Whittier Narrows Earthquake struck Los Angeles, and the 1989 Loma Prieta Earthquake struck the San Francisco Bay area; neither had been predicted. Furthermore, as indicated in the Senate report accompanying the 1990 reauthorization bill, the application of NEHRP research findings to earthquake preparedness was considered slow and inadequate. The efforts of the four agencies were perceived as uncoordinated and unfocused. Finally, the goal of *earthquake control* was criticized as unrealistic and unattainable in the near future.

A mental exercise illustrates the problems facing the goal of earthquake control. An experiment by earthquake scientists in 1969 had shown that small earthquakes in an oil field at Rangely, Colorado, could be turned on and off by increasing the amount of water injected into or withdrawn from the oil field. When water was withdrawn, earthquake activity decreased. The added water pressure along existing faults in the oil field weakened the fault zones and caused them to move, producing earthquakes. As in the case of filling the reservoir behind Oroville Dam, human activity was shown to have an effect on earthquakes.

The suggestion was then made: could this be done on a larger scale at a major fault, where the results could mitigate the earthquake hazard there? Specifically, could it be done for the San Andreas Fault? The idea was simple: drill several very deep boreholes along the thinly populated 1857 rupture zone of the San Andreas Fault in central California and inject water, thereby weakening the fault. The idea was to weaken the fault enough to trigger a smaller earthquake of, say, M 6.5 to M 7 rather than wait for another earthquake as large as the 1857 rupture, which was M 7.9. The smaller earthquake, or series of smaller earthquakes, would cause much less damage than a repeat of the 1857 earthquake.

There are two problems with this idea. First, the cost of drilling the holes for injection of water would be exorbitantly high, many millions of dollars to inject water deep enough to have an influence on the earthquake source 10 miles or more beneath the surface. Second, what would be the legal implications of a triggered earthquake? What is the legal recourse for a person whose home or business is severely damaged in a triggered M 7 earthquake as opposed to the next M 7.9 earthquake which might not have struck during his lifetime? What about the possibility of people being killed during the smaller event? Questions such as these led to the conclusion that earthquake control was not attainable in the near future, at least not by injecting fluids into a major active fault zone.

The 1990 reauthorization bill passed by Congress eliminated some references to earthquake prediction and control, and expanded efforts in public education and in research on lifelines, earthquake insurance, and land-use policy. It marked the beginning of the shift from a predominantly research program toward an implementation and outreach program. The role of FEMA as lead agency was clarified, including presentation of program budgets, reports to Congress, an education program, and block grants to states. New federal buildings were required to have seismic safety regulations, and seismic standards were established for existing federal buildings.

In the 1994 reauthorization, Congress again expressed concern about implementation and about coordination among the four agencies to achieve a unified, focused program. This led to an executive review by the White House Office of Science and Technology Policy (OSTP) and by the Office of Technology Assessment of the U.S. Congress. The OSTP review led to the establishment of the National Earthquake Loss-Reduction Program (NEP), under the leadership of FEMA, with newly formulated goals to be developed in five-year plans by the principal agencies that are officially part of the federal earthquake program. The goals of NEP are to speed up the application of earthquake research to benefit society, to reduce the vulnerability of communities to earthquakes. At the present time, both NEP and NEHRP are both in existence, although it was earlier believed that one would replace the other.

The amount allocated for NEHRP was less than $60 million in FY (Fiscal Year) 1978 and around $100 million in FY 1994. In terms of constant 1978 dollars, the program received less money in 1994 than it did at its startup in 1978. In addition, there was commonly a disparity between the amount *authorized* and the amount actually *appropriated* by Congress. This disparity was greatest in FY 1979 and 1980 and again in FY 1992 and 1993. The effects of individual earthquakes was apparent. The only boost in constant dollars came in 1990 after the Loma Prieta "World Series" Earthquake in the San Francisco Bay Area, and the only time in the past ten years that appropriations were the same as authorization was after the Northridge Earthquake of 1994. On the other hand, the Landers Earthquake, which struck a thinly populated area in the Mojave Desert of California in 1992, had no impact on funding, even though it was larger than either the Loma Prieta Earthquake or the Northridge Earthquake.

The lesson here is that politicians respond to an immediate crisis, but they have short memories for solving the problem in the long haul, particularly after the last earthquake fades into memory. It is again a difference in the perception of time, as discussed in Chapter 1. To an earth scientist, the 1989 and 1994 California earthquakes, or the two 1993 Oregon earthquakes, are part of a continuum, a response to the slow but inexorable movement of tectonic plates. To a public official, and indeed to the public at large, the earthquake is an instant calamity that must be dealt with in the short term, without serious consideration for when and where the next earthquake will strike.

We now consider the role of individual federal agencies, first those officially part of NEHRP, and then other agencies that play an important role in earthquake research but are not an official part of the coordinated NEHRP or NEP programs.

Federal Emergency Management Agency (FEMA)

The Federal Emergency Management Agency (FEMA) has two roles within NEHRP: (1) leadership and coordination of NEHRP, and (2) implementation of mitigation measures. In the early years of its involvement in the program, it served mainly as a coordinator rather than as a leader, resulting in congressional criticism in hearings before the 1990 and 1994 reauthorization bill. By 1994,

FEMA's leadership responsibilities included (1) preparation of NEHRP plans and reports to Congress, (2) assessment of user needs, (3) support of earthquake professional organizations, (4) arranging interagency coordination meetings, (5) support of problem-focused studies, and (6) outreach programs, especially for small businesses.

In its implementation role, FEMA contributes to developing standards in new construction and retrofits, and to applying engineering design knowledge to upgrading building codes. Through its State and Local Hazards Reduction Program, FEMA provides grants to state governments and to multistate consortia to support earthquake hazard mitigation. Usually, a state agency exists with objectives similar to those of FEMA. Hazards include not only earthquakes, but also floods, wildfires, hurricanes, and other disasters. Activities include education, outreach, adoption of building codes, and training exercises. In the Northwest, this is coordinated by the FEMA regional offices in Bothell, Washington, and in San Francisco.

At present, twenty-eight of the forty-three states and territories at some degree of seismic risk participate in this program. FEMA supports the program 100 percent in the first year, but requires 25 percent and 35 percent matches by the states in the second and third years, respectively, and 50 percent matches thereafter. The idea is for state and local government to take over part of the financial responsibility after the first year: if it's worth doing, the federal government should not have to pay for it all. Participation by some states has declined when the 50 percent match year approached, and some states have not participated at all.

FEMA plays the lead role in preparing the federal government for national emergencies. Public Law 93-288 established a Federal Response Plan to coordinate federal assistance in any situation where a presidential disaster declaration is likely to be issued. The Federal Response Plan outlines the responsibilities, chain of command, and sequence of events for federal and local authorities to deal with the emergency. These activities include carrying out training exercises, getting local agencies to agree on emergency response plans, and supporting urban search and rescue teams.

When the president declares an area struck by an earthquake as a disaster area, FEMA swings into action. A coordinating officer is appointed, who sets up a disaster field office to manage the response, including rescue and small loans to businesses or individuals. The disaster field office coordinates response from other federal agencies and the Red Cross. The emergency response team deals with twelve support functions: transportation, communications, public works/engineering, firefighting, information planning, mass care, resource support, health/medical services, urban search and rescue, hazardous materials, food, and energy.

In most cases, the governor of a state requests the president to declare a disaster area, as was done recently in the 1996 floods in the Pacific Northwest; however, the president may do so without the request of the governor. The disaster declaration varies from one disaster to the next. For example, the disaster declaration for Klamath Falls following the 1993 earthquake limited assistance to nonprofit organizations. Klamath County was able to combine FEMA funds with a bond issue to build a new county courthouse to replace the structure severely damaged during the earthquake. So far, in the presidential declarations that have been issued in the last few years, this organization has worked reasonably well. However, the system in the Pacific Northwest has yet to be tested by an emergency of the magnitude of the Northridge Earthquake, let alone a subduction-zone earthquake.

Another FEMA initiative is HAZUS, which uses a software program to map building inventories, soil conditions, known faults, and lifelines to estimate economic losses and casualties from a disaster. The three-county Portland metropolitan area was designated as a test site, and the losses were estimated by the National Institute of Building Sciences from a M 6.5 earthquake on the Portland Hills Fault, which extends along the base of the Portland Hills through downtown Portland. The study was completed in 1997. There is an effort to do this for the nation as a whole, building up from local census tract data. In 1997, Congress appropriated funds for a FEMA program called Building Disaster Resistant Communities, with Seattle selected as one of the seven communities for the pilot project. Rather than a top-down approach, the idea is for individual communities to develop their own plans to reduce their potential losses in any disaster, including hurricanes as well as earthquakes.

U.S. Geological Survey

The USGS receives the largest share of NEHRP funding, more than half in FY 1994. Funds are used to pursue four goals: (1) understanding what happens at the earthquake source, (2) determining the potential for future earthquakes, (3) predicting the effects of earthquakes, and (4) developing applications for earthquake research results. Research ranges from fundamental study of earthquake processes to mapping expected ground motions to proposing building design codes.

More than two-thirds of NEHRP funding is spent internally to support USGS scientists in regional programs, laboratory and field studies, national hazard assessment programs, and the operation of seismic networks, including the Pacific Northwest regional network operated cooperatively with the University of Washington and the Northern California network operated with the University of California at Berkeley. The remainder is spent on grants to outside researchers in universities, consulting firms, and state agencies and partial support of the Southern California Earthquake Center. The external grants program is based on objectives established within the USGS with advice from outside. Grant proposals must address one or more of these objectives, which may change from year to year. The external grants program encourages the best minds in the country, not only those of government scientists, to focus on earthquake hazard mitigation.

Much of the geographic focus has been on California, which received almost one-third of earthquake research funds in FY 1995. But starting in the mid-1980s, the USGS began a series of focused studies in urban areas at seismic risk, starting with the Salt Lake City urban corridor. After the identification of the Pacific Northwest as a seismically hazardous area, the Puget Sound-Portland metropolitan region was selected for a focused program in the late 1980s, a program that is still in progress. The results of this program were summarized in 1996 in U.S. Geological Survey Professional Paper 1560, *Assessing Earthquake Hazards and Reducing Risk in the Pacific Northwest.*

Most of the present understanding of earthquake hazards in the Pacific Northwest has been due to research by USGS scientists directly and by nongovernment scientists funded by the external-grants program. The Pacific Northwest program is managed from a USGS office in Seattle; other USGS scientists working on Northwest problems work out of offices in Vancouver, Washington, Menlo Park, California, Denver, Colorado, and Reston, Virginia.

Although this program has worked amazingly well over the past two decades, it nearly ran off track in 1995-96 as a result of the Contract with America from the new Republican majority in Congress. One of the objectives of the Contract was to eliminate several government agencies, and the USGS was one of those targeted. As the USGS fought for its existence and tried to save the jobs of permanent staff members, the external-grants program of NEHRP suddenly found itself eliminated by a committee in the House of Representatives. The program was finally restored, thanks to assistance from Pacific Northwest senators including Slade Gorton (R., Washington) and Mark Hatfield (R., Oregon), as well as Barbara Boxer (D., California). But before grants could be awarded, the government was temporarily shut down in early 1996, and the Department of the Interior, which includes the USGS, was forced to operate by continuing resolutions of the Congress for most of FY 1996 at significantly lower-than-normal appropriations. The side effects of that political disaster are still being felt. A year of earthquake research was lost.

The USGS provides financial support to the Southern California Earthquake Center and has also assisted in organizing the Cascadia Region Earthquake Workgroup (CREW), an organization discussed more fully in the next chapter. The USGS also operates the National Earthquake Information Center in Golden, Colorado, to locate damaging earthquakes around the world as rapidly and accurately as possible and to collect and distribute seismic information for earthquake research.

National Science Foundation

The National Science Foundation (NSF) receives about one-fourth of NEHRP funding, divided into two areas, administered by two directorates within NSF. The largest amount goes to earthquake engineering, including direct grants to individual investigators. Part of the budget goes to three earthquake-engineering research centers in New York (established in 1986), Illinois, and California (both established in 1997). The new Pacific Earthquake Engineering Research Center will be operated at the University of California at Berkeley, one of the leading institutions in the world for earthquake engineering research.

Part of the budget of the engineering research centers comes from NSF, but an equal amount is expected to come from nonfederal sources. The Buffalo, New York, center has received money from the Federal Highway Administration for research into the seismic vulnerability of the national highway system. Other research includes geotechnical engineering studies of liquefaction, tsunamis, and soil response to earthquakes, and the response of structures to ground motion. A category called earthquake systems integration includes research in the behavioral and social sciences and in planning, including issues of code enforcement and how to decide whether or not to demolish or repair a building.

The directorate of NSF that includes the geosciences funds grants to individual investigators and to three university consortia, the Incorporated Research Institutions for Seismology (IRIS), the Southern California Earthquake Center (which also receives support from the USGS), and the University Navstar Consortium, which provides technical assistance and equipment for geodetic studies of crustal deformation. IRIS (which includes a station in Corvallis, Oregon) is building a global network of state-of-the-art digital seismograph stations. IRIS provides NEHRP with assessments of the frequency of earthquakes worldwide and of their expected ground motion. It is developing a program to deploy seismographs in the field immediately after a large earthquake or volcanic event. The Data Management Center of IRIS is housed in Seattle.

Direct grants from NSF to individual investigators include research into the study of earthquake sources, of active faults and paleoseismology, and of shallow crustal seismicity. In FY 1990, instrument-based studies in seismology and geodesy received the bulk of the funding. In FY 1996, an initiative in active tectonics led to a new relatively modest program which includes investigations in earthquake geology; one study funded under this program is investigating rates of deformation of structures on the Oregon continental shelf and slope.

The Ocean Sciences Directorate in NSF has thus far shown little interest in focused earthquake studies except as piggyback projects attached to oceanographic cruises with other primary objectives. For example, the first of the sea-floor faults that cut across the Cascadia Subduction Zone (Figure 4-1) was discovered in an NSF-sponsored cruise in preparation for a research drilling program off Cascadia in 1992. A set of seismic-reflection profiles, also preparatory to the drilling project, imaged the plate-boundary fault directly, as illustrated in Figure 4-2. The tube worm and clam communities in the vicinity of the Cascadia Subduction Zone, described in Chapter 4, were discovered on a cruise to work out the migration of fluids in subduction zones; those fluids were found to travel along active faults. An earthquake-related proposal funded to Oregon State University in 1993-94 resulted in the discovery of at least nine of these sea-floor faults as far north as offshore central Washington and as far south as southern Oregon (Figure 4-8). Nonetheless, earthquake studies have not ranked high enough in the Ocean Sciences Directorate to permit a significant allocation of ship time.

National Institute of Standards and Technology (NIST)

The National Institute of Standards and Technology (NIST), the old National Bureau of Standards, has received the least amount of funding of the four agencies comprising NEHRP. Its main role has been in applied engineering research and in code development. Its initial budget for earthquake research was less than $500,000 per year and now stands at $1.9 million. In FY 1994, it received a supplemental appropriation to respond to the Northridge Earthquake, resulting in a budget of $3.6 million. The 1990 reauthorization directed NIST to carry out "research and development to improve building codes and standards and practices for structures and lifelines."

National Oceanic and Atmospheric Administration

The agencies discussed in this section are not part of NEHRP and apparently will not be part of NEP. Yet two of these agencies contribute in a major way to earthquake research because of their technological focus on the sea floor (National Oceanic and Atmospheric Administration, NOAA) and in space (National Aeronautics and Space Administration, NASA). There are, of course, frequent informal working relationships between NEHRP agencies and other parts of the federal government, but the lack of formal structure inevitably leads to a lack of focus. Nonetheless, NOAA and NASA have both managed to make critical contributions to an understanding of earthquakes and earthquake hazard mitigation.

NOAA is the principal federal agency responsible for tsunami hazard mitigation (see Chapter 9 and Bernard 1998). Earthquake and tsunami data are distributed through its National Geophysical Data Center in Colorado. NOAA also provides real-time tsunami warnings for the United States and its territories through tsunami warning centers in Alaska and Hawaii (described in Chapter 9). A tsunami inundation mapping center has been established in Newport, Oregon. After a tsunami generated by the 1992 Petrolia Earthquake was detected on the northern California coast, Congress gave NOAA additional funds and responsibilities and established the National Tsunami Hazard Mitigation Program, designed to reduce risks from tsunamis. NOAA is the lead federal agency, with participation by FEMA, USGS, and NSF. Among the objectives of the new initiative are a better understanding of why tsunamis affect some coastal communities more than others, a better warning system, and a better understanding by the general public of the dangers from a tsunami.

In 1997, NOAA deployed two sea-floor pressure sensors, one off Oregon and one off Alaska, to detect tsunamis in the deep ocean where they are undetectable from ships at sea. These sensors provide the most accurate information about a tsunami before it strikes, more accurate than local tide gauges that are influenced by sea-bottom configuration, and more reliable than locating and characterizing an earthquake, which may or may not generate a tsunami. Tsunami warnings based only on earthquakes have led to false alarms.

The U.S. Navy has declassified arrays of hydrophones (called SOSUS) on the sea floor that were used during the Cold War to monitor military ship traffic in the oceans and has allowed them to be used by NOAA. These hydrophones, in addition to recording ship engine noise and whale calls, monitor earthquake waves transmitted directly through water, called *T-phase waves*. These waves permit the location of earthquakes on the sea floor with much higher accuracy and to a much lower magnitude threshold than is possible from land-based seismographs. An example of the success of this program can be seen by examining the seismicity map of the Juan de Fuca Plate in Figure 6-1. This map, depicting earthquakes located by land-based seismographs, shows the earthquakes associated with the Blanco Fracture Zone to lie consistently north of the fracture zone. The SOSUS data show this to be a location error; these earthquakes fall directly on the Blanco Fracture Zone. Furthermore, NOAA has located many times the number of earthquakes in and adjacent to the Juan de Fuca Plate than the land-based seismograph network.

Just as the USGS is responsible for topographic mapping, NOAA is responsible for mapping the topography (or *bathymetry*) of the sea floor using a ship-borne mapping device called SeaBeam. Earlier mapping techniques relied on individual soundings of water depth, followed later by profiles of the sea floor by depth recorders mounted in the hulls of passing ships. SeaBeam and similar techniques developed by the French and Japanese map a swath of sea floor based on the echos of sounds transmitted from several locations mounted in the ship's hull. NOAA swath bathymetry results in topographic maps of the sea bottom comparable in accuracy to topographic maps of dry land constructed by the USGS.

Once thought to be a barren featureless landscape, the sea floor is now known to be marked by canyons, great faults, volcanoes, landslides, and active folds (Figures 4-3, 4-4, and 8-10). Detailed understanding of the sea floor topography has allowed scientists to map directly the Cascadia Subduction Zone and its related faults and folds off the coast of Oregon. These tectonic features of the subduction zone are not altered by erosion to the degree that land structures are.

The SeaBeam topographic maps have in the past been classified by the U.S. Navy. The SeaBeam map of offshore Oregon is available for public use, but the map of offshore Washington is still classified, apparently because of the presence of a submarine base at Bangor, Washington. The arguments for declassifying swath bathymetry and making it available for public use are strong. Detailed bathymetry is necessary for determining which coastal communities are at greatest risk from tsunamis. With SeaBeam, submarine cables and pipelines can be positioned in places where they are least likely to be ruptured by trawlers or by submarine landslides. And, as shown in Oregon, swath bathymetry allows the direct mapping of active faults. Yet, despite the end of the Cold War, the Navy has refused to release its classified SeaBeam bathymetry off Washington to the public.

The bathymetry is recorded digitally so that it can be displayed as a computer model in which the water has been stripped away, as shown in Figures 4-3 and 4-4. (Similarly, the USGS has digitized its land topographic maps permitting a new and revealing perspective on the tectonic forces that produce the topography above sea level, as illustrated in Figure 6-17 and the onshore portion of Figure 8-10.) SeaBeam bathymetry directs submersibles with observers and reomote-controlled robotic vehicles to observe and map faults on the sea floor. An active research program involving submersibles, funded by NOAA's National Undersea Research Program (NURP), has led to new detailed information on the Cascadia Subduction Zone and active faults and folds on the continental shelf.

Because NOAA is not part of NEHRP, programs such as NURP earthquake hazards research and SeaBeam bathymetric mapping are at risk from budget cutters because except for tsunamis, earthquake hazard research is not a primary mission of NOAA.

National Aeronautics and Space Administration

When LANDSAT cameras returned images of the Earth from space several decades ago, it changed our perspective forever. Faults like the San Andreas were viewed in unprecedented clarity and other, previously unknown earthquake-producing structures were also revealed. The Geodynamics Program at NASA was developed to take advantage of the new space platforms as a means to learn about the Earth, including plate tectonics, mineral resources, and an understanding of earthquakes. These activities are now coordinated in a program called Mission to Planet Earth.

More than twenty years ago, it was discovered that faint radio signals from quasars, billions of light years away in outermost space, could be used to detect the relative motion of radio telescopes many thousands of miles apart. By using only a few years of radio-telescope observations of quasar signals, the motion of tectonic plates could be detected directly. It was found that the motion of plates based on geologic data spanning millions of years is at the same rate as that based on only a few years of geodetic data: plate tectonics in real time. The motion of the Pacific Plate with respect to the North American Plate could be measured by comparing the change in position of points on the California coast and in Hawaii with those in Texas and Massachusetts.

The next step was to change the focus of space-based geodesy from plate tectonics to the measurement of crustal strain using satellites providing data at regional rather than intercontinental scale. Since the 1980s, data from a constellation of NAVSTAR satellites orbiting the Earth at an altitude of 12,000 miles has led to a revolution in surveying techniques. Instead of locating a benchmark with respect to another benchmark by line-of-sight land surveying instruments, both benchmarks can be located relative to each other by locking onto NAVSTAR satellites using the *Global Positioning System (GPS)*. Satellite locations are so accurate that during the Gulf War, "smart bombs" could be directed to very precise targets in Iraq. This produced a problem of military classification, because the military was reluctant to allow the general public to locate features to the accuracy possible with GPS. However, in tectonic studies, the important measurement is not the absolute position but the relative change of position of stations over a period of time, and this can be accomplished without compromising the security requirements of the military.

GPS receivers are fairly inexpensive, and a site can be occupied and measured in only a few minutes. Permanent GPS arrays allowing hundreds of measurements between stations are now being constructed in southern California with the cooperation of NASA's Jet Propulsion Laboratory operating as part of the Southern California Earthquake Center. In addition, the Canadians have a permanent GPS network covering southern Vancouver Island, the Straits of Juan de Fuca, and the adjacent mainland of Canada, and a consortium of universities called PANGA is extending this network throughout the Pacific Northwest. These networks are measuring the deformation of the crust to unprecedented detail and in real time. As GPS measurements are collected over the next few decades, some scientists hope to be able to detect anomalous crustal movements before an earthquake strikes.

Space satellites have produced one more surprise for the study of earthquakes: *radar interferometry*. A French team (Massonet 1997) found that by comparing radar images of the same area taken from the same point in space before and after the 1992 Landers Earthquake, the deformation of the crust accompanying the earthquake could be mapped in unprecedented detail. Other earthquakes have been studied in the same way by the French and by a group at the Jet Propulsion Lab in Pasadena, California.

Other Federal Agencies

Earthquake research by other non-NEHRP agencies principally involves the earthquake safety of those critical facilities that are their responsibility. The Nuclear Regulatory Commission (NRC) has sponsored research into earthquake hazards related to the safety of nuclear power plants. With nuclear plants at Trojan at

St. Helens, Oregon (since deactivated) and an unsuccessful effort
to build a plant east of Aberdeen, Washington, as well as plants at
Hanford, the NRC took a strong interest in evaluating the
earthquake hazard in the Pacific Northwest as early as the 1970s.
The Department of Energy (DOE) has also taken an interest in the
earthquake safety of nuclear power plants as well as sites for nuclear
waste disposal, including those formerly planned for Hanford.
Surprisingly, the early DOE work did not focus on active faults
and folds at Hanford, but the present planned site at Yucca
Mountain, Nevada, has been evaluated for its earthquake potential
in great detail.

Dams are critical facilities as well, and this has resulted in
research by the Army Corps of Engineers and the Bureau of
Reclamation of the Department of Interior. These agencies,
together with the Veterans Administration, have been responsible
for installing instruments to measure strong ground motion. The
Department of Defense has funded investigations through the
Office of Naval Research and the Air Force Office of Scientific
Research, which provides some support for IRIS and other seismic
monitoring for nuclear test ban compliance.

Role of the Canadian Government

Canada does not have an equivalent of NEHRP, possibly because
Canada has never experienced an earthquake with the losses of
Northridge, Loma Prieta, or even the 1906 San Francisco
Earthquake. However, individual Canadian agencies are actively
involved in earthquake research and in planning for natural
disasters.

Earthquake research is centered in the Geological Survey of
Canada (GSC), with offices in Ottawa and at the Pacific Geoscience
Centre in Sidney, on Vancouver Island. Coincidentally, both
centers are located in seismically active areas, although southwest
British Columbia is clearly the most seismically hazardous part of
Canada. The GSC maintains a state-of-the-art seismic network as
well as a geodetic network tracking the deformation of the crust
in southwest British Columbia. Geological studies have lagged
behind, principally because no active fault has ever been found
in British Columbia, despite an extensive search. However, the
Canadians have studied their own marsh deposits on Vancouver
Island that subsided during subduction-zone earthquakes.

There are Canadian equivalents of NSF (Research Council of
Canada) and FEMA (Emergency Preparedness Canada), but in
general, earthquake activities are more decentralized than in the
United States, requiring more leadership by the Province of British
Columbia.

Getting the Word Out to the Public

Scientists and engineers in the NEHRP program and in other federal agencies have made great advances in the understanding of earthquakes and of how to strengthen our society against future earthquakes. But how well has NEHRP succeeded in getting its research results out to society at large? Educating the public was one of the objectives of the original Earthquake Hazards Reduction Act of 1977, and this objective has been stated many times since, particularly at the prodding of Congress. Yet the public, twenty years later, is still poorly informed about earthquakes. Why?

Many government scientists and their supervisors believe that their job is done when their research results are published in a government document such as USGS Professional Paper 1560, discussed earlier in this chapter, which focused on earthquake hazards of the Pacific Northwest. But the publications branch of USGS is underfunded and inefficient. Professional Paper 1560 was not published until several years after the research was completed, and even then, only part of it was published. Because the papers represent the official position of a federal agency, they had to be approved not only by other scientists but also by USGS management.

But most people have never heard of Professional Paper 1560, even that part of it that has been published. It must be ordered from a list of government publications, and that list is not easy for the nonpractitioner to find. And if you are successful in finding the list and purchasing the publication, you discover that it is written for other scientists and engineers, not for the general public. The papers are full of technical jargon, and a background in earthquake science is necessary to understand fully the results. Many USGS scientists, frustrated by bureaucratic delays in their own publications branch, publish their results in scientific journals. Non-USGS scientists do the same. This fulfills the scientist's professional obligation, but still does not inform the public.

As an example of this problem, consider Diann Walker, the hazard coordinator in 1991 for the Klamath Falls Chapter of the American Red Cross. As part of her job, Walker wanted some information about earthquakes, even though Klamath Falls had never suffered damage from an earthquake. She contacted the USGS, whose Public Information Office referred her to its authority, George Walker, who had supervised the preparation of a geologic map of Oregon but who was not a specialist on earthquakes. After many phone calls, the request came down to Dave Sherrod of the Cascade Volcano Observatory in Vancouver, Washington. Sherrod had been mapping the Klamath Falls region, including a set of active faults (some of which were described in Chapter 6).

Sherrod sent Walker some materials, but he recognized that the government publications were written for other scientists and would be of little use to her. Even the general-interest publications of the USGS, although well written, do not cover enough background material to allow people like Walker to take full advantage of USGS results in carrying out their own responsibilities. So Sherrod offered to help by giving a public presentation, at no expense to the Red Cross.

Before going to Klamath Falls, Sherrod turned to Steve Brantley, public information officer at the USGS Vancouver office, who expressed interest in participating if the workshop could be expanded by the Red Cross to involve the Oregon State Police, city and county fire departments, National Guard staff from nearby Kingsley Field, public works managers from the city and county, and others who needed to know about emergency response. The workshop was held in early 1993.

It was a great success, mainly because Diann Walker was persistent, and the Red Cross, being local, was able to organize the workshop and involve the community in a meaningful way. Six months later, Klamath Falls was struck by two large earthquakes, as described in Chapter 6. The contacts were already in place for USGS people to return the month following the earthquakes and again four months later, when the people of Klamath Falls were trying to cope with the hundreds of aftershocks that continued to rattle the area.

Two things coincided: a local official willing to do the detective work necessary to find government scientists who could shed light on the earthquake hazard, and USGS scientists who were willing to take time from their own projects to educate the public.

In general, though, the public is educated not by government documents, regardless of how well they are written, but by the broadcast and print media. A television reporter is interested in a breaking news story, like an earthquake, not in public education. When a large earthquake strikes, my telephone rings off the hook for a day or a week, depending on how the story develops. Earthquake scientists, including myself, prefer to go about their lives unbothered by microphones or television cameras. During an earthquake, however, we get our fifteen minutes (or twenty-four hours) of fame, and any public education message has to be threaded into our response to the news story. That message often ends up on the cutting-room floor.

Since Klamath Falls, the USGS has held press conferences on its initiatives involving earthquakes, generally in coordination with state agencies. In addition, the USGS has participated actively in public hearings, such as those held by the Oregon Building Codes Division to consider upgrading the Oregon coast to Seismic Zone 4 (see following chapter).

In the long run, the best way to get the word out is in the classroom, starting in elementary schools, where children are fascinated by earthquakes and volcanoes, just as they are by dinosaurs. Earthquakes and volcanoes are generally included in courses in earth science in high school, but these courses are not required and often are not even recommended in high school. Many high schools lack a teacher qualified or interested in teaching an earth science course that would include a unit on earthquakes.

Summary and a Word about the Future

NEHRP, and more recently NASA's Mission to Planet Earth and NOAA's Tsunami Initiative, are mission-oriented, applied programs, not basic research programs. In the words of Sen. Barbara Mikulski (D., Maryland), this is strategic rather than curiosity-driven research. And yet NEHRP has been responsible for fundamental discoveries not only about earthquakes but about how the earth deforms and behaves through time. Not only this, but NEHRP has led to world leadership in earthquake science for the United States since its beginning in the 1970s. Most of what has been presented in this book is the result of federally funded research. The program in the U. S. is the best in the world, even though it has not yet been able to weave an understanding of earthquake science and engineering into the fabric of society.

But the leadership of the U.S. is now being challenged by the Japanese. The cost of the 1995 Kobe Earthquake was ten times that of the Northridge Earthquake, and an additional cost was to the confidence of the Japanese in coping with the earthquake peril. Accordingly, the Japanese government has ratcheted up its budget for earthquake hazards research to a much higher level than the American program, or that of any other country, possibly because so much of their country is at great risk from earthquakes. The U.S. responded to the Northridge Earthquake with a one-year special appropriation with no long-range followup, but instead, an attempt by the Republican Congress in 1995 to dissolve the USGS, the principal agency responsible for earthquake research. Perhaps this is because earthquakes are still perceived as a California problem, despite the fact that earthquakes have caused great damage in places like Missouri, South Carolina, Alaska, Hawaii, Tennessee, and Massachusetts, in addition to Pacific Northwest states. Most people, if asked to list the things they would like the federal government to do, would not list earthquakes in the top ten, unless they live in an area that was recently struck by an earthquake. Because of this prevailing public attitude, leadership in earthquake studies may return to where it was at the beginning of the 20th century, to Japan.

Suggestions for Further Reading

Bernard, E.N. 1998. Program aims to reduce impact of tsunamis on Pacific states. *EOS, Transactions American Geophysical Union*, vol. 79, pp. 258, 262-63.

Hanks, T.C. 1985. The National Earthquake Hazards Reduction Program—Scientific Status. U.S. Geological Survey Bull. 1659, 40p.

Office of Technology Assessment, Congress of the United States. 1995. Reducing earthquake losses. Washington, D.C.: Government Printing Office, OTA-ETI-623, 162p.

Page, R.A., D.M. Boore, R.C. Bucknam, and W.R. Thatcher. 1992. Goals, opportunities, and priorities for the USGS Earthquake Hazard Reduction Program. U.S. Geological Survey Circular 1079, 60p.

U.S. Geological Survey. 1996. USGS Response to an Urban Earthquake Northridge '94. U.S. Geological Survey Open-File Report 96-263, 78p.

∽ 14 ∽
The Role of State and Local Government

Quakex 94

10:35 a.m., Wednesday, April 13. It was a beautiful spring morning. Children were at school, people were at work, cars were on the highways. A normal day, except for one difference: at that moment, an earthquake of M 8.5 ruptured the Cascadia Subduction Zone off the coast of Oregon.

No one would forget where he or she was when the strong shaking began. Each person dealt with the earthquake as a one-on-one unequal encounter as buildings collapsed, bricks showered sidewalks, bridges tilted crazily and sank into their support structures, and school gymnasium roofs collapsed onto students in gym class. And the shaking went on—and on, as if it would never stop. Some buildings survived the first back-and-forth, and the next, and the next, but finally, after three-quarters of a minute, storefronts began to fall into the street, and apartment buildings dropped into their carports, shrinking by one story. Finally, after 70 seconds, it was over, and a vast region of southwest Washington and western Oregon lay in ruins and chaos.

Suddenly, the power was out. Lockout alarms shut down Bonneville Power transformers at Tillamook, Toledo, Wendson, Tahkenitch, and Reedsport. Portland Gas and Electric alarms were tripped at McLoughlin and Gresham. Ninety percent of communications, power, and water went out in Lane County, although Eugene fared a little better, losing only 60 percent. The Marion County Dispatch Center was immediately overloaded with calls and could not be reached.

By 10:36, as strong shaking came to an end, major buildings began to come apart. City Hall collapsed in Dallas, with major destruction in the downtown historical district. At Independence, the bridge to Salem fell into the Willamette River, and the elementary school collapsed, trapping or killing children and teachers in their classrooms. The Monmouth City Hall and Police Department brick building disintegrated into a mass of rubble, and major failures and collapses occurred in the downtown business district and historical section. In Marion County, there were landslides on Highway 22 near Detroit Dam and Mill City and failures of the Highway 22 overpasses at Cordon Road and Lancaster Drive. The large plate glass windows of the County Health Department shattered, and the gym wall at Monitor Elementary school fell in. People knew only of the damage and casualties at the place where they happened to be at that moment, due to failed communications.

At Tualatin, the I-205-65th Street overpass and the I-5-Nyberg Road overpass collapsed; parts of five cars were visible under the rubble at the Nyberg Road intersection. There was major damage at the Council Building, with liquefaction at its southwest corner, causing the building to tilt. One person sustained liquid plastic burns at Bonar Plastics; other companies were also experiencing hazardous waste spills and trying to cope with them on their own.

At Oregon State University, the north section of Snell Hall disintegrated, and the Pharmacy Building suffered major damage. The roof in the Womens Building fell into the swimming pool, and the glass front of the Electrical Computer Engineering Building shattered, injuring seven students arriving early for an eleven o'clock class. All power was off in Albany and Corvallis. Fire Station No. 1 in Corvallis was put out of action, and Station No. 2 suffered moderate structural damage. A building crumpled at 5th and Van Buren, trapping people inside. The facade and ceilings of the Benton Hotel on Fourth and Monroe partially fell in, causing injuries. The Harrison Street Bridge across the Willamette suffered major damage, and the Van Buren Street Bridge dropped into the Willamette River. The railroad tracks between Jefferson and Jackson streets shifted sideways 14 inches, derailing an engine and eleven cars. The 19th-century Benton County Courthouse suffered severe damage, jamming doors and cracking exterior walls.

10:45 a.m. There was an aftershock of M 5.7. The water tower at Aumsville fell on the police station, causing major damage. The Woodburn High School gym wall and locker room were shaken down, trapping about two dozen students under the debris. The gym ceiling and the front portion of Silverton High School fell, burying many students in the rubble. A brick wall at the fire station fell on an engine at the same time that a building down the street was reported on fire.

10:46 a.m. The first preliminary report on the earthquake was made available, but could be heard by most people only on portable radios or car radios. The University of Washington gave a preliminary location offshore, and a tsunami warning was issued. It was now apparent that many high schools, elementary schools, county courthouses, and city halls had suffered massive damage and major casualties. Many freeway overpasses were down, but some were still functioning. Most highways across the Coast Range and Cascades were blocked by landslides, including I-84 in the Columbia Gorge. There was flooding east of Dayton due to a sudden shift in the channel of the Willamette River. The phones came back on at Woodburn at 10:47. At Gervais, fires broke out, but there was no water pressure in the mains to fight the fires. At Dayton, engines were trapped inside the damaged fire station and could not respond to fire calls. A two-million-gallon reservoir for the Silverton water plant failed, and the Franzen Reservoir in Marion County was damaged.

10:55 a.m. The first tsunami wave reached Coos Bay; one minute later, it reached Florence with a maximum wave height of 23.3 feet, and two minutes later, it reached Mapleton and Yachats with a wave height of 24 feet. The tsunami reached Astoria at 11:05. Land along the coast at Florence had already dropped up to one foot as far as a quarter of a mile inland, adding to the area inundated by the tsunami. The second tsunami wave reached Coos Bay at 11:30 and reached Astoria at 11:40. At 12:06, the third tsunami crested at Oceanside at 21.8 feet and at Netarts at 25.7 feet. The fourth tsunami crested at Netarts at 18.8 feet at 12:56.

You hadn't heard about this earthquake? It "occurred" in 1994, the year following the two earthquakes at Scotts Mills and Klamath Falls, as part of a statewide exercise sponsored by Oregon Emergency Management to see how federal, state, and local agencies would react to a major earthquake. The dimensions of the disaster were as realistic as scientists could make them, and the effects on buildings, utilities, transportation arteries, and people were based on preliminary assessments of specific structures, public and private.

Quakex-94 was a twelve-day disaster exercise involving more than two hundred federal, state, county, city, volunteer, and private industry organizations to enable them to test their individual emergency response plans. Some agencies participated for the entire twelve days; others for only a small part of that time. Those agencies participating were able to test the effectiveness of interagency coordination, cooperation, and communication during a large-scale simulated disaster. The destruction visited on each community was built into the scenario based on realistic assumptions of risk, to see how each agency would respond. Each jurisdiction tested an Emergency Operations Plan which outlined the roles and responsibilities of agencies and individuals during the emergency.

There were three distinct phases of Quakex-94. The first phase, the first part of which was described above, simulated the first seventy-two hours of the disaster. During this time, local public utilities had to respond to repair outages, local government responded to medical emergencies and threatening situations such as fire, dam failure, building collapses with people inside, flooding, tsunamis, hazardous waste spills, and coastal subsidence. Government began collecting information about the extent of the disaster, dispatching assistance as needed.

The second phase was a continuation of the first, with an emphasis on collecting initial damage assessments from local and state agencies. In a real disaster situation, this assessment would be used to advise the governor about declaring a state disaster area and to provide factual backup for a request to the president to declare a national disaster area, thereby bringing in federal assistance.

The third and final phase simulated the recovery after a disaster. With the help of the Federal Emergency Management Agency (FEMA), a damage assessment was conducted in the areas heavily impacted by the earthquake. The assumption was made that Oregon would receive a presidential Major Disaster Declaration, allowing federal and state agencies to work together, processing disaster assistance applications from individuals as well as businesses and local government. After the exercise, there was an after-action report to determine whether the objectives set out for each participating organization had been met.

In the section that follows, the major state agencies in Oregon that deal with earthquake hazards are described. Oregon is used as an example, although some mention is made of the role of Washington, California, and British Columbia. Other states have more or less the same system, with California's earthquake response system the best developed.

Oregon Office of Emergency Management

The Oregon Office of Emergency Managament (OEM), part of the Oregon State Police, is highlighted as an example of how disasters are handled at the state level. In Washington, the equivalent agency is the Washington State Emergency Management Office; in California, it's the Office of Emergency Services; and in British Columbia, it's the Provincial Emergency Program.

In 1972, the Oregon Emergency Response System was established by the governor, the first of its kind in the United States. It is managed by OEM as the primary point of contact for state notification of an emergency or disaster. Operations assigned to OEM include the statewide 9-1-1 emergency number, search and rescue, and a state Emergency Coordination Center. This center is activated during a disaster to provide information, direction, and coordination during the disaster, and to provide liaison with the FEMA regional office in Bothell, Washington.

The governing legislation for OEM is ORS 401, which establishes rules for coordination with local government. Each county in Oregon is required to have an emergency operations plan, an emergency operations center, and an emergency program manager. Some counties also have a citizens' emergency management council, involving the community. Although not required, cities may also have an emergency management program, and three in Oregon do so. There is also an earthquake coordinator for Portland Metro, which includes Portland and satellite cities making up the Portland metropolitan area.

The Emergency Coordination Center (ECC) is located at OEM headquarters in Salem and consists of twenty-two state agencies. When a disaster happens, the ECC is the primary contact with the governor and legislature as well as local jurisdictions.

OEM conducts training exercises such as Quakex-94. Another training exercise was planned for 1996, but the February floods in the Willamette Valley allowed OEM to deal with the real thing. The agency provides planning and technical assistance to local governments, and assists with public education, including hazard identification and analysis. It serves as the primary state contact with FEMA and the Federal Response Plan, described in the previous chapter.

OEM responds to a disaster if the city or county fails to act responsibly, if the disaster involves two or more counties, or if a major disaster is imminent or strikes a large area in the state. For Quakex-94, it was obvious that a disaster would be declared, so everybody swung into action. The priorities are to save lives and protect public health and safety, provide basic life-support needs, and to protect emergency-response equipment, in that order. Of lower priority is the protection of public and private buildings. In a nutshell: *lives first, buildings later*.

Seven presidential disaster declarations have been issued for Oregon during this decade: three floods (1990, 1995, 1996), one windstorm (1995), the El Niño and drought of 1994 (which included a salmon-related economic disaster), and the two earthquakes in 1993. Thus OEM is getting plenty of practice in real emergencies, preparing it for a future earthquake much larger than the two that occurred in 1993, including planning for an earthquake on the Cascadia Subduction Zone.

Pending legislation: Oregon requires each county to have an emergency management system to respond to a declaration of a state of emergency. Although all would agree that this is an important thing to have, it represents, at least in part, an unfunded mandate. It is an expression of the propensity of legislatures to pass worthy legislation (*authorization*) without providing the money to carry it out at the local level (*appropriation*).

In 1997, a bill was introduced in Salem to allocate money to create a disaster reserve trust fund, to be administered by OEM, not to exceed $30 million. Money would also be allocated to create and run the emergency management programs of the state and eligible jurisdictions to provide, among other things, statewide uniformity in an operation that requires close coordination for it to work in an emergency. Finally, money would be used as grants, to be awarded competitively to local jurisdictions or nonprofit organizations to implement hazard mitigation projects. Funds for this bill would come from the state lottery, from a tax on insurers against hazards including earthquakes, and from the general fund. With the financial restrictions facing the state legislature in 1997, this bill did not pass.

In November 1996, British Columbia held its third earthquake response exercise in its Thunderbird Series in the Greater Victoria area, responding to an imaginary M 6.9 earthquake 15 miles from downtown Victoria. The main purpose was to train provincial response coordinators, with a secondary goal of evaluating a local community college as a coordinating and communications center in the event of an earthquake.

Building Codes Division

The starting point for building codes is the Uniform Building Code (UBC), published and updated by the International Conference of Building Officials, which has as its objective "to provide minimum standards to safeguard life or limb, health, property, and public welfare while regulating and controlling design and construction." Priority is given to protecting the inhabitants of a building over the prevention of damage to the building itself. Building codes represent minimum standards; the owner may well choose to have higher standards than those required by the code. In Oregon, the UBC is adopted and amended as the Oregon Structural Specialty Code.

In Oregon, the agency responsible for building codes, the Building Codes Division, is part of the new Department of Consumer and Business Services, established in 1993. The agency operates under ORS Chapter 455, and its objective is that the building code system should protect the life, health, and safety of the citizens of Oregon. As stated earlier, lives first, property second.

In California, building codes began to take seismic resistance into consideration after the 1906 San Francisco Earthquake, although these codes carefully avoided reference to earthquakes because it was perceived as being bad for business as San Francisco rebuilt. (The disaster was later referred to as the "San Francisco

Fire.") After the 1933 Long Beach Earthquake, the state legislature passed the Field and Riley acts to require that schools and other public buildings meet certain seismic resistance standards. Later, these standards were applied to bridges, hospitals, and dams. Subsequent upgrades to the building codes, generally triggered by large earthquakes such as the 1971 San Fernando and 1989 Loma Prieta events, have resulted in the highest earthquake-resistant building standards in the United States.

The first Oregon Structural Specialty Code, including the assignment of Oregon to Seismic Zone 2, was established in 1974, based on the 1973 edition of the Uniform Building Code with Oregon amendments. Before that time, earthquake shaking was not taken into consideration in regulating building construction. ORS Chapter 455 regulates how the building code is enforced. If a city chooses to enforce the code, it is empowered to do so. If not, the county may elect to enforce the code. If neither the city nor the county takes responsibility, the state Building Codes Division is charged with enforcement. In general, local government has taken on code enforcement in the Willamette Valley, whereas enforcement responsibility on the coast and east of the Cascades has, for the most part, been left to the state. Each year, local government must decide whether or not to enforce the code and to declare any change in their role by January 1, to take effect the following July. Smaller counties that cannot afford full-time building-code officials may contract with private engineering firms for plan review and inspection.

In 1988, after a consensus was reached among scientists that Oregon faced a major earthquake hazard (as described in the Introduction), the International Conference of Building Officials upgraded the Oregon Structural Specialty Code to Seismic Zone 2B. After the 1989 Loma Prieta Earthquake, proposals for further revisions were made to the Building Codes Division Advisory Board. The board recommended a public hearing at which scientists, including myself, testified about the earthquake hazard to Oregon, and structural engineers, most notably Roger McGarrigle of Portland, testified about the need for stronger building codes. Based on this hearing, changes were proposed under the leadership of Walter Friday, then a structural engineer with the Building Codes Divison. A recommendation was made by the Board to the Building Codes Division Administrator, and the codes were changed. In 1993, western Oregon was upgraded to Seismic Zone 3; interestingly enough, this upgrade included Klamath County east of the Cascades prior to the Klamath Falls Earthquake later that year. Figure 14-1 shows the increase in seismic resistance to earthquakes required by the Structural Specialty Code over time. In the following year, Seattle and most of southwest

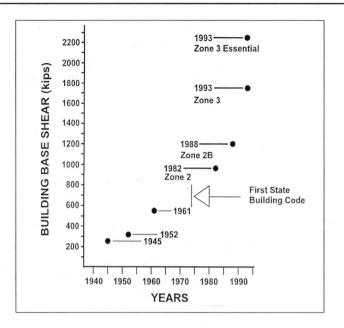

Figure 14-1. Change in building codes in Oregon since 1945 for a typical mid-rise building with respect to seismic base shear force (horizontal) measured in kips (1 kip = 1,000 pounds per square inch). With this diagram and the age of the building, it can be determined how much shear resistance was allowable in the building when it was constructed. The higher rating for "Zone 3 Essential" is for critical facilities. From Grant Davis, KPFF Consulting Engineers, courtesy of Franz Rad, Portland State University.

Washington followed Oregon's lead and upgraded building codes to Seismic Zone 3.

Two cautions should be made about building codes. The first tradeoff is cost. Upgrading seismic resistance may add up to 5 percent of the cost of a new building, and for retrofitting, the percentage increase is higher. For a new building, the revised codes set the standard, and the owner must decide whether to exceed these standards or not. For a retrofit, the decision is more difficult, because of the added cost to a business, or the added cost to taxpayers if a public building is retrofitted. Without better insight into earthquake forecasting than is now available, the decision is a gamble.

The second caution is that upgrading the building code does not automatically make the area safe against earthquakes. New buildings will meet the standard, as will major remodels of buildings. But old buildings that are not remodeled will continue in the building inventory, and when these are unreinforced masonry (URM), they are potential time bombs. The greatest loss of life in the 1971 Sylmar Earthquake was in those buildings at the Veterans Administration Hospital that had not been retrofitted after the 1933 Long Beach Earthquake. Oregon has numerous school buildings, city halls, public-housing projects, retirement homes, churches, dams, and bridges that have not been upgraded. Destruction to unreinforced masonry buildings in Molalla (Figure 14-2) and Klamath Falls (book cover) were the result. So the 1993 seismic upgrade will not become fully effective until well into the next millenium.

*Figure 14-2.
Damage to
Molalla High
School, a URM
building, from the
Scotts Mills
Earthquake of
1993. Bricks from
the URM gable
over the doorway
fell on the steps
and sidewalk.
Fortunately, the
earthquake
occurred early in
the morning, and
no students were
in the building.
Photo courtesy of
Yumei Wang,
Oregon
Department of
Geology and
Mineral Industries.*

Following the 1993 seismic upgrade of building codes, the Oregon legislature, through Senate Bill 1057, established a Seismic Rehabilitation Task Force in 1995 to provide recommendations about how to eliminate those structures that are earthquake hazards. At the same time, the City of Portland, through its Bureau of Buildings, established its own task force to consider the seismic strengthening of existing buildings.

The state task force recommended that all unreinforced masonry (URM) buildings be rehabilitated within seventy years, with the more dangerous within thirty years, following a statewide inventory of buildings by the year 2004 to be conducted by the Building Codes Division. Mandatory strengthening would be required for appendages outside a building such as parapets and signs that could fall on people below during an earthquake. Essential and hazardous URM buildings would be repaired by the year 2019. Essential buildings would include fire and police stations and emergency communications centers. Hazardous facilities would include structures housing hazardous or toxic materials that could be released during an earthquake. A program for rehabilitating hospitals was also proposed.

Other buildings would be rehabilitated based on *passive triggers*: actions within the control of the owner that would require the building to be strengthened. These triggers would include (1) changes in use that would increase the risk to occupants, (2) renovations that are substantial relative to the value of the building, and (3) renovations or additions that could potentially weaken the existing structure.

To encourage and facilitate the strengthening of buildings, a state tax credit equal to 35 percent of the investment for seismic rehabilitation retroactive to the year western Oregon was upgraded to Seismic Zone 3, and a local property tax abatement equal to 35 percent of the seismic rehabilitation cost were proposed.

Implementation of the program would be assigned to the Department of Geology and Mineral Industries (DOGAMI).

These recommendations were incorporated into House Bill 2139, introduced in the 1997 legislative session. However, this bill failed to pass.

An opinion survey was conducted among four hundred Portland residents. When asked to rank earthquakes among several social and environmental concerns, earthquakes were ranked relatively high, behind crime and violence, cancer, motor vehicle accidents, and fire. However, none of the categories was listed as "high risk." Respondents were also asked to rank on a scale of 1 to 10 (1 = no money should be spent to strengthen the facility, 10 = it is absolutely essential to strengthen the facility) their priority ratings for strengthening key buildings and infrastructure facilities. Hospitals, buildings for storing hazardous wastes, emergency communications buildings, bridges and overpasses, and schools received ratings above 8.

The insurance industry has established a system to grade the effectiveness of building codes, considering the quality of inspection and plan review as well as construction standards. A high score may lead to discounts on insurance premiums for new construction, similar to discounts based on fire insurance grading systems.

The International Code Council is now hard at work developing the 2000 International Building Code, which will take into consideration the largest-magnitude earthquake expected for a region, a more precise use of shaking criteria, and a use of contour maps developed by the USGS to quantify the seismic hazard.

Grading Ordinances and Regulation of Building Sites

Building codes deal with the safety of buildings, but how about the site on which the building is constructed? A good example of a poor building site is the Leaning Tower of Pisa. The tower itself is in good shape, but the soils beneath the building are unable to hold it up, and it is settling differentially, causing it to lean.

A perfectly sound building is unsafe if it is built on an old landslide, or on a sea cliff subject to wave erosion, or on soils subject to liquefaction, or on an active fault. As part of its responsibility for public safety, a city or county may take responsibility for evaluation of the safety of a building site, just as it takes responsibility for the structural integrity of a building. Ordinances passed for this purpose are called *grading ordinances*. Grading—which is one of the first steps in virtually any building project—may include excavation by a bulldozer or backhoe or it may involve placement of fill material to provide a flat surface for building. In either case, the natural landscape is altered, and regulation is required to ensure that the alteration of the landscape will not harm residents of other sites, particularly those downhill, in addition to the potential residents or workers in buildings on the site in question.

Grading ordinances call into question the fundamental right of individuals to do with their land what they want. This differs from building codes, which may require a more expensive structure to be built for safety reasons, but would not prevent some sort of structure from being built on a site. It is difficult for a landowner to accept the fact that the property may contain hidden geologic fatal flaws such as active faults or landslides that could prevent it from being developed. A site with a beautiful view over a steep hillslope should not be developed if the steep hillslope providing the view is the scarp of an active fault or a landslide.

In 1952, the City of Los Angeles adopted the first grading ordinance in the United States and set up a grading section within the Department of Building and Safety. The city was growing out of the lowlands and up into the surrounding hills, and building sites there were found to be subject to major landslides, with extensive property losses. In 1963, the grading ordinance was upgraded to require both engineering and geologic reports to be submitted, and to require that grading operations be supervised by both a *soils engineer* and an *engineering geologist*. Although responsibilities overlap, the soils engineer or geotechnical engineer deals directly with the strength and bearing capacity of earth materials on which a structure is to be built and on the propensity of a hillslope to slide, and an engineering geologist takes more account of the past geologic history of a building site, including old landslides, evidence of faulting, and the inclination of bedding and fracturing of rock formations on site.

The standard reference for grading was Chapter 70 of the Uniform Building Code, which is written in the form of an ordinance which can be modified to fit the situation in the city or county where it is adopted. The 1997 edition of the code places the Grading Code in Chapter A-33. The local building official decides which sites pose a potential threat to life and public safety, requiring an evaluation of the site and supervision of grading. For commercial developments, Chapter A-33 makes provision for both a report by geotechnical and geological consultants employed by the developer and a review of the findings by soils engineers and geologists employed by the city or county for that purpose. The cost of plan review, like the cost of building inspection, is borne by the developer in the form of permit fees. A plan reviewer may ask questions such as: Is provision for drainage off the property adequate so that other property owners are not affected? Are cut slopes gentle enough that they would not be expected to fail by landsliding? Is the bearing strength of the soil sufficient to hold up the building? Do potentially active faults cross the property (this is covered by Chapter 16 of the Code)?

California then passed an addition to its Health and Safety Code that required that all cities and counties adopt the UBC Grading Code or its equivalent. Unfortunately, many cities and counties lack the professional expertise to regulate grading effectively. In addition, implementation of the Grading Code in some communities has been opposed by developers and building contractors, as well as some politically well-connected landowners. However, where the Grading Code has been used, including review by consultants for the city or county, losses related to geologic conditions have dropped by 90 to 95 percent. The law works!

Accompanying the increase in standards for grading is an increase in the number of lawsuits. If a development is approved, but a landslide subsequently destroys homes on the property, the landowner, the contractor, the engineering and geological firm, the city or county approving the plans, even the bank lending the money for the development may be sued. Were any of the parties negligent in approving the development? As the standards of practice are raised, so, then, are the conditions under which someone could be found negligent.

Oregon and Washington are far behind California in establishing grading ordinances. The ones that exist are largely in the metropolitan areas of Portland and Seattle. Some cities require engineering and geologic reports subject to city review, more do not. This may change after the floods of February and December 1996, when many homes, including some worth hundreds of thousands of dollars, were destroyed by active landslides. According to Scott Burns of Portland State University, the Portland, Oregon, metropolitan area suffered more than seven hundred landslides, resulting in seventeen houses being red-tagged (meaning that they would have to be demolished) and sixty-four houses yellow-tagged (meaning that the occupants could not return until certain repairs had been made). In most cases, these landslides could have been identified by a geologist prior to the development. This has led to a flurry of lawsuits including some against cities and counties. The plaintiff, who may have lost his million-dollar home to a landslide, argues that the city *should have known* that the site was unsafe, since establishing that fact is standard practice in other parts of the country. Many cities are (or should be) watching these lawsuits with interest and perhaps trepidation.

In 1990, the state of Washington passed its Growth Management Act to require comprehensive planning in its most rapidly growing counties and cities. This act required these cities and counties to designate and protect critical areas subject to geological hazards, including landsliding and seismic hazards. In 1991, the act was broadened to require the designation of critical areas in all Washington's cities and counties. The dampening effect this law has had on rapid development around metropolitan areas has led to attempts to amend it in the legislature, and even to repeal it outright.

A problem faced in the Northwest is the difference between what can be done—"state of the art"—and what is the standard level of practice in the area. Clearly the standard level of practice is much higher in the Los Angeles and San Francisco metropolitan regions than it is for Oregon or Washington, although the "state of the art" is the same in all those areas. For example, it is quite straightforward to evaluate a building site for liquefaction and ground-shaking potential, and Chapter 16 of the Uniform Building Code presents sample ordinances to do this. But it is not standard practice for most of the Pacific Northwest, and it is not carried out, despite the existence of maps of metropolitan Portland, Salem, and Victoria that point to areas of potential hazard from liquefaction, ground shaking, and earthquake-induced landsliding.

Jim Slosson, an engineering-geology consultant and former state geologist of California, is the source of what has come to be called Slosson's Law, a corollary to Parkinson's Law: *The quality of professional work will sink to the lowest level that government will accept.* This applies to building codes as well as grading ordinances.

Identification of Zones of Active Faulting

After the 1906 San Francisco Earthquake, ground rupture was recognized along the San Andreas Fault, which led to its being mapped from northern California to the Salton Sea in southeastern California. Other active faults were also mapped. Some, like the Hayward and Calaveras faults in the east San Francisco Bay area, extend through cities and towns, commonly under individual houses and commercial buildings. The 1971 earthquake in Sylmar, a suburb of Los Angeles, was accompanied by surface rupture that caused considerable damage to structures, and the problem was taken up by the California legislature.

The result was the Alquist-Priolo Act of 1972, which directed the California state geologist to identify faults that are sufficiently active and well defined to require regulatory zoning (Hart and Bryant 1997). This led to identification of many active faults throughout the state as Alquist-Priolo Special Studies Zones, including several in northern California adjacent to the Cascadia Subduction Zone. The criteria for inclusion were relatively restrictive, including paleoseismologic evidence that the fault had ruptured during the Holocene (past ten thousand years). But many faults were not zoned, even though geologists considered them to be active. Hard evidence was required.

In northern California, the Mad River and Little Salmon fault zones are sufficiently well defined that they can be zoned under the Alquist-Priolo Act. Even though these faults have not ruptured in historical earthquakes, paleoseismic evidence from backhoe trenches shows that they have ruptured during the Holocene (Figure 6-26).

The philosophy of Alquist-Priolo was *mitigation by avoidance*, that is, do not place certain types of structures within zones of active faulting as defined by the state. The California Seismic Mapping Act of 1990, in addition, addressed the hazards of strong ground motion, liquefaction, landslides, and other hazards caused by earthquakes. Preliminary seismic hazard maps were issued for the Los Angeles region, comparable to those issued for Portland and Salem. In contrast to the Alquist-Priolo philosophy of mitigation by avoidance, the Seismic Mapping Act allows for *mitigation by engineering design.*

After passage of the Seismic Mappng Act, it became clear that certain types of active geologic structures were not covered by Alquist-Priolo, because they were not sufficiently well defined, yet they constituted a major hazard. Principal among these were *fold scarps* above blind faults, characterized by local steepening of bedding dips and intensity of ground fracturing, but not by a throughgoing surface fault. Regulations now being considered in California would requre special studies for such zones, but would permit structures in these zones to be specially designed to withstand deformation during an earthquake.

At present, there are no comparable laws governing the Pacific Northwest north of California. But west of the Cascades, most mapped faults—including the Seattle Fault and those faults mapped in the Willamette Valley, including the Mount Angel Fault that was the probable source of the 1993 Scotts Mills Earthquake— could not be characterized as "sufficiently active and well defined" to be zoned under Alquist-Priolo or even under the Seismic Hazards Mapping Act. No active faults with demonstrated Holocene rupture have been found in onshore southwestern British Columbia. However, some faults cutting Pleistocene marine terraces along the coast are being investigated for evidence for Holocene displacement. In addition, active faults with Holocene displacement have been mapped in the back country of eastern Oregon. Faults in Bend, Klamath Falls, and La Grande could be zoned under a law like Alquist-Priolo, but evidence of Holocene activity on these faults has not yet been demonstrated.

Those provisions of California's Seismic Hazards Mapping Act dealing with liquefaction, strong ground motion, and earthquake-induced landslides could be useful in the Pacific Northwest. Low-lying areas around Portland, Tacoma, Seattle, and Vancouver could be severely damaged by strong ground shaking and liquefaction. And as Pacific Northwest cities spread out into the hills, earthquake-triggered landsliding (as well as landsliding accompanying heavy rains) will become an increasingly important concern. Northwest cities are growing at the rate that southern California cities grew three decades ago. Rapid urbanization led to protective legislation in California; it may lead to legislation in Washington and Oregon as well. Washington's Growth Management Act marks the first step.

Chapter 16 of the Uniform Building Code contains sample regulations that cover geotechnical tests for liquefaction and ground shaking that should be considered by all cities.

Department of Geology and Mineral Industries (DOGAMI)

This agency has undergone a dramatic shift in its mission in the past ten years. In earlier years, it focused on the search for and the regulation of the extraction of natural resources, including sand and gravel, groundwater, minerals, and fuels. Geologic hazards were also considered to some extent in reports issued by the agency.

With the recognition of an earthquake hazard in the late 1980s, the legislature in 1989 passed Senate Bill 955, which directed DOGAMI to improve the state's understanding of earthquakes and other geologic hazards and to use this knowledge to reduce the loss of life and property due to these hazards. DOGAMI's responsibilities are established by several statutes, starting with ORS 516 with administrative rules, in which the agency is the state repository of information about geologic hazards, including earthquakes. DOGAMI conducts research programs in coordination with the federal government, other state agencies, local government, and universities, commonly with federal grants rather than state funding. It is the lead agency in coordinating the issuance of permits for facilities for metal mining and chemical leach mining. It also archives all site-specific seismic reports for critical and essential facilities in Oregon.

As described in Chapter 8, DOGAMI has produced earthquake hazard maps of the Portland and Salem metropolitan areas, in which these areas are divided into zones of increasing earthquake hazard based on ground shaking, liquefaction, and potential for landsliding. Plans are underway to construct similar maps for other metropolitan areas. One use of these maps is to superimpose a building inventory on the earthquake zones, as the Portland Bureau of Buildings has done. This highlights the unreinforced masonry buildings that lie in the highest earthquake hazard zone and assists in establishing retrofit priorities. These maps are suitable for the application of Chapter 16 of the Uniform Building Code to regulate construction on ground subjected to these earthquake hazards.

Senate Bill 379, passed by the Oregon legislature in 1995 and implemented as ORS 455.446 and 455.447, restricts the construction of critical facilities and special-occupancy structures in tsunami flooding zones. In response, George Priest of DOGAMI, in cooperation with scientists outside the agency, constructed tsunami runup maps for the entire Oregon coast. These maps take into consideration the range of sizes of the next earthquake on the Cascadia Subduction Zone as well as a detailed understanding of the configuration of the sea floor, which focuses tsunami waves as they approach the coast. In addition, DOGAMI has done a detailed tsunami study of the Siletz Bay area of Lincoln City and is engaged in detailed studies at Newport and Seaside. A tsunami inundation map of Newport, prepared by DOGAMI, NOAA, and the Oregon Graduate Institute of Science and Technology, is shown as Figure 9-8.

Other duties of the agency include serving as the lead technical agency in the Oregon Emergency Response Plan, the installation of strong-motion accelerographs in new buildings, the review of plans for dams and power plants, and participation in the Oregon Seismic Safety Policy Advisory Commission (OSSPAC). This commission was established by executive order in 1990 by Governor Neil Goldschmidt after the Loma Prieta Earthquake and then confirmed by Senate Bill 96 in 1991.

Assignment of responsibilities to DOGAMI has not always been accompanied by sufficient state funds to do the job. The National Earthquake Hazards Reduction Program, through its focus on the Puget Sound-Portland metropolitan area, provided grants for research in earthquake hazards to both DOGAMI and the Washington Division of Geology and Earth Resources, and this was supplemented by individual grants to scientists within DOGAMI and in universities. FEMA and NOAA have also been sources of money. Federal funds made it possible to hire an earthquake geologist, Ian Madin, who served as a highly visible point man for informing the public about earthquake hazards in

Oregon. More recently, the state has allocated funds to DOGAMI to carry out its earthquake-related mission, although, as stated above in another context, appropriation still lags behind authorization.

Oregon has established regulations for the seismic safety of buildings to protect lives. If a local jurisdiction chooses not to administer building codes, the state does so. Is the same protection available regarding the stability of a building site to ground shaking, liquefaction, or landsliding? As discussed above, the answer is yes for most of California, but no for most of Oregon and Washington, unless special ordinances are in place. If you purchase a house that lies on an unstable site such as a landslide or an active fault, no inspection to protect you is required by the state that is comparable to the building code. One county in Oregon specifically disengaged itself from any responsibility for site stability because of its fear of lawsuits. DOGAMI has a responsibility to map and describe geologic hazards such as landsliding, but in most cases the potential homeowner is not made aware of these findings, and in any event, the DOGAMI maps refer to a general region and are not site specific.

Lawsuits are claiming that a landslide was triggered because of alteration of a site upslope by paving or the construction of buildings, causing water to run off rather than sink into the ground, or because an upslope owner diverted water onto a downslope property that was damaged. In most cases, state and

Figure 14-3. Map showing most recent faults in Oregon, adjacent states, and the offshore region. Solid line: faults with demonstrated movement in the last 20,000 years; irregular solid line at left margin marks Cascadia Subduction Zone. Dashed line: faults with demonstrated movement in last 780,000 years. Dotted line: faults with movement in last 1,600,000 years. Faults shown in dashed and dotted lines could be active, but this has not been demonstrated on geological evidence. From Geomatrix Consultants (1995) and Department of Geology and Mineral Industries.

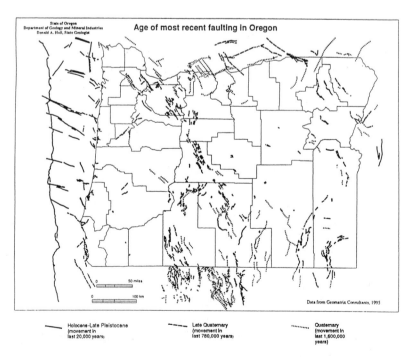

local governments are staying out of these lawsuits, except to provide general information for planning purposes and the maintenance of public safety. However, the availability of ordinances regulating hillside development almost certainly will result in local governments being named as codefendants in future lawsuits.

Senate Bill 198 was introduced in the 1997 Oregon legislature to require a seller to disclose any unsafe condition prior to sale of a property. Sample questions, to which the seller would be required to answer "yes" or "no," are: "To your knowledge, is the property or any portion of it within a designated hazard area or zone, including floodway, floodplain, landslide or slump area, groundwater or drainage hazard area, erosion-hazard area, dune-hazard area, or earthquake-related hazard area?" "To your knowledge, is the property . . . subject to special zoning or other land use requirements for development that are related to the hazards listed [above]?" If the seller is not aware of geologic hazards (note the phrase "to your knowledge"), he/she simply answers, "No." Or the seller will simply state that the property is being sold "as is,—with all defects, if any." Senate Bill 198 would not have offered much protection, but it would have been better than what the citizens of Oregon have now! But like other legislation related to earthquakes or geologic hazards, the 1997 legislature failed to pass this consumer-protection bill.

In contrast, the state of California requires property owners to disclose the fact that a property is in a seismic hazard zone or an Alquist-Priolo fault zone. Effective March 1, 1998, the law requires disclosure when one of two conditions are met: (1) the seller has actual knowledge that the property is within a seismic hazard zone, or (2) a map that includes the property has been provided to the city and county by the state geologist, and a notice has been posted at the offices of the county recorder, county assessor, and county planning agency.

The British Columbia Geological Survey is engaged in an earthquake hazard mapping project, focused in urban areas where rapid growth of population is expected. A pilot project was done in the small town of Chilliwack, east of Vancouver, and a map of the Capital Regional District, including Victoria, has just been completed.

State Universities

It is widely perceived that the Oregon University System (OUS) has a legislated responsibility in earthquake hazards reduction. But it has none. Oregon citizens are fortunate in that the three major state universities, Oregon State University, University of Oregon, and Portland State University, have hired faculty members with expertise in earthquake geology, seismology, or earthquake engineering. The work that they do in earthquake science is nearly all funded by the federal government, as described in the previous chapter, and in small part by state and local government. Faculty members have testified as private citizens to the state legislature and other commissions about earthquake hazards as part of their public service obligation, but not as representatives of OUS.

On the other hand, universities have been given the responsibility, through federal funding, to operate regional seismic networks. These include the Pacific Northwest Network operated by the University of Washington and the Northern California Network, which includes part of southern Oregon, operated by the University of California at Berkeley.

Regional Organizations

The Western States Seismic Policy Council (WSSPC) is established as a partnership of emergency managers and state geoscience organizations to work on earthquake hazard mitigation, earthquake preparedness, emergency response, and recovery. It includes all the mountainous western states, Alaska, Hawaii, and Pacific island territories. Federal agencies that are part of WSSPC include the Department of Transportation, FEMA, NOAA, and USGS.

WSSPC is very much involved in training and technology transfer, in getting the message out to the general public. It holds an annual conference, collects publications on earthquake matters produced by its member organizations, and helps find money to work on earthquake research.

Another working group in the Pacific Northwest is the Cascadia Region Earthquake Workgroup (CREW), focused on mitigation against a Cascadia Subduction Zone earthquake. CREW includes representatives from FEMA, state and provincial emergency services agencies, the scientific community represented by USGS, universities, and state and provincial geological surveys, and private industry. The involvement of the private sector may be the most important hallmark of CREW. In addition to the expected concerns about loss of life and property, industries in the Pacific

Northwest are concerned about loss of market share in the event of a catastrophic earthquake. An example of the loss of market share is provided by the Port of Kobe, Japan, which became inoperable after the 1995 Kobe earthquake. As a result, other ports in Japan took over the business that had previously gone to Kobe. It is unclear at present if the Port of Kobe has regained its pre-earthquake level of business.

A Final Word

The recent earthquakes in California and Oregon have led to an increased involvement in earthquake preparedness at the federal and state level, and much of this can be attributed to the success of NEHRP through USGS and FEMA. However, these programs suffer from the short interest span of the general public and government officials about earthquake hazards. For example, DOGAMI is making a concerted effort to publicize the tsunami hazard on the Oregon coast, including all-weather signs describing what happens in a tsunami, publications for schools, even tsunami bookmarks. But most people remain unaware of tsunami hazards and continue to build in low-lying areas. Many coastal counties and cities express little or no interest.

The public suddenly becomes concerned about earthquakes when one strikes. Media attention is intense for a few days, then the interest dies down, and the public turns its attention to other things. Gradually, largely through FEMA and local emergency management agencies, more people are becoming involved in earthquake hazard mitigation. Individuals like Diane Merten of Corvallis, concerned about the large number of children in Oregon educated in unreinforced masonry school buildings, are taking leadership roles in involving more people in advocacy roles to reduce the danger from earthquakes.

Everybody wants to survive an earthquake and not suffer losses. But there is a price: increased taxes to retrofit unreinforced masonry school buildings and courthouses, increased consumer costs as businesses retrofit commercial buildings, more government control over how land with geologic hazards should be developed. Society has met similar challenges in the past to mitigate hazards from asbestos in buildings and from hazardous waste disposal. The earthquake hazard is less obvious, particularly when it is not known that an earthquake will occur in the lifetime of a structure, or of its owner. My own hope is for education in the schools. If children in grade school and high school learn about the danger from earthquakes, they will go home and tell their parents.

Suggestions for Further Reading

California Division of Mines and Geology. 1997. Guidelines for evaluating and mitigating seismic hazards in California. Calif. Div. Mines and Geology Spec. Pub. 117.

International Conference of Building Officials. 1997. 1997 Uniform Building Code in 3 volumes, available in hard copy or CD-ROM. Whittier, CA: ICBO, web page www.icbo.org

Jochim, C.L., W.P. Rogers, J.O. Truby, R.L. Wold, Jr., G. Weber, and S.P. Brown. 1988. Colorado landslide hazard mitigation plan. Colorado Geological Survey Bull. 48, 149p.

Oregon Structural Specialty Code, coordinated with the 1994 Uniform Building Code, available through ICBO, Whittier, CA, web page www.icbo.org

Scullin, C.M. Excavation and grading code administration, inspection, and enforcement (available through ICBO, Whittier, CA, web page www.icbo.org).

Mader, G. G., et al. 1988. Geology and planning: The Portola Valley experience. Portola Valley, CA: Spangle, W., and Associates, Inc., 75p.

∽ 15 ∽

Preparing for the Next Earthquake

"Five minutes before the party is not the time to learn to dance."
   Snoopy, 1982.

Introduction

W e are in denial about earthquakes. During the past ten years, scientists have reached a consensus that great earthquakes have struck the Pacific Northwest, and more will arrive in the future. Government has responded by upgrading building codes and establishing an infrastructure of emergency services down to the county level. Media reports take it as a given that there will be future damaging earthquakes. Yet if the average person were to list the ten top concerns in his or her daily life, earthquakes would probably not make the list.

In terms of public perception, earthquakes may not be all that different from other disasters such as floods or forest fires. Television reports showed new expensive homes in Keizer, Oregon, flooded out in February 1996, but when the waters rose again in November, only nine months later, people from Keizer were quoted on television as expressing great astonishment and dismay when more new houses, or even some of the same ones, were flooded again. Forest fires swept through rural subdivisions east of the Cascades, but after the fires were put out, more homes were built in the forest with the same potential for destruction in a future fire. Nobody seems to learn anything.

I am reminded of the story about the sheep grazing at the edge of a field. A wolf comes out of the forest, grabs a sheep, and carries it off. The other sheep scatter and bleat for a few minutes, then return to their grazing. The forest is still there, and the wolf will come back, but the sheep graze on. So it is with earthquakes. The Scotts Mills Earthquake struck, a flurry of excitement followed, and newspaper editorials referred to the earthquake as a wake-up call (see the *Oregonian* cartoon at the beginning of the book). Then the earthquake dropped out of the news, and we settled back into our lives and forgot about it.

It is in light of such public apathy that this chapter is written. You will be asked to organize your household, then your neighborhood, and then your children's schools, but your efforts may result in your being compared to Chicken Little, warning that the sky is falling. If you're serious, you must be determined and patient and have a thick skin. It won't be easy.

Getting Your Home Ready

Chapter 11 focused on steps you can take to make your home and its contents more resistant to earthquake damage. This chapter presents ways you can prepare yourself and members of your family to survive an earthquake and to help others survive as well. It is analogous to the fire drills we have to take in school or aboard an ocean-going ship. We are pretty sure that our school or the ship will not catch fire, but we have the fire drills all the same. Fire drills are built into our culture. By law, earthquake drills are conducted in schools in some states, but they generally are not taken seriously, even by the school officials who conduct them.

Several things could happen to your house in an earthquake. Seismic shaking could cause a chimney to collapse, plate-glass windows to break , tall pieces of furniture to fall over, or a garage to cave in. Liquefaction or landsliding beneath your foundation could cause your house to move downslope, breaking up as it does so, and snapping underground utility lines. Here the recent landslides in Portland and southwest Oregon give us a clue as to what's in store. If severe flooding results in dozens of landslides, a M 7 earthquake could result in thousands of landslides, with some more than a mile across. If you live on the coast, your house may be in danger of a tsunami, in which case you have twenty-five minutes or less to get to high ground, above the tsunami run-up line.

Some of the steps outlined here are not unique to earthquakes. They would apply if you were marooned by a flood or a landslide that cut off access to your house. But a large earthquake (a Northridge rather than a Scotts Mills Earthquake) is unique in the large number of people impacted. The 9-1-1 emergency number would be overwhelmed and essentially useless. You may lose your phone service, electric power, water, sewer, and gas for days or even weeks. Police and ambulance services would be diverted to the most serious problems like collapsed apartment buildings or major fires. Access to your house or from your house to the nearest hospital could be cut off by a damaged bridge or a major landslide.

For these reasons, you should be prepared to survive without assistance or any public utilities (gas, water, sewer, electric power, or phone service) for up to three days. If you are at work, or your children are at school when the earthquake strikes, you should have a plan in place outlining what each member of the family should do. Designate a contact person *outside the potential disaster area* that everyone should contact if your family is separated.

Earthquake Preparedness Kit

Designate a kitchen cabinet or part of a hall closet in your house as the location of an earthquake preparedness kit. Everyone should know where it is and what's in it. It should be easy to reach in a damaged house. (The crawl space in your basement is not a good place, especially if you have not reinforced your cripple wall.) The kitchen is a good place, and so is an unused and cleaned-out garbage can in your garage, unless the garage collapses due to "soft-story" problems. Many of the items listed below are handy in an*y* emergency, not just an earthquake.

First-aid kit, fully equipped, including an instruction manual. Check expiration dates of medicines and replace when necessary. Liquids and glass bottles should be sealed in zip-lock storage bags. Keep your previous prescription glasses here; your prescription may have changed, but the glasses will do in an emergency.

Flashlights, one per person, preferably with alkaline batteries. Replace batteries every year. Keep extra batteries in the package they came in until ready for use. Several large *candles* for each room, together with matches. *Coleman lantern*, with an extra can of gas for it.

Portable radio with spare batteries. If the power is off, this will be your only source of information about what's going on. Your portable phone won't work if your phone service is cut off. Your *cell phone* may work, but heavy usage may make it hard to get through.

Food, in large part what you would take on a camping trip. Granola bars, unsalted nuts, trail mix, lots of canned goods (fish, fruit, juice, chili, beef stew, beans, spaghetti). Dried fruit, peanut butter, honey (in plastic containers, not glass), powdered or canned milk. We're talking about survival, not gourmet dining, but try to stock with food your family likes. Keep a manual can opener and other cooking and eating utensils separate from those you use every day. If you lose power, eat the food in your freezer first. It will keep for several days if the freezer door is kept shut as much as possible.

Fire extinguishers. Keep one in the bedroom, one in the kitchen, and one in the garage. Attach them firmly to wall studs so that they don't shake off. Keep a bucket of sand near your fireplace during the winter, when the fireplace is in frequent use.

Drinking water. You'll need one gallon per person per day for at least three days; more is better. Large plastic containers can be filled with water and stored; change the water once a year. $2^1/_2$-gallon containers are available, but one-gallon containers are easier to carry. Your water heater and toilet tank are water sources, but if the water heater is not strapped, and it falls over, its glass lining may break, requiring the water to be filtered through a cloth. Empty the water heater by turning off the heater (remove its fuse or shut off its circuit breaker) and its hot-water source, then turn on a hot water faucet and fill containers. Water purification will be necessary. Do not use toilet tank water if the water has been chemically treated to keep the bowl clean (turns blue after flushing). Swimming pool or hot tub water is okay for washing but not for drinking.

Turn off your house water supply at the street to prevent sewage from backing up into your house water system. Also plug bathtub and sink drains.

If you are a backpacker, you already know about hand-operated water pumps, filters, and purifying tablets. A system called FirstNeed is commonly available at outdoor stores. Iodine purifying tablets make the water taste terrible, but you can add other tablets to neutralize the taste. Store these with your preparedness kit, and use them if there is any doubt about the water, including water from the water heater or toilet tank. You can also use liquid bleach in a plastic container, but do *not* use *granular* bleach!

Tools. Keep a hammer, axe, screwdriver, pliers, crowbar, shovel, and Swiss army knife in your kit, along with work gloves and duct tape. You can purchase a special wrench to turn off your gas at the source. Keep this at the gas valve, and make sure everyone knows where it is and how to use it. If you smell gas, turn your gas supply off imm*ediately*; the pilot light on your furnace would be enough to catch your house on fire. Don't turn it on again yourself; let a professional do it. Similarly, keep a wrench at the water meter to shut off your water at the source.

If your water is shut off, you won't be able to use the bathroom. Use your shovel to dig a hole in your yard for a temporary latrine. Line the hole with a large plastic garbage bag; alternatively, sprinkle with lime after each use (purchase the lime from a hardware store). If you are able to get to your bathroom, you could line the toilet with a small garbage bag, use the toilet, and dispose of the bag.

Camping gear. Keep tents, sleeping bags, tarps, mattresses, ponchos, Coleman stoves and lanterns, and gas to supply them together so that they are as accessible as your preparedness kit. Picnic plates and cups, plastic spoons, paper napkins, and paper towels should be in your kit.

Other items. Large, zip-lock plastic bags, large and intermediate size garbage bags with twist ties, toothbrushes and toothpaste, soap, shampoo, face cloths, towels, dish pan and pot, toilet paper, sanitary napkins, shaving items (your electric razor won't work), baby needs.

Kits for elsewhere. Under your bed, keep a day pack with a flashlight, shoes, work gloves, glasses, car and house keys, and clothes to put on in an emergency. Keep another day pack, along with a fire extinguisher, in the trunk of your car, and, if you work in an isolated area, at your workplace.

Other Preparations

After a major earthquake, civil authorities will inspect your neighborhood to see if there is damage, and they may determine that your house is dangerous to live in. This is due to fear that the structure might collapse with you inside. If your house is labeled with a *red tag*, you will not be permitted to live in it, and the house will have to be torn down. If your house is labeled with a *yellow tag*, you will be ordered to leave, and will not be allowed to return until the necessary repairs are made, and it is determined that your house is safe to live in. Accordingly, you should have ready those items you need if you are forced to leave your home for an extended period of time.

It's nice to have a first-aid kit, but make sure that you and your family know how to use it. Take a first aid course and a CPR class (lots of reasons to do this, not just earthquake preparedness). You may be called on to help your neighbor, and access to a hospital may be blocked.

Neighborhood Plan

Many neighborhoods already have a neighborhood watch plan for security. Arrange a meeting once a year to discuss your contingency plans in case of an earthquake. Are some of your neighbors handicapped or elderly? Are there small children? Do some of your neighbors have special skills? Here the advantages of having a plumber, carpenter, nurse, or doctor for a neighbor become apparent. Do each of you know where your neighbors' gas shut-off valves are located? Be prepared to pool your resources.

You can make lifelong friends during a major calamity. Your county emergency services coordinator, police department, and Red Cross office will be glad to help you get organized—it's their job.

Benton County, Oregon, through the leadership of a concerned citizen, Diane Merten of Corvallis, has organized an emergency management council which brings people in emergency services, law enforcement, and fire protection together with civic and school leaders to plan for a disaster. Public involvement raises the priority for disaster preparedness among local officials. A website address is provided for additional information on setting up similar councils elsewhere in the Pacific Northwest.

Your Child's School and Other Buildings You Use

When you head for the principal's office or the school board meeting, be prepared to be called Chicken Little. Our schools have many problems: too few teachers, controversies over curriculum, and too little money. When you say "earthquake" and point to an unreinforced masonry building like Molalla Union High School, severely damaged by the 1993 Scotts Mills Earthquake, the response may be "Yes, but what can we do?"

But there are steps your school can take that cost little or no money, only time. Work through the PTA to ensure that the school has its own earthquake-preparedness supplies, an evacuation plan, and earthquake drills. Earthquake drills are required by law in Oregon, but school officials commonly do not take them seriously. Ask questions about the specifics of staff training and responsibilities. What is the school's plan to release children (or to house them in the school building) after an earthquake?

Even if there is no money to replace that unreinforced masonry time bomb, you could ask the school board to reinforce the building enough that students would survive the earthquake, even if the building did not. In your petition, there is strength in numbers. If you are the only petitioner, you are not likely to be taken seriously. But if you are organized and can get the PTA on your side, you have a fighting chance. But safety comes with a price tag. Are you willing to vote for and campaign for a bond issue to make your schools more resistant to earthquakes? Some areas have taken the initiative, including Portland, with a multimillion-dollar plan to retrofit unsafe school buildings.

A few years ago, I learned that Oregon State University had been selected for a model study of its physical plant to bring it up to modern standards. I was astonished to learn that the San Francisco engineering firm doing the study was not authorized to consider seismic hazards in its study, even though it was qualified to do so. Fortunately, OSU had recently hired Tom Miller, a specialist in earthquake engineering. He had his engineering class do a preliminary examination of the physical plant. The students found that nearly half the buildings would fare badly during a large earthquake. These include the administration building, several dormitories, and the lift-slab building housing my office in the Department of Geosciences. You don't solve the problem by changing to another state university campus. Other campuses are in at least as bad shape, but the risk is more poorly known.

Earthquakes seem to pick on universities. The 1989 Loma Prieta Earthquake caused more than $160 million in damage to Stanford University, including the building housing the Department of Geology. The university had previously been damaged severely by the 1906 San Francisco Earthquake; at that time it was a relatively new campus. The 1994 Northridge Earthquake trashed the physical plant of California State University at Northridge, again including the Department of Geology, which was still in temporary quarters two years later.

Oregon State University will get a start on retrofitting dangerous buildings with a grant from FEMA to restore Weatherford Hall, a historic but hazardous building that had been closed because of a lack of funds to repair it.

Let's pray that the earthquake doesn't strike on Sunday morning. Most Pacific Northwest cities have large church buildings constructed of unreinforced masonry. In most cases, the churches do not have earthquake insurance, nor do they have the money to bring their buildings up to code.

And how about those historic courthouses, built in the 19th century? Lovely to look at, but dangerous to work in. The Klamath County Courthouse was rendered useless after the 1993 earthquake. And the State Capitol building in Salem was damaged in the Scotts Mills Earthquake, as noted in Chapter 6, and visitors were not permitted to enter the rotunda due to the possibility of falling masonry.

During the Earthquake

The strong shaking *will* stop. For a M6 to M7 earthquake, strong shaking will last less than a minute, and in most cases less than thirty seconds, but it may seem the longest minute of your life. A subduction-zone earthquake may produce strong shaking of one to three minutes, but it, too, will stop.

The earthquake mantra is *duck, cover, and hold. Duck* under something such as a table or desk, and *cover* your face and neck with your arms. *Hold* on until the shaking stops. Teach this to your children, and make it part of your own family earthquake drill.

The greatest danger is something collapsing on you. So get under a big desk or table. Stay away from windows, chimneys, or tall pieces of furniture such as a refrigerator or china cabinet. Standing in a doorway is not a good option, unless you happen to live in an adobe house in a third-world country. The doorway may be in a wall that is not braced against shear, and both wall and doorway may collapse. Do not run outside, because you may be hit by debris or glass falling from the building. Remember Bill Given, the bartender at the Busy Bee Restaurant in Seattle, who saved lives by keeping frightened patrons from the front door during the 1949 Puget Sound earthquake, as described in Chapter 5? Had people been allowed to go out to the sidewalk, they would have been buried by tons of falling bricks.

If you can't get under something, sit or lie down with your feet and hands against a wall. Turn away from glass windows or mirrors. Don't try to hold or pick up your dog or cat; the animal will be so confused that for the first time in its life, it may bite you. Stay where you are until the strong shaking stops. If a vase is about to topple from a table, don't try to catch it.

Should you be at a stadium or theater, cover your head with your coat and stay where you are. Do not rush to the exits. The behavior of the California crowd when the Loma Prieta Earthquake struck at the beginning of the World Series game in October 1989 was exemplary. There was no panic, and people did not trample over others trying to get out of the ball park. There were no injuries. The important thing to remember is that there is no reason to leave. After the shaking stops, there will be plenty of time to leave.

At work, get away from tall heavy furniture, or get under your desk. The fire sprinklers may come on. Stand against an inside wall. If you are in a tall building, do not try to use the elevator. If the lights go out, just stay where you are.

If you are in a wheelchair, lock your wheels and stay where you are. If you are out in the open, move only if you are close to a building where debris may fall on you.

Should you be outside in a business district with tall buildings, get as far away as you can from buildings, where plate glass may shatter, and masonry parapets may come crashing down on you. Stay away from tall trees. Watch for downed power lines.

If you are in your vehicle (with seat belt fastened), pull over to the side of the road. Do not stop under an overpass or on a bridge. Look for places where sections of roadway may have dropped, as the Highway 18 bridge across the Yamhill River at Dayton did during the Scotts Mills Earthquake, catching driver Ricky Bowers by surprise. If wires fall on your car, stay in your car, roll up the windows, and wait for someone to help you. You may be waiting a long time, but the alternative, electrocution, makes the wait a safer if more boring choice.

After the Earthquake

Look for fires in your own home and the homes of your neighbors. Look out for downed power lines. Has anyone has been injured? Is your house damaged enough to require it to be evacuated? Consider your chimney as a threat to your life until you have assured yourself that it is undamaged. Check for gas leaks, and if you smell gas, turn off the main gas valve to your house, which will extinguish all your pilot lights.

In case of a fire, try to put it out with your fire extinguisher or your bucket of sand. The most likely place for a fire is your woodstove if it has turned over. You have a few minutes to put the fire out; if the fire gets away from you, evacuate everybody from the house.

An earthquake may cause electric and telephone lines to snap. Even if you have lost power to your house, do not touch any downed power lines.

This is not the time to get in your car and try to drive around town looking at the damage. Roads will be clogged, making life tough for emergency vehicles. Stay where you are, and turn on your portable radio. You will be given status reports and told what to do and what not to do. If you are told to evacuate your neighborhood, do so. You will be told where to go. Do not decide on your own that you can tough it out where you are. Lock your house, unless it is too damaged to do so, to protect against looters.

Aftershocks or a Foreshock?

The 1949 and 1965 Puget Sound earthquakes were "slab" earthquakes that originated in the Juan de Fuca Plate. They had almost no aftershocks. A big shake and that was it. But crustal earthquakes and subduction-zone earthquakes have many aftershocks, and they will cause a lot of alarm. In a large earthquake, aftershocks will continue for months and even years after the main event. Many of these will be felt, and some can cause damage to already weakened buildings. This is one of the reasons you may be asked to leave your house. It may be still standing after the main earthquake, but it might not survive a large aftershock. Warn your family members that there will be aftershocks.

However, there is always the possibility that the earthquake you just experienced may be a foreshock to an even larger one. The great 1857 Earthquake on the San Andreas Fault of M 7.9 was preceded by a foreshock of about M 6 at Parkfield. The Chinese have based their successful earthquake predictions on foreshocks, in some cases many foreshocks. Normal-fault earthquakes, occurring in crustal regions that are being extended or pulled apart, such as the Basin and Range of southeastern Oregon, are more likely to have foreshocks. The 1993 Klamath Falls Earthquake had a small foreshock, but there was too little instrumentation and too little experience for anyone to take action on it. It was only identified after the earthquake.

Special Problems with Tsunamis

If you live on the coast, you will have the problems everybody else has with shaking and unstable ground. But you will have an additional problem, the threat of inundation from a large wave from the ocean.

In the case of a distant tsunami, such as the one that originated in Alaska and struck the Pacific Northwest coast in 1964, a warning will be issued by the tsunami warning service in Alaska. You will have hours to evacuate to high ground. It is critical that you have a portable radio turned on to listen for evidence of a tsunami. Most of the people at the coast who got into trouble in the Easter weekend tsunami of 1964 were just enjoying a normal spring holiday, without enough concern for events in the rest of the world to keep up with the news. With satellite communication and tsunami warning systems throughout much of the Pacific, the warning of a distant tsunami should be reliable, but you have to have your radio on to hear it. A coastal community should have a siren to warn those that aren't listening to their radio or watching television.

In the case of an earthquake on the Cascadia Subduction Zone, or on an offshore structure such as the Stonewall Bank Blind Fault, you will have a much shorter time to react, twenty minutes or less. For this reason, if your area is subjected to very strong shaking, don't wait for a tsunami warning. Leave immediately for high ground and stay there until you are told you can return home.

There is no direct correlation between tsunami height and magnitude of the earthquake. A subduction-zone earthquake off the Pacific coast of Nicaragua on September 2, 1992, generated an unusually large tsunami for the size of the earthquake. It was determined later that fault rupture occurred much closer to the surface, and fault motion took place much more slowly than for most subduction-zone earthquakes. Earthquakes like this one are sometimes called *tsunami earthquakes*; the tsunami is much more extreme than the seismic shaking would predict. The lesson here is that you should leave for high ground even if the radio announces that the earthquake is only M 7 to 7.5.

The other problem in coping with tsunamis is the period of the waves. Frequently, the first wave is not the largest one. The people of Crescent City, California, found this out the hard way. The first waves were small and caused little damage, and people returned to the shoreline, only to be struck by much larger waves that crashed through the town.

Unlike ordinary storm waves, the period of a tsunami wave may be as much as an hour. So when the first wave rushes up and then recedes, for the next half hour or so, you will notice only the ordinary surf. But don't think the tsunami is over. Wait at least two hours before you return. And just as a tsunami rises higher than ordinary waves, causing great damage, the tsunami also causes the water to recede much farther out to sea, exposing ocean floor not ordinarily seen even at the lowest tides. The temptation to rush to the beach at that time could be fatal, as it was for people in Crescent City.

Psychological Issues

Children are especially traumatized by earthquakes. All their familiar surroundings, everything that is supposed to stay put in their lives, suddenly moves, is damaged, or becomes a threat. Children may have to leave home for an extended period of time. They will fear that the shaking and destruction will get worse, or will continue again and again.

Assuring the physical safety of your child is only the first step. Include the child in all your activities, continue talking, and encourage the child to talk out fears. It may be necessary for your child to sleep with you for a few days until things return, more or less, to normal. Plenty of reassurance and just being present will be a great help in your child's overcoming fears after an earthquake. Encourage the school to plan group activities that relate to the psychological recovery from an earthquake.

Elderly or disabled persons may also feel a sense of helplessness and fear due to an earthquake. Some individuals of any age are prone to a "disaster syndrome." This illness may not come on immediately after the disaster, but it builds up over days and weeks, with evidence of the disaster everywhere, and with the telling and retelling of the stories of the event. In severe cases, these people will need counseling and may need to leave the area until they have recovered.

Suggestions for Further Reading

American Red Cross. 1985. The emergency survival handbook (local Red Cross office).

Health Plus. 1986. Getting ready for the big one. San Francisco, CA.

Kimball, V. 1988. *Earthquake Ready*. Santa Monica, CA: Roundtable Publishing, 225p.

Lafferty and Associates, Inc. 1989. Earthquake preparedness— for office, home, family, and a community. La Canada, CA.

Morgan, L. 1993. *Earthquake Survival Manual*. Seattle: Epicenter Press, 160p.

National Science Teachers Association. 1988. *Earthquakes: A teacher's guide for K-6 grades*. Washington, DC.

Yanev, P. 1974. *Peace of Mind in Earthquake Country: How to save your home and life*. San Francisco: Chronicle Books.

An Uncertain Appointment with a Restless Earth

"In its relation to man, an earthquake is a cause. In its relation to the Earth, it is chiefly an incidental effect of an incidental effect."

G.K. Gilbert, 1912, preface to *U.S. Geological Survey Professional Paper 69.*

A Catastrophe Is Coming to the Pacific Northwest

This is more acceptable in a geologic time frame of thousands of years, because the evidence is strong that the region is visited by great earthquakes every few centuries. The recognition that the Pacific Northwest is subject to earthquakes was slow in coming, but in the past decade, it has been accepted by the scientific community as a major paradigm change. As a result, the structural engineering community has seen to it that building codes have been upgraded, resulting in much higher safety standards for new buildings than was the case ten or fifteen years ago. The governors of California, Oregon, and Washington and the premier of British Columbia would probably all agree now that there is an earthquake problem within their jurisdictions. Earthquake drills are conducted in schools, and partnerships are building between government and private industry in taking steps to deal with the earthquake hazard.

Yet there is a feeling of unreality about it all, and this feeling even extends to those people whose careers are in earthquake studies and preparedness. For example, I know that the place where I live and work has a potential for earthquakes, yet I have not taken all of the steps called for in Chapters 11 and 15 to safeguard my home and family against earthquakes. I asked a friend of mine, a well-known seismologist, if he had earthquake insurance. He hung his head a bit sheepishly and replied, "No."

I had my own experience with an earthquake in the autumn of 1978 in Mexico City, where my friend Chuck Denham and I were sitting in the bar of a small hotel, planning an ascent of Mount Popocatépetl. We were having a beer at nine o'clock in the morning because we didn't trust the water, and we didn't want to get sick halfway up the mountain.

Out of the corner of my eye, I noticed a chandelier start to sway. At first, I thought I was imagining things, but then I gained enough confidence in my senses to say something to Chuck. At that instant, the first strong waves struck. Glasses and bottles toppled from the bar, chairs scraped back, and people began to yell in Spanish. The entire building began to rumble, like the noise of a train. *Earthquake*, I thought. The movement of the chandelier registered the P wave, and the strong shaking marked the S wave and the surface waves.

Despite all my wisdom about what to do in an earthquake, Chuck and I ran outside. I knew that it was the wrong thing to do, but rationality fled with the strong shaking. Fortunately, we were not bombarded by masonry or plate glass.

The scene in the street was surreal. The hotel was built very close to neighboring buildings, and each was vibrating independently of the others so that their walls bounced together, like hands clapping. We waited for pieces of the building to fall off into the street, realizing at that instant how stupid it had been for us to run outside. Light poles were waving back and forth. Parked cars rolled forward to hit the car in front, then backward to hit the car behind. The ground seemed like a thin sheet of plywood, bucking up and down, making it difficult to stand. I dropped to one knee.

Then it was over. A siren wailed in the distance; otherwise it was deathly quiet. The buildings had not collapsed where we were, although we would learn later that lives had been lost in other parts of the city due to building destruction.

Although aftershocks continued throughout the day, the whole experience seemed unreal, as though we had seen a UFO, or heard a ghost in the attic. To this day, I find it hard to believe that the earthquake actually happened, even though every part of the experience is as vivid today as it was two decades ago. It was like a bad dream.

Perhaps this is our problem about earthquakes. An earthquake is an act of devastation, like the bombing of the World Trade Center, which happens, causes great damage and loss of life, and then is over. It is difficult for us to recognize this act of devastation as part of a continuum of Earth processes, of plate tectonics, of the building of the Cascade and Olympic mountain ranges.

The shaking of the Earth, considered as a normal process by geologists, is thought of as a bizarre aberration of Earth processes by everyone else, and perhaps even by geologists at the gut level, despite the level of knowledge gained by space satellites and seismographs. It is what scientists *feel* as opposed to what they *know*. Most people have only the feeling of unreality that an earthquake (or even the expectation of an earthquake) brings. An earthquake is so "unnatural" that it is almost impossible to believe, even when a person has experienced one.

One could describe this book as a morality play: the scientist points out the earthquake hazard to the public official, who refuses to take action, either through ignorance or greed. Taxpayers and their elected representatives decide against paying for retrofit of buildings, living for today and gambling that they will be long gone and out of the game before the earthquake arrives to cash in its chips.

Our cholesterol level or our blood pressure is too high, or we smoke too much. But our personal feeling is that heart attacks, strokes, and cancer will always happen to the other guy. So it is with earthquakes. Even though an earthquake strikes a blow to Los Angeles or San Francisco, it is unbelievable that an even larger earthquake might strike Vancouver or Seattle. It can't happen here.

Dealing with the earthquake threat may be similar to dealing with the U.S. national debt. The debt is in the trillions of dollars, and our descendants will be the ones that have to deal with it. But this threat is so unreal that, like earthquakes, we put it out of our mind and allow our politicians to continue to spend money rather than pay off the debt.

When Nikita Khrushchev banged his shoe on a table at the United Nations and said about the Soviet Union, "We will bury you," there was a great media outcry, and many people began to build bomb shelters. After a while, though, the bomb shelter craze passed, even though the threat of nuclear annihilation increased. It didn't seem real, and then, when the Soviet Union collapsed, it turned out that it hadn't mattered after all. We ignored the nuclear threat, and for the most part, it went away.

Surely there is a middle path, and perhaps we are taking it. The upgrading of building codes is an encouraging response of government to the earthquake problem. When the next earthquake strikes, I want to be in a building constructed under Seismic Zone 3 rather than in an older building constructed under earlier codes. In a few generations, the older unreinforced masonry buildings will be gone, and if an earthquake does not arrive beforehand, it may have proven sufficient.

Or maybe not.

The pressure needs to be kept on state, provincial, and national governments to protect their citizens against earthquakes, just as we now require protection against fires and windstorms. We must be sure that regional economies do not collapse, and insurance companies are not forced out of business in the event of a Cascadia Subduction Zone earthquake. Nuclear power plants, dams, hospitals, and government command centers must be able to operate after a major earthquake.

And, finally, research must continue into the sources of earthquakes, just as we must continue to support research toward a cure for AIDS or for cancer. The Japanese took the Kobe Earthquake as a wake-up call, and they greatly boosted their efforts in preparedness and in research. North Americans have not done the same, perhaps because the national command centers and population centers in Canada and the United States are on the east coast, whereas the larger danger is on the west coast.

To be ready for our uncertain appointment with the next earthquake, we as taxpayers and voters need to keep the earthquake issue high on the list of priorities of our elected officials and our neighbors. A politician who fails to act must pay a political price.

The effort starts with you and me.

Glossary

abrasion—The mechanical wearing, grinding, scraping, or rubbing away of rock surfaces by friction and impact.

acceleration—Rate of increase in speed of an object.

accelerometer—A seismograph for measuring ground acceleration as a function of time.

active fault—A fault along which there is recurrent movement, which is usually indicated by small, periodic displacements or seismic activity.

active tectonics—Tectonic movements that are expected to occur within a future time span of concern to society.

aftershock—Smaller earthquakes following the largest earthquake of a series concentrated in a restricted crustal volume.

amplitude—Maximum height of a wave crest or depth of a wave trough.

anticline—A fold, generally convex upward, whose core contains the stratigraphically older rocks.

asperity—Roughness on the fault surface subject to slip. Region of high shear strength on the fault surface.

asthenosphere—The layer or shell of the Earth below the lithosphere, which is weak and in which isostatic adjustment take place, magmas may be generated, and seismic waves are strongly attenuated.

attenuation—The reduction in amplitude of a wave with time or distance traveled.

basalt—A general term for dark-colored mafic igneous rocks, commonly extrusive but locally intrusive (e.g. as dikes), composed chiefly of calcic plagioclase and clinopyroxene. The principal constituent of oceanic crust, which includes gabbro, the coarse-grained equivalent of basalt.

base isolation—A process of foundation construction whereby forces from the ground are not transmitted upward into the building.

bathymetry—Topography of the sea floor; the science of measuring depths in the sea.

blind fault—A fault that does not break the surface, but may be expressed at the surface as a fold or broad warp.

body wave—A seismic wave thaty travels through the interior of an elastic material.

brittle—1. Said of a rock that fractures at less than 3-5 percent deformation or strain.
2. In structural engineering, describes a building that is unable to deform without collapsing.

capable fault—A fault along which it is mechanically feasible for sudden slip to occur.

characteristic earthquake—An earthquake with a size and generating mechanism typical for a particular fault source.

colluvial wedge—In cross section, a wedge of coarser grained material forming the debris slope and wash slope of a fault scarp, commonly taken as evidence in a backhoe trench of a surface dip-slip faulting event.

colluvium—A general term applied to any loose, heterogeneous, and incoherent mass of soil material and/or rock fragments deposited by rainwash, sheetwash, or slow, continuous downslope creep, usually collecting at the base of gentle slopes or hillsides.

continent—One of the Earth's major land masses, including both dry land and continental shelves.

continental crust—That type of the Earth's crust which underlies the continents and the continental shelves, ranging in thickness from about 35 km to as much as 60 km under mountain ranges. The density of the upper layer of the continental crust is ~ 2.7 g/cm^3, and the velocities of compressional seismic waves through it are less then ~ 7.0 km/sec.

core (of Earth)—The central part of the Earth below a depth of 2900 km. It is thought to be composed mainly of iron and silicates and to be molten on the outside with a solid central part.

creep (along a fault)—slow slip unaccompanied by earthquakes.

cripple wall—Short studs between the mudsill and foundation and the floor joists of the house.

critical facility—A structure that is essential to survive a catastrophe because

287

of its need to direct rescue operations or treat injured people or because if it were destroyed (such as a dam or nuclear power plant), the effects of that destruction could be catastrophic to society.

crust—The outermost layer or shell of the Earth, defined according to various criteria, including seismic velocity, density and composition; that part of the Earth above the Mohorovičić discontinuity.

crystalline rock—An inexact but convenient term designating an igneous or metamorphic rock as opposed to a sedimentary rock.

density—mass per unit volume.

deterministic forecast—An estimation of the largest earthquake or most severe ground shaking to be found on a fault, or in a region, the **maximum credible earthquake**, or MCE.

diaphragm—horizontal element of a building, such as a floor or a roof, that transmits horizontal forces between vertical elements such as walls.

dip—The angle between a layer or fault and a horizontal plane, measured in a plane perpendicular to strike.

dip-slip fault—A fault in which the relative displacement is in the direction of fault dip.

ductile—1. Said of a rock that is able to sustain, under a given set of conditions, 5-10 percent deformation before fracture or faulting 2. In structural engineering, the ability of a building to bend and sway without collapsing.

earthquake segment—That part of a fault zone or fault zones that have ruptured during individual earthquakes.

elastic limit—The greatest stress that can be developed in a material without permanent deformation remaining when the stress is released.

epicenter—The point on the Earth's surface that is directly above the focus (hypocenter) of an earthquake.

epoch—A geologic-time unit shorter than a period.

era—A geologic-time unit next in order of magnitude above a period; e.g., the Paleozoic, Mesozoic, and Cenozoic Eras.

eustatic—Pertaining to worldwide changes of sea level that affect all the oceans.

Eustatic changes may have various causes, but the changes dominant in the last few million years were caused by additions of water to, or removal of water from, the continental icecaps.

fault—A fracture or a zone of fractures along which there has been displacement of the sides relative to one another parallel to the fracture.

fault creep—Steady or episodic movement along a fault unaccompanied by earthquakes.

feldspar—A group of abundant rock-forming minerals of general formula: $MAl(Al,Si)_3O_8$, where M = K, Na, Ca, Ba, Rb, Sr, and Fe. Feldspars are the most widespread of any mineral group and constitute 60 percent of the Earth's crust.

felsic—Said of an igneous rock having abundant light-colored minerals.

first motion—On a seismogram, the direction of motion at the beginning of the arrival of a P wave. Conventionally, upward motion indicates a compression of the ground; downward motion, a dilatation.

focal depth—The depth of the focus below the surface of the Earth.

focus—The place at which rupture commences.

footwall—The underlying side of a fault.

forecast (of an earthquake)—A specific area is identified as having a higher statistical probability of an earthquake measured in a time window of months or years.

foreshocks—smaller earthquakes preceding the largest earthquake of a series concentrated in a restricted crustal volume.

frequency—Number of waves per unit time; unit is Hertz, or 1 cycle per second.

free face—exposed surface of a scarp resulting from faulting or succeeding gravity spalling.

friction—The resistance to motion of a body sliding past another body along a surface of contact.

g—Acceleration due to the gravitational attraction of the Earth, a rate of 32 feet (9.8 meters) per second, per second

geodesy—The science concerned with the determination of the size and shape of the Earth and the precise location of points on its surface.

geomorphology—The science that treats the general configuration of the Earth's surface; specifically the study of the classification, description, nature, origin, and development of present landforms and their relationships to underlying structures, and of the history of geologic changes as recorded by these surface features.

geothermal gradient—The rate of increase of temperature in the Earth with depth.

GPS—Global Positioning System, in which surveying is accomplished by determining the position with respect to the orbital positions of several NAVSTAR satellites. Repeated surveying of ground stations may reveal tectonic deformation of the Earth's crust.

graben—A crustal block of rock, generally long and narrow, that has dropped down along boundary faults relative to adjacent rocks.

granite—A plutonic (deep-seated) rock in which quartz constitutes 10 to 50 percent of the light-colored mineral components and in which the alkali feldspar/total feldspar ratio is generally restricted to the range of 65 to 90 percent. Broadly applied, any completely crystalline, quartz-bearing plutonic rock.

Gutenberg-Richter recurrence relationship—The observed relationship that, for large areas and long time periods, numbers of earthquakes of different magnitudes occur systematically with the relationship M = a - bN, where M is magnitude, N is the number of events per unit area per unit time, and a and b are constants representing, respectively, the overall level of seismicity and the ratio of small to large events.

hangingwall—The overlying side of a fault.

hazard—Risk, danger.

Holocene—The last 10,000 years; an epoch of the Quaternary.

indemnity—Insurance against, or repayment for, loss or damage.

inertia—The tendency of matter to remain at rest or continue in a fixed direction unless acted upon by an outside force.

intensity (of earthquakes)—A measure of ground shaking, obtained from the damage done to structures built by humans, changes in the Earth's surface, and felt reports.

isoseismal—Contour lines drawn to separate one level of seismic intensity from another.

isostasy—That condition of equilibrium, comparable to floating, of the units of the lithosphere above the asthenosphere.

Law of Large Numbers—The larger the number of insurance contracts a company writes, the more likely the actual results will follow the predicted results based on an infinite number of contracts.

left-lateral fault—A strike-slip fault on which the displacement of the far block is to the left when viewed from either side.

liquefaction—The act or process transforming any substance into a liquid.

lithosphere— A layer of strength relative to the underlying asthenosphere for deformation at geologic rates. It includes the crust and part of the upper mantle and is of the order of 100 km in thickness.

load—The forces acting on a building. The weight of the building itself is its **dead load**. Weight of contents, or of snow on the roof, etc., are **live loads**.

mafic—Said of an igneous rock composed chiefly of one or more ferromagnesian, dark-colored minerals.

magma—Naturally occurring mobile rock material, generated within the Earth and capable of intrusion and extrusion, from which igneous rocks are thought to have been derived through solidification and related processes.

magnitude (of earthquakes)—A measure of earthquake size, determined by taking the common logarithm (base 10) of the largest ground motion recorded during the arrival of a seismic wave type and applying a standard correction for distance to the epicenter

mantle—The zone of the Earth below the crust and above the core, which is divided into the upper mantle and the lower mantle, with a transition zone between.

meizoseismal region—The area of strong shaking and significant damage in an earthquake.

mitigate—To moderate or to make milder or less severe.

modulus of elasticity—The ratio of stress to its corresponding strain under given conditions of load, for materials that deform elastically, according to Hooke's law.

Mohorovičić discontinuity—The boundary surface or sharp seismic-velocity discontinuity that separates the Earth's crust from the subjacent mantle. It marks the level in the Earth at which P-wave velocities change abruptly from 6.7-7.2 km/sec in the lower crust to 7.6-8.6 km/sec or average 8.1 km/sec at the top of the upper mantle.

moment (of earthquakes)— A measure of earthquake size related to the leverage of the forces (couples) across the area of fault slip; the rigidity of the rock times the area of faulting times the amount of slip. Dimensions are dyne-cm or Newton-meters.

moment magnitude (Mw)—Magnitude of an earthquake estimated by using the seismic moment.

moment-resistant frame—Steel frame structures with rigid welded joints, more flexible than shear-wall structures.

mudsill—The lowest board between a house and its foundation.

neotectonics—The study of the post-Miocene structures and structural history of the Earth's crust. The study of recent deformation of the crust, generally Neogene (post-Oligocene). Tectonic processes now active, taken over the geologic time span during which they have been acting in the presently observed sense, and the resulting structures.

normal fault—A fault in which the hangingwall appears to have moved downward relative to the footwall.

ocean basin—The area of the sea floor between the base of the continental margin, usually the foot of the continental rise, and the mid-ocean ridge.

olivine—An olive-green, grayish-green, or brown orthorhombic mineral: $(Mg,Fe)_2SiO_4$. A common rock-forming mineral of basic, ultrabasic, and low-silica igneous rocks (basalt, peridotite, dunite).

orthoclase— A mineral of the alkali-feldspar group:$KAlSi_3O_8$. A common rock-forming mineral occurring especially in granite, acid igneous rocks, and crystalline schists.

P wave—The primary or fastest wave traveling away from a seismic event through the rock and consisting of a train of compressions and dilatations of the material.

paleoseismology—That part of earthquake studies that deals with geological evidence for earthquakes and fault rupture.

paradigm—A pattern, example, or model.

peridotite—Rock composed predominantly of the minerals pyroxene and olivine; the major component of the Earth's mantle.

peril—The risk, contingency, event, or cause of loss insured against, as in an insurance policy.

period—1. The time interval between successive crusts in a wave train; the period is the inverse of the frequency of a cyclic event. 2. The fundamental unit of the geological time scale, subdivided into epochs, and subdivisions of an era.

plagioclase—A group of triclinic feldspars of general formula $(Na,Ca)Al(Si,Al)Si_2O_8$. A common rock-forming mineral in continental and oceanic crust.

plate—A large, relatively rigid segment of the Earth's lithosphere that moves in relation to other plates over the deeper interior.

plate tectonics—A theory of global tectonics in which the lithosphere is divided into a number of plates whose pattern of horizontal movement is that of torsionally rigid bodies that interact with one another at their boundaries, causing seismic and tectonic activity along these boundaries.

Pleistocene—An epoch of the Quaternary Period, after the Pliocene and before the Holocene.

precursor—A change in the geological conditions that is a forerunner to earthquake generation on a fault.

prediction (of earthquakes)—The forecasting in time, place, and magnitude of an earthquake.

premium—An amount payable for an insurance policy.

probability—The number of cases that actually occur divided by the total number of cases possible.

probability of exceedance of a given earthquake size—The odds that the size of a future earthquake will exceed some specified value.

pyroxene—A group of dark rock-forming silicate minerals, closely related in crystal form and composition and having the general formula: $ABSi_2O_6$, where $A = Ca$, Na, Mg, or Fe^{+2} and $B = Mg$, Fe^{+2}, Fe^{+3}, Fe, Cr, Mn, or Al, with silicon sometimes replaced by aluminum.

quartz—Crystalline silica, an important rock-forming mineral: SiO_2.

Quaternary—The second period of the Cenozoic era, following the Tertiary, consisting of the Pleistocene and Holocene Epochs.

radiometric—Pertaining to the measurement of geologic time by the study of parent and/or daughter isotopic abundances and known disintegration rates of the radioactive parent isotopes.

recurrence interval—The average time interval between earthquakes in a seismic region or along a fault.

reinsurance—A contract in which the insurer becomes protected by effecting insurance upon a risk that he or she, as first insurer, has assumed.

retrofit—Reinforcement or modification of a building that is already constructed.

reverse fault—A fault that dips toward the block that has been relatively raised.

Richter scale—Logarithm to the base 10 of the maximum seismic-wave amplitude, in thousandths of a millimeter, recorded on a Wood-Anderson seismograph at a distance of 100 km from the earthquake epicenter.

rheology—The study of the deformation and flow of matter.

right-lateral fault—A strike-slip fault on which the displacement of the far block is to the right when viewed from either side.

rigidity—An index of the resistance of an elastic body to shear. The ratio of the shearing stress to the amount of angular rotation it produces in a rock sample.

S wave—The secondary seismic wave, traveling more slowly than the P wave and consisting of elastic vibrations transverse to the direction of travel.

sand—A rock fragment or detrital particle smaller than a granule and larger than a coarse silt grain, having a diameter in the range of 62 to 2000 microns (2 mm).

sea-floor spreading—A hypothesis that the oceanic crust is increasing by convective upwelling of magma along the mid-oceanic ridges or world rift system and by a moving-away of the new material at a rate of one to ten centimeters per year.

seismic gap—An area in an earthquake-prone region where there is a below-average release of seismic energy

seismic moment *See* moment (of earthquakes).

seismic wave—An elastic wave in the Earth usually generated by an earthquake or explosion.

seismicity—The occurrence of earthquakes in space and time.

seismogenic—Characterized by earthquakes.

seismograph—An instrument for recording as a function of time the motions of the Earth's surface that are caused by seismic waves.

seismology—1. The study of earthquakes. 2. The study of earthquakes, and of the structure of the Earth, by both naturally and artificially generated seismic waves.

seismotectonics—That subfield of active tectonics concentrating on the seismicity, both instrumental and historical, and dealing also with geological and other geophysical data sets.

serpentine—Green, streaky rock formed by the hydration (addition of water) to peridotite.

shear wall— A wall of a building that has been strengthened to resist horizontal forces.

silicic—Said of a silica-rich igneous rock or magma.

silt—A rock fragment or detrital particle smaller than a very fine sand grain and larger than coarse clay having a diameter in the range of 4 to 62 microns.

shoreline angle—The boundary between a freshly-cut sea cliff and the marine abrasion platform.

slip—The relative displacement of formerly-adjacent on opposite sides of a fault, measured in the fault surface.

soft story—A section or horizontal division of a building extending from the floor to the ceiling or roof above it characterized by large amounts of open space that reduces its resistance to horizontal forces, such as a two-car garage or a ballroom in a hotel.

soil—1. A natural body consisting of layers or horizons of mineral and/or organic constituents of variable thicknesses, which differ from the parent material in their morphological, physical, chemical, and mineralogical properties and their biological characteristics. 2. All unconsolidated materials above bedrock (engineering).

stick slip—A jerky, sliding motion associated with fault movement.

strain—Change in the shape or volume of a body as a result of stress.

stress—Force per unit area.

stress drop—The sudden reduction of stress across the fault plane during rupture.

strike—The direction of trend taken by a structural surface as it intersects the horizontal.

strike slip—In a fault, the component of movement that is parallel to the strike of the fault.

strike-slip fault—A fault on which the movement is parallel to the fault's strike.

subduction—The process of one lithospheric plate descending beneath another.

subduction zone—A long, narrow belt in which subduction takes place.

surface-wave magnitude (Ms)—Magnitude of an earthquake estimated from measurements of the amplitude of surface waves.

surface waves—Seismic waves that follow the Earth's surface only, with a speed less than that of S waves. There are two types of surface waves —Rayleigh waves and Love waves.

swarm (of earthquakes)—A series of earthquakes in the same locality, no one earthquake being of outstanding size.

syncline—A fold of which the core contains the stratigraphically younger rocks; it is generally concave upward.

tectonic geomorphology—The study of landforms that result from tectonic processes.

tectonics—A branch of geology dealing with the broad architecture of the outer part of the Earth, that is, the regional assembling of structural or deformational features, a study of their mutual relations, origin, and historical evolution.

tephrochronology—The collection, preparation, petrographic description, and approximate dating of tephra (pyroclastic material from a volcano).

teleseism—An earthquake that occurs at a distant place, usually overseas.

thrust fault—A fault with a dip of 45° or less over much of its extent, on which the hanging wall appears to have moved upward relative to the footwall.

topography—The general configuration of a land surface or any part of the Earth's surface, including its relief and the position of its natural and man-made features.

trace—The intersection of a geological surface with another surface, e.g., the trace of bedding on a fault surface, or the trace of a fault or outcrop on the ground surface.

transform fault—A plate boundary that ideally shows pure strike-slip displacement.

trend—A general term for the direction or bearing of the outcrop of a geological feature of any dimension.

trench—1. Long, narrow, arcuate depression on the sea floor which results from the bending of the lithospheric plate as it descends into the mantle at a subduction zone. 2. Shallow excavation, dug by bulldozer, backhoe, or by hand, revealing detailed information about near-surface geological materials.

triple junction—Point where three plates meet.

tsunami—A long ocean wave usually caused by sea-floor movements in an earthquake, submarine volcanic eruption, or landslide.

turbidite—A sediment or rock deposited from a turbidity current, a flow of sediment-charged water.

ultimate strength—The maximum differential stress that a material can sustain under the conditions of deformation.

ultramafic—Said of an igneous rock composed chiefly of mafic minerals, e.g. pyroxene and/or olivine.

underwriting—The writing of one's signature at the end of an insurance company, thereby assuming liability in the event of specific loss or damage.

uniformitarianism—The fundamental principle or doctrine that geologic processes and natural laws now operating to modify the Earth's crust have acted in the same regular manner and with the same intensity throughout geologic time, and that past geologic events can be explained by phenomena and forces observable today.

URM—Unreinforced masonry, a type of construction that is not strengthened against horizontal forces from an earthquake.

viscosity—The property of a substance to offer internal resistance to flow; its internal friction. The ratio of the shear stress to the rate of shear strain.

volcanology—The branch of geology that deals with volcanism, its causes and phenomena.

Wadati-Benioff zone—A narrow zone, defined by earthquake foci, that is tens of kilometers thick dipping from the surface under the Earth's crust.

wavelength—The distance between two successive crests or trough of a wave.

Bibliography

Principal Data Sources

Alaska Tsunami Warning Center, 910 S. Felton Street, Palmer, AK 99645, 907-745-4212.

British Columbia Geological Survey, P.O. Box 9320, Stn. Provincial Government, Victoria, BC V8W 9N3, 250-952-0429.

California Division of Mines and Geology, P.O. Box 2980, Sacramento, CA 95812-2980, 916-445-5716.

California Office of Emergency Services, 11200 Lexington Drive, Bldg. 283, Los Alamitos, CA 90720-5002, 310-795-2900; Coastal Region Earthquake Program, 1300 Clay Street, Suite 400, Oakland, CA 94612-1425; 510-286-0873.

Federal Emergency Management Agency, P.O. Box 70274, Washington, DC 20024.

Federal Emergency Management Agency, Region X, 130 228ath Street SW, Bothell, WA 98021-9796, 206-487-4600.

Humboldt Earthquake Education Center, Humboldt State University, Arcata, CA 95521-8299. 707-826-3931.

International Tsunami Information Center, Box 50027, Honolulu, HI 96850-4993, 808-541-1658

Nature of Oregon Information Center, 800 NE Oregon St. #5, Suite 177, Portland, OR 97232, 503-731-4444.

Oregon Department of Geology and Mineral Industries, 800 NE Oregon St. #28, Suite 965, Portland, OR 97232, 503-731-4100; Nature of the Northwest Information Center, 800 NE Oregon St. #5, 503-872-2750

Oregon Emergency Management, 595 Cottage St. NE, Salem, OR 97310, 503-378-2911.

Pacific Tsunami Warning Center, 91-270 Fort Weaver Road, Ewa Beach, HI 96706-2928, 808-689-8207.

Provincial Emergency Program, 455 Boleskine Road, Victoria, BC V8Z 1E7.

Southern California Earthquake Center, University of Southern California, University Park, Los Angeles, CA 90089-0742.

U.S. Geological Survey, Earth Science Information Center, 345 Middlefield Road, Menlo Park, CA 94025, 415-329-4390.

University of Washington Geophysics Program, Seattle, WA 98195.

Washington Department of Natural Resources, Division of Geology and Earth Resources, Mail Stop PY-12, Olympia, WA 98504.

Western States Seismic Policy Council, 121 Second Street, 4th Floor, San Francisco, CA 94105.

Web Sites and E-mail Addresses

More than fifty sites for earthquake information can be accessed through Earthquake Net at http://www.eqnet.org/index.html Web sites are expanding and changing daily; this list should be updated frequently. List below begins with http://

Association of Bay Area Governments: www.abag.ca.gov

California Division of Mines and Geology: www.consrv.ca.gov/dmg(seismic hazard information about California).

California Universities for Research in Earthquake Engineering: curee.eerc.berkeley.edu/curee.html

Canadian Centre for Emergency Preparedness: www.ccep.ca

Cascadia Regional Earthquake Workgroup (CREW): www.geophys.washington.edu/CREW

Earthquake Engineering Research Center: nisee.ce.berkeley.edu www.eerc.berkeley.edu/

Earthquake Engineering Research Institute: www.eeri.org/

Earthquake Information: geology.usgs.gov/quake.html

Earthquake Program, California Office of Emergency Services: www.oes.ca.gov:8001/html/eqprog/eqprog.html

Federal Emergency Management Agency (FEMA): fema.gov/homepage.html

FEMA Region X: www.fema.gov/fema/regx.html

Insurance Institute for Property Loss Reduction: iiplr@aol.com

Incorporated Research Institutions in Seismology: www.iris.washington.edu

Institute for Business and Home Safety: www.iiplr.org

International Conference of Building Officials: www.icbo.org (latest information on building codes)

National Center for Earthquke Engineering Research: nceer.eng.buffalo.edu

National Earthquake Information Center: gldss7.cr.usgs.gov e-mail neic@usgs.gov

National Information Service for Earthquake Engineering: nisee.ce.berkeley.edu

National Landslide Information Center: e-mail nlic@usgs.gov

National Oceanic and Atmospheric Administration (NOAA) Geophysical Data Center: www.ngdc.noaa.gov/ngdc.html

NOAA Tsunami Program: www.pmel.noaa.gov/tsunami-hazard

National Science Foundation (NSF): www.nsf.gov

Northern California Earthquake Data Center: quake.geo.berkeley.edu

Pacific Geoscience Centre, Sidney, BC: www.pgc.nrcan.gc.ca or www.pgc.emr.ca

Pacific Disaster Center (tsunami warnings): www.pdc.org

Paleoseismology Information: inqua.nlh.no/commpl/paleoseism.html

Provincial Emergency Program (British Columbia): hoshi.cic.sfu.ca/~pep/

Southern California Earthquake Center (SCEC): www.scec.org

SCEC: Recent earthquakes in northern and southern California, with maps: www.scecdc.scec.org/recenteqs www.scecdc.scec.org/earthquakes/current.txt (text)

www.scecdc.scec.org/earthquakes/current.gif (map)

U. S. Geological Survey (USGS): www.usgs.gov

USGS Menlo Park office: quake.wr.usgs.gov/

USGS National Earthquake Information Center: gldfs.cr.usgs.gov

University of Washington Seismic Network: www.geophys.washington.edu/SEIS/

Seismo-surfing: www.geophys.washington.edu/seismosurfing.html

Western States Seismic Policy Council: www.wsspc.org For online discussion group, e-mail wsspc@wsspc.org

References

Adams, J. 1984. Active deformation of the Pacific Northwest continental margin. *Tectonics*, vol. 3, pp. 449-72.

Adams, J. 1990. Paleoseismicity of the Cascadia subduction zone: Evidence from turbidites off the Oregon-Washington margin. *Tectonics*, vol. 9, pp. 569-83.

Algermissen, S.T., S.T. Harding, L.V. Steinbrugge, and W.K. Cloud. 1965. The Puget Sound, Washington, earthquake of April 29, 1965. Preliminary Seismological Engineering Report, U.S. Coast and Geodetic Survey, 26p.

Allen, J.E., M. Burns, and S.C. Sargent. 1986. Cataclysms on the Columbia. Portland: Timber Press, 211p.

American Red Cross. 1985. The Emergency Survival Handbook (local Red Cross office).

Association of Bay Area Governments. 1992. Seismic retrofit incentive programs: A handbook for local governments. Association of Bay Area Governments Publ. P92001BAR, P. O. Box 2050, Oakland, CA 94604.

Atwater, B.F. 1987. Evidence for great Holocene earthquakes along the outer coast of Washington State. *Science*, vol. 236, pp. 942-44.

Atwater, B.F. 1992. Geologic evidence for earthquakes during the past 2000 years along the Copalis River, southern coastal Washington. *Journal of Geophysical Research*, vol. 97, pp. 1901-19.

Atwater, B.F., and A.L. Moore. 1992. A tsunami about 1000 years ago in Puget Sound, Washington. *Science*, vol. 258, pp. 1614-17.

Atwater, B.F., and others. 1995. Summary of coastal geologic evidence for past great earthquakes at the Cascadia subduction zone. *Earthquake Spectra*, vol. 11, pp. 1-18.

Atwater, B.F., and Yamaguchi, D.E., 1997,

Basham, P., S. Halchuk, D. Weichert, and J. Adams. 1997. New seismic hazard assessment for Canada. *Seismological Research Letters*, vol. 68, pp. 722-26.

Bernard, E.N., et al. 1991. *Tsunami Hazard: A Practical Guide for Tsunami Hazard Reduction*. Dordrecht, The Netherlands: Kluwer Academic Publishers.

Bolt, B.A. 1993. *Earthquakes*. Newly revised and expanded. New York: W.H. Freeman and Co., 331p.

Q1.5323

QC811.J4

Nature Q1 N2
Geology QE1.157

Bott, J.D.J., and I.G. Wong. 1993. Historical earthquakes in and around Portland, Oregon. DOGAMI, *Oregon Geology*, vol. 55, no. 6. pp. 116-22.

Bucknam, R.C., E. Hemphill-Haley, and E.B. Leopold,. 1992. Abrupt uplift within the past 1700 years at southern Puget Sound, Washington. *Science*, vol. 258, pp. 1611-14.

Burns, S. 1998. Landslide hazards in Oregon, in Burns, S., ed., *Environmental, Groundwater and Engineering Geology Applications from Oregon*. Association of Engineering Geologists Special Pub. 11, Star Publishing Co., 940 Emmett Ave., Belmont, CA 94002, pp. 303-15.

Burns, S. 1998. Landslides in the Portland area resulting from the storm of February, 1996, in Burns, S., ed., *Environmental, Groundwater and Engineering Geology Applications from Oregon*. Association of Engineering Geologists Special Pub. 11, Star Publishing Co., 940 Emmett Ave., Belmont, CA 94002, pp. 353-65.

Burns, S., and L. Palmer. 1996. Homeowner's Landslide Guide. Oregon Emergency Management, Federal Emergency Management Agency Region 10, and Oregon Department of Geology and Mineral Industries, 10p.

California Division of Mines and Geology. Guidelines for Evaluating and MitigatingSeismic Hazards in California. CDMG SP 117.

California Office of Emergency Services. An Ounce of Prevention: Strengthening Your Wood Frame House for Earthquake Safety. Video and booklet.

Campbell, N.P., and R.D. Bentley. 1981 Late Quaternary deformation of the Toppenish Ridge uplift in south-central Washington. *Geology*, vol. 9, pp. 519-24.

Cassidy, J.F., R.M. Ellis, and G.C. Rogers. 1988. The 1918 and 1957 Vancouver Island earthquakes. *Seismological Society of America Bulletin*, vol. 78, pp. 617-35.

Clague, J.J. 1997. Evidence for large earthquakes at the Cascadia Subduction Zone. *Reviews of Geophysics*, vol. 35, pp. 439-60.

Clague, J.J., and P.T. Bobrowski. 1994. Evidence for a large earthquake and tsunami 100400 years ago on wesern Vancouver Island, British Columbia. *Quaternary Research*, vol. 41, pp. 176-84.

Clarke, S.H., Jr., and G.A. Carver. 1992. Late Holocene tectonics and paleoseismicity, southern Cascdia subduction zone. *Science*, vol. 255, pp. 188-92.

Coastal Natural Hazards Policy Working Group. 1994. Improving natural hazards management on the Oregon coast. Corvallis: Oregon State University, Oregon Sea Grant Publ. ORESU-T-94-001, 128p.

Cope, V. 1993. *The Oregon Earthquake Handbook*. Portland: Vern Cope, 140p.

Crosson, R.S., and T.J. Owens. 1987. Slab geometry of the Cascadia subduction zone beneath Washington from earthquake hypocenters and teleseismic converted waves. *Geophysics Research Letters*, vol. 14, pp. 824-27.

D'Antonio, M. 1993. Atomic Harvest: Hanford and the Lethal Toll of America's Nuclear Arsenal. New York: Crown Publishers, 304p.

Darienzo, M.E., and C.D. Peterson. 1990. Episodic tectonic subsidence of late Holocene salt marshes, northern Oregon coast, central Cascadia margin, U.S.A. *Tectonics*, vol. 9, pp. 1-22.

Dragert, H., R.D. Hyndman, G.C. Rogers, and K. Wang. 1994. Current deformation and the width of the seismogenic zone of the northern Cascadia subduction thrust. *Journal of Geophysical Research*, vol. 99, pp. 653-68.

Dragovich, J.D., and P.T. Pringle.1995. Liquefaction susceptibility map of the Sumner 7.5-minute quadrangle, Washington, with a section on liquefaction analysis by S.P. Palmer. Washington Division of Geology and Earth Resources Geologic Map GM-44, 1 sheet, 1:24,000, text 26p.

Dudley, W.C., and M. Lee. 1988. *Tsunami!* Honolulu: University of Hawaii Press.

Earthquake Engineering Research Institute. 1996. Construction quality, education, and seismic safety. EERI Endowment Fund White Paper: Earthquake Engineering Research Institute, 499 14th Street, Suite 320, Oakland, CA 95612-1934, 68p.

Earthquake Engineering Research Institute. 1996. Public policy and building safety. EERI Endowment Fund White Paper. Earthquake Engineering Research Institute, 499 14th Street, Suite 320, Oakland, CA 95612-1934, 57p.

Fratessa, P. 1994. *Buildings: Practical Lessons from the Loma Prieta Earthquake.* Washington, DC: National Academy Press.

Geller, R.J. 1997. Predictable publicity. *Seismological Research Letters*, vol. 68, pp. 477-80, reprinted from *Astronomy & Geophysics*, journal of the Royal Astronomical Society.

Gerstel, W.J., M.J. Brunengo, W.S. Lingley, Jr., R.L. Logan, H. Shipman, and T.J. Walsh. 1997. Puget Sound bluffs: The where, why, and when of landslides following the holiday 1996/97 storms. *Washington Geology*, vol. 25, no. 1, pp. 17-31.

Geomatrix Consultants. 1995. Seismic design mapping, State of Oregon. Final report prepared for the Oregon Department of Transportation, Project 2442, Salem, OR.

Gere, J.M., and H.C. Shah. 1984. *Terra Non Firma.* San Francisco, CA: W.H. Freeman and Co., 203p.

Glen, W. 1982. *The Road to Jaramillo.* Stanford, CA: Stanford University Press.

Goldfinger, C. 1990. Evolution of the Corvallis fault and implications for the Oregon Coast Range. Corvallis: Oregon State University MS thesis, 118p.

Goldfinger, C., et al. 1992. Transverse structural trends along the Oregon continental margin: Implications for Cascadia earthquake potential and coastal rotations. *Geology*, vol. 20, pp. 141-44.

Griffin, W. 1984. *Crescent City's Dark Disaster.* Crescent City Printing Co., 381 H Street, Crescent City, CA 95531, 188p.

Hanks, T.C. 1985. The National Earthquake Hazards Reduction Program—Scientific Status. U.S. Geological Survey Bull. 1659, 40p.

Hart, R., and C. Peterson. 1997. Episodically buried forests in the Oregon surf zone. *Oregon Geology*, vol. 59, pp. 131-44.

Health Plus. 1986. Getting ready for the big one. 694 Tennessee St., San Francisco, CA 94107.

Heaton, T.H., and S.H. Hartzell. 1987. Earthquake hazards on the Cascadia subduction zone. *Science*, vol. 236, pp. 162-68.

Heaton, T.H., and H. Kanamori. 1984. Seismic potential associated with subduction in the northwestern United States. *Seismological Society of America Bulletin*, vol. 74, pp. 933-41.

Hemphill-Haley, M.A. 1987. Quaternary stratigraphy and late Holocene faulting along the base of the eastern escarpment of Steens Mountain, southeastern Oregon. Arcata, CA: Humboldt State University MS thesis, 87p.

Humboldt Earthquake Information Center. How to survive earthquakes and tsunamis on the north coast. Humboldt State University, Arcata CA 95521-8299, 23p.

Hyndman, R.D. 1995. Giant earthquakes of the Pacific Northwest. *Scientific American,* vol. 273, no. 6, pp. 50-57.

Hyndman, R.D. 1995 The Lithoprobe corridor across the Vancouver Island continental margin: the structural and tectonic consequences of subduction. *Canadian Journal of Earth Science*, vol. 32, pp. 1777-1802.

Hyndman, R.D., and K. Wang. 1995. The rupture zone of Cascadia great earthquakes from current deformation and the thermal regime. *Journal of Geophysical Research*, vol. 100, pp. 22,133-154.

Hyndman, R.D., G.C. Rogers, H. Dragert, K. Wang, J.J. Clague, J. Adams, and P.T. Bobrowski. 1996. Giant earthquakes beneath Canada's west coast. *Geoscience Canada*, vol. 23, no. 2, pp. 63-72.

Insurance Service Office, Inc. 1996. Homeowners insurance: Threats from without, weakness within. ISO Insurance Issues Series, 62p.

International Conference of Building Officials. 1997. 1997 Uniform Building Code in three volumes, available in hard copy or CD-ROM. ICBO, 5360 Workman Mill Road, Whittier, CA 90601-2298.

Jacoby, G.C., P.L. Williams, and B.M. Buckley. 1992. Tree ring correlation between prehistoric landslides and abrupt tectonic events in Seattle, Washington. *Science*, vol. 258, pp. 1621-23.

Jibson, R.W. 1996. Using landslides for paleoseismic analysis, in McCalpin, J.P., ed., *Paleoseismology.* San Diego, CA: Academic Press, pp. 297-438.

Kagan, Y.Y., and D.D. Jackson. 1991. Seismic gap hypothesis: Ten years after. *Journal of Geophysical Research*, vol. 96, pp. 21,419-31.

Karlin, R.E., and S.E.B. Abella. 1992. Paleoearthquakes in the Puget Sound region recorded in sediments from Lake Washington, U.S.A. *Science*, vol. 258, pp. 1617-20.

Karlin, R.E., and S.E.B. Abella. 1996. A history of Pacific Northwest earthquakes recorded in Holocene sediments from Lake Washington. *Journal of Geophysical Research*, vol. 101, pp. 6137-50.

Kearey, P., and F.J. Vine. 1990. *Global Tectonics*. London: Blackwell Scientific Publications, 302p.

Keefer, D.K. 1984. Landslides caused by earthquakes. *Geological Society of American Bulletin*, vol. 95, pp. 406-71.

Keller, E.A. 1988. *Environmental Geology*. Fifth Edition. Columbus, OH: Merrill Publishing Co., 540p.

Kelsey, H.M., and G.A. Carver. 1988. Late Neogene and Quaternary tectonics associated with northward growth of the San Andreas Transform Fault, northern California. *Journal of Geophysical Research*, vol. 93, pp. 4797-819.

Kelsey, H.M., D.C. Engebretson, C.E. Mitchell, and R.L. Ticknor. 1994. Topographic form of the Coast Ranges of the Cascadia margin in relation to coastal uplift rates and plate subduction. *Journal of Geophysical Research*, vol. 99, pp. 12,245-55.

Kimball, V. 1988. *Earthquake Ready*. Santa Monica, CA: Roundtable Publishing, 225p.

Komar, P.D. 1997. *The Pacific Northwest Coast: Living with the Shores of Oregon and Washington*. Durham, NC: Duke University Press, 195p.

Kramer, S.L. 1996. *Geotechnical Earthquake Engineering*. Englewood Cliffs, NJ: Prentice-Hall.

Krinitsky, E., J. Gould, and F. Edinger. 1993. *Fundamentals of Earthquake Resistant Construction*. Wiley Series of Practical Construction Guides. New York: J. Wiley & Sons.

Lafferty and Associates, Inc. 1989. Earthquake preparedness—for office, home, family, and community. P.O. Box 1026, La Canada, CA 91012.

Lagorio, H.J. 1990 *Earthquakes: An Architect's Guide to Nonstructural Seismic Hazards*. New York: J. Wiley & Sons.

Lasmanis, R., ed. 1994. Growth management in Washington State. *Washington Geology*, vol. 22, no. 2, pp. 3-45. Series of articles on the Growth Management Act.

Lillie, R.J. 1998. *Whole-Earth Geophysics*. Englewood Cliffs, NJ: Prentice-Hall, **in press.**

Lindeburg, M. *Seismic Design of Building Structures*. 7th edition. Belmont, CA: Professional Publications.

Lomnitz, C. 1994. *Fundamentals of Earthquake Prediction*. New York: John Wiley & Sons, 326p.

Ma Z., Z. Fu, Y. Zhang, C. Wang, G. Zhang, and D. Liu. 1990. *Earthquake Prediction: Nine Major Earthquakes in China (1966-1976)*. Beijing: Seismologicical Press, and Berlin: Springer-Verlag, 332p.

Mabey, M.A., D.B. Meier, and S,P. Palmer. 1995. Relative earthquake hazard map of the Mount Tabor quadrangle, Multnomah County, Oregon, and Clark County, Washington. Oregon Dept. of Geology and Mineral Industries Geol. Map Series GMS-89: map 1:24,000, text. For other Portland-area maps, see GMS-59, GMS-75, O-74-1, O-90-2, O-93-6, O-93-14.

Madin, I.P., and M.M. Mabey. 1996. Earthquake hazard maps for Oregon. DOGAMI Geological Map Series GMS-100.

Madin, I.P., and others. 1993. March 25, 1993, Scotts Mills earthquake—western Oregon's wake-up call. DOGAMI, *Oregon Geology*, vol. 55, no. 3, pp. 51-57.

Mann, G.M. and G.E. Meyer. 1993. Late Cenozoic structure and correlations to seismicity along the Olympic-Wallowa Lineament, northwest United States. *Geological Society of America Bulletin*, vol. 105, pp. 853-71.

Massonnet, D. 1997. Satellite radar interferometry. *Scientific American*, vol. 276, no. 2, pp. 46-53.

Mathewes, R.W., and J.J. Clague. 1994. Detection of large prehistoric earthquakes in the Pacific Northwest by microfossil analysis. *Science*, vol. 264, pp. 688-91.

McCaffrey, R., and C. Goldfinger. 1995. Forearc deformation and great subduction earthquakes: Implications for Cascadia offshore earthquake potential. *Science*, vol. 267, pp. 856-59.

McInelly, G.W., and H.M. Kelsey. 1990. Late Quaternary tectonic deformation in the

Cape Arago-Bandon region of coastal Oregon as deduced from wave-cut platforms. *Journal of Geophysical Research*, vol. 95, pp. 6699-714.

Meyers, R.A., D.G. Smith, H.M. Jol, and C.D. Peterson. 1996. Evidence for eight great earthquake-subsidence events detected with ground-penetrating radar, Willapa barrier, Washington. *Geology*, vol. 24, pp. 99-102.

Mitchell, C.E., P. Vincent, R.J. Weldon, II, and M.A. Richards. 1994. Present-day vertical deformation of the Cascadia margin, Pacific Northwest, United States. *Journal of Geophysical Research*, vol. 99, pp. 12,257-77.

Monahan, P.A., V.M. Levson, E.J. McQuarrie, S.M. Bean, P. Henderson, and A. Sy. **In press.** Earthquake hazard map of Greater Victoria showing areas susceptible to amplification of ground motion, liquefaction and earthquake-induced slope instability. British Columbia Geological Survey, Open-File Report.

Morgan, L. 1993. *Earthquake Survival Manual*. Seattle, WA: Epicenter Press, 160p.

Muir, J. 1912. *The Yosemite*. The Century Company, republished by Doubleday and Co, Inc., New York.

Naiem, F. ed. 1989. *The Seismic Design Handbook*. London: Chapman and Hall.

Nance, J.J. 1988. *On Shaky Ground*. New York: William Morrow, 416 p.

National Science Teachers Association. 1988. *Earthquakes: A teacher's guide for K-6 grades*. NSTA Publications, 1742 Connecticut Ave. NW, Washington, DC 20009.

Nelson, A.R., et al. 1995. Radiocarbon evidence for extensive plate-boundary rupture about 300 years ago at the Cascadia subduction zone. *Nature*, vol. 378, pp. 371-74.

Nelson, A.R., I. Shennan, and A.J. Long. 1996. Identifying coseismic subsidence in tidal-wetland stratigraphic sequences at the Cascadia subduction zone of western North America. *Journal of Geophysical Research*, vol. 101, pp. 6115-35.

Noson, L.L., A. Qamar, and G.W. Thorsen. 1988. Washington State earthquake hazards. Washington Division of Geology and Earth Resources, Information Circular 85, 77p.

Obermeier, S.F. 1996. Using liquefaction-induced features for paleoseismic analysis, in McCalpin, J.P., ed., *Paleoseismology*. San Diego: Academic Press, p. 331-96.

Office of Technology Assessment, Congress of the United States. 1995. *Reducing Earthquake Losses*. Washington, Government Printing OFfice, OTA-ETI-623, 162p.

Olson, R.S. 1989. *The Politics of Earthquake Prediction*. Princeton, NJ: Princeton University Press, 187p.

Oppenheimer, D., et al. 1993. The Cape Mendocino, California earthquakes of April, 1992: Subduction at the triple junction. *Science*, vol. 261, pp. 433-38.

Oregon Department of Geology and Mineral Industries. Landslides in Oregon. Free circular.

Oregon Department of Geology and Mineral Industries. 1991-1996: Earthquake hazards maps of Portland and Salem metropolitan areas. GMS 79, 89-92, 104-105.

Oregon Department of Geology and Mineral Industries. 1997. Relative earthquake hazard map of the Portland Metro Region, Clackamas, Multnomah, and Washington Counties, Oregon. Interpretive Map Series IMS-1.

Oregon Department of Geology and Mineral Industries. 1997. Tsunami hazard map of lthe Yaquina Bay area, Lincoln County, Oregon. Oregon Interpretive Map Series IMS-2.

Oregon Structural Specialty Code, coordinated with the 1994 Uniform Building Code. ICBO, 5360 Workman Mill Road, Whittier, CA 90601-2298.

Palm, R., M. Hodgson, R.D. Blanchard, and D. Lyons. 1990. *Earthquake Insurance in California: Environmental Policy and Individual Decision Making*. Boulder, CO: Westview Press.

Palmer, S.P. 1994. Revision to the 1994 Uniform Building Code Seismic Zone Map for Washington and Oregon. *Washington Geology*, vol. 22, no. 2, p. 35.

Palmer, S.P., H.W. Schasse, and D.K. Newman. 1994. Liquefaction susceptibility for the Des Moines and Renton 7.5-minute quadrangles, Washington. Washington Division of

Geology and Earth Resources Geologic
Map GM-41, 2 sheets, scale 1:24,000, text
15p.

Palmer, S.P., T.J. Walsh, R.L. Logan, and W.J.
Gerstel. Liquefaction susceptibility for
the Auburn and Poverty Bay 7.5-minute
quadrangles, Washington. Washington
Division of Geology and Earth Resources
Geologic Map GM-43, 2 sheets, scale
1:24,000, text 15p.

Petersen, M. 1996. Probabilistic seismic
hazard assessment for the State of
California. Calif. Div. Mines and Geology
Open-File Report OFR 96-8.

Pezzopane, S.V., and R.J. Weldon. 1993.
Tectonic role of active faulting in central
Oregon. *Tectonics*, vol. 12, pp. 1140-69.

Priest, G.R. 1995. Explanation of mapping
methods and use of the tsunami hazard
maps of the Oregon coast. Oregon Dept.
of Geology and Mineral Industries Open-
File Report O-95-67, 95p.

Priest, G.R. 1995. Explanation of mapping
methods and use of the tsunami hazard
map of the Siletz Gay area, Lincoln
County, Oregon. Oregon Department of
Geology and Mineral Industries
Geologica Map Series Report.

Richter, C.F. 1958. *Elementary Seismology.* San
Francisco, CA: W.H. Freeman & Co.,
468p.

Rogers, A.M., T.J. Walsh, W.J. Kockelman,
and G.R. Priest, eds. 1996. Assessing
earthquake hazards and reducing risk in
the Pacific Northwest. USGS Prof. Paper
1560, vol. 1, 306p (vol. 2 awaits USGS
funding).

Rogers, G.C. 1988. An assessment of the
megathrust earthquake potential of the
Cascadia subduction zone. *Canadian
Journal of Earth Sciences*, vol. 25, pp. 844-
52.

Rogers, G.C. 1994. Earthquakes in the
Vancouver area, in Geology and
Geological Hazards of the Vancouver
Region, Southwestern British Columbia.
Geological Survey of Canada Bull. 481, pp.
221-29.

Rogers, G.C., and H.S. Hasegawa. 1978. A
second look at the British Columbia
earthquake of June 23, 1946.
Seismological Society of America Bulletin,
vol. 68, pp. 653-75.

Roth, R.J., Jr. 1997. Earthquake basics:
Insurance. What are the principles of

insuring natural disasters? Earthquake
Engineering Research Institute, Suite 320,
499-14th Street, Oakland, CA 94612-
1934.

Satake, K. 1992, Tsunamis, in *Encyclopedia of
Earth Sciences*, vol. 4, pp. 389-97.

Satake, K., K. Shimazaki, Y. Tsuji, and K.
Ueda. 1996. Time and size of a giant
earthquake in Cascadia inferred from
Japanese tsunami records of January
1700. *Nature* vol. 379, pp. 246-49.

Savage, J.C., and M. Lisowski. 1991. Strain
measurements and the potential for a
great subduction earthquake off the coast
of Washington. *Science*, vol. 252, pp. 101-
103.

Savage, J.C., M. Lisowski, and W.H. Prescott.
1991. Strain accumulation in western
Washington. *Journal of Geophysical
Research*, vol. 96, pp. 14,493-503.

Scholz, C.H. 1997. Whatever happened to
earthquake prediction? *Geotimes*, vol. 42,
no. 3, pp. 16-19.

Schuster, R.L., R.L. Logan, and P.T. Pringle.
1992. Prehistoric rock avalanches in the
Olympic Mountains, Washington. *Science*,
vol. 258, pp. 1620-21.

Schwartz, D.P., and K.J. Coppersmith. 1984.
Fault behavior and characteristic
earthquakes: Examples from the Wasatch
and San Andreas faults. *Journal of
Geophysical Research*, vol. 89, pp. 5681-98.

Scullin, C.M. Excavation and grading code
administration, inspection, and
enforcement. ICBO, 5360 Workman Mill
Road, Whittier, CA 90601-2298.

Shedlock, K.S., and C.S. Weaver. 1991.
Program for earthquake hazards
assessment in the Pacific Northwest. U.S.
Geol. Survey Circular 1067, 29p.

Shennan, I., et al. 1997. Tidal marsh
stratigraphy, sea-level change and large
earthquakes: I: A 5000-year record in
Washington, USA. *Quaternary Science
Reviews*, vol. 15, pp. 1023-58.

Sieh, K., and S. LeVay, S. 1998. *Earthquakes,
Volcanoes, and their Human Impact.* New
York: W.H. Freeman & Co., in press.

Southern California Earthquake Center.
1995. Putting down roots in earthquake
country. SCEC, University of Southern
California, University Park, Los Angeles,
CA 90089-0742

Spence, W., R.B. Herrmann, A.C. Johnston,
and G. Reagor. 1993. Responses to Iben

Browning's prediction of a 1990 New Madrid, Missouri, earthquake. U.S. Geol. Survey Circular 1083, 248p.

Stein, R.S., and R.S. Yeats. 1989. Hidden earthquakes. *Scientific American*, vol. 260, no. 6, pp. 48-57.

Sunset Magazine. 1990. Quake, two-part series in October and November 1990 issues; available as reprints (Sunset Quake '90 Reprints) from Sunset Publishing Co., 80 Willow Road, Menlo Park, CA 94025.

Taber, J.J., Jr., and S.W. Smith. 1985. Seismicity and focal mechanisms associated with the subduction of the Juan de Fuca plate beneath the Olympic Peninsula, Washington. *Seismological Society of America Bulletin*, vol. 75, pp. 237-49.

Thomas, G., and M.M. Witts. 1971. *The San Francisco Earthquake*. New York: Dell Publishing Co., 301p.

Thorsen, G.W., compiler. 1986. The Puget Lowland earthquakes of 1949 and 1965. Washington Division of Geology and Earth Resources, Information Circular 81, 113p.

Toppozada, T., and others. 1995. Planning scenario in Humboldt and Del Norte Counties, California, for a great earthqauke on the Cascadia subduction zone. California Division of Mines and Geology Special Pub. 116, 157p.

U.S. Geological Survey. 1996. USGS Response to an Urban Earthquake Northridge '94. U.S. Geological Survey Open-File Report 96-263, 78p.

U.S. Geological Survey. Next big earthquake in the Bay Area may come sooner than you think. U.S. Geological Survey, 345 Middlefield Rd., Menlo Park, CA 94025, 24p.

U.S. Geological Survey. Earthquake hazard map showing earthquake ground accelerations, from USGS website http://geohazards.cr.usgs.gov/eq/

Walsh, T.J., and P.T. Pringle. Suggestions for growth management planning for seismic hazards, and C.J. Manson. Washington earthquake hazards: A select bibliography. Unpublished report available from the Washington Division of Geology and Earth Resources.

Wang, Y.M., and G.R. Priest. 1995. Relative earthquake hazard maps of the Siletz Bay area, coastal Lincoln County, Oregon.

Oregon Dept. of Geology and Mineral Industries Geol. Map Series GMS-93: map 1:24,000, text 13p.

Wang, Y.M., and W.J. Leonard. 1996. Relative earthquake hazard maps of the Salem East and Salem West quadrangles, Marion and Polk Counties, Oregon. Oregon Department of Geology and Mineral Industries Geol. Map Series GMS-105: maps 1:24,000, text 10p.

Washington State Department of Natural Resources. 1994. *Washington Geology*, vol. 22, no. 2. Articles on the Growth Management Act.

Weaver, C.S., and G.E. Baker. 1988. Geometry of the Juan de Fuca plate beneath Washington and northern Oregon from seismicity. *Seismological Society of America Bulletin,* vol. 78, pp. 264-75.

Weaver, C.S., and S.T. Smith. 1983. Regional tectonic and earthquake hazard implications of a crustal fault zone in southwestern Washington. *Journal of Geophysical Research*, vol. 88, pp. 10,371-83.

Werner, K., J. Nabelek, R. Yeats, and S. Malone. 1992. The Mount Angel fault: Implications of seismic reflection data and the Woodburn, Oregon, earthquake sequence of August, 1990. *Oregon Geology*, vol. 54, pp. 112-17.

Wicander, R., and J.S. Monroe. 1980. *Historical Geology*. St. Paul, MN: West Publishing Co., 578p.

Wiley, T.J., and others. 1993. Klamath Falls earthquakes, September 20, 1993—including the strongest quake ever measured in Oregon. DOGAMI *Oregon Geology*, vol. 55, no. 6, pp. 127-36.

Wong, I.G., and W.J. Silva. 1990. Preliminary assessment of potential strong earthquake ground shaking in the Portland, Oregon, metropolitan area. *Oregon Geology*, vol. 52, pp. 131-34.

Wong, I.G., and J.D.J. Bott. 1995. A look back at Oregon's earthquake history, 1841-1994. DOGAMI, *Oregon Geology*, vol. 57, no. 6, pp. 125-39.

Yamaguchi, D.K., B.F. Atwater, D.E. Bunker, B.E. Benson, and M.S. Reid. 1997. Tree-ring dating the 1700 Cascadia earthquake. *Nature*

Yanev, P. 1974. *Peace of Mind in Earthquake Country: How to save your home and life.* San Francisco, CA: Chronicle Books.

Yelin, T.S., and H.J. Patton. 1991,
    Seismotectonics of the Portland, Oregon,
    region. *Seismological Society of America
    Bulletin*, vol. 81, pp. 109-30.
Yeats, R.S., E.P. Graven, K.S. Werner, C.
    Goldfinger, and T.A. Popowski. 1996.
    Tectonics of the Willamette Valley,
    Oregon. U.S. Geological Survey
    Professional Paper 1560, pp. 183-222,
    map 1:100,000 scale.
Yeats, R.S., L.D. Kulm, C. Goldfinger, and L.
    C. McNeill. 1998. Stonewall anticline: An
    active fold on the Oregon continental
    shelf. *Geological Society of America Bulletin*,
    vol. 110, pp. 572-87.
Yeats, R.S., K. Sieh, and C.R. Allen. 1997. *The
    Geology of Earthquakes*. New York: Oxford
    University Press, 568p.

Index